HERMAN MELVILLE
Mariner and Mystic
RAYMOND M. WEAVER

Engraved on wood, by L. F. Grant.
From a photograph.

Herman Melville

HERMAN MELVILLE

MARINER AND MYSTIC

BY

RAYMOND M. WEAVER

Introduction by Mark Van Doren

New York: PAGEANT BOOKS, INC.: 1961

PUBLISHED BY
PAGEANT BOOKS, INC.
128 OLIVER STREET
PATERSON 1, NEW JERSEY

PRINTED IN THE UNITED STATES OF AMERICA

TO

PROFESSOR FRANKLIN T. BAKER

"— il maestro cortese"

To Professor Carl Van Doren, to Miss Cora Paget, and to Mrs. Eleanor Melville Metcalf, I am, in the writing of this book, very especially indebted. By Professor Van Doren's enthusiasm and scholarship I was instigated to a study of Melville. It has been my privilege to enjoy Miss Paget's very valuable criticism and assistance throughout the preparation of this volume. Mrs. Metcalf gave me access to all the surviving records of her grandfather: Melville manuscripts, letters, journals, annotated books, photographs, and a variety of other material. But she did far more. My indebtedness to Mrs. Metcalf's vivid interest, her shrewd insight, her keen sympathy can be stated only in superlatives. To Mrs. and Mr. Metcalf I owe one of the richest and most pleasant associations of my life.

RAYMOND M. WEAVER.

October 1, 1921.

Most of the letters of Melville to Hawthorne included in this volume are quoted from *Nathaniel Hawthorne and His Wife,* by Julian Hawthorne. These letters, and other citations from Mr. Hawthorne's memoir, are included through the courtesy of Messrs. Houghton Mifflin Company.

CONTENTS

ILLUSTRATIONS

INTRODUCTION

It is given to few biographies to make as much difference in the reputations of their subjects as this book
made in the reputation of Herman Melville. There is
a legend that it made all the difference: Melville had
no reputation before Raymond Weaver discovered him,
or at the best he had one only as a writer of romances
about the sea. If this last is more or less literally the
case, the legend errs in minimizing the extent of Melville's fame among those who read of waves and whales;
it was a very substantial fame, and Weaver himself was
able to cite John Masefield's magnificent tribute to
Moby Dick. At any rate the legend exists; and like all
legends it contains a core of truth. In 1921, when
Weaver published his book, Melville was not unknown;
I can remember, for instance, that as a student I had
bought three of his works, *Typee, Omoo,* and *Moby
Dick,* out of Everyman's Library; yet the ignorance.
concerning him was wide and deep, and almost nobody
had any conception of the amazing riches there had
been in his mind. Passing references were made to his
mysticism or his madness, but there was no search to see
if there was method in him, or at least consistency.

Raymond Weaver sailed into the subject as into an
uncharted sea. He says in his acknowledgments that
Carl Van Doren had instigated the study; this was at
Columbia University, where both were teachers and
where my brother, who conducted research in American

literature, had recently made his own discovery of Melville in the course of writing *The American Novel* (1921). The section of that book devoted to Melville was to be sure only half a chapter, against whole ones for Cooper, Hawthorne, Mark Twain, and Henry James; but it did ample justice to Melville's power, and it suggested if not explored his depths. The exploration was even then bearing fruit in Weaver's volume, soon to appear with its significant subtitle: *Mariner and Mystic*. Mariner, it went without saying; but what of the mystic? Weaver's contribution was decisive on both sides. He set forth the full circumstances of Melville's engagement with the sea, and he plunged straight into the billows of his thought, whether about the sea or about the monsters that infest dry land.

Weaver could not have done all this without the documents placed at his disposal by Mrs. Eleanor Melville Metcalf, the subject's granddaughter. He acknowledges that assistance too, and indicates that it consisted of more than the lending of materials. I·can add at this late date my own memories of the association between relative and writer, each of whom was indispensable to the other in an enterprise they undertook together, Weaver on his part being always most generous in his recognition of the help he received. But there was one important thing he had to do for himself: he had to scour the secondhand bookstores of the country, and of England, for copies of Melville's works, many of which when he found them were as bits of driftwood long buried under sand. He found them all, I think, in first editions. One day as I entered his room in Livingston Hall he tossed me a fat book which he said was one of three first editions of *Moby Dick*. He had paid fifty cents for it, and since there were so many on his hands, this was mine. I accepted the gift with no intimation of the value it was soon to have: a value created by

Weaver's biography. Perhaps I can show most simply what the effect of the biography was by revealing that in 1928 the copy of *Moby Dick* which had been tossed to me was sold for five hundred dollars—sold jointly by Weaver and me, for he would never take back the gift itself, though I pressed it on him.

Now it would again be dabbling in legend to say that *Herman Melville: Mariner and Mystic* performed such a miracle entirely by itself. The world was ready for the book. Not only was there some sort of Melville audience already in existence, as I have said; but the special climate of the time was propitious. It was after the first World War; it was after the publication of *The Education of Henry Adams;* it was when *The Waste Land* was preparing to appear. Pessimism was ceasing to be bad taste; indeed, it was taking over. Not for the most part the raging pessimism of Melville, which has few enough parallels in any age; but at the very least, a boredom with optimism and progress, and a willingness to indulge the dark, the dolorous, the wild. Melville, who in Victorian days had talked as it were to himself, and said devastating things, now had his public at last. Add to this his enormous eloquence, and it follows that the ears of the world opened wide to take him in. His vogue, in the years immediately subsequent to Weaver's book, was instantaneous and immense. And the book was the efficient cause. So that legend is right once more: Raymond Weaver made all the difference a biographer can hope to make.

Not that he said the last word. Four decades have brought forth further biographies and critical studies, until there is a library of Melville literature. Weaver's book, however, is still somehow basic to it all. His was the first enthusiasm, the first reconnaisance on a broad front, the first outright claim that Melville was what we have come to think of him as being, namely, an author of world importance. To have witnessed Weaver as he worked in this exciting faith was itself a privilege. His relish was vast, his dedication not to be doubted. It is reassuring to know that his book will circulate again.

MARK VAN DOREN

HERMAN MELVILLE

CHAPTER I

DEVIL'S ADVOCATE

"IF ever, my dear Hawthorne," wrote Melville in the summer of 1851, "we shall sit down in Paradise in some little shady corner by ourselves; and if we shall by any means be able to smuggle a basket of champagne there (I won't believe in a Temperance Heaven); and if we shall then cross our celestial legs in the celestial grass that is forever tropical, and strike our glasses and our heads together till both ring musically in concert: then, O my dear fellow mortal, how shall we pleasantly discourse of all the things manifold which now so much distress us." This serene and laughing desolation—a mood which in Melville alternated with a deepening and less tranquil despair—is a spectacle to inspire with sardonic optimism those who gloat over the vanity of human wishes. For though at that time Melville was only thirty-two years old, he had crowded into that brief space of life a scope of experience to rival Ulysses', and a literary achievement of a magnitude and variety to merit all but the highest fame. Still did he luxuriate in tribulation. Well-born, and nurtured in good manners and a cosmopolitan tradition, he was, like George Borrow, and Sir Richard Burton, a gentleman adventurer in the barbarous outposts of human experience. Nor was his a kid-gloved and expensively staged dip into studio savagery. "For my part, I abominate all honourable respectable toils, trials, and tribulations of every kind whatsoever," he declared. And as proof of this abomination he went forth penniless as a common sailor to view the watery world. He spent his youth and early man-

15

hood in the forecastles of a merchantman, several whalers, and a man-of-war. He diversified whale-hunting by a sojourn of four months among practising cannibals, and a mutiny off Tahiti. He returned home to New England to marry the daughter of Chief Justice Shaw of Massachusetts, and to win wide distinction as a novelist on both sides of the Atlantic. Though these crowded years had brought with them bitter hardship and keen suffering, he had sown in tears that he might reap in triumph. But when he wrote to Hawthorne he felt that triumph had not been achieved. Yet he needed but one conclusive gesture to provoke the world to cry this as a lie in his throat: one last sure sign to convince all posterity that he was, indeed, one whom the gods loved. But the gods fatally withheld their sign for forty years. Melville did not die until 1891.

None of Melville's critics seem ever to have been able to forgive him his length of days. "Some men die too soon," said Nietzsche, "others too late; there is an art in dying at the right time." Melville's longevity has done deep harm to his reputation as an artist in dying, and has obscured the phenomenal brilliancy of his early literary accomplishment. The last forty years of his history are a record of a stoical—and sometimes frenzied—distaste for life, a perverse and sedulous contempt for recognition, an interest in solitude, in etchings and in metaphysics. In his writings after 1851 he employed a world of pains to scorn the world: a compliment returned in kind. During the closing years of his life he violated the self-esteem of the world still more by rating it as too inconsequential for condemnation. He earned his living between 1866 and 1886 as inspector of Customs in New York city. His deepest interest came to be in metaphysics: which is but misery dissolved in thought. It may be, to the all-seeing eye of truth, that Melville's closing years were the most glorious of his life. But to the mere critic of literature, his strange career is like a star that drops a line of streaming fire down the vault of the sky—and then the dark and blasted shape that sinks into the earth.

There are few more interesting problems in biography than

this offered by Melville's paradoxical career: its brilliant early achievement, its long and dark eclipse. Yet in its popular statement, this problem is perverted from the facts by an insufficient knowledge of Melville's life and works. The current opinion was thus expressed by an uncircumspect critic at the time of Melville's centenary in 1919: "Owing to some odd psychological experience, that has never been definitely explained, his style of writing, his view of life underwent a complete change. From being a writer of stirring, vivid fiction, he became a dreamer, wrapping himself up in a vague kind of mysticism, that rendered his last few books such as *Pierre: or The Ambiguities* and *The Confidence Man: His Masquerade* quite incomprehensible, and certainly most uninteresting for the average reader."

Unhampered by diffidence—because innocent of the essential facts—critics of Melville have been fluent in hypothesis to account for this "complete change." A German critic patriotically lays the blame on Kant. English-speaking critics, with insular pride, have found a sufficiency of disruptive agencies nearer at home. Some impute Melville's decline to Sir Thomas Browne; others to Melville's intimacy with Hawthorne; others to the dispraise heaped upon *Pierre*. Though there is a semblance of truth in each, such attempts at explanation are, of course, too shallow and neat to merit reprobation. But there is another group of critics, too considerable in size and substance to be so cavalierly dismissed. This company accounts for Melville's swift obscuration in a summary and comprehensive manner, by intimating that Melville went insane.

Such an intimation is doubtless highly efficacious to mediocrity in bolstering its own self-esteem. But otherwise it is without precise intellectual content. For insanity is not a definite entity like leprosy, measles, and the bubonic plague, but even in its most precise use, denotes a conglomerate group of phenomena which have but little in common. Science, it is true, speaking through Nordau and Lombroso, has attempted to show an intimate correlation between genius and degeneracy; and if the creative imagination of some of the disciples of Freud is to be trusted, the choir invisible is little more than a glorified bedlam. Plato would have accepted this verdict with approval. "From insanity," said Plato, "Greece has derived its greatest benefits." But the dull and decent Philistine, untouched by Platonic heresies, justifies his sterility in a boast of sanity. The America in which Melville was born and died was exuberantly and unquestionably "sane." Its "sanity" drove Irving abroad and made a recluse of Hawthorne. Cooper alone throve upon it. And of Melville, more ponderous in gifts and more volcanic in energy than any other American writer, it made an Ishmael upon the face of the earth. With its outstanding symptoms of materialism and conformity it drove Emerson to pray for an epidemic of madness: "O Celestial Bacchus! drive them mad.—This multitude of vagabonds, hungry for eloquence, hungry for poetry, starving for symbols, perishing for want of electricity to vitalise this too much pasture, and in the long delay indemnifying themselves with the false wine of alcohol, of politics, of money."

From this it would appear that a taste for insanity has been widespread among poets, prophets and saints: men venerated more by posterity than by their neighbours. It is well for Socrates that Xantippe did not write his memoirs: but there was sufficient libel in hemlock. In ancient and mediæval times, of course, madness, when not abhorred as a demoniac possession, was revered as a holy and mysterious visitation. To-day, witch-burning and canonisation have given place to more refined devices. The herd must always be intolerant of all who violate its sacred and painfully reared traditions. With an easy conscience it has always exterminated in the flesh those who sin in the flesh. In times less timid than the present it dealt with sins of the spirit with similar crude vindictiveness. We boast it as a sign of our progress that we have outgrown the days of jubilant public crucifixions and bumpers of hemlock: and there is ironic justice in the boast. Openly to harbour convictions repugnant to the herd is still the unforgivable sin against that most holy of ghosts—fashionable opinion; and carelessly to let live may be more cruel than officiously to cause to die.

Melville sinned blackly against the orthodoxy of his time.

In his earlier works, he confined his sins to an attack upon Missionaries and the starchings of civilisation: sins that won him a *succes de scandal*. The London Missionary Society charged into the resulting festivities with its flag at half mast. Cased in the armour of the Lord, it with flagrant injustice attacked his morals, because it smarted under his ideas. But when Melville began flooding the very foundations of life with torrents of corrosive pessimism, the world at large found itself more vulnerable in its encasement. It could not, without absurdity obvious even to itself, accuse Melville of any of the cruder crimes against Jehovah or the Public. Judged by the bungling provisions of the thirty-nine articles and the penal code, he was not a bad man: more subtle was his iniquity. As by a divine visitation, the Harper fire of 1853 effectually reduced *Pierre*—his most frankly poisonous book—to a safely limited edition. And the public, taking the hint, ceased buying his books. In reply, Melville earned his bread as Inspector of Customs. The public, defeated in its righteous attempts at starvation, hit upon a more exquisite revenge. It gathered in elegiacal synods and whispered mysteriously: "He went insane."

To view Melville's life as a venturesome romantic idyll frozen in mid-career by the *deus ex machina* of some steadily descending Gorgon is possible only by a wanton misreading of patent facts. Throughout Melville's long life his warring and untamed desires were in violent conflict with his physical and spiritual environment. His whole history is the record of an attempt to escape from an inexorable and intolerable world of reality: a quenchless and essentially tragic Odyssey away from home, out in search of "the unpeopled world behind the sun." In the blood and bone of his youth he sailed away in brave quest of such a harbour, to face inevitable defeat. For this rebuff he sought both solace and revenge in literature. But by literature he also sought his livelihood. In the first burst of literary success he married. Held closer to reality by financial worry and the hostages of wife and children, the conflict within him was heightened. By a vicious circle, with brooding disappointment came ill health. "Ah, muskets the gods have made to carry infinite combustion," he wrote in *Pierre*, "and yet made them of clay." The royalties from his books proved inadequate for the support of his family, so for twenty years he earned a frugal living in the customs houses in New York. During his leisure hours he continued to write, but never for publication. Two volumes of poetry he privately printed. His last novel, surviving in manuscript, he finished a few months before his death. Though it is for the second half that his critics have felt bound to regret, it seems that in serenity and mental equipoise, the last state of this man was better than the first.

In his early manhood he wrote in *Mardi:* "Though essaying but a sportive sail, I was driven from my course by a blast resistless; and ill-provided, young, and bowed by the brunt of things before my prime, still fly before the gale. . . . If after all these fearful fainting trances, the verdict be, the golden haven was not gained;—yet in bold quest thereof, better to sink in boundless deeps than float on vulgar shoals; and give me, ye gods, an utter wreck, if wreck I do." To the world at large, it has been generally believed that the Gods ironically fulfilled his worst hopes.

One William Cranston Lawton, in an *Introduction to the Study of American Literature*—a handy relic of the parrot judgment passed upon Melville during the closing years of his life—so enlightens young America: "He holds his own beside Cooper and Marryat, and boy readers, at least, will need no introduction to him. Nor will their enjoyment ever be alloyed by a Puritan moral or a mystic double meaning." And Barrett Wendell, in *A Literary History of America*—a volume that modestly limits American literature of much value not only to New England, but even tucks it neatly into the confines of Harvard College—notes with jaunty patronage: "Herman Melville with his books about the South Seas, which Robert Louis Stevenson is said to have declared the best ever written, and his novels of maritime adventure, began a career of literary promise, which never came to fruition."

These typical pronouncements, unperverted by the remotest touch of independent judgment, transcend Melville's worst fears. "Think of it!" he once wrote to Hawthorne. "To go down to posterity is bad enough, any way; but to go down as a 'man who lived among the cannibals!' When I think of posterity in reference to myself, I mean only the babes who will probably be born in the moment immediately ensuing upon my giving up the ghost. I shall go down to them, in all likelihood. *Typee* will be given to them, perhaps, with their gingerbread." In that mythical anomaly known as the "popular mind," Melville has, indeed, survived as an obscure adventurer in strange seas and among amiable barbarians. *Typee* and *Omoo* have lived on as minor classics. Though there have been staccato and sporadic attacks upon the ludicrous inadequacy of the popular judgment upon Melville, not until recently, and then chiefly in England has there been any popular and concerted attempt to take Melville's truer and more heroic dimensions. An editorial in the London *Nation* for January 22, 1921, thus bespeaks the changing temper of the times:

"It is clear that the wind of the spirit, when it once begins to blow through the English literary mind, possesses a surprising power of penetration. A few weeks ago it was pleased to aim a simultaneous blast in the direction of a book known to some generations of men as *Moby-Dick*. A member of the staff of *The Nation* was thereupon moved in the ancient Hebrew fashion to buy and to read it. He then expressed himself on the subject, incoherently indeed, but with signs of emotion as intense and as pleasingly uncouth as Man Friday betrayed at the sight of his long-lost father. While struggling with his article, and wondering what the deuce it could mean, I received a letter from a famous literary man, marked on the outside 'Urgent,' and on the inner scroll of the manuscript itself 'A Rhapsody.' It was about *Moby-Dick*. Having observed a third article on the same subject, of an equally febrile kind, I began to read *Moby-Dick* myself. Having done so I hereby declare, being of sane intellect, that since letters began there never was such a book, and that the mind of man is not constructed so as to produce such another; that I put its author with Rabelais, Swift, Shakespeare, and other minor and disputable worthies; and that I advise any adventurer of the soul to go at once to the morose and prolonged retreat necessary for its deglutition."

Having earlier been hailed in France as an "American Rabelais;" prized in England by the author of *The City of Dreadful Night;* greeted by Stevenson with slangy enthusiasm as a "howling cheese;" rated by Mr. Masefield as unique among writers of the sea; the professed inspirer of Captain Hook of Sir James Barrie's *Peter Pan,* Melville is beginning to appear as being vastly more than merely a "man who lived among the cannibals" and who returned home to write lively sea stories for boys.

The wholesale neglect of Melville at the hands of his countrymen—though explained in some part as a consummation of Melville's best efforts—has not been merely unintelligent, but thoroughly discreditable. For Melville, from any point of view, is one of the most distinguished of our writers, and there is something ludicrous in being before all the world—as, assuredly, we sometimes are—in recognising our own merit where it is contestable, and in neglecting it where it is not.

It has been our tradition to cherish our literature for its embodiment of Queen Victoria's fireside qualities. The repudiation of this tradition—as a part of our repudiation of all tradition—has made fashionable a wholesale contempt for our native product. "I can't read Longfellow" is frequently remarked; "he's so subtle!" Our critical estimates have laboured under the incubus of New England provincialism: a provincialism preserved in miniature in the first pages of Lowell's essay on Thoreau. At present we need to have the eminence of the section recalled to us; but during the period of Melville's productivity, it was at its apex, and in its bosom Melville wrote. This man, whose closest literary affinities were Rabelais, Zola, Sir Thomas Browne, Rousseau, Meredith, and Dr. John Donne,—a combination to make the unitiated blink with incredulity—was indebted to Nathaniel Hawthorne for the best makeshift for companionship he was ever to know: one of the most subtly ironical associations the imps of comedy ever brought about. Nor was the comedy lessened by Mrs. Hawthorne's presence upon the scene. Shrewd was her instinctive resentment of her husband's friend. Viewed by his neighbours "as little better than a cannibal and a 'beach comber' "—such was the report of the late Titus Munson Coan in a letter to his mother written immediately after a pilgrimage to Melville in the Berkshires—Melville turned to Hawthorne for understanding. Frank Preston Stearns, in his *Life and Genius of Nathaniel Hawthorne* (1906) says that for Hawthorne "the summer of 1851 in Lenox was by no means brilliant. . . . Hawthorne's chief entertainment seems to have been the congratulatory letters he received from distinguished people. . . . For older company he had Herman Melville and G. P. R. James, whose society he may have found as interesting as that of more distinguished writers." But Mrs. Hawthorne had studied Melville with a closer scrutiny and was not so easily convinced of Melville's insignificance. Melville had visited the Hawthornes in the tiny reception room of the Red House, where Mrs. Hawthorne "sewed at her stand and read to the children about Christ;" in the drawing room, where she disposed "the embroidered furniture," and where, in the farther corner, stood "Apollo with his head tied on;" in Hawthorne's study, which to Mrs. Hawthorne's wifely adoration was consecrated by "his presence in the morning." Mrs. Hawthorne looked from the "wonderful, wonderful eyes" of her husband—each eye "like a violet with a soul in it,"—to Melville's eyes, and confessed to her mother her grave and jealous suspicion of Melville: "I am not quite sure that *I do not think him* a very great man. . . . A man with a true, warm heart, and a soul and an intellect,—with life to his finger-tips; earnest, sincere and reverent; very tender and *modest.* . . . He has very keen perceptive power; but what astonishes me is, that his eyes are not large and deep. He seems to see everything very accurately; and how he can do so with his small eyes, I cannot tell. They are not keen eyes, either, but quite undistinguished in any way. His nose is straight and rather handsome, his mouth expressive of sensibility and emotion. He is tall, and erect, with an air free, brave and manly. When conversing, he is full of gesture and force, and loses himself in his subject. There is no grace nor polish. Once in a while, his animation gives place to a singularly quiet expression, out of these eyes to which I have objected; an indrawn, dim look, but which at the same time makes you feel that he is at that moment taking deepest note of what is before him. It is a strange, lazy glance, but with a power in it quite unique. It does not seem to penetrate through you, but to take you into itself. I saw him look at Una so, yesterday, several times."

Mrs. Hawthorne must ever enjoy a lofty eminence as one of Melville's most penetrating critics. Her husband dwelt apart, and less because he found the atmosphere of New England wholly uncongenial than because he shared his wife's conviction that he was like a star. And shrewdly his wife resented the presence of a second luminary—treacherously veiled and of heaven knows what magnitude!—in her serene New England sky. Time may yet harp her worst fears aright.

For despite his comparative obscurity, Melville is—as cannot be too frequently iterated—one of the chief and most unusual figures in our native literature. And his claim to such high distinction must rest upon three prime counts.

First—because most obvious—Melville was the literary discoverer of the South Seas. And though his ample and rapidly multiplying progeny includes such names as Robert Louis Stevenson, Charles Warren Stoddard, John La Farge, Jack London, Louis Becke, A. Safroni-Middleton, Somerset Maugham, and Frederick O'Brien, he is still unsurpassed in the manner he originated. On this point, all competent critics are agreed.

Melville's second achievement is most adequately stated by the well-known English sea-writer, W. Clark Russell, in *A Claim of American Literature* (reprinted from *The North American Review* in *The Critic* for March 26, 1892). "When Richard Henry Dana, and Herman Melville wrote," says Russell, "the commercial sailor of Great Britain and the United States was without representation in literature. . . . Dana and Melville were Americans. They were the first to lift the hatch and show the world what passes in a ship's forecastle; how men live down in that gloomy cave, how and what they eat, and where they sleep; what pleasures they take, what their sorrows and wrongs are; how they are used when they quit their black sea-parlours in response to the boatswain's silver summons to work on deck by day and by night. These secrets of the deep Dana and Melville disclosed. . . . Dana and Melville created a new world, not by the discovery, but by the interpretation of it. They gave us a full view of the life led by tens of thousands of men whose very existence, till these wizards arose, had been as vague to the general land intelligence as the shadows of clouds moving under the brightness of the stars." And to Melville and Dana, so Russell contends, we owe "the first, the best and most enduring revelation of these secrets." On this score, Conrad, Kipling, and Masefield must own Melville as master.

Melville's third and supreme claim to distinction rests upon a single volume, which, after the order of Melchizedek, is without issue and without descent: "a work which is not only unique in its kind, and a great achievement" to quote a recent judgment from England, "but is the expression of an imagination that rises to the highest, and so is amongst the world's great works of art." This book is, of course, *Moby-Dick,* Melville's undoubted masterpiece. "In that wild, beautiful romance"—the words are Mr. Masefield's—"Melville seems to have spoken the very secret of the sea, and to have drawn into his tale all the magic, all the sadness, all the wild joy of many waters. It stands quite alone; quite unlike any other book known to me. It strikes a note which no other sea writer has ever struck."

The organising theme of this unparalleled volume is the hunt by the mad Captain Ahab after the great white whale which had dismembered him of his leg; of Captain Ahab's unwearied pursuit by rumour of its whereabouts; of the final destruction of himself and his ship by its savage onslaught. On the white hump of the ancient and vindictive monster Captain Ahab piles the sum of all the rage and hate of mankind from the days of Eden down.

Melville expresses an ironical fear lest his book be scouted "as a monstrous fable, or still worse and more detestable, a hideous and intolerable allegory." Yet fabulous allegory it is: an allegory of the demonism at the cankered heart of nature, teaching that "though in many of its visible aspects the world seems formed in love, the invisible spheres were formed in fright." Thou shalt know the truth, and the truth shall make you mad. To the eye of truth, so Melville would convince us, "the palsied universe lies before us as a leper;" "all deified Nature absolutely paints like a harlot, whose allurements cover nothing but the charnal house within." To embody this devastating insight, Melville chooses as a symbol, an albino whale. "Wonder ye then at the fiery hunt?"

An artist who goes out to find sermons in stones does so at the peril of converting his stone pile into his mausoleum. His danger is excessive, if, having his sermons all ready, he makes it his task to find the stones to fit them. Allegory justifies itself only when the fiction is the fact and the moral the induction; only when its representation is as imaginatively real as its meaning; only when the stones are interesting boulders in a rich and diversified landscape. So broadly and vividly is *Moby-Dick* based on solid foundation that even the most literal-minded, innocent of Melville's dark intent, have found this book of the soul's daring and the soul's dread a very worthy volume. One spokesman for this congregation, while admitting that "a certain absorption of interest lies in the nightmare intensity and melodramatic climax of the tale," finds his interest captured and held far more by "the exposition of fact with which the story is loaded to the very gunwale. No living thing on earth or in the waters under the earth is so interesting as the whale. How it is pursued, from the Arctic to the Antarctic; how it is harpooned, to the peril of boat and crew; how, when brought to the side, 'cutting in' is accomplished; how the whale's anatomy is laid bare; how his fat is redeemed—to be told this in the form of a narrative, with all manner of dramatic but perfectly plausible incidents interspersed, is enough to make the book completely engrossing without the white whale and Captain Ahab's fatal monomania."

So diverse are the samples out of which *Moby-Dick* is compounded, yet so masterful is each of its samples, that there is still far from universal agreement as to the ground colour of this rich and towering fabric. Yet by this very disagreement is its miraculous artistry affirmed.

In *Moby-Dick*, all the powers and tastes of Melville's complex genius are blended. *Moby-Dick* is at once indisputably the greatest whaling novel, and "a hideous and intolerable allegory." As Mr. Frank Jewett Mather, Jr. has said, "Out of the mere episodes and minor instances of *Moby-Dick*, a literary reputation might be made. The retired Nantucket captains Bildad and Peleg might have stepped out of Smollett. Father Mapple's sermon on the book of Jonah is in itself a masterpiece, and I know few sea tales that can hold their own with the blood feud of Mate Rodney and sailor Steelkilt." Captain Hook of *Peter Pan* is but Captain Boomer of *Moby-Dick* with another name: and this an identity founded not on surmise, but on Sir James Barrie's professed indebtedness to Melville. There are, in *Moby-Dick,* long digressions, natural, historical and philosophical, on the person, habits, manners and ideas of whales; there are long dialogues and soliloquies such as were never spoken by mortal man in his waking senses, conversations that for sweetness, strength and courage remind one of passages from Dekker, Webster, Massinger, Fletcher and the other old dramatists loved both by Melville and by Charles Lamb; in the discursive tradition of Fielding, Sir Thomas Browne and the anatomist of melancholy, Melville indulges freely in independent moralisings, half essay, half rhapsody; withal, scenes like Ishmael's experience at the "Spouter-Inn" with a practising cannibal for bed-fellow, are, for finished humour, among the most competent in the language. When Melville sat down to write, always at his knee stood that chosen emissary of Satan, the comic spirit: a demoniac familiar never long absent from his pages.

There are those, of course, who would hold against Dante his moralising, and against Rabelais his broad humour. In like manner, peculiarity of temperament has necessarily coloured critical judgment of *Moby-Dick*. But though critics may mouth it as they like about digressions, improbability, moralising reflections, swollen talk, or the fetish of art now venerated with such articulate inveteracy, all wonderfully agree upon the elementary force of *Moby-Dick,* its vitality, its thrilling power. That it achieves the effect of illusion, and to a degree peculiar to the highest feats of the creative imagination, is incontestable. No writer has more. On this point it is simply impossible to praise Melville too highly. What defects *Moby-Dick* has are formal rather than substantial. As Thackeray once impatiently said of Macaulay: "What critic can't point them out?" .It was the contention of James Thomson that an overweening concern for formal impeccability is a fatal sign of weakened vitality. Intensity of imagination—and Melville exhibited it prodigally in *Moby-Dick*—is an infinitely rarer and more precious gift than technical sophistication. Shakespeare has survived, despite his "monstrous irregularities." But since Shakespeare, as Francis Thompson has observed, there has been a gradual decline from imperfection. Milton, at his most typical, was far too perfect; Pope was ruined by his quest for the quality. No thoughtful person can contemplate without alarm the idolatry bestowed upon this quality by the contemporary mind: an idolatry that threatens to reduce all art to the extinction of unendurable excellence. How insipid would be the mere adventures of a Don Quixote recounted by a Stevenson.

The astonishing variety of contradictory qualities synthesised in *Moby-Dick* exists nowhere else in literature, perhaps, in such paradoxical harmony. These qualities, in differences of combination and emphasis, are discoverable, however, in all of Melville's writings. And he published, besides anonymous contributions to periodicals, ten novels and five volumes of poetry (including the two volumes privately printed at the very close of his life). There survives, too, a bulk of manuscript material: a novel, short stories, and a body of verse. And branded on everything that Melville wrote is there the mark of the extraordinary personality that created *Moby-Dick.*

Though some of Melville's writing is distinctly disquieting in devastating insight, and much of it is very uneven in inspiration, none of it is undistinguished. Yet only four of his books have ever been reprinted. The rest of his work, long since out of print, is excessively rare, some of it being practically unavailable. The scarcity of a book, however, is not invariably a sign of its insignificance. It is one of the least accessible of Melville's books that Mr. Masefield singles out for especial distinction. "The book I love best of his," says Mr. Masefield, "is one very difficult to come by. I think it is his first romance, and I believe it has never been reprinted here. It is the romance of his own boyhood. I mean *Redburn*. Any number of good pens will praise the known books, *Typee* and *Omoo* and *Moby-Dick* and *White-Jacket,* and will tell their qualities of beauty and romance. Perhaps *Redburn* will have fewer praises, so here goes for *Redburn;* a boy's book about running away to sea." Even more difficult of access is *Pierre*—a book at the antipodes from *Redburn*. Far from being a boy's book, *Pierre* was prophetic of the pessimism of Hardy and the subtlety of Meredith. From *Redburn* to *Pierre;* from *Typee,* a spirited travel-book on Polynesia, to *Clarel,* an intricate philosophical poem in two volumes: these mark the antithetical extremes of the art that mated poetry and blubber, whaling and metaphysics. The very complexity and versatility of Melville's achievement has been an obstacle in the way of his just appreciation. Had Mandeville turned from his *Travels,* to write *The City of Dreadful Night,* the incompatibility would have been no less extraordinary or bewildering.

Indeed, Melville's complete works, in their final analysis, are a long effort towards the creation of one of the most complex, and massive, and original characters in literature: the character known in life as Herman Melville. "I am like one of those seeds taken out of the Egyptian Pyramids," he wrote to Hawthorne while he was in the middle of *Moby-Dick,* "which, after being three thousand years a seed and nothing but a seed, being planted in English soil, it developed itself, grew to greenness, and then fell to mould. So I. Until I was twenty-five, I had no development at all. From my twenty-fifth year I date my life. But I feel that I am now come to the inmost leaf of the bulb, and that shortly the flower must fall to the mould. It seems to me now that Solomon was the truest man who ever spoke, and yet that he *managed* the truth with a view to popular conservatism."

Blighted by disillusionment, and paralysed by doubt, Melville came to treat as an irrelevancy, the making of books. "He informed me that he had 'pretty much made up his mind to be annihilated,' " wrote Hawthorne in his *Note-book,* after Melville visited him in Southport, England, in 1856; "but still he does not seem to rest in that anticipation. It is strange how he persists—as he has persisted ever since I knew him, and probably long before—in wandering to and fro over these deserts, as dismal and monotonous as the sandhills amidst which we were sitting. He can neither believe nor be comfortable in his unbelief; and he is too honest and courageous not to try to do one or the other." If, in contempt for the orthodox interpolations by which pious scribes attempted to sweeten Solomon's bitter message, Melville ever *managed* truth as he saw it, it was more to violate popular conservatism than to propitiate it. "We incline to think that God cannot explain His own secrets," he editorially wrote Hawthorne in 1851, "and that He would like a little information upon certain points Himself. We mortals astonish Him as much as He us." And as Melville grew in disillusionment, he grew in astonishment. In his relentless pessimism he boasted himself "in the happy condition of judicious, unencumbered travellers in Europe; they cross the frontiers into Eternity with nothing but a carpet bag,—that is to say, the Ego." It was his ripest conviction that the exclamation point and the triumphant perpendicular pronoun were interchangeable signs. But to the end, he bristled with minor revelations.

Though he boasted that he crossed the frontier into Eternity with nothing but a carpet bag, he had, in fact, sent more bulky consignments on ahead. And at the final crack of doom, this dead and disappointed mariner may yet rise to an unexpected rejoicing. For at that time of ultimate reckoning, according to the eschatology of Mr. Masefield, "then the great white whale, old Moby-Dick, the king of all the whales, will rise up trom his quiet in the sea, and go bellowing to his mates. And all the whales in the world—the sperm-whales, the razor-back, the black-fish, the rorque, the right, the forty-barrel Jonah, the narwhal, the hump-back, the grampus and the thrasher—will come to him, 'fin-out,' blowing their spray to the heavens. Then Moby-Dick will call the roll of them, and from all the parts of the sea, from the north, from the south, from Callao to Rio, not one whale will be missing. Then Moby-Dick will trumpet, like a man blowing a horn, and all that company of whales will 'sound' (that is, dive), for it is they that have the job of raising the wrecks from down below.

"Then when they come up the sun will just be setting in the sea, far away to the west, like a ball of red fire. And just as the curve of it goes below the sea, it will stop sinking and lie there like a door. And the stars and the earth and the wind will stop. And there will be nothing but the sea, and this red arch of the sun, and the whales with the wrecks, and a stream of light upon the water. Each whale will have raised a wreck from among the coral, and the sea will be thick with them— row-ships and sail-ships, and great big seventy-fours, and big White Star boats, and battleships, all of them green with the ooze, but all of them manned by singing sailors. And ahead of them will go Moby-Dick, towing the ship our Lord was in, with all the sweet apostles aboard of her. And Moby-Dick will give a great bellow, like a fog-horn blowing, and stretch 'fin-out' for the sun away in the west. And all the whales will bellow out an answer. And all the drowned sailors will sing their chanties, and beat the bells into a music. And the whole fleet of them will start towing at full speed towards the sun, at the edge of the sky and water. I tell you they will make white water, those ships and fishes.

"When they have got to where the sun is, the red ball will swing open like a door, and Moby-Dick, and all the whales, and all the ships will rush through it into an anchorage in Kingdom Come. It will be a great calm piece of water, with land close aboard, where all the ships of the world will lie at anchor, tier upon tier, with the hands gathered forward, sing- ing. They'll have no watches to stand, no ropes to coil, no mates to knock their heads in. Nothing will be to do except singing and beating on the bell. And all the poor sailors who went in patched rags, my son, they'll be all fine in white and gold. And ashore, among the palm-trees, there'll be fine inns for the seamen." And there, among a numerous company, will be Fayaway, and Captain Ahab, and Jack Chase, and Jarl, and Toby, and Pierre, and Father Mapple, and Jackson, and Doctor Long Ghost, and Kory-Kory, and Bildad, and Peleg, and Fedallah, and Tashetego, and Marnoo, and Queequeg. But it seems hardly likely that Melville will there find Hawthorne to tempt by a basket of champagne into some little shady corner, there to cross their legs in the celestial grass that is forever tropical, and to discourse pleasantly of all the things manifold which once so much distressed them. In my Father's house are many mansions.

CHAPTER II

GHOSTS

"We are full of ghosts and spirits; we are as grave-yards full of buried dead, that start to life before us. And all our dead sires, verily, are in us; *that* is their immortality. From sire to son, we go on multiplying corpses in ourselves; for all of which, are resurrections. Every thought's a soul of some past poet, hero, sage. We are fuller than a city." —HERMAN MELVILLE: *Mardi.*

THE High Gods, in a playful and prodigal mood, gave to Melville, to Julia Ward Howe, to Lowell, to Kingsley, to Ruskin, to Whitman, and to Queen Victoria, the same birth year. On August 1, 1819, Herman Melville was born at No. 6 Pearl Street, New York City.

Melville's vagabondage as a common sailor on a merchantman, on whaling vessels, and in the United States Navy, together with his Bohemian associations with cannibals, mutineers, and some of the choicest dregs of our Christian civilisation, must have wrenched a chorus of groans from a large congregation of shocked ancestral ghosts. For Melville was descended from a long and prolific line of the best American stock. Through his mother, Maria Gansevoort, he traced back to the earliest Dutch emigrants to New York; through his father, Allan Melville, to pre-revolutionary Scotch-Irish emigrants to New England. Both of his grandfathers distinguished themselves in the Revolutionary War. His ancestors, on both sides, came to this country in the days when some of the best blood of Europe was being transferred to America.

Though Melville was too ironic a genius ever to have been guilty of the ill-breeding that makes an ostentation of ancestry, still he looked back upon his descent with self-conscious pride: a pride drawn by childhood absorption from his parents who, by resting on the achievements of their forebears, added several cubits to their stature. Lacking the prophetic vision to glory in being ancestors, they chose the more comfortable rôle of parading as descendants. Melville's father, Allan, was sufficiently absorbed in his genealogy to compile, in 1818, an elaborately branching family tree that sent its master root back to one Sir Richard de Melvill, del Compte de Fife, a worthy of the thirteenth century. And at the proud conclusion of his labours he inscribed the Melville motto, *Denique Coelum* — "Heaven at last." Melville's mother, Maria Gansevoort, though too absorbed in domesticity to compete with Allan in drawing up a parallel document, still sat opposite her spouse with a stiff spine, conscious that she could counter his ancestry, grandfather for grandfather. It is true, she had no thirteenth century count to fall back upon; and though her line lost itself in a cluster of breweries, they were very substantial breweries, and owned by a race of stalwart and affluent and uncompromising burghers. Her ancestor, Harmen Harmense Van Gansevoort, was brewing in Beverwyck as early as 1660, and with sufficient success to acquire such extended investments in land that he bequeathed to his heirs a baronial inheritance. During the centuries following his death his name crossed itself with that of the Van Rensselaers, the Ten Broeks, the Douws, the Van Schaicks,—with the proudest names that descended from the earlier Colonial Dutch families. Melville's mother, Maria, is remembered as a cold, proud woman, arrogant in the sense of her name, her blood, and the affluence of her forebears.

She was the only daughter and oldest child in a family of six, of General Peter Gansevoort and Catharine Van Schaick. Her father, born in Albany, New York, July 17, 1749, was among the outstanding patriots of the American Revolution. He was among the troops which accompanied Schuyler, in 1775, in his advance towards Canada. In December of the same year he was with Montgomery, as Major, in the unfortunate assault upon Quebec. In the summer of 1777, when Burgoyne's semi-barbarous invading army was slowly advancing down Lake Champlain and the Hudson, he was Colonel in command of Fort Stanwix. By his obstinate and gallant defence of Fort Stanwix in August, 1777, he prevented the junc-

ture of St. Leger with Burgoyne, and so changed the course
of the whole subsequent campaign. Washington keenly and
warmly recognised this, and Congress passed a vote of thanks
to Colonel Gansevoort. Peter Gansevoort did other brilliant
service in the Revolutionary War, and in 1809, when the War
of 1812 was approaching, he was made brigadier general in
the United States army. He was sheriff of Albany County
from 1790 to 1792, and regent of the University of New York
from 1808 until his death in 1812.

Of his sons, Hon. Peter Gansevoort, who was born in Albany in 1789, was long one of the most prominent and honoured citizens of Albany. The elder son, General Herman
Gansevoort, from whom Melville received his name, lived at
Gansevoort, a village in the township of Northumberland,
Saratoga County, New York. In 1832-33, the brothers built
on the site of the birthplace of their father what is now the
Stanwix Hotel. As a boy, Melville spent most of his summers
as guest of the Gansevoorts, and in his novel *Pierre,* the childhood recollections of his hero are transparent autobiographical
references to his own early memories. "On the meadows
which sloped away from the shaded rear of the manorial mansion, far to the winding river, an Indian battle had been fought,
in the earlier days of the colony, and in that battle the great-
grandfather of Pierre, mortally wounded, had sat unhorsed
on his saddle in the grass, with his dying voice still cheering
his men in the fray. . . . Far beyond these plains, a day's
walk for Pierre, rose the storied heights, where in the Revolutionary War his grandfather had for several months de-
fended a rude but all-important stockaded fort, against the repeated combined assaults of Indians, Tories and Regulars.
From behind that fort, the gentlemanly but murderous half-
breed, Brandt, had fled, but survived to dine with General
(Gansevoort) in the amiable times that followed that vindictive war. All the associations of Saddle-Meadows were full
of pride to Pierre. The (Gansevoort) deeds by which their
estate had been so long held, bore the cyphers of three Indian
kings, the aboriginal and only conveyancers of those noble
woods and plains. Thus loftily, in the days of his circum-

scribed youth, did Pierre glance along the background of his race. . . . Or how think you it would be with this youthful Pierre if every day, descending to breakfast, he caught sight of an old tattered British banner or two, hanging over an arched window in the hall: and those banners captured by his grandfather, the general, in fair fight?"

On February 22, 1832, so it is recorded in Joel Munsell, *The Annals of Albany* (Vol. IX, Albany, 1859) "the military celebrated the centennial anniversary of the birthday of Washington. Col. Peter Gansevoort, on this occasion, presented to the artillery a large *brass Drum,* a trophy of the revolution, taken from the British on the 22nd August, 1777, at Fort Stanwix, by his father, General Peter Gansevoort." The sound of this drum was tapping in Melville's memory, when he goes on to ask: "Or how think you it would be if every time he heard the band of the military company of the village, he should distinctly recognise the peculiar tap of a British kettle-drum also captured by his grandfather in fair fight, and afterwards suitably inscribed on the brass and bestowed upon the Saddle-Meadows Artillery Corps? Or how think you it would be, if sometimes of a mild meditative Fourth of July morning in the country, he carried out with him into the garden by way of ceremonial cane, a long, majestic, silver-tipped staff, a Major-General's baton, once wielded on the plume-nodding and musket-flashing review by the same grandfather several times here-in-before mentioned?"

Not content to leave this a rhetorical query, Melville answers his own catechism in unambiguous terms: "I should say that considering Pierre was quite young and very unsophisticated as yet, and withal rather high-blooded; and sometimes read the History of the Revolutionary War, and possessed a mother who very frequently made remote social allusions to the epaulettes of the Major-General his grandfather;—I should say that upon all these occasions, the way it must have been with him was a very proud, elated sort of way."

Melville did not preserve throughout his long life this early and proud elation in his descent, and in later years he thought it necessary to apologise for the short-sighted and provincial self-satisfaction that he absorbed from his parents in his early youth. "And if this seem but too fond and foolish in Pierre," he pleads in a mood both of apology and of prophecy; "and if you tell me that this sort of thing in him showed him no sterling Democrat, and that a truly noble man should never brag of any arm but his own; then I beg you to consider again that this Pierre was but a youngster as yet. And believe me, you will pronounce Pierre a thorough-going Democrat in time; perhaps a little too Radical altogether to your fancy."

Radical he came to be, indeed: it was the necessary penalty of being cursed with an intelligence above that of the smug and shallow optimism of his country and his period. Democratic he may have been, but only in the most unpopular meaning of that once noble term. He was a democrat in the same relentless sense that Dante or Milton were democrats. Lucifer rebelled, let it be remembered, to make Heaven "safe for Democracy:" the first experiment in popular government. "Hell," says Melville, "is a democracy of devils." In *Mardi,* Melville indulges lengthy reflections on a certain "chanticleer people" who boast boisterously of themselves: "Saw ye ever such a land as this? Is it not a great and extensive republic? Pray, observe how tall we are; just feel of our thighs; are we not a glorious people? We are all Kings here; royalty breathes in the common air." Before the spectacle of this lusty republicanism, Melville exhibits unorthodox doubts. "There's not so much freedom here as these freemen think," he makes a strolling deity observe; "I laugh and admire. . . . Freedom is more social than political. And its real felicity is not to be shared. *That* is of a man's own individual getting and holding. Little longer, may it please you, can republics subsist now, than in days gone by. Though all men approached sages in wisdom, some would yet be more wise than others; and so, the old degrees would be preserved. And no exemption would an equality of knowledge furnish, from the inbred servility of mortal to mortal; from all the organic causes, which inevitably divide mankind into brigades and battalions, with captains at their heads. Civilisation has not ever been the brother of equality."

As Melville grew away from boyhood, he came to distinguish between the accidentals and the essentials that distinguish man from man. At his mother's breast he had absorbed with her milk a vivid and exaggerated belief that the accidents concomitant upon birth that range men into artificial classes, were ingrain in the very woof of the universe. When he later discovered that his parents tinted life with a very perishable dye, he also found, set below their cheap calico patterns, an unchangeable texture of sharper and deeper and more variegated colours. And he discovered, too, that his uncritical boyhood pride in his blood was, withal, not entirely a mere savage delight in calico prints.

He was, as he boasts in the sub-title of *Redburn,* "the son-of-a-gentleman," reared in an environment rich with the mellowing influences of splendid family traditions. And these associations left an indelible stamp upon him. In *Mardi,* in speaking of the impossibility of belying one's true nature while at sea and in the fellowship of sailors, he offers himself as an example to point. "Aboard of all ships in which I have sailed," he says, "I have invariably been known by a sort of drawing-room title. Not,—let me hurry to say,—that I put hand in tar bucket with a squeamish air, or ascended the rigging with a Chesterfieldian mince. No, no, I was never better than my vocation. I showed as brown a chest, and as hard a hand, as the tarriest tar of them all. And never did shipmate of mine upbraid me with a genteel disinclination to duty, though it carried me to truck of main-mast, or jib-boom-end, in the most wolfish blast that ever howled. Whence, then, this annoying appellation? for annoying it most assuredly was. It was because of something in me that could not be hidden; stealing out in an occasional polysyllable; an otherwise incomprehensible deliberation in dining; remote, unguarded allusions to belle-lettres affairs; and other trifles superfluous to mention."

Though his grandfather, General Peter Gansevoort, had been dead seven years when Melville was born, so vital were the relics of him that surrounded Melville's boyhood, so reverently was his memory tended by his first child and only daughter, that the image of Peter Gansevoort was one of the most potent influences during Melville's most impressionable years. The heroic presence that dominated Melville's imagination, "measured six feet four inches in height; during a fire in the old manorial mansion, with one dash of the foot, he had smitten down an oaken door, to admit the buckets of his negro slaves; Pierre had often tried on his military vest, which still remained an heirloom at Saddle-Meadows, and found the pockets below his knees, and plenty additional room for a fair-sized quarter-cask within its buttoned girth; in a night scuffle in the wilderness before the Revolutionary War, he had annihilated two Indian savages by making reciprocal bludgeons of their heads. And all this was done by the mildest hearted, the most blue-eyed gentleman in the world, who, according to the patriarchal fashion of those days, was a gentle, white-haired worshipper of all the household gods; the gentlest husband and the gentlest father; the kindest master to his slaves; of the most wonderful unruffledness of temper; a serene smoker of his after dinner pipe; a forgiver of many injuries; a sweet-hearted, charitable Christian; in fine, a pure, cheerful, child-like, blue-eyed, divine old man; in whose meek, majestic soul the lion and the lamb embraced—fit image of his God." His portrait was to Melville "a glorious gospel framed and hung upon the wall, and declaring to all people, as from the Mount, that man is a noble, god-like being, full of choicest juices; made up of strength and beauty." Most of the images of God that Melville met in actual secular embodiment, suffered tragically by comparison with this image of mortal perfection which Melville nursed in his heart. Most men that Melville met, in falling short of the mythical excellence of Peter Gansevoort, whom he never knew in the flesh, seemed to Melville, to be libels upon their Divine Original. According to Melville's account, he could never look upon his grandfather's military portrait without an infinite and mournful longing to meet his living aspect in actual life. Yet such was the temper of Melville's mind, his life such a tragic career of dreaming of elusive perfection, dreams invariably to be dashed and bruised and shattered by an incompatible reality, that it is safe to sur-

mise—with no impiety to the memory of Peter Gansevoort—
that had Melville known his maternal grandfather, the old
General's six feet four of blood and bone would have shrunk,
with his extravagance of all human excellence, to more truly
historical dimensions.

Melville's paternal grandfather, Major Thomas Melville,
who died in 1832, when Melville was thirteen years old, inspired his grandson to no such glowing tributes. Born in
Boston, in 1751, an only child, he was left an orphan at the
age of ten. It appears by the probate records on the appointment of his guardian in 1761, that he inherited a considerable
fortune from his father. He was reared by his maternal
grandmother, Mrs. Mary Cargill. Mrs. Mary Cargill's brother
was the celebrated and eccentric dissenter and polemic writer,
John Abernethy of Dublin, who in his *Tracts* (collected in
1751) measured swords with Swift himself triumphantly; her
son, David, was both a celebrated warrior against the Indians,
and the father of twenty-three children, fifteen of whom were
sons. Whatever the immediate male relatives of Mrs. Mary
Cargill did, it would appear, they did vigorously, and on an
enterprising scale. She was herself an old lady of very independent ideas about the universe, and her grandson, Thomas
Melville—Melville's grandfather,—perpetuated much of her
independence. Indifferent to the caprices of fashion, Thomas
Melville persisted until his death in 1832, in wearing the old-
fashioned cocked hat and knee breeches. Oliver Holmes said
of him: "His aspect among the crowds of a later generation
reminded me of a withered leaf which has held to its stem
through the storms of autumn and winter, and finds itself still
clinging to its bough while the new growths of spring are
bursting their buds and spreading their foliage all around it."

And so the Autocrat wrote:

> "I saw him once before,
> As he passed by the door,
>   And again
> The pavement stones resound
> As he totters o'er the ground
>   With his cane.

GENERAL PETER GANSEVOORT

MELVILLE'S GRANDFATHERS

MAJOR THOMAS MELVILLE

They say that in his prime,
Ere the pruning-knife of Time
   Cut him down,
Not a better man was found
By the Crier on his round
   Through the town.

But now he walks the streets,
And he looks at all he meets
   Sad and wan.
And he shakes his feeble head
And it seems as if he said,
   'They are gone.'

The mossy marbles rest
On the lips that he has pressed
   In their bloom,
And the names he loved to hear
Have been carved for many a year
   On the tomb.

My grandmamma has said,—
Poor old lady, she is dead
   Long ago—
That he had a Roman nose,
And his cheek was like a rose
   In the snow:

But now his nose is thin,
And it rests upon his chin
   Like a staff,
And a crook is in his back,
And a melancholy crack
   In his laugh.

I know it is a sin
For me to sit and grin
   At him here;
But the old three-cornered hat,
And the breeches, and all that,
   Are so queer!

And if I should live to be
The last leaf upon the tree
   In the spring,
Let them smile as I do now,
At the old forsaken bough,
   Where I cling."

In his boyhood, Thomas Melville was sent by his grandmother (who lived on till her grandson was thirty years old, clinging as tenaciously to life as to every other good thing she set hands upon) to the College of New Jersey, now Princeton. He was graduated in 1769. From both Princeton and Harvard he later received an M.A. Between 1771 and 1773 he visited his relatives in Scotland. During this visit he was presented with the freedom of the city of St. Andrews and of Renfrew. He returned to Boston to become a merchant and to enter with spirit into the patriotic ferment then so actively brewing. He was a member of the Long Room Club, in sympathy with the Sons of Liberty, and with Paul Revere, one of the "Indians" to take part in the Boston Tea Party of December 16, 1773. There still survive a few unbrewed leaves from this cargo of tea: the carefully preserved shakings from Major Melville's shoes, resurrected when he relaxed into slippers immediately upon his return home from the excitements of revolutionary defiance. Though Major Melville was, throughout his life, an extreme conservative, it was his very conservatism that fired him to revolution. He believed that what needed to be conserved was the constitutional—British constitutional—rights of his country, not the innovation of Hanoverian tyranny. He commanded a detachment sent to Nantucket, the centre of whaling, to watch the movement of the British fleet; in the expedition into Rhode Island, in 1778, he took the rank of Major in Croft's regiment of Massachusetts artillery. His resignation, dated Boston, Oct. 21, 1778, states "that he had been almost three years in said service and would willingly continue to serve, but owing to inadequate pay and subsequent inability to support his family he felt compelled to resign his commission." In 1789 he was commissioned by Washington as naval officer of the port of Boston: a commission renewed by all succeeding presidents down to Andrew Jackson's time in 1824. Major Melville was the nearest surviving male relative of the picturesque General Robert Melville, who was the first and only Captain General and Governor-in-Chief of the islands ceded to England by France in 1763, and at the time of his death in

1809, with one exception, the oldest General in the British Army.

In 1779, Major Melville was elected fire ward of Boston, and when he resigned in 1825, he was offered a vote of thanks "for the zeal, intrepidity and judgment with which he has on all occasions discharged his duties as fire ward for forty-six years in succession, and for twenty-six as chairman of the board." In those days, volunteer fire companies were fashionable sporting clubs, and such was the distinction attached to membership that a premium was often paid for the privilege of belonging to such an exclusive and diverting fraternity. Melville's father-in-law, Lemuel Shaw, Chief Justice of Massachusetts, was Fire Warden between 1818 and 1821. Melville's grandfather and future father-in-law may have met at many a fire and, for all we know to the contrary, the intimacy between the Shaws and the Melvilles that culminated in Herman's marriage, may have been first kindled by a burning house.

The tradition survives of Major Melville that the excitement of running to fire grew upon him like gambling upon more sedentary mortals, and that his death was caused by over-fatigue and exposure at a fire near his house he attended at the age of eighty-one.

Of Melville's two grandmothers, Catharine Van Schaick and Priscilla Scollay, there is no mention in any of his writings. It is a peculiarity of Melville's writings indeed, completely to disregard all of his female relatives,—with the notable exceptions of his mother, his mother-in-law, and his wife.

Major Thomas Melville, by his marriage with Priscilla Scollay, is said to have aggravated an already ample fortune, though the terms of his resignation from the Revolutionary army argue a dwindling of income during unsettled times. The Scollays, one of the oldest of Boston families, were related to Melville not only by direct blood descent, but Melville's great-great-uncle, John Melville (who died in London in 1798) married Deborah Scollay, Melville's great-aunt. Deborah Scollay, Priscilla's sister, was the first of thirteen children; Priscilla the tenth. The Scollays, in brave competition

with the Melvilles and the Gansevoorts, seem to have devoutly
accepted the Mosaic edict to increase and multiply: they were,
as Carlyle says of Dr. Thomas Arnold, of "unhastening, un-
resting diligence." Major Thomas Melville had eleven children by his wife Priscilla, Melville's father Allan being the
fourth child and second son. Of the influence of Allan's numerous brothers and sisters upon Melville there are scant records to show. His aunt Priscilla, however, mentioned him
in her will.

Allan's oldest sister, Mary (1778-1859) married Captain
John DeWolf II. of Bristol, Rhode Island. In *Moby-Dick,*
in offering instances of ships being charged upon by whales,
Melville quotes from the *Voyages* of Captain Langsdorff, a
member of Admiral Krusenstern's famous Discovery Expedition in the beginning of the last century. In the passage
quoted by Melville is mentioned a Captain D'Wolf. "Now,
the Captain D'Wolf here alluded to as commanding the ship
in question," says Melville, "is a New Englander, who, after
a long life of unusual adventures as a sea captain, this day
resides in the village of Dorchester, near Boston. I have the
honour of being a nephew of his. I have particularly questioned him concerning this passage in Langsdorff. He sub-
stantiates every word." In *Redburn,* Melville speaks of "an
uncle of mine, an old sea-captain, with white hair, who used
to sail to a place called Archangel in Russia, and who used
to tell me that he was with Captain Langsdorff, when Captain
Langsdorff crossed over by land from the sea of Okotsk in
Asia to St. Petersburg, drawn by large dogs in a sled. . . .
He was the very first sea captain I had ever seen, and his white
hair and fine handsome florid face made so strong an impression upon me that I have never forgotten him, though I only
saw him during this one visit of his to New York, for he was
lost in the White Sea some years after." Just what, if anything besides two contradictory statements—Melville owed to
this uncle it would be worthless to surmise.

Another of Melville's uncles, however, Thomas—Allan's
older brother—played an important rôle in Melville's development. After an eventful residence of twenty-one years in

France, Thomas returned to America with his wife Françoise Raymonde Eulogie Marie des Douleurs Lamé Fleury, shortly before the War of 1812. Enlisted in the army, he was sent to Pittsfield, Massachusetts, with the rank of Major. After the war he continued in Pittsfield, and with his family set up at what is now Broadhall.

Broadhall, built by Henry Van Schaek in 1781, bought by Elkanah Watson in 1807, was, in 1816, acquired by Major Thomas Melville of the cocked hat. His son, Major Thomas Melville of the French wife, lived in Broadhall until 1837, when he moved to Galena, Illinois, where he died on August 1—Melville's birthday—1845. By a parallel irony of fate, just as the Stanwix House of the Gansevoorts is now a hotel, Broadhall of the Melvilles is now a country club.

It was a strange transplanting, that of Major Thomas Melville and his wife, Marie des Douleurs, from Paris to the rustic crudities of the farming outskirts of civilisation. Marie des Douleurs rapidly pined and wilted in the harsh brusque air. A bundle of her letters survive, written in a delicate drooping hand: letters that might have been written by a wasted and homesick nun. In 1814, within the space of a single month, Mrs. Thomas Melville and two of her children died of consumption. Thomas, of more vigorous stock, survived to marry again—this time to Mary Anna Augusta Hobard, and to take actively to farming. He achieved a local reputation for his successful devotion to the soil; presiding at meetings of the Berkshire Agricultural Association, and winning a first prize at a ploughing match at the Berkshire Fair. As a boy, Melville was sent to alternate his visits to the Gansevoorts by trips to his uncle at Pittsfield. The single record of his life at Broadhall is preserved in *The History of Pittsfield* (1876) "compiled and written, under the general direction of a committee, by J. E. A. Smith." Melville says:

"In 1836 circumstances made me the greater portion of a year an inmate of my uncle's family, and an active assistant upon the farm. He was then grey haired, but not wrinkled; of a pleasing complexion, but little, if any, bowed in figure; and preserving evident traces of the prepossessing good looks

of his youth. His manners were mild and kindly, with a faded
brocade of old French breeding, which—contrasted with his
surroundings at the time—impressed me as not a little interesting, not wholly without a touch of pathos.

"He never used the scythe, but I frequently raked with him
in the hay field. At the end of the swath he would at times
pause in the sun and, taking out his smooth worn box of satin-
wood, gracefully help himself to a pinch of snuff, while leaning on his rake; quite naturally: and yet with a look, which—
as I recall it—presents him in the shadowy aspect of a courtier
of Louis XVI, reduced as a refugee to humble employment in
a region far from gilded Versailles.

"By the late October fire, in the great hearth of the capacious kitchen of the old farm mansion, I remember to have
seen him frequently sitting just before early bed time, gazing
into the embers, while his face plainly expressed to a sympathetic observer that his heart, thawed to the core under the influence of the general flame—carried him far away over the
ocean to the gay boulevards.

"Suddenly, under the accumulation of reminiscences, his eye
would glisten and become humid. With a start he would check
himself in his reverie, and give an ultimate sigh; as much as to
say 'ah, well!' and end with an aromatic pinch of snuff. It
was the French graft upon the New England stock, which produced this autumnal apple: perhaps the mellower for the frost."

It was immediately following upon the heels of this sojourn
in Pittsfield in 1836, that Melville went down to the sea and
shipped before the mast. Of Melville's companionship with
his Pittsfield cousins during this visit, nothing seems to be
known. Melville's uncle, Thomas, had two children living at
the time: Anna Marie Priscilla, who died in Pittsfield in 1858,
and Pierre François Henry Thomas Wilson, thirteen years
Melville's senior, who in 1842 died in the Sandwich Islands.
That Pierre's adventures to the far corners of the earth may
have had some influence upon Melville's taking to a ship is a
tempting surmise; but a surmise whose only cogency is its possibility.

Whatever the influence of Pittsfield in sending Melville to

sea, it was to Pittsfield he finally returned, when, after wide
wanderings, he faced homeward. The old Major, his uncle,
was dead, and Broadhall, descended to one of his sons, was
rented as a hotel. During the summer of 1850, Melville and
his wife boarded at Broadhall. In October of the same year,
they settled in Pittsfield, not at Broadhall, as has been repeatedly stated, but at a neighbouring farm, christened Arrowhead
by Melville. Arrowhead was Melville's home for the following thirteen years.

Melville's great-grandfather, Allan—father of *The Last
Leaf*—came to America in 1748, and settled in Boston as
a merchant. This Allan was the son of Thomas Melville, a
clergyman of the Scotch Kirk. This Thomas Melville was
from 1718 to 1764 minister of Scoonie Parish, Levin, Fife-
shire. In 1769 he "ended his days in a state of most cheerful
tranquillity."

Thomas Melville of Scoonie was second in lineal descent
from Sir John Melville of Carnbee: a worthy knighted by
James VI. According to Sir Robert Douglas' *The Baronage
of Scotland* (Edinburgh, 1798), this Sir John Melville of
Carnbee was thirteenth in direct blood descent from one Sir
Richard Melvill, a man of distinction in the reign of Alexander III, and who in 1296 was compelled to swear allegiance
to Edward I of England when he overran Scotland.

If this remote tracing of Melville's descent were a discovery
of facts unknown to Melville, it would be an ostentatious irrelevancy to flaunt it in his biography. But Melville was
ironically conscious of his lineage, and when his earlier novels
had won him reputation at home and in England as an entertaining literary vagabond, in France (see the typically patronising *Études sur la Littérature et les Mœurs des Anglo-Améri-
cains du XIXe Siècle*—Paris, 1851—by M. Philarete Chasles)
as a representative product of a crude and traditionless civilisation, he took satirical unction to his soul at the illustrious
associations that clung around his ancient name. In his own
person he felt that he contradicted the conceit of the European
world "that in demagogical America the sacred Past hath no
fixed statues erected to it, but (that) all things irreverently

seethe and boil in the vulgar caldron of an everlasting, uncrys-
tallising Present." Founding his defence upon the knowledge
of his own ancestry, he maintained in *Pierre* that if America so
chose to glorify herself, she could make out a good general
case with England in the little matter of long pedigrees—pedigrees, that is, without a flaw. In monarchical Europe, Melville
takes pains to contend, the proudest families are but grafted
families that successively live and die on the eternal soil of
a name. In the pride of unbroken lineal blood descent from
a thirteenth century count, he matched his blood and patronym
with the most honoured in England. "If Richmond, and St.
Albans, and Grafton, and Portland, and Buccleugh, be names
almost as old as England herself, the present Dukes of those
names stop in their own genuine pedigrees at Charles II., and
there find no very fine fountain; since what we would deem the
least glorious parentage under the sun, is precisely the parentage of a Buccleugh, for example; whose ancestress could not
well avoid being a mother, it is true, but had incidentally
omitted the preliminary rites. Yet a King was the sire. . . .
All honour to the names, and all courtesy to the men; but if St.
Albans tell me he is all-honourable and all-eternal, I must
politely refer him to Nell Gwynne." Melville bitterly resented
the fashionable foreign imputation that his was a rootless and
upstart people. Through its grilling of bars sinister, he viewed
the superior pretensions of monarchical aristocracy with his
finger at his nose. "If in America," he boasted, "the vast mass
of families be as the blades of grass, yet some few there are
that stand as the oak; which, instead of decaying, annually puts
forth new branches; whereby Time, instead of subtracting, is
made to capitulate into a multiple virtue."

If Melville took over-elaborate pains to point to himself as
swinging at the dizzy crest of such a patriarchal tree, it was
not to derive personal glory from mere altitude. By exhibiting
the humorous incompatibility between his destiny and his descent, he strove to show, at one and the same time, both the absurdity of all pride in blood, and the ironic poignancy of his
own apparent defeat.

Melville's parents, however, qualified their ancestral pride

with no such ironic considerations. With whole-hearted gratitude they thanked God for their descent; nor did they, in their
thanksgiving, fail to acknowledge, with becoming humility, a
Heavenly Father who, in power and glory, transcended even
terrestrial counts and brewers.

Allan was always a man of devout protestations; and although he always signed his own name with an underscoring of
tangled flourishes, he wrote the name of God—and his correspondence is liberally scattered with Deity—with three conspicuous capitals of his most ornate penmanship. Melville was
patently modelling the father of Pierre after his own male par-
ent, when he recorded Pierre's father's platitudinous insist-
ence "that all gentlemanhood was vain, all claims to it prepos-
terous and absurd, unless the primeval gentleness and golden
humanities of religion had been so thoroughly wrought into
the complete texture of the character, that he who pronounced
himself gentleman, could also rightly assume the meek but
knightly style of Christian."

Allan, proud in the sense of this humility, in untangling his
descent back to Sir John Melville of Carnbee, seems to have
rested serenely in the pious faith that he had established his
kinship to all the titled and illustrious Melvilles in history. So
he carried his head high—as he felt a republican should—and
with a generous and comprehensive fraternity claimed as his
more than kith—as indeed they were—an impressive congregation of courtiers, scholars and divines.

So prolific has been the Melville family, so extended its history, that its intricate branchings from the veritable Aaron's
rod in which it had its source, have never been completely un-
tangled by even the most arduous genealogical historians.
With what directness and potency the different Melville strains
were active in Melville's blood it would be utterly absurd to
pretend to determine. But if not forces in Melville's blood,
Allan made them vital presences in his son's boyhood imagination.

The most illustrious of this shadowy company of adopted
ancestors was the old Viking, Andrew Melville (1545-1622),
the dauntless "Episcopomastrix" or "Scourge of Bishops,"

second in fame among Scotch reformers only to John Knox. In October, 1577, at an interview between Andrew and the Regent Morton, the latter, irritated at the intrepidity of the assembly, exclaimed: "There will never be quiet in this country till half a dozen of you be hanged!" Whereupon Andrew, in language Morton dared not resent, exclaimed: "Hark! Sir; threaten your courtiers after that manner. It is the same to me whether I rot in the air or in the ground. The earth is the Lord's. Patria est ubicunque est bene." Another Andrew (1624-1706) among these ghostly presences was a soldier of fortune who in the preface of his *Memoires de M. de Chevalier de Melville* (Amsterdam, 1704) was eulogised for his valour and his protestantism.

Conspicuous in Allan's library was a copy of the *Memoirs of His Own Life by Sir James Melvil of Hallhill* (London, 1683), bearing the autograph of Allan's great-grandfather, Thomas Melville of Scoonie. This volume had been brought to America by Allan's grandfather in 1746, and was cherished by Melville's father as a record of the part played by his exuberant ancestors in the turbulent affairs of Elizabeth and Mary, Queen of Scots. From this volume Allen taught his children of Sir James' father, John Melville, Lord of Raith in Fife, who, "although there was not the least suspicion of anie fault, yitt lost he his head, becaus he was known to be one that unfainedlie favoured the truthe;" of Sir James' brother, William, who was able to speak perfectly "the Latin, the Dutche, the Flemyn, and the Frenche tongue;" of another brother of Sir James, Sir Robert Melville, who "spak brave and stout language to the consaill of England, so that the quen herself boisted him of his lyf." But all of the details of Sir James' racy account of his own adventures were not fit entertainment for the sons of New England Unitarians. Yet many of these unpuritan accounts are in Melville's own vein, as witness the recounting of the incident that befell Sir James at the age of fourteen, when, in company with the French Ambassador, Monluc, Bishop of Valence, he was entertained in Ireland by one O'Docherty who lived in "a dark tour." It appears that the Bishop paid such disquieting attention to O'Docherty's daughter that the father substituted another bait to the Prelate's susceptibilities: a substitution that produced an awkward scene in etiquette. For the second lady mistook a phial "of the maist precious balm that grew in Egypt, which Soliman the great Turc had given in a present to the same bishop" for something to eat; and this "because it had an odoriphant smell." "Therefore she licked it clean out." During this process of consumption, O'Docherty's daughter, disengaged from the Bishop, turned to Sir James for solace, with an offer to elope. Sir James was cautious for his fourteen years, and convinced the lady of the superfluousness of migratory impulses.

Contemporary with Allan, there lived in Scotland, direct descendants of these Elizabethan Melvilles. One year before Herman's birth, Allan, with admirable republican simplicity, decided, during one of the frequent business trips that took him across the Atlantic, to look up his titled Scotch cousins, and pay them the compliments of his dutiful respects. The record of this adventure is preserved in Allan's journal, bound in vellum of a lurid emerald green. The entries are characteristically business-like, and stoically naked of personal reflections:

May 22, 1818—Visited Melville house, the seat of the Earl of Leven & Melville at 2 P.M., 14 miles— the Earl & Family being absent, left them at 4 A.M. & dined at the New Inn at the Junction of the Perth, Cupar & Dundee Roads, 6 miles.

May 26, 1818—Reached Melville house at ½ past 3 P.M.— 10 miles—& met with a very hospitable & friendly reception from his lordship & family.

May 27, 1818—Left Melville house at ½ past 11 in his lordship's gig with a lacquey to meet the coach at the New Inn.

It would, perhaps, be entertaining to know just exactly what Alexander, 7th Earl of Levin and 6th Earl of Melville, who was also Viscount Kirkaldie, Lord Melville of Monymaill, Lord Bolgonie, and Lord Raith, Monyraill and Balwearie, thought in his heart of Allan Melville of Boston, merchant, and importer of commodities from France.

CHAPTER III

PARENTS AND EARLY YEARS

"In general terms we have been thus decided in asserting the great
genealogical and real-estate dignity of some families in America, because
in so doing we poetically establish the richly aristocratic condition of
Master Pierre Glendinning, for whom we have claimed some special
family distinction. And to the observant reader the sequel will not fail
to show how important is this circumstance, considered with reference
to the singularly developed character and most singular life-career of our
hero. Nor will any man dream that the last chapter was merely intended for a foolish bravado, and not with a solid purpose in view."
—HERMAN MELVILLE: *Pierre.*

SAMUEL BUTLER, who with Thomas Huxley cherished certain unorthodox convictions as to "the unfathomable injustice
of the Universe," found the make-shift of family life not the
least of natural evils. In a more benevolent adjustment of
the human animal to its environment, so Butler declared, children would be spared the incubus of parents. After the ease-
ful death of their progenitors, they would be hatched, cocoon-
like, from an ample and comfortable roll of bank-notes of high
denomination. And it is a foregone surety that, had Samuel
Butler known Herman Melville's parents, he would not have
been moved to soften his impeachment of the way of all flesh.
For the household of Allan Melville bore striking resemblances
to that of the most self-important of the Pontifexes. Both
John Pontifex and Allan Melville, judged either by the accepted standards of their own time or to-day, were good men:
to his God, his neighbours, his wife, his children, each did his
duty relentlessly. And each, as Melville, with obvious autobiographical reference, says of the father of Pierre, "left behind
him in the general voice of the world, a marked reputation as a
Christian and a gentleman; in the heart of his wife, a green
memory of many healthy days of unclouded and joyful wedded
life." But each also left behind him a son who in the end was
to cherish his memory with some misgivings. Allan was less

fortunate than John Pontifex in that though he died rich in virtue, he died with no corresponding abundance of corruptible riches. Nothing in his life so ill became him as his bequest of poverty to his widow and eight children.

Herman, the second son and third child, was thirteen years old at the time of Allan's decease: young enough to cherish up into early manhood the most fantastic idealisation of his father. "Children begin by loving their parents," a modern cynic has said; "later the children grow to understanding, and sometimes, they forgive." As Melville grew in maturity of years, he did not grow in charity toward his parents. In his novel *Pierre* he seems to draw malicious delight in pronouncing, under a thin disguise, an imaginary libel upon his father's memory. There he desecrated in fiction what he had once fondly cherished in life. Aside from its high achievement as a work of art, this dark wild book of incest and death is of the greatest importance as a document in autobiography. Most of the characters in *Pierre* are unmistakably idealisations of clearly recognisable originals. The hero, Pierre Glendinning, is a glorification of Melville; the widowed mother, Marie Glendinning, owes much more to Melville's mother, Maria Gansevoort, than the initials of her name. And in this book, Melville exorcises the ghost of his father, and brings him forth to unearth from the past a skeleton that Melville seems to have manufactured in the closet of a vindictive subconsciousness.

"Blessed and glorified in his tomb beyond Prince Mausolus," wrote Melville at the age of thirty-three, "is that mortal sire, who, after an honourable, pure course of life, dies, and is buried, as in a choice fountain, in the filial breast of a tenderhearted and intellectually appreciative child. But if fate preserve the father to a later time, too often the filial obsequies are less profound, the canonisation less ethereal."

As has been said, Melville was thirteen when, in 1832, his father died. And at that time, as for years following, there survived from Allan in Melville's memory "the impression of a bodily form of rare manly virtue and benignity, only rivalled by the supposed perfect mould in which his virtuous heart had been cast." In *Redburn* he says of his youthful idealisation of

Allan: "I always thought him a marvellous being, infinitely purer and greater than I was, who could not by any possibility do wrong or say an untruth." And as a gesture expressive of this piety for his father's memory, he took but one book with him to Liverpool when at the age of seventeen he worked his way across the Atlantic in a merchantman. This was an old dog-eared guide-book that had belonged to his father. On the map in this book, Allan, with characteristic precision, had traced with a pen a number of dotted lines radiating in all directions from Riddough's Hotel at the foot of Lord Street: marks that delineated his various excursions in the town. As Melville planned his itinerary while in Liverpool, he was in the first place to visit Riddough's Hotel, where his father had stopped more than thirty years before; and then, with the map in his hand, to follow Allan through the town, according to the dotted lines in the diagram. "For this," says Melville, "would be performing a filial pilgrimage to spots which would be hallowed to my eyes." Because Melville had failed to take into account the mutability of cities, he was disappointed to find some of the shrines hallowed by his father's visits no longer in existence. But the very bitterness of his disappointment was an eloquent tribute to his father's memory.

Allan himself was born in 1782, second son, and fourth child, in a family of eleven children. Of his early life, almost nothing is known. Though he was born into a well-to-do family of considerable cultivation, he seems never to have been exposed to the boasted advantages of a university education. He was, however, a rather extensively travelled man. At the age of eighteen, as if to set a precedent for his son, he made his first trip abroad. But whereas Melville went as a sailor before the mast, to land in Liverpool as a penniless itinerant, Allan was two years in Paris as a guest, in comfortable circumstances, of a well-to-do uncle. Before his marriage in 1814, Allan made five other pilgrimages to Europe; and once, after his marriage, he crossed the Atlantic again. This last trip he would not have taken but from urgency of business: "It will be a most painful sacrifice to part from my beloved wife and children," he says, in prospect of the journey; "but duty towards them requires it." Allan acclimated himself to France as a young man, and so acquired a mastery of the French language. He is said to have spoken French like a native: a bilingual accomplishment that Melville never even remotely acquired. Melville boasted a smattering of a Polynesian dialect or two: but so imperfect was this smattering that it moved Stevenson to complain that Melville, like Charles Lamb, "had no ear."

In the journal which Allan kept from 1800 to 1831, there survives a meticulously accurate account of his wanderings up and down upon the face of Christendom. On the fly-leaf of the journal, under the title "Recapitulations of Voyages and Travels from 1800 to 1822 both inclusive," he gives, in ledger-like summary, this statement of his peregrinations:

> "by land 24425 miles.
> by water 48460 miles.
> days at sea, etc. 643."

That part of his early life that he spent outside of Europe, he distributed between Boston and Albany. Allan was a man to turn to account all of his resources. His knowledge of French he converted into a business asset, by setting up as a merchant-importer trafficking in dry-goods and notions from France: "razors, children's white leather gloves, leghorn hats, and taffeta ribbons" being a typical shipment.

It was in Albany that Allan met Maria Gansevoort: a meeting of which his journal is austerely ignorant. If there ever were any romance in Allan's life he must have emulated Pepys and recorded it in cipher, and then, with a caution deeper than Pepys', have burned the cryptic revelation. It is true that in *Pierre*, Melville attempts to brighten his father's pre-marital years by imputing to him a lively vitality in his youth: but the evidence for this imputation hangs upon a most tenuous thread of ambiguities. Yet now that it has transpired that even the sober Wordsworth under similar circumstances succumbed to the flesh, it is not impossible, on the face of it, that Allan, in the unredeemed years before his comparatively late

From a Painting
made in Paris, 1810.

marriage, may have been anointed in mortality. But in his later life—as was Wordsworth—he was a paragon of propriety, and he must be acquitted of indiscretion until more damning facts are mustered to accuse him. All surviving evidence presents him as a model of rigid decorum. In so far as he has revealed himself, all but the most restrained and well-behaved and standardised emotions fell within the forbidden degrees. It is certain that no flower ever gave *him* thoughts too deep for tears.

His courtship seems to have been a model of discretion, and might well have been modelled after Mrs. Hannah More's *Coelebs in Search of a Wife*. There survive two gifts that he made while he was meditating on the serious verge of matrimony. A year before his marriage he bought, fresh from the press, a copy of *The Pleasures of Imagination* by Mark Akenside, M.D., with a critical essay on the poem, by Mrs. Barbauld, prefixed. Whether either Allan or Maria ever read a line of Dr. Akenside we do not know : Maria's copy, it must be confessed, is suspiciously well-preserved. But Allan had the authority of *Coelebs* that "the condensed vigour, so indispensable to blank verse, the skilful variation of the pause, the masterly structure of the period, and all the occult mysteries of the art, can, perhaps, be best learned from Akenside." That the poet's object was "to establish the infinite superiority of mind over unconscious matter, even in its fairest terms," gave Allan opportunity to pay Maria a veiled compliment.

This same Anna Letitia Barbauld, whose introductory essay gave the final stamp of respectability to Dr. Akenside, had, in a chapter of advice to young girls, earlier remarked, and with best-intentioned seriousness, that "An ass is much better adapted than a horse to show off a lady." It may be so. In any event, Allan inscribed on the fly-leaf of Dr. Akenside's effusion :

> MISS MARIA GANSEVOORT
> FROM HER FRIEND
> A. M.

The emotions that smouldered beneath this chaste inscription he vented, and with no compromise to himself, in a tropical tangle of copy-book flourishes that he made below his initials.

The second gift is also a book—Mrs. Chapone's *Letters on the Improvement of the Mind*. Lydia Languish, it is true, had, on a memorable occasion, with unblushing deceit, placed Mrs. Chapone and the reverend Fordyce ostentatiously on a table together. But it is certain that Allan was not consciously furnishing Miss Gansevoort with any of the stage-properties of hypocrisy. Mrs. Chapone's pronouncements were then being accepted by the adoring middle class as Protestant Bulls. And Allan purchased Mrs. Chapone's little volume with his ear to the verdict of Mrs. Delany, who wrote: "They speak to the heart as well as to the head; and I know no book (next to the Bible) more entertaining or edifying."

It was within a few months before his marriage that Allan, in the most orthodox manner of that "Happy Half Century" so happily celebrated by Miss Agnes Repplier, undertook to heighten the virtues of Miss Maria Gansevoort by exposing her to the "pure and prevailing superiority" of Mrs. Chapone. For Allan was a cautious man, and marriage, he knew, was a step not lightly to be made. "I do not want a Helen, or a Saint Cecilia, or a Madame Dacier," said Coelebs, in sketching an ideal wife; "yet must she be elegant or I could not love her; sensible, or I could not respect her; prudent, or I could not confide in her; well-informed, or she could not educate my children; well-bred, or she could not entertain my friends; pious, or I should not be happy with her, because the prime comfort in a companion for life is the delightful hope that she will be a companion for eternity."

Maria was patently elegant, well-bred and pious. The present of Dr. Akenside and Mrs. Chapone gave her generous opportunity of coming to be well-informed. But Allan did not hesitate to make further and more direct contributions to her information. Prudence he rated prime among virtues; and he approached marriage with Miltonic preconceptions. By no means confident that the eternal truths enunciated by Mrs.

Chapone would penetrate Maria's female intellect, Allan prudently summarised the most sacred verities of the volume in two manuscript introductions. Maria's copy of the *Letters* bears three inscriptions made by Allan on three separate flyleaves. The first is in a formal upright hand, rigid in propriety:

"Prudence should be the governing principle of Woman's existence, domestick life her peculiar sphere; no rank can exempt her from an observation of the laws of the former, from an attention to the duties of the latter. To neglect both is to violate the sacred statutes of social happiness, and to frustrate the all-wise intention of that Providence who framed them."

In the second inscription, made with acknowledgment to Miss Owensong, Allan takes all the precautions of a Coelebs to make certain that at his table "the eulogist of female ignorance might dine in security against the intrusion and vanity of erudition." The inscription reads:

"The liberal cultivation of the female *mind* is the best security for the virtues of the female *heart;* and genius, talents and grace, where regulated by prudence and governed by good sense, are never incompatible with domestic qualities or meek and modest virtues."

On the third fly-leaf, this double pronouncement is presented to "Miss Maria Gansevoort" and "from A. M." Allan had doubtless learned from Mrs. Chapone that "our feelings are not given us for ornament, but to spur us on to right action." And Miss Maria may have taken to heart Mrs. Chapone's dictum that "compassion is not impressed upon the human heart, only to adorn the fair face with tears and to give an agreeable languor to the eyes." There survives no trace of a record of Allan's indulging emotions for decorative purposes. How far his sentiments were moved in "right action" to melt Miss Maria to becoming compassion can never be known. During the months immediately before the marriage, however, the even tenor of Allan's journal is jolted by the unusual acknowledgment of the existence of his sisters, and the bald mention of a specified number of miles covered in a "pleasure wagon." Miss Maria, when not his undisputed property by rites of holy matrimony, he never mentions in his journal.

Maria kept no journal; if she presented Allan with inscribed volumes, Allan has eradicated all such breaches of maiden modesty. The only intimate records of Maria that survive are three of her letters, comments upon her in Allan's letters, Melville's elaborate idealisation of her in the person of the mother of Pierre, and a vague memory handed down orally by her descendants.

Maria was born in 1791 and died in 1871. Of her girlhood, little or nothing is very specifically known. After Melville's marriage, she spent the greater part of the remaining years of her life as a dependant in his household, and the oral traditions that survive of her do not halo her memory. She is remembered in such terms as "cold," "worldly," "formal," "haughty" and "proper"; as putting the highest premium upon appearances; as frigidly contemptuous of Melville's domestic economy, and of the home-made clothes of his four children. Though she condescended eight times to motherhood, such was her animal vigour and her ferocity of pride that she preserved to her death a remarkable regality of appearance. She is said to have made a completely competent wife to Allan, superior both to any undue intellectual distractions, and to any of the demoralisations of domesticity. She managed his household, she bore and reared his children, and she did both with a vigorous and unruffled efficiency, without sign of worry or regret. There persists the story—significant even if apocryphal—that each afternoon, enthroned upon a high four-poster, she would nap in order to freshen herself for Allan's evening arrival, her children seated silently on a row of low stools ranged on the floor at the side of her bed. In his death, as in his life, she cherished the image of Allan—with that of her father, General Gansevoort—as the mirror of manly perfection.

In *Pierre,* Melville is said to have drawn an essentially accurate portrait of his mother in the character and person of Mrs. Glendinning. Mrs. Glendinning is presented as a "haughty widow; a lady who externally furnished a singular example of the preservative and beautifying influences of unfluctuating rank, health, and wealth, when joined to a fine mind of medium culture, uncankered by any inconsolable grief, and never worn by sordid cares. In mature age, the rose still miraculously clung to her cheek; litheness had not yet completely uncoiled itself from her waist, nor smoothness unscrolled itself from her brow, nor diamondness departed from her eyes." Proudly conscious of this preservation, never, even in the most intimate associations of life, did she ever appear "in any dishabille that was not eminently becoming." For "she was vividly aware how immense was that influence, which, even in the closest ties of the heart, the merest appearances make upon the mind." And to her pride of appearance she added "her pride of birth, her pride of affluence, her pride of purity, and all the Semiramian pride of woman:" a pride "which in a life of nearly fifty years had never betrayed her into a single published impropriety, or caused her one known pang of the heart." . . . "Infinite Haughtiness had first fashioned her; and then the haughty world had further moulded her; nor had a haughty Ritual omitted to finish her." Nor must Allan's moralisings, and Dr. Akenside, and Mrs. Barbauld, and Mrs. Chapone, be denied their due credit in contributing to the finished product.

Between Maria and her son there existed a striking personal resemblance. From his mother, too, Melville seems to have inherited a constitution of very remarkable vigour, and all the white intensity of the Gansevoort aptitude for anger. But here the resemblance ceased. In the youthful Pierre, Mrs. Glendinning felt "a triumphant maternal pride," for in her son "she saw her own graces strangely translated into the opposite sex." But of his mother's love for him, Pierre entertained precocious and Meredithian suspicions: "She loveth me, ay;—but why? Had I been cast in a cripple's mould, how then? Now do I remember that in her most caressing love, there ever gleamed some scaly, glittering folds of pride. . . . Before my glass she stands—pride's priestess—and to her mirrored image, not to me, she offers up her offering of kisses."

Strangely must she have been baffled by this mirrored image of herself,—fascinated, and at the same time contemptuously revolted. What sympathy, what understanding could she know for this thing of her blood that in obscurity, in poverty, a failure in the eyes of the world, returned from barbarism to dream wild dreams that were increasingly unsalable? As a boy, all his passionate cravings for sympathy, for affection, were rebuffed by her haughty reserve, and recoiled within him. Fatherless and so mothered, he felt with Pierre, "that deep in him lurked some divine unidentifiableness, that owed no earthly kith or kin. Yet was this feeling entirely lonesome and orphan-like. He felt himself driven out an infant Ishmael into the desert, with no maternal Hagar to accompany and comfort him." In *Redburn,* with the mother image like a fury in his heart, he describes himself as "a sort of Ishmael." "Call me Ishmael," is the striking opening sentence of *Moby-Dick;* and its no less striking close: "On the second day, a sail drew near, nearer, and picked me up at last. It was the devious cruising *Rachel,* that in retracing search after her missing children, only found another orphan." Of his mother he is reported to have said in later life: "She hated me."

It seems not altogether fantastic to contend that the Gorgon face that Melville bore in his heart; the goading impalpable image that made his whole life a pilgrimage of despair: that was the cold beautiful face of his mother, Maria Gansevoort. One shudders to think how such a charge would have violated Maria's proprieties. But in the treacherous ambiguities of *Pierre,* Melville himself hovers on the verge of this insight. Pierre is haunted by a mysterious face, which he thus invokes: "The face!—the face!—The face steals down upon me. Mysterious girl! who art thou? Take thy thin fingers from me; I am affianced, and not to thee. Surely, thou lovest not me? —that were most miserable for thee, and me. What, *who* art thou? Oh! wretched vagueness—too familiar to me, yet inexplicable,—unknown, utterly unknown!" To the mind of Pierre it was a face "backward hinting of some irrevocable sin; forward, pointing to some inevitable ill; hovering between Tartarian misery and Paradisaic beauty." In *Pierre,* this face, "compounded so of hell and heaven," is the instrument by which the memory of Pierre's father is desecrated, Pierre's mother is driven to insanity and death, and Pierre himself is utterly ruined. *Pierre* is a book to send a Freudian into ravishment.

Allan Melville, aged thirty-two, and Maria Gansevoort, nine years younger, were married on the fourth of October, 1814. In his journal, Allan has left this record of their wedding-trip.

October 4, 1814—Left Albany at 11 A.M. in a hack with Mrs. M. and Helen (his youngest sister, in her sixteenth year). Dined at Stottard's, Lapan, & slept at Beths Lebanon.

October 5, 1814—Left Lebanon at 9, dined at Pittsfield & slept at Worthington.

October 6, 1814—Left Worthington at ½ past 9, dined at Southampton & slept at Belchertown.

October 7, 1814—Left Belchertown at 9, dined at Brookfield & slept at Worcester.

October 8, 1814—Left Worcester at ½ past 9, dined at Farmingham & arrived at Boston at 5 P.M.

For five years following this initial daily shifting of bed and board, Allan and his wife lived in Albany. The monotony of this residence was broken by the birth of two children,—Gansevoort, and Helen Marie,—and Allan's trip to Europe in the spring of 1818: the enforced business trip, already mentioned, that took him to the home of his titled Scotch cousins. Upon his return he resolved to leave Albany, and settle in what he appreciatively called "the greatest universal mart in the world." On May 12, 1819, he records in his journal: "Commenced Housekeeping at No. 6 Park Street, New York.

Mrs. M. & the children who had been to a visit to her Mother at Albany since 6th April, having joined me on this day, to my great joy."

Three months after Allan's moving to "the greatest universal mart in the world," Maria presented him with a third child, and second son, who was christened after Maria's brother, Herman. At this time, Allan seems to have accepted the excitements of childbirth so casually that Melville's birth passed unrecorded in his father's journal. The first surviving record of Melville's existence is unromantic enough. In a letter dated October 7, 1820, Allan wrote: "Helen Marie suffers most from what we term the whooping cough but which I am sometimes suspicious is only influenza. But Gansevoort and Herman are as yet slightly affected."

At this time, Allan seems to have prospered in business, for on September 20, 1820, he reported to his mother: "We have hired a cook & nurse and only want a waiter to complete our domestic establishment."

Herman's infancy seems to have been untroubled by any event more startling than a growing aggregation of brothers and sisters, occasional trips to Boston, and periodic pilgrimages to Albany with his mother to be exhibited to his grandmother Gansevoort. There are frequent references to his ailing health. In April, 1824, Allan complains that "Gansevoort has lost much of his ruddy appearance, while Herman who has never entirely regained his health again looks pale, thin and dejected."

At this time Allan signed "a 4 yrs. lease at $300 per annum free of taxes, for a new brick 2 story house replete with conveniences, to be handsomely furnished in the most modern style under my own direction & a vacant lot of equal size attached to it which will be invaluable as a play ground for the children. It is situated in Bleecker, the first south, and parallel to Bond St. . . . An open, dry & elevated location equidistant from Broadway & the Bowery, in plain sight of both & almost uniting the advantages of town & country, but its distance from my store, nearly two miles, will compel me to dine from my family most of the time, a serious objection to

In 1820

MARIA GANSEVOORT MELVILLE

In 1865

us all, but we shall be amply compensated by a residence which will obviate the necessity of their leaving town every summer, which deprives me altogether of their society.   I shall also remove professionally on the 1st of May to No. 102 Pearl St. upstairs in the very focus of Business & surrounded by the auction rooms which have become the Rialto of the modern merchants but where I dare say even Shylock would be shy of making his appearance."

By December 29, 1824, we hear of Herman that "he attends school regularly but does not appear so fond of his Book as to injure his health.   He has turned into a great tease & daily puts Gansevoort's patience to flight who cannot bear to be plagued by such a little fellow."

On the same date, Maria writes to her brother about pickling oysters, 500 of which she sent to Albany as a gift to his family.   The picture of her life that she then gives is evidence that she had cherished the counsels that "her friend A. M." had appended to Mrs. Chapone.   She tells of a call she received before eleven o'clock.   "Although the hour was early, all things were neat & in order & my ladyship was dressing herself preparatory to sitting down to her sewing."   She boasts of this fact, she says, in shamed recollection of the time her brother and Mr. Smyth were ushered into a parlour out of order.   "It is the first time a thing of this kind has ever happened to me & for my credit as a good housekeeper, I hope it will be the last."   In conclusion she reports: "This afternoon Mr. M. & myself, induced by the enlivening rays of the setting sun, strolled down the Bowery & after an agreeable walk returned home with renovated spirits."

In December, 1825, Allan is moved to "lament little Herman's melancholy situation, but we trust in humble confidence that the GOD of the widow and the fatherless will yet restore him."   By the following May, Allan's humble confidence seems to have been rewarded not only by Herman's recovery, but by the birth of another child.   In the midst of a business letter—the usual repository of Allan's raptures—he with unwonted vivacity so celebrates his paternal felicity: "The Lovely Six!! are all well, and, while the youngest though both last &

least is a sweet child of promise, & bids fair to become the fairest of the fair—so much for affection, now for business."

On August 10, 1826, Melville was sent out upon his first trip from home unaccompanied by his parents. His destination was his mother's people in Albany, and his custodian during the trip a Mr. Walker. Allan shifts his responsibility for his son on the shoulders of his brother-in-law, Peter Gansevoort, in these terms:

"I now consign to your especial care & patronage my beloved son Herman, an honest hearted double-rooted Knickerbocker of the true Albany stamp, who, I trust, will do equal honour in due time to ancestry, parentage & kindred. He is very backward in speech & somewhat slow in comprehension, but you will find him as far as he understands men and things both solid & profound & of a docile & amiable disposition. If agreeable, he will pass the vacation with his grandmother & yourself & I hope he may prove a pleasant auxiliary to the Family circle—I depend much on your kind attention to our dear Boy who will be truly grateful to the least favour—let him avoid green fruit & unseasonable exposure to the Sun & heat, and having taken such good care of Gansevoort last Summer I commit his Brother to the same hands with unreserved confidence. & with love to our good mother and yourself in which Maria, Mary & the children most cordially join I remain very truly Your Friend & Brother, Allan Melville."

At the foot of this document, Allan appended in pencil: "please turn over." On the reverse of the letter is scribbled a breathless last request: "Have the goodness to procure a pair of shoes for Herman, time being insufficient to have a pair made here."

When Allan here pronounces Melville "very backward in speech & somewhat slow in comprehension," he puts his son in a large class of genius conspicuous for a deferred revelation of promising intelligence. Scott, occupied in building up romances, was dismissed as a dunce; Hume, the youthful thinker, was described by his mother as "uncommon weak minded." Goldsmith was a stupid child; Fanny Burney did not know her letters at the age of eight. Byron showed no aptitude for school work. And Chatterton, up to the age of six and a half, was, on the authority of his mother, "little better than an absolute fool." Allan scorned to take solace from such facts, however. He consoled himself with the fact that though his son was dull, he was at least "docile & amiable."

Melville spent the summer of 1826 with the Gansevoorts. And he looked back upon it as perhaps the most fortunate privilege of his youth, that this first visit to Albany set the precedent for a whole series of similar summers. He is idealising from his own experience when he says of Pierre: "It had been his choice fate to have been born and nurtured in the country, surrounded by scenery whose uncommon loveliness was the perfect mould of a delicate and poetic mind; while the popular names of its finest features appealed to the proudest patriotic and family associations of the historic line of Glendinning." Nor does he hesitate to reiterate that Pierre's was a "choice fate": "For to a noble American youth this indeed —more than in any other land—this indeed is a most rare and choice lot." Each summer, for as long as his school vacations would permit, Melville shared the choice lot of Pierre. But Allan, unconverted to Melville's Wordsworthian creed, regularly recalled his son to the city with the opening of school.

This is the recall for the year 1826, dated "12 Sept. Tuesday, 4 P.M.": "We expect Gansevoort on Sunday, at fartherest, when we wish Herman also to be here, that they may recommence their studies together on Monday next, with equal chances of preferment, & without any feelings of jealousy or ideas of favoritism—besides they may thus acquire a practical lesson whose influence may endure forever, for if they understand early, that inclination must always yield to Duty, it will become a matter of course when their vacations expire to bid a fond adieu to friends & amusements, & return home cheerfully to their books, & they will consequently imbibe habits of Order & punctuality, which bear sweet blossoms in the dawn of life, golden fruits in 'the noon of manhood' & a rich harvest for the garners of old age—business is about as dull and unprofitable as the most bitter foe to general prosperity, if such a being exists in human shape, could desire it, & it requires a keener vision than mine, to discern among the signs of the times, any real symptoms of future improvement."

The summer of 1827 Melville spent with his grandparents in Boston; the two following summers in Albany.

On February 28, 1828, Allan reported to his brother-in-law Peter Gansevoort: "We have taken a house on Broadway (No. 675—if I mistake not) for 5 years @ $575 without taxes— being the 2d beyond the marble buildings & nearly opposite Bond Street. The house is a modern 2 stories built 4 years since for the owner & has only been occupied by his family. The lot is 200 feet deep through to Mercer St., Maria is charmed with the house & situation."

But Allan never lived to see this lease expire. The dull business of which he earlier complained settled upon him, and in 1830 the prospects in New York were so hopeless that he moved back to Albany, to die two years later, leaving his wife and eight children practically penniless.

But before Allan moved away from New York, Herman had time to write the earliest manuscript of his that survives. It reads:

11th of October, 1828.

DEAR GRANDMOTHER

This is the third letter that I ever wrote so you must not think it very good. I now study geography, gramar, writing, Speaking, Spelling, and read in the Scientific class book. I enclose in this letter a drawing for my dear grandmother. Give my love to grandmamma, Uncle Peter and Aunt Mary. And my Sisters and also to allan,

Your affectionate grandson
HERMAN MELVILLE.

In *Redburn,* Melville speaks "of those delightful days before my father was a bankrupt, and died, and we moved from the city"; or again, speaking of Allan: "he had been shaken by many storms of adversity, and at last died a bankrupt." Allan's journal, however, which he kept until within a few months of his death, is proudly superior to anything suggestive of the outrageousness of fortune: its hard glazed surface betrays to the end no crack in the veneer. Beyond a persistent tradition, and Melville's iterated statement, no further evidence of Allan's financial reverses has transpired.

It is certain, however, that after Allan's death his family found themselves in straitened circumstances. After 1830, the most specific evidence known to exist about the whereabouts and condition of Melville's family is preserved in old Albany Directories, as follows:

1830: no Melvilles mentioned.
1831: Melville, Allan, 446 s. Market.
   house 338 n. Market.
1832: Melville, Gansevoort, fur store, 364 s. Market.
   Melville, widow Maria, cor. of n. Market & Steuben.
1833: Melville, Gansevoort, fur store, 364 s. Market.
   Melville, widow Maria, 282 n. Market.
1834: Melville, Gansevoort, fur and cap store, 364 s. Market,
   res. 3 Clinton Square n. Pearl.
   Melville, Herman, clerk in N. Y. State Bank, res. 3
   Clinton Square n. Pearl.
   Melville, widow Maria, 3 Clinton Square n. Pearl.
1835: Melville, Gansevoort, fur and cap store, 364 s. Market,
   res. 3 Clinton Square n. Pearl.
   Melville, Herman, clerk at 364 s. Market, res. 3 Clinton Square n. Pearl.
   Melville, widow Maria, 3 Clinton Square n. Pearl.

After 1835 the family scattered, Melville to begin his wanderings on land and sea,—Gansevoort to drift about Albany for two years, Maria and the rest of the children to move to Lansingburg—now a part of Albany.

The publication of the *Celebration of the Semi-Centennial Anniversary of the Albany Academy* (Albany, 1862) in its list of alumni, and the date of their entrance, offers the following record:

    1831: Melville, Allan.
    1830: Melville, Gansevoort.
    1830: Melville, Herman.

This Semi-Centennial Anniversary Celebration took place in Tweedle Hall, which, so says the publication, "was crowded with an appropriate audience." "The meeting was presided over by the Honourable PETER GANSEVOORT, the President of the Board of Trustees," the publication goes on to say, "and by his side were his associates and the guests of the festival, among whom was warmly welcomed HERMAN MELVILLE, whose reputation as an author has honoured the Academy, world-wide." As Melville sat there, "the Rev. Doc. FERRIS . . . made prayer to Heaven the source of that knowledge which shall not vanish away;" Orlando Mead, LL.D., read a Historical Discourse; and "at successive periods the exercises were diversified by the music of *Home, Sweet Home* or *Rest, Spirit, Rest,* and of other appropriate harmonies." What recollections of his school-days at the Albany Academy were then passing through Melville's head, we haven't sufficient knowledge of his schooling to guess. As part of the celebration, Alexander W. Bradford, who was a student at the Academy between 1825 and 1832, spoke of the "domestic discords and fights between the Latins and the English, and the more fierce and bitter foreign conflicts waged between the Hills and the Creeks, the latter being a pugnacious tribe of barbarians who inhabited the shores of Fox Creek;" of "the weekly exhibitions in the Gymnasium grand with the beauty of Albany;" of "the lectures and experiments in chemistry, which being in the evening, were favoured by the presence of young ladies as well as gentlemen." In what capacity, if any, Melville figured in these activities there is no way of knowing.

Dr. Henry Hun, now President of the Albany Academy, in answer to a request for information about Melville, answers: "Unfortunately, the records of the Albany Academy were burned in 1888. It is impossible to say how long he remained in the school or what results he achieved. He probably took the Classical Course, as most of the brighter boys took it. It was really a Collegiate Course, and the Head-master (or Principal as he was then called) Dr. T. Romeyn Beck was an extraordinary man, but one who did not spare the rod, but gave daily exhibitions in its use." In a postscript Dr. Hun adds: "It was a God-fearing school."

Joseph Henry, at one time teacher at the Albany Academy, later head of the Smithsonian Institute, in an address before the Association for the Advancement of Science, in session in Albany in 1851, said of Melville's Alma Mater: "The Albany Academy was and still is one of the first, if not the very first, institution of its kind in the United States. It early opposed the pernicious maxim that a child should be taught nothing but what it could perfectly understand, and that the sole object of instruction is to teach a child to think."

Since Melville was in 1834 employed as clerk in the New York State Bank (a post he doubtless owed to his uncle, Peter Gansevoort, who was one of the Trustees) he must have ceased to enjoy the advantages of the Albany Academy before that date. During the time of Melville's attendance, the same texts were used by all students alike during their first three years at the Albany Academy. This, then, would seem to be a list of the texts (offered by the courtesy of Dr. Hun) studied by Melville:

1st Year:

Latin Grammar
Historia Sacra
Turner's Exercises (begun)
Latin Reader
Irving's Universal History

2d Year:

Latin Reader continued
Turner's Exercises
Cornelius Nepos
Irving's Grecian and Roman Histories
Roman Antiquities

3d Year:

Cæsar, Ovid, Latin Prosody
Turner's Exercises, Translations
Irving's Grecian Antiquities
Mythology and Biography
Greek Grammar

J. E. A. Smith, in the *Biographical Sketch of Herman Melville* that in 1891 he wrote for *The Evening Journal* of Pittsfield, Massachusetts, says of Melville's school-days:

"In 1835, Professor Charles E. West . . . was president of the Albany Classical Institute for boys, and Herman Melville became one of his pupils. Professor West now remembers him as a favourite pupil, not distinguished for mathematics, but very much so in the writing of 'themes' or 'compositions' and fond of doing it, while the great majority of pupils dreaded it as a task, and would shirk it if they could."

In 1835, Melville was clerk in his brother's shop. If J. E. A. Smith's record is accurate, Melville was at the time alternating business with education.

The greater part of 1836 was spent by Melville, according to his own account, already quoted, in the household of his uncle Major Thomas Melville, at Pittsfield, Massachusetts.

J. E. A. Smith in his *Biographical Sketch* so supplements Melville's account: "Besides his labours with his uncle in the hay field, he was for one term teacher of the common school in the 'Sykes district' under Washington mountain, of which he had some racy memories—one of them of a rebellion in which some of the bigger boys undertook to 'lick' him—with what results, those who remember his physique and character can well imagine."

The only other records we have of Melville's boyhood and early youth are the scattered recollections preserved in his published works. Such, throughout his life, were the veering whims of his blood, that he recalled these earlier years with no unity of retrospect. The confessions of St. Augustine are a classical warning of the untrustworthiness of even the most conscientious memory. To call memory the mother of the Muses, is too frequently but a partial and euphemistic naming of her offspring. So when Melville writes of early years, now in rhapsody and then in bitterness, the result, though always valuable autobiography, is not invariably, of course, strict history.

Some of his idealisations of his life with the Gansevoorts have already been given. Through the refracting films of memory he at times looked back upon "those far descended Dutch meadows . . . . steeped in a Hindooish haze" and proud of his name and his "double revolutionary descent," he viewed himself with Miltonic self-esteem as a "fine, proud, loving, docile, vigorous boy." And there is no reason to suspect him of perverting the truth. Behind these are "certain shadowy reminiscences of wharves, and warehouses, and shipping, which a residence in a seaport during early childhood had supplied me." And with them he blended remembrances "of winter evenings in New York, by the well-remembered sea-coal fire, when my father used to tell my brother and me of the monstrous waves at sea, mountain high; of the masts bending like twigs; and all about Havre, and Liverpool, and about going up into the ball of St. Paul's in London. Indeed, during my early life, most of my thoughts of the sea were connected with the land; but with fine old lands, full of mossy cathedrals and churches, and long, narrow crooked streets without sidewalks, and lined with strange houses. And especially I tried hard to think how such places must look on rainy days and Saturday afternoons; and whether indeed they did have rainy days and Saturdays there, just as we did here, and whether the boys went to school there, and studied geography and wore their shirt collars turned over, and tied with a black ribbon; and whether their papas allowed them to wear boots instead of shoes, which I so much disliked, for boots looked so manly."

Melville confesses here to a precocious exercise of the poetic imagination: a type of imagination for which the consistent disappointments of his life were to be the invariable penalty. In the prosaic man, in Benjamin Franklin, for example, the imagination does not, as it did with Melville, enrich the immediate facts of experience with amplifications so vivid that the reality is in danger of being submerged. In the prosaic man, the imagination works in a safely utilitarian fashion, combining images for practical purposes under the supervision of a matter-of-fact judgment. And though it may indeed bring the lightning from the clouds, it makes the transfer not to glorify the firmament, but to discipline the lightning and to make church steeples safe from the wrath of God. Melville's was the type of imagination whose extreme operation is exemplified in William Blake. "I assert for myself," said Blake, "that I do not behold the outward creation, and that it is to me hindrance and not action. 'What,' it will be questioned, 'when the sun rises, do you not see a round disk of fire something like a guinea?' Oh! no! no! I see an innumerable company of the heavenly host, crying, 'Holy, holy, holy is the Lord God Almighty!' I question not my corporeal eye any more than I would question a window concerning a sight. I look through it, and not with it." Though Allan Melville chose as courtship gift a copy of *Pleasures of Imagination,* the pleasures he derived from the exercise of this faculty were of a sort that both Blake and his son would have thought tame in the extreme. Allan saw the world with his eyes alone, he proudly believed, the world as it really is. It was both the blessing and the curse of his son that his was the gift of "second sight."

"We had several pieces of furniture in the house," says Melville, speaking of his childhood days, "which had been brought from Europe": furniture that had been imported by Allan, some of which is still in the possession of Melville's descendants. "These I examined again and again, wondering where the wood grew: whether the workmen who made them still survived, and what they could be doing with themselves now." Could Allan have known what was going on in the head of his son, he would have been as alarmed as was the father of Anatole France when the young Thibault undertook to emulate St. Nicholas of Patras and distribute his riches to the poor.

Even as a child, he was lured by the romance of distance, and he confesses how he used to think "how fine it would be, to be able to talk about remote barbarous countries; with what reverence and wonder people would regard me, if I had just returned from the coast of Africa or New Zealand: how dark and romantic my sunburnt cheeks would look; how I would bring home with me foreign clothes of rich fabric and princely make, and wear them up and down the streets, and how grocers' boys would turn their heads to look at me, as I went by. For I very well remembered staring at a man myself, who was pointed out to me by my aunt one Sunday in church, as the person who had been in stony Arabia and passed through strange adventures there, all of which with my own eyes I had read in the book which he wrote, an arid-looking book in a pale yellow cover.

" 'See what big eyes he has,' whispered my aunt, 'they got so big, because when he was almost dead in the desert with famishing, he all at once caught sight of a date tree, with the ripe fruit hanging on it.' Upon this, I stared at him till I thought his eyes were really of an uncommon size, and stuck out from his head like those of a lobster. When church was out, I wanted my aunt to take me along and follow the traveller home. But she said the constables would take us up, if we did; and so I never saw the wonderful Arabian traveller again. But he long haunted me; and several times I dreamt of him, and thought his great eyes were grown still larger and rounder; and once I had a vision of the date tree."

It is one of the few certainties of life that a child who has once stood fixed before a piece of household furniture worrying his head about whether the workman who made it still be alive; who after seeing an Arabian traveller in church goes home and has a vision of a date tree: such a child is not going to die an efficiency expert. At the age of fifteen Melville found himself faced with the premature necessity of coming to some sort of terms with life on his own account. Helped by his uncle, he tried working in a bank. The experiment seems not to have been a success. His next experiment was clerk in his brother's store. But banking and clerking seem to have been equally repugnant. Melville had a taste for landscape, so his next experiment was as farmer and country school-keeper. But farming, interspersed with pedagogy and pugilism, fired Melville to a mood of desperation. "Talk not of the bitterness of middle age and after-life," he later wrote; "a boy can feel all that, and much more, when upon his young soul the mildew has fallen. . . . Before the death of my father I never thought of working for my living, and never knew there were hard hearts in the world. . . . I had learned to think much, and bitterly, before my time." So he decided to slough off the tame respectabilities of his well-to-do uncles, and cousins, and aunts. Goaded by hardship, and pathetically lured by the glamorous mirage of distance, with all the impetuosity of his eighteen summers he planned a hegira. "With a philosophical flourish Cato throws himself upon his sword; I quietly take to the ship. This is my substitute for pistol and ball."

CHAPTER IV

A SUBSTITUTE FOR PISTOL AND BALL

"When I go to sea, I go as a simple sailor, right before the mast, plumb down into the forecastle, aloft there to the royal mast-head. True, they rather order me about some, and make me jump from spar to spar, like a grasshopper in a May meadow. And at first, this sort of thing is unpleasant enough. It touches one's sense of honour, particularly if you come of an old established family in the land, the Van Rensselaers, or Randolphs, or Hardicanutes. And more than all, if just previous to putting your hand into the tar-pot, you have been lording it as a country schoolmaster, making the tallest boys stand in awe of you, the transition is a keen one, I assure you, from a schoolmaster to a sailor, and requires a strong decoction of Seneca and the Stoics to enable you to grin and bear it." —HERMAN MELVILLE: *Moby-Dick.*

WHEN, at the age of seventeen, Melville cut loose from his mother, his kind cousins and aunts, and sympathising sisters, he was stirred by motives of desperation, and by the immature delusion that happiness lies elusive and beckoning, just over the world's rim. It was a drastic escape from the intolerable monotony of prosaic certainties and aching frustrations. "Sad disappointments in several plans which I had sketched for my future life," says Melville, "the necessity of doing something for myself, united with a naturally roving disposition, conspired within me, to send me to sea as a sailor."

In *Redburn: His First Voyage. Being the Sailor-boy Confessions and Reminiscences of the Son-of-a-Gentleman* (1849) Melville has left what is the only surviving record of his initial attempt "to sail beyond the sunset." Luridly vivid and exuberant was his imagination, flooding the world of his childhood and fantastically transmuting reality. At the time of his first voyage, Melville was, it is well to remember, a boy of seventeen. He was not old enough, not wise enough, to regard his dreams as impalpable projections of his defeated desires: desires inflamed by what Dr. Johnson called the "dangerous prevalence of imagination," and which, in "sober probability" could find no actual satisfaction. Had Melville been a nature

of less impetuosity, or of less abundant physical vitality, he
might have moped tamely at home and "yearned." But with
the desperate Quixotic enterprise of a splendid but embittered
boy, he sallied forth into the unknown to put his dreams to the
test. When it was reported to Carlyle that Margaret Fuller
made boast: "I accept the universe," unimpressed he remarked: "Gad! she'd better." Melville, when only seventeen,
had not yet come to Carlyle's dyspeptic resignation to the cosmic order. "As years and dumps increase; as reflection lends
her solemn pause, then," so Melville says, in substance, in a
passage on elderly whales, "in the impotent, repentant, admon-
itory stage of life, do sulky old souls go about all alone among
the meridians and parallels saying their prayers." Lacking
Dr. Johnson's elderly wisdom, Melville believed there to be
some correlation between happiness and geography. He was
not willing to take resignation on faith. Not through "spontaneous striving towards development," but through necessity
and hard contact with nature and men does the recalcitrant
dreamer accept Carlyle's dictum. With drastic experience,
most men come at last to have a little commonsense knocked
into their heads,—and a good bit of imagination knocked out,
as Wordsworth, for one, discovered.

Melville's recourse to the ocean in 1837, as that of Richard
Henry Dana's three years before, was a heroic measure, calculated either to take the nonsense out of both of them, or else
to drive them straight either to suicide, madness, or rum-
soaked barbarism. To both boys, it was a crucial test that
would have ruined coarser or weaker natures. Dana came
from out the ordeal purged and strengthened, toned up to the
proper level, and no longer too fine for everyday use. Though
as years went by, so says C. F. Adams, his biographer, "the
freshness of the great lesson faded away, and influences which
antedated his birth and surrounded his life asserted themselves,
not for his good."

Because of lack of contemporary evidence, the immediate
influences of Melville's first experience in the forecastle, cannot be so positively stated. *Redburn,* the only record of the
adventure, was not written until twelve years after Melville

had experienced what it records.   Extraordinarily crowded was this intervening span of twelve years.   But despite the fulness of intervening experience—or, maybe, because of it—the universe still stuck in his maw: it was a bolus on which he gagged.   *Redburn* is written in embittered memory of Melville's first hegira.   In the words of Mr. H. S. Salt: "It is a record of bitter experience and temporary disillusionment—the confessions·of a poor, proud youth, who goes to sea 'with a devil in his heart' and is painfully initiated into the unforeseen hardships of a sea-faring life."   In 1849 he was still unadjusted to unpalatable reality, and in *Redburn* he seems intent upon revenging himself upon his early disillusion by an inverted idealism,—by building for himself, "not castles, but dungeons in Spain,"—as if, failing to reach the moon, he should determine to make a Cynthia of the first green cheese. And this inverted idealism he achieves most effectively by recording with photographic literalness the most hideous details of his penurious migration.   His romantic realism—reminding one of Zola and certain pages out of Rousseau—he alternates with malicious self-satire, and its obverse gesture, obtrusive self-pity.   To those austere and classical souls who are proudly impatient of this style of writing, it must be insisted with what Arnold called "damnable iteration" that *Redburn* purports to be the confessions of a seventeen-year-old lad.   Autobiographically, the book is, of course, of superlative interest.   But despite its unaccountable neglect, and Melville's ostentation of contempt for it, it is none the less important, in the history of letters, as a very notable achievement.   Mr. Masefield and W. Clark Russell alone, of competent critics, seem to have been aware of its existence.   It is *Redburn* that Mr. Masefield confesses to loving best of Melville's writings: this "boy's book about running away to sea."   Mr. Masefield thinks, however, that "one must know New York and the haunted sailor-town of Liverpool to appreciate that gentle story thoroughly."

When Melville wrote *Redburn* in 1849, there was no book exactly like it in our literature, its only possible forerunners being Nathaniel Ames' *A Mariner's Sketches* (1830) and

Dana's *Two Years before the Mast* (1840). The great captains had written of their voyages, it is true; or when they themselves left no record, their literary laxity was usually corrected by the querulousness of some member of their ship's company. Great compilations such as Churchill's, or Harris', or Hakluyt's *The Principal Navigations, Voyages, Traffiques and Discoveries of the English Nation: made by sea or overland to the remotest and farthest different quarters of the earth at any time within the Compass of these 1600 years,* or no less luxuriously entitled works, such as the fine old eighteenth century folio of Captain Charles Johnson's *A General History of the Lives and Adventures of the Most Famous Highwaymen, Murderers, Street Robbers, etc., To which is added, A Genuine Account of the Voyages and Plunders of the Most Notorious Pyrates, interspersed with several diverting tales, and pleasant songs, and adorned with the Heads of the Most Remarkable Villains, curiously Engraven,* are monuments to the prodigious wealth of the early literature of sea adventure. The light of romance colours these maritime exploits, and even upon the maturest gaze there still lingers something of the radiance with which the ardent imagination of boyhood gilds the actions and persons of these fierce sea-warriors, treacherous, cruel and profligate miscreants though the most picturesque of them were.

But these hardy adventurers were men of action; men proud of their own exploits, but untouched by any corrupt self-consciousness of their Gilbert-and-Sullivan, or Byronic possibilities; men untempted to offer any superfluous encouragement to the deep blue sea to "roll." And though many of them—Captain Cook, for example—ran away to sea to ship before the mast, they in later years betray no temptings to linger with attention over their days of early obscurity. Even *The Book of Things Forgotten* passes over the period of Cook's life in the forecastle. He began as an apprentice, he ended as a mate. That is all. As regards the life he led as a youth on board the merchant ship there is no account: a silence that forces Walter Besant in his *Captain Cook* to a page or two of surmise as a transition to more notable sureties. An appreciation of the romance of the sea, and of the humbler details of the life of the common sailor is one of our most recent sophistications.

In fiction, it is true, Smollett had his sailors, as did Scott, and Marryat, and Cooper,—to mention only the most notable names. Provoked to originality by a defiant boast, Cooper wrote the earliest first-rate sea-novel: a story concerning itself exclusively with the sea. Remarkable is the clearness and accuracy of his description of the manœuvres of his ships. He makes his vessels "walk the waters like a thing of life." "I have loved ships as I have loved men," says Melville. And Cooper before him, as Conrad after him, have by similar love given personality to vessels. Among his company of able seamen, Cooper has his Long Tom Coffin: and these are more picturesque, and perhaps more real than his Lord Geoffrey Cleveland, his Admiral Bluewater, his Griffith, and his other quarterdeck people. But sea-life as Cooper knew it was sea-life as seen from the quarterdeck, and from the quarterdeck of the United States navy.

Marryat, it is true, makes his Newton Foster a merchant sailor. But Marryat knew nothing of the hidden life of the merchant service. He had passed his sea-life in the ships of the States, and he knew no more of what passed in a merchantman's forecastle than the general present day land intelligence knows of what passes in a steamer's engine room. Dana and Melville were the first to lift the hatch and show the world what passes in a ship's forecastle. Dana disclosed these secrets in a single volume; Melville in a number of remarkable narratives, the first of which was *Redburn*.

Dana's is a trustworthy and matter-of-fact account in the form of a journal; a vigorous, faithful, modest narrative. With very little interest exhibited in the feeling of his own pulse, he recounts the happenings aboard the ship from day to day. Melville's account is more vivid because more intimate. As is the case with George Borrow, his eye is always riveted upon himself. He minutely amplifies his own emotions and sensations, and with an incalculable gain over Dana in descriptive vividness. One would have to be colour blind to purple patches to fail to recognise in *Redburn* streaks of the purest Tyrean dye.   Between Melville and Dana the answer is obvious as to "who fished the murex up?"

"It was with a heavy heart and full eyes," says Melville, "that my mother parted from me; perhaps she thought me an erring and a wilful boy, and perhaps I was; but if I was, it had been a hard-hearted world, and hard times that had made me so."

Dressed in a hunting jacket; one leg of his trousers adorned with an ample and embarrassing patch; armed with a fowling piece which his older brother Gansevoort had given him, in lieu of cash, to sell in New York; without a penny in his pocket: Melville arrived in New York on a fine rainy day in the late spring of 1837.   Dripping like a seal, and garbed like a housebreaker, he walked across town to the home of a friend of Gansevoort's, where he was dried, warmed and fed.

Philo of Judea has descended to posterity blushing because he had a body.   Melville survives, rosy in animality: but his was never Philo's scarlet of shame.   Melville was a boy of superb physical vigour: and his blackest plunges of discouragement and philosophical despair were always wholesomely amenable to the persuasions of food and drink.   It was Carlyle's conviction that with stupidity and a good digestion man can bear much: had Melville been gifted with stupidity, he would have needed only regular meals to convert him into a miracle of cheerful endurance.   "There is a savour of life and immortality in substantial fare," he later wrote; "we are like balloons, which are nothing till filled."   When Melville sat down to the well-stocked table at his friend's house in New York he was a very miserable boy.   But his misery was not invulnerable.   "Every mouthful pushed the devil that had been tormenting me all day farther and farther out of me, till at last I entirely ejected him with three successive bowls of Bohea.   That night I went to bed thinking the world pretty tolerable after all."

Next day, accompanied by his brother's friend, whose true name Melville disguises under the anonymity of Jones, Melville walked down to the water front.

At that time, and indeed until as recently as thirty years ago, the water front of a great sea-port town like New York showed a towering forest of tall and tapering masts reaching high up above the roofs of the water-side buildings, crossed with slender spars hung with snowy canvas, and braced with a maze of cordage: a brave sight that Melville passes over in morose silence. He postpones until his arrival in Liverpool the spicing of his account with the blended smells of pitch, and tar, and old-ropes, and wet-wood, and resin and the sharp cool tang of brine. Nor does Melville pause to conjure up the great bowsprits and jib-booms that stretched across the street that passed the foot of the slips. Though Melville has left a detailed description of the Liverpool docks—not failing to paint in with a dripping brush the blackest shadows of the low life framing that picturesque scene—it was outside his purpose to give any hint of the maritime achievement of the merchant service in which he was such an insignificant unit.

The maritime achievement of the United States was then almost at the pinnacle of its glory. At that time, the topsails of the United States flecked every ocean, and their captains courageous left no lands unvisited, no sea unexplored. From New England in particular sailed ships where no other ships dared to go, anchoring where no one else ever dreamed of looking for trade. And so it happened, as Ralph D. Paine in his *The Old Merchant Marine* has pointed out, that "in the spicy warehouses that overlooked Salem Harbour there came to be stored hemp from Luzon, gum copal from Zanzibar, palm oil from Africa, coffee from Arabia, tallow from Madagascar, whale oil from the Antarctic, hides and wool from the Rio de la Plata, nutmeg and cloves from Malaysia." With New England originality and audacity, Boston shipped cargoes of ice to Calcutta. And for thirty years a regular trade in Massachusetts ice remained active and lucrative: such perishable freight out upon a four or five months' voyage across the fiery Equator, doubling Da Gama's cape and steering through the furnace heat of the Indian Ocean. In those days the people of the Atlantic seacoast from Maryland northward found their interests vitally allied with maritime adventure. There was

a generous scattering of sea-faring folk among Melville's forebears of our early national era; and Melville's father, an im-
porting merchant, owed his fortunes in important part, to
the chances of the sea. The United States, without railroads,
and with only the most wretched excuses for post-roads,
were linked together by coasting ships. And thousands of
miles of ocean separated Americans from the markets in which
they must sell their produce and buy their luxuries. Down
to the middle of the last century, one of the most vital interests of the United States was in the sea: an interest that
deeply influenced the thought, the legislature and the literature
of our people. And during this period, as Willis J. Abbott,
in his *American Merchant Ships and Sailors* has noted, "the
sea was a favourite career, not only for American boys with
their way to make in the world, but for the sons of wealthy
men as well. That classic of New England seamanship *Two
Years Before the Mast* was not written until the middle of the
19th century, and its author went to sea, not in search of
wealth, but of health. But before the time of Richard Henry
Dana, many a young man of good family and education—a
Harvard graduate, like him, perhaps—bade farewell to a
home of comfort and refinement and made his berth in a
smoky, fetid forecastle to learn the sailor's calling. There
was at that time less to engage the activities and arouse the
ambitions of youth than now, and the sea offered a most promising career. . . . Ships were multiplying fast, and no really
lively and alert seaman need stay long in the forecastle." The
brilliant maritime growth of the United States, after a steady
development for two hundred years, was, when Melville sailed
in 1837, within twenty-five years of its climax. It was to
reach its peak in 1861, when the aggregate tonnage belonging
to the United States was but a little smaller than that of Great
Britain and her dependencies, and nearly as large as the combined tonnage of all other nations of the world, Great Britain
excepted. Vanished fleets and brave memories—a chronicle
of America which had written its closing chapters before the
Civil War!

But this state of affairs,—if, indeed, he was even vaguely

conscious of its existence,—left Melville at the time of his first shipping, completely cold. It is doubtless true that Maria would have respected him more if he had attempted to justify his sea-going by assuring her that at that time it was to no degree remarkable for seamen to become full-fledged captains and part owners at the age of twenty-one, or even earlier. And Maria would have listened impressed to such cogent evidence as the case of Thomas T. Forbes, for example, who shipped before the mast at the age of thirteen, and was commander of the *Levant* at twenty; or the case of William Sturges, afterwards the head of a firm which at one time controlled half the trade between the United States and China, who shipped at seventeen, and was a captain and manager in the China trade at nineteen. But such facts touched Melville not at all. "At that early age," he says, "I was as unambitious as a man of sixty." Melville's brother, Tom, came to be a sea-captain. Melville's was a different destiny.

So he trudged with his friend among the boats along the water front, where, after some little searching, they hit upon a ship for Liverpool. In the cabin they found the suave and bearded Captain, dapperly dressed, and humming a brisk air as he promenaded up and down: not such a completely odious creature, despite Melville's final contempt for him. The conversation was concluded by Melville signing up as a "boy," at terms not wildly lucrative for Melville.

"Pray, captain," said Melville's amiable bungling friend, "how much do you generally pay a handsome fellow like this?"

"Well," said the captain, looking grave and profound, "we are not so particular about beauty, and we never give more than three dollars to a green lad."

Melville's next move was to sell his gun: an experience which gives him occasion to discourse on pawn shops and the unenviable hardships of paupers. With the two and a half dollars that he reaped by the sale of his gun, and in almost criminal innocence of the outfit he would need, he bought a red woollen shirt, a tarpaulin hat, a belt, and a jack-knife. In his improvidence, he was ill provided, indeed, with everything calculated to make his situation aboard ship at all comfortable, or even tolerable. He was without mattress or bed-clothes, or table-tools; without pilot-cloth jackets, or trousers, or guernsey frocks, or oil-skin suits, or sea-boots and the other things which old seamen used to carry in their chests. As he himself says, his sea-outfit was "something like that of the Texan rangers, whose uniform, they say, consists of a shirt collar and a pair of spurs." His purchases made, he did a highly typical thing: "I had only one penny left, so I walked out to the end of the pier, and threw the penny into the water."

That night, after dinner, Melville went to his room to try on his red woollen shirt before the glass, to see what sort of a looking sailor he would make. But before beginning this ritual before the mirror, he "locked the door carefully, and hung a towel over the knob, so that no one could peep through the keyhole." It is said that throughout his life Melville clung to this practice of draping door-knobs. "As soon as I got into the shirt," Melville goes on to say, "I began to feel sort of warm and red about the face, which I found was owing to the reflection of the dyed wool upon my skin. After that, I took a pair of scissors and went to cutting my hair, which was very long. I thought every little would help in making me a light hand to run aloft."

Next morning, before he reached the ship, it began raining hard, so it was plain there would be no getting to sea that day. But having once said farewell to his friends, and feeling a repetition of the ceremony would be awkward, Melville boarded the ship, where a large man in a large dripping pea-jacket, who was calking down the main-hatches, directed him in no cordial terms to the forecastle. Rather different was Dana's appearance on board the brig *Pilgrim* on August 14, 1834, "in full sea-rig, with my chest containing an outfit for a two or three years' voyage." Nor did Dana begin in the forecastle.

In the dark damp stench of that deserted hole, Melville selected an empty bunk. In the middle of this he deposited the slim bundle of his belongings, and penniless and dripping spent the day walking hungry among the wharves: a day's peregrination that he recounts with vivid and remorseless realism.

At night he returned to the forecastle, where he met a thick-headed lad from Lancaster of about his own years. Glad of any companionship, Melville and this lubber boy crawled together in the same bunk. But between the high odour of the forecastle, the loud snoring of his bed-fellow, wet, cold and hungry, he went up on deck, where he walked till morning. When the groceries on the wharf opened, he went to make a breakfast of a glass of water. This made him qualmish. "My head was dizzy, and I went staggering along the walk, almost blind."

By the time Melville got back to the ship, everything was in an uproar. The pea-jacket man was there ordering about men in the riggings, and people were bringing off chickens, and pigs, and beef, and vegetables from the shore. Melville's initial task was the cleaning out of the pig-pen; after this he was sent up the top-mast with a bucket of a thick lobbered gravy, which slush he dabbed over the mast. This over, and, in the increasing bustle everything having been made ready to sail, the word was passed to go to dinner fore and aft. "Though the sailors surfeited with eating and drinking ashore did not touch the salt beef and potatoes which the black cook handed down into the forecastle: and though this left the whole allowance to me; to my surprise, I found that I could eat little or nothing; for now I only felt deadly faint, but not hungry."

Only a lunatic, of course, would expect to find very commodious or airy quarters, any drawing-room amenities, Chautauqua uplift, or Y.M.C.A. insipidities aboard a merchantman of the old sailing days. Nathaniel Ames, a Harvard graduate who a little before Melville's time shipped before the mast, records that on his first vessel, men seeking berths in the forecastle were ordered to bring certificates of good character from their clergymen: an unusual requirement, surely. In more than one memoir, there is mention of a " religious ship ": an occasional mention that speaks volumes for the heathenism of the majority. Dana says of one of the mates aboard the *Pilgrim:* "He was too easy and amiable for the mate of a merchantman. He was not the man to call a sailor a 'son of a bitch' and knock him down with a handspike." And J. Grey Jewell, sometime United States Consul at Singapore, in his book *Among Our Sailors* makes a sober and elaborately documented attempt to strip the life of a sailor of its romantic glamour, to show that it is not a "round of fun and frolic and jollity with the advantages of seeing many distant lands and people thrown in" : an effort that would seem to be unnecessary except to boy readers of Captain Marryat and dime thrillers.

Melville's shipmates were, it goes without saying, rough and illiterate men. With typical irony, he says that with a good degree of complacency and satisfaction he compared his own character with that of his shipmates: "for I had previously associated with persons of a very discreet life, so that there was little opportunity to magnify myself by comparing myself with my neighbours." In a more serious mood, he says of sailors as a class: "the very fact of their being sailors argues a certain restlessness and sensualism of character, ignorance, and depravity. They are deemed almost the refuse of the earth; and the romantic view of them is principally had through romances." And their chances of improvement are not increased, he contends, by the fact that "after the vigorous discipline, hardships, dangers and privations of a voyage, they are set adrift in a foreign port, and exposed to a thousand enticements, which, under the circumstances, would be hard even for virtue to withstand, unless virtue went about on crutches." It was a tradition for centuries fostered in the naval service that the sailor was a dog, a different human species from the landsman, without laws and usages to protect him. This tradition survived among merchant sailors as an unhappy anachronism even into the twentieth century, when an American Congress was reluctant to bestow upon seamen the decencies of existence enjoyed by the poorest labourer ashore. Melville's shipmates did not promise to be men of the calibre of which Maria Gansevoort would have approved.

With his ship, the *Highlander,* streaming out through the

Narrows, past sights rich in association to his boyish recollection; streaming out and away from all familiar smells and sights and sounds, Melville found himself "a sort of Ishmael in the ship, without a single friend or companion, and I began to feel a hatred growing up in me against the whole crew." In other words, Melville was a very homesick boy. But he blended common sense with homesickness. "My heart was like lead, and I felt bad enough, Heaven knows; but I soon learnt that sailors breathe nothing about such things, but strive their best to appear all alive and hearty." And circumstances helped him live up to this gallant insight. For, as he says, "there was plenty of work to be done, which kept my thoughts from becoming too much for me."

Melville was a boy of stout physical courage, game to the marrow, and in texture of muscle and bone a worthy grandson of General Gansevoort. What would have ruined a sallow constitution, he seems to have thriven upon. "Being so illy provided with clothes," he says, "I frequently turned into my bunk soaking wet, and turned out again piping hot and smoking like a roasted sirloin, and yet was never the worse for it; for then, I bore a charmed life of youth and health, and was daggerproof to bodily ill." With alacrity and good sportsmanship, he went at his duties. Before he had been out many days, he had outlived the acute and combined miseries of homesickness and seasickness; the colour was back in his cheeks, he is careful to observe with Miltonic vanity. Soon he was taking especial delight in furling the top-gallant sails and royals in a hard wind, and in hopping about in the riggings like a Saint Jago's monkey. "There was a wild delirium about it," he says, "a fine rushing of the blood about the heart; and a glad thrilling and throbbing of the whole system, to find yourself tossed up at every pitch into the clouds of a stormy sky, and hovering like a judgment angel between heaven and earth; both hands free, with one foot in the rigging, and one somewhere behind you in the wind."

The food, of course, was neither dainty nor widely varied: an unceasing round of salt-pork, stale beef, "duff," "lobscouse," and coffee. "The thing they called *coffee*," says

Melville with keen descriptive effort, "was the most curious tasting drink I ever drank, and tasted as little like coffee as it did like lemonade; though, to be sure, it was generally as cold as lemonade. But what was more curious still, was the different quality and taste of it on different mornings. Sometimes it tasted fishy, as if it were a decoction of Dutch herring; and then it would taste very salt, as if some *old horse* or sea-beef had been boiled in it; and then again it would taste a sort of cheesy, as if the captain had sent his cheese-parings forward to make our coffee of; and yet another time it would have such a very bad flavour that I was almost ready to think some old stocking heel had been boiled in it. Notwithstanding the disagreeableness of the flavour, I always used to have a strange curiosity every morning to see what new taste it was going to have; and I never missed making a new discovery and adding another taste to my palate."

Withal, Melville might have fared much worse, as contemporaneous accounts more than adequately prove. Even in later days, Frank T. Bullen was able to write: "I have often seen the men break up a couple of biscuits into a pot of coffee for breakfast, and after letting it stand for a minute or two, skim off the accumulated scum of vermin from the top—maggots, weevils, etc., to the extent of a couple of tablespoonsful, before they could shovel the mess into their craving stomachs." Melville never complains of maggots or weevils in his biscuits, nor does he complain of being stinted food; during this period, both common enough complaints. The cook, it is true, did not sterilise everything he touched. "I never saw him wash but once," says Melville, "and that was at one of his own soup pots one dark night when he thought no one saw him." But as has already been imputed to Melville for righteousness, his was not a squeamish stomach, and despite the usual amount of filth on board the *Highlander,* his meals seem to have gone off easily enough. He has left this pleasant picture of the amenities of food-taking: "the sailors sitting crosslegged at their chests in a circle, and breaking the hard biscuit, very sociably, over each other's heads, which was very convenient, indeed, but gave me the headache, at least for the first four or five days till I got used to it; and then I did not care much about it, only it kept my hair full of crumbs; and I had forgot to bring a fine comb and brush, so I used to shake my hair out to windward over the bulwarks every evening."

Though the forecastle was, to characterise it quietly, a cramped and fetid hole, dimly lighted and high in odour, Melville came to be sufficiently acclimated to it to enjoy lying on his back in his bunk during a forenoon watch below, reading while his messmates slept. His bunk was an upper one, and right under the head of it was a bull's-eye, inserted into the deck to give light. Here he read an account of *Shipwrecks and Disasters at Sea,* and a large black volume on *Delirium Tremens:* Melville's share in the effects of a sailor whose bunk he occupied, who had, in a frenzy of drunkenness, hurled himself overboard. Here Melville also struggled to read Smith's *Wealth of Nations.* "But soon I gave it up for lost work," says Melville; "and thought that the old backgammon board we had at home, lettered on the back *The History of Rome,* was quite as full of matter, and a great deal more entertaining."

The forecastle, however, was not invariably the setting for scenes so idyllic. Drunkenness there was aplenty, especially at the beginning of the voyage both from New York and from Liverpool. Of the three new men shipped at Liverpool, two were so drunk they were unable to engage in their duties until some hours after the boat quit the pier; but the third, down on the ship's papers as Miguel Saveda, had to be carried in by a crimp and slung into a bunk where he lay locked in a trance. To heighten the discomforts of the forecastle, there was soon added to the stench of sweated flesh, old clothes, tobacco smoke, rum and bilge, a new odour, attributed to the presence of a dead rat. Some days before, the forecastle had been smoked out to extirpate the vermin over-running her: a smoking that seemed to have been fatal to a rodent among the hollow spaces in the side planks. "At midnight, the larboard watch, to which I belonged, turned out; and instantly as every man waked, he exclaimed at the now intolerable smell, sup-posed to be heightened by the shaking up of the bilge-water, from the ship's rolling.

"'Blast that rat!' cried the Greenlander.

"'He's blasted already,' said Jackson, who in his drawers had crossed over to the bunk of Miguel. 'It's a water-rat, shipmates, that's dead; and here he is'—and with that he dragged forth the sailor's arm, exclaiming 'Dead as a timber-head!'

"Upon this the men rushed toward the bunk, Max with the light, which he held to the man's face. 'No, he's not dead,' he cried, as the yellow flame wavered for a moment at the seaman's motionless mouth. But hardly had the words escaped when, to the silent horror of all, two threads of greenish fire, like a forked tongue, darted out between his lips; and in a moment the cadaverous face was crawled over by a swarm of worm-like flames.

"The light dropped from the hand of Max, and went out; while covered all over with spires and sparkles of flame, that faintly crackled in the silence, the uncovered parts of the body burned before us, precisely like a phosphorescent shark in a midnight sea. The eyes were open and fixed; the mouth was curled like a scroll, while the whole face, now wound in curls of soft blue flame, wore an aspect of grim defiance, and eter-nal death. Prometheus blasted by fire on the rock.

"One arm, its red shirt-sleeve rolled up, exposed the man's name, tattooed in vermilion, near the hollow of the middle joint; and as if there was something peculiar in the painted flesh, every vibrating letter burned so white that you might read the flaming name in the flickering ground of blue.

"'Where's that damned Miguel?' was now shouted down among us by the mate.

"'He's gone to the harbour where they never weigh anchor,' coughed Jackson. 'Come down, sir, and look.'

"Thinking that Jackson intended to beard him, the mate sprang down in a rage; but recoiled at the burning body as if he had been shot by a bullet. 'Take hold of it,' said Jackson at last, to the Greenlander; 'it must go overboard. Don't stand

shaking there, like a dog; take hold of it, I say!—But stop!'
and smothering it all in the blankets, he pulled it partly out of
the bunk.

"A few minutes more, and it fell with a bubble among the
phosphorescent sparkles of the sea, leaving a coruscating wake
as it sank."

After this, Melville ceased reading in the forecastle. And
indeed no other sailor but Jackson would stay in the forecastle alone, and none would laugh or sing there: none but
Jackson. But he, while the rest would be sitting silently smoking on their chests, or on their bunks, would look towards the
nailed-up bunk of Miguel and cough, and laugh, and invoke
the dead man with scoffs and jeers.

Of Melville's shipmates, surely this Jackson was the most
remarkable: a fit rival to Conrad's Nigger of the Narcissus.
Max and the Greenlander were merely typical old tars. Mr.
Thompson, the grave negro cook, with his leaning towards
metaphysics and his disquisitions on original sin, together with
his old crony, Lavendar the steward, with his amorous back-
slidings, his cologne water, and his brimstone pantaloons,
though mildly diverting, were usual enough. Blunt, too, with
his collection of hair-oils, and his dream-book, and his flowing
bumpers of horse-salts, though picturesque, was pale in comparison with Jackson. Larry, the old whaler, with his sentimental distaste for civilised society, was a forerunner of Mr.
H. L. Mencken; and as such, deserves a more prominent mention. "And what's the use of bein' *snivelized?*" he asks Melville; "snivelized chaps only learn the way to take on 'bout
life, and snivel. Blast Ameriky, I say. I tell ye, ye wouldn't
have been to sea here, leadin' this dog's life, if you hadn't
been snivelized. Snivelization has been the ruin on ye; and it's
sp'iled me complete: I might have been a great man in Mada-
gasky; it's too darned bad! Blast Ameriky, I say."

But flat, stale and unprofitable seem the whole ship's company in comparison with the demoniacal Jackson. Sainte-
Beuve, in reviewing an early work of Cooper's, speaks enthu-
siastically of Cooper's "faculté créatrice qui enfante et met au
monde des caractères nouveaux, et en vertu de laquelle Rabelais

a produit 'Panurge,' Le Sage 'Gil Blas,' et Richardson 'Clarissa.' " In *The Confidence Man* Melville spends a chapter discussing "originality" in literature. The phrase "quite an original" he maintains, in contempt of Sainte-Beuve, is "a phrase, we fancy, oftener used by the young, or the unlearned, or the untravelled, than by the old, or the well-read, or the man who has made the grand tour." This faculty of creating "originals"—which is, after all, as both Melville and Flaubert clearly saw, but a quality of observation—Melville had to an unusual degree. In this incongruous group of striking "originals" Jackson deserves, as Melville says, a "lofty gallows."

"Though Tiberius come in the succession of the Cæsars, and though unmatchable Tacitus has embalmed his carrion," writes Melville in the luxurious cadence of Sir Thomas Browne which some of his critics have stigmatised as both the sign and cause of his later "madness," "yet do I account this Yankee Jackson full as dignified a personage as he, and as well meriting his lofty gallows in history, even though he was a nameless vagabond without an epitaph, and none but I narrate what he was. For there is no dignity in wickedness, whether in purple or rags: and hell is a democracy of devils, where all are equals. In historically canonising on earth the condemned below, and lifting up and lauding the illustrious damned, we do but make ensamples of wickedness; and call upon ambition to do some great iniquity to be sure of fame."

When Melville came to know Jackson, nothing was left of him but the foul lees and dregs of a man; a walking skeleton encased in a skin as yellow as gamboge, branded with the marks of a fearful end near at hand: "like that of King Antiochus of Syria, who died a worse death, history says, than if he had been stung out of the world by wasps and hornets." In appearance he suggests Villon at the time when the gallows spared him the death-penalty of his vices. He looked like a man with his hair shaved off and just recovering from the yellow fever. His hair had fallen out; his nose was broken in the middle; he squinted in one eye. But to Melville that squinting eye "was the most deep, subtle, infernal-looking eye that I ever saw lodged in a human head. I be-

lieve that by good rights it must have belonged to a wolf, or
starved tiger; at any rate I would defy any oculist to turn out
a glass eye half so cold and snaky and deadly." He was a
foul-mouthed bully, and "being the best seaman on board, and
very overbearing every way, all the men were afraid of him,
and durst not contradict him or cross his path in anything."
And what made this more remarkable was, that he was the
weakest man, bodily, of the whole crew. "But he had such
an over-awing way with him; such a deal of brass and impudence, such an unflinching face, and withal was such a hideous
mortal, that Satan himself would have run from him." The
whole crew stood in mortal fear of him, and cringed and
fawned before him like so many spaniels. They would rub
his back after he was undressed and lying in his bunk, and run
up on deck to the cook-house to warm some cold coffee for
him, and fill his pipe, and give him chews of tobacco, and mend
his jackets and trousers, and watch and tend and nurse him
every way. "And all the time he would sit scowling on them,
and found fault with what they did: and I noticed that those
who did the most for him were the ones he most abused."
These he flouted and jeered and laughed to scorn, on occasion
breaking out in such a rage that "his lips glued together at
the corners with a fine white foam."

His age it was impossible to tell: for he had no beard, and
no wrinkles except for small crow's-feet about the eyes. He
might have been thirty, or perhaps fifty years. "But according to his own account, he had been at sea ever since he was
eight years old, when he first went to sea as a cabin-boy in
an Indiaman, and ran away at Calcutta." And according to
his own account, too, he had passed through every kind of
dissipation and abandonment in the worst parts of the world.
He had served in Portuguese slavers on the coast of Africa,
and with diabolical relish would tell of the middle passage
where the slaves were stowed, heel and point, like logs, and the
suffocated and dead were unmanacled and weeded out from the
living each morning before washing down the decks. Though
he was apt to be dumb at times, and would sit with "his eyes
fixed, and his teeth set, like a man in the moody madness,"

yet when he did speak his whole talk was full of piracies, plagues, poisonings, seasoned with filth and blasphemy. "Though he never attended churches and knew nothing of Christianity; no more than a Malay pirate; and though he could not read a word, yet he was spontaneously an atheist and an infidel; and during the long night watches, would enter into arguments to prove that there was nothing to be believed; nothing to be loved, and nothing worth living for; but everything to be hated in the wide world. He was a Cain afloat; branded on his yellow brow with some inscrutable curse; and going about corrupting and searing every heart that beat near him."

The last scene in his eventful history took place off Cape Cod, when, in a stiff favourable breeze, the captain was impatient to make his port before a shift of wind. Four sullen weeks previous to this had Jackson spent in the forecastle without touching a rope. Every day since leaving New York Jackson had seemed to be growing worse and worse, both in body and mind. "And all the time, though his face grew thinner and thinner, his eyes seemed to kindle more and more, as if he were going to die out at last, and leave them burning like tapers before his corpse." When, after these four weeks of idleness, Jackson, to the surprise of the crew, came up on deck, his aspect was damp and death-like; the blue hollows of his eyes were like vaults full of snakes; and issuing so unexpectedly from his dark tomb in the forecastle, he looked like a man raised from the dead.

"Before the sailors had made fast the reef-tackle, Jackson was tottering up the rigging; thus getting the start of them, and securing his place at the extreme weather-end of the topsail yard—which in reefing is accounted the place of honour. For it was one of the characteristics of this man that though when on duty he would shy away from mere dull work in a calm, yet in tempest time he always claimed the van and would yield to none.

"Soon we were all strung along the main-topsail yard; the ship rearing and plunging under us like a runaway steed; each man griping his reef-point, and sideways leaning, dragging the sail over towards Jackson, whose business it was to confine the reef corner to the yard.

"His hat and shoes were off; and he rode the yard-arm end, leaning backward to the gale, and pulling at the earing-rope like a bridle. At all times, this is a moment of frantic exertion with sailors, whose spirits seem then to partake of the commotion of the elements as they hang in the gale between heaven and earth; and then it is, too, that they are the most profane.

" 'Haul out to windward!' coughed Jackson, with a blasphemous cry, and he threw himself back with a violent strain upon the bridle in his hand. But the wild words were hardly out of his mouth when his hands dropped to his side, and the bellying sail was spattered with a torrent of blood from his lungs.

"As the man next him stretched out his arm to save, Jackson fell headlong from the yard, and with a long seethe, plunged like a diver into the sea.

"It was when the ship had rolled to windward, which, with the long projection of the yard-arm over the side, made him strike far out upon the water. His fall was seen by the whole upward-gazing crowd on deck, some of whom were spotted with the blood that trickled from the sail, while they raised a spontaneous cry, so shrill and wild that a blind man might have known something deadly had happened.

"Clutching our reef-joints, we hung over the stick, and gazed down to the one white bubbling spot which had closed over the head of our shipmate; but the next minute it was brewed into the common yeast of the waves, and Jackson never arose. We waited a few minutes, expecting an order to descend, haul back the fore-yard, and man the boats; but instead of that, the next sound that greeted us was, 'Bear a hand and reef away, men!' from the mate."

CHAPTER V

DISCOVERIES ON TWO CONTINENTS

"If you read of St. Peter's, they say, and then go and visit it, ten to
one, you account it a dwarf compared to your high-raised ideal. And,
doubtless, Jonah himself must have been much disappointed when he
looked up to the domed midriff surmounting the whale's belly, and surveyed the ribbed pillars around him. A pretty large belly, to be sure,
thought he, but not so big as it might have been."
—HERMAN MELVILLE: *Redburn.*

THE merchantman on which Melville shipped was not a
Liverpool liner, or packet-ship, plying in connection with a
sisterhood of packets. She was a *regular trader* to Liverpool;
sailing upon no fixed days, and acting very much as she pleased,
being bound by no obligation of any kind, though in all her
voyages ever having New York or Liverpool for her destination. Melville's craft was not a greyhound, not a very fast
sailer. The swifter of the packet ships then made the passage
in fifteen or sixteen days; the *Highlander,* travelling at a more
matronly pace, was out on the Atlantic a leisurely month.

"It was very early in the month of June that we sailed,"
says Melville; "and I had greatly rejoiced that it was that
time of year; for it would be warm and pleasant upon the
ocean I thought; and my voyage would be like a summer excursion to the seashore for the benefit of the salt water, and a
change of scene and society." But the fact was not identical
with Melville's fancy, and before many days at sea, he found
it a galling mockery to remember that his sisters had promised
to tell all enquiring friends that he had gone *"abroad"*: "just
as if I was visiting Europe on a tour with my tutor." Though
his thirty days at sea considerably disabused him—for the
time—of the unmitigated delights of ocean travel in the forecastle; still always in the vague and retreating distance did he
hold to the promise of some stupendous discovery still in store.
Finally, one morning when he came on deck, he was thrilled

to discover that he was, in sober fact, within sight of a foreign land: a shore-line that in imagination he transformed into the seacoast of Bohemia. "A foreign country actually visible!" But as he gazed ashore, disillusion ran hot upon the heels of his romantic expectations.

"Was that Ireland? Why, there was nothing remarkable about that; nothing startling. If *that's* the way a foreign country looks, I might as well have stayed at home. Now what, exactly, I had fancied the shore would look like, I can not say; but I had a vague idea that it would be something strange and wonderful."

The next land they sighted was Wales. "It was high noon, and a long line of purple mountains lay like a bank of clouds against the east. But, after all, the general effect of these mountains was mortifyingly like the general effect of the Kaatskill Mountains on the Hudson River."

It was not until midnight of the third day that they arrived at the mouth of the Mersey. Before the following daybreak they took the first flood.

"Presently, in the misty twilight, we passed immense buoys, and caught sight of distant objects on shore, vague and shadowy shapes, like Ossian's ghosts." And then it was that Melville found leisure to lean over the side, "trying to summon up some image of Liverpool, to see how the reality would answer to my concept."

As the day advanced, the river contracted, and in the clear morning Melville got his first sharp impression of a foreign port.

"I beheld lofty ranges of dingy ware-houses, which seemed very deficient in the elements of the marvellous; and bore a most unexpected resemblance to the ware-houses along South Street in New York. There was nothing strange, nothing extraordinary about them. There they stood; a row of calm and collected ware-houses; very good and substantial edifices, doubtless, and admirably adapted to the ends had in view by the builders: but yet, these edifices, I must confess, were a sad and bitter disappointment to me."

Melville was six weeks in Liverpool. Of this part of his

adventure, he says in *Redburn:* "I do not mean to present a diary of my stay there. I shall here simply record the general tenor of the life led by our crew during that interval; and will proceed to note down, at random, my own wanderings about town, and impressions of things as they are recalled to me now after the lapse of so many (twelve) years."

Not the least important detail of these six weeks is the fact that Melville and his ship-mates were very well fed at the sign of the Baltimore Clipper. "The roast beef of Old England abounded; and so did the immortal plum-puddings and the unspeakably capital gooseberry pies." Owing to the strict but necessary regulations of the Liverpool docks, no fire of any kind was allowed on board the vessels within them. And hence, though the sailors of the *Highlander* slept in the forecastle, they were fed ashore at the expense of the ship's owners. This, in a large crew remaining at Liverpool more than six weeks, as the *Highlander* did, formed no inconsiderable item in the expenses of the voyage. The Baltimore Clipper was one of the boarding houses near the docks which flourished on the appetite of sailors. At the Baltimore Clipper was fed not only the crew of the *Highlander,* but, each in a separate apartment, a variety of other crews as well. Since each crew was known collectively by the name of its ship, the shouts of the servant girls running about at dinner time mustering their guests must have been alarming to an uninitiated visitor.

"Where are the *Empresses of China?*—Here's their beef been smoking this half-hour"—"Fly, Betty, my dear, here come the *Panthers*"—"Run, Molly, my love; get the salt-cellars for the *Splendids*"—"You, Peggy, where's the *Siddons'* pickle-pot?"—"I say, Judy, are you never coming with that pudding for the *Sultans?*"

It was to the Baltimore Clipper that Jackson immediately led the ship's crew when they first sprang ashore: up this street and down that till at last he brought them to their destination in a narrow lane filled with boarding-houses, spirit-vaults and sailors. While Melville's shipmates were engaged in tippling and talking with numerous old acquaintances of theirs in the neighbourhood who thronged about the door, he sat alone in the dining-room appropriated to the *Highlanders* "meditating upon the fact that I was now seated upon an English bench, under an English roof, in an English tavern, forming an integral part of the British empire."

Melville examined the place attentively. "It was a long narrow little room, with one small arched window with red curtains, looking out upon a smoky, untidy yard, bounded by a dingy brick wall, the top of which was horrible with pieces of broken old bottles stuck into mortar. A dull lamp swung overhead, placed in a wooden ship suspended from the ceiling. The walls were covered with a paper, representing an endless succession of vessels of all nations continually circumnavigating the apartment. From the street came a confused uproar of ballad-singers, bawling women, babies, and drunken sailors."

It was during this disenchanting examination that the realisation began to creep chillingly over Melville that his prospect of seeing the world as a sailor was, after all, but very doubtful. It seems never to have struck him before that sailors but hover about the edges of terra-firma; that "they land only upon wharves and pier-heads, and their reminiscences of travel are only a dim recollection of a chain of tap-rooms surrounding the globe."

Melville's six weeks in Liverpool offered him, however, opportunity to make slightly more extended observations. During these weeks he was free to go where he pleased between four o'clock in the afternoon and the following dawn. Sundays he had entirely at his own disposal. But withal, it was an excessively limited and distorted version of England that was open for his examination. Except for his shipmates, his very distant cousin, the Earl of Leven and Melville and Queen Victoria and such like notables, he knew by name no living soul in the British Isles. And neither his companions in the forecastle, nor the remote and elaborately titled strangers of Melville House, offered encouragement of an easy and glowing intimacy. With but three dollars as his net capital—money advanced him in Liverpool by the ship—and without a thread of presentable clothing on his back, he could not hope promiscuously to ingratiate himself either by his purse or the adorn-

ments of his person. Thus lacking in the fundamentals of
friendship, his native charms stood him in little stead. So
alone he walked the streets of Liverpool and gratuitously saw
the sights.

While on the high seas, Melville had improved his fallow
hours by poring over an old guide-book of Liverpool that had
descended to him from his father. This old family relic was
to Melville cherished with a passionate and reverent affection.
Around it clustered most of the fond associations that are the
cords of man. It had been handled by Allan amid the very
scenes it described; it bore some "half-effaced miscellaneous
memoranda in pencil, characteristic of a methodical mind, and
therefore indubitably my father's": jottings of "a strange, sub-
dued, old, midsummer interest" to Melville. And on the flyleaves were crabbed inscriptions, and "crayon sketches of wild
animals and falling air-castles." These decorations were the
handiwork of Melville and his brothers and sisters and cousins.
Of his own contributions, Melville says: "as poets do with their
juvenile sonnets, I might write under this horse, *'Drawn at the
age of three years,'* and under this autograph, *'Executed at the
age of eight.'* " This guide-book was to Melville a sacred volume, and he expresses a wish that he might immortalise it.
Addressing this unpretentious looking little green-bound,
spotted and tarnished guide-book, he exclaims: "Dear book! I
will sell my Shakespeare, and even sacrifice my old quarto Hogarth, before I will part from you. Yes, I will go to the hammer myself, ere I send you to be knocked down in the auc-
tioneer's scrambles. I will, my beloved; till you drop leaf
from leaf, and letter from letter, you shall have a snug shelf
somewhere, though I have no bench for myself."

To the earlier manuscript additions to this guide-book, Melville added, while on the Atlantic, drawings of ships and anchors, and snatches of Dibdin's sea-poetry. And as he lay in
his bunk, with the aid of this antiquated volume he used to
take "pleasant afternoon rambles through the town, down St.
James street and up Great George's, stopping at various places
of interest and attraction" so familiar seemed the features of
the map. But in this vagabondage of reverie he was but pre-

paring for himself a poignant disillusionment. Lying in the dim, reeking forecastle, with his head full of deceitful day-dreams, he was being tossed by the creaking ship towards a bitter awakening. The Liverpool of the guide-book purported to be the Liverpool of 1808. The Liverpool of which Melville dreamed was, of course, without date and local habitation. When Melville found himself face to face with the solid reality of the Liverpool of 1837, he was offered an object-lesson in mutability. As the brute facts smote in the face of his cherished sentimentalisings, he sat his concrete self down on a particular shop step in a certain street in Liverpool, reflected on guide-books and luxuriated in disenchantment. "Guide-books," he then came to see, "are the least reliable books in all literature : and nearly all literature, in one sense, is made up of guide-books. Old ones tell us the ways our fathers went; but how few of those former places can their posterity trace." In the end he sealed his moralising by the pious reflection that "there is one Holy Guide-Book that will never lead you astray if you but follow it aright." There can be no doubt that the ghost of Allan, retracing its mundane haunts at that moment trailed its shadowy substance through the offspring of its discarded flesh.

If this same paternal ghost, recognising its kinship with this obstruction of blood and bone, tracked in futile affection at Melville's heels through Liverpool, only a posthumous survival of its terrestrial Calvinism could have spared it an agonised six weeks; only the sardonic optimism of a faith in predestination could have saved Allan's shade from consternation and fear at the chances of Melville's flesh. Or it may be that Allan was sent as a disembodied spectator to haunt Melville's wake, by way of penance for his pre-ghostly theological errors. In any event, Melville, on occasion, took Allan through the most hideous parts of Liverpool. Of evenings they strolled through the narrow streets where the sailors' boarding-houses were. "Hand-organs, fiddlers, and cymbals, plied by strolling musicians, mixed with the songs of seamen, the babble of women and children, and groaning and whining of beggars. From the various boarding-houses proceeded the noise of rev-

elry and dancing: and from the open casements leaned young
girls and old women chattering and laughing with the crowds
in the middle of the street." In the vicinity were "notorious
Corinthian haunts which in depravity are not to be matched by
anything this side of the pit that is bottomless." Along
Rotten-row, Gibraltar-place and Boodle-alley Melville surveyed
the "sooty and begrimed bricks" of haunts of abomination
which to Melville's boyish eyes (seen through the protecting
lens of Allan's ghost) had a "reeking, Sodom-like and murderous look." Melville excuses himself in the name of propriety from particularising the vices of the residents of this
quarter; "but kidnappers and resurrectionists," he declares,
"are almost saints and angels to them."

Melville satirically pictures himself as pathetically innocent
to the iniquities of the flesh and the Devil when he left home
to view the world. He was, he says, a member both of a Juvenile Total Abstinence Association and of an Anti-Smoking Society organised by the Principal of his Sunday School. With
dire compunctions of conscience—which had been considerably
weakened by sea-sickness—Melville had his first swig of spirits
—administered medicinally to him by a paternal old tar,—before they were many hours out upon the Atlantic. But neither
on the high seas nor in England does he seem to have been
prematurely tempted by the bottle. And this, for the adequate reason that united to his innocence of years, his very
limited finances spared him the solicitations of toping companions as well as the luxury of precocious solitary tippling.
Though at the beginning of the voyage he refused the friendly
offer of a cigar, he less austerely eschewed tobacco by the time
he again struck land. Melville did not, throughout his life,
hold so strictly to the puritanical prohibitions of his boyhood.

The youthful member of the Anti-Smoking Society came
in later years to be a heroic consumer of tobacco, and the
happiest hours of his life were haloed with brooding blue haze.
"Nothing so beguiling," he wrote in 1849, "as the fumes of
tobacco, whether inhaled through hookah, narghil, chibouque,
Dutch porcelain, pure Principe, or Regalia." On another occasion he expressed a desire to "sit cross-legged and smoke out

Tuesday Dec 16 [Continued from last journal]

1856

Wandered about in vicinity of Wallpohne till nearly dusk; lost myself, & finally came out at a gate on the Sea of Marmora. Returned to Tophanna by kayak. Interesting appearance of the walls here. Owing to the height of the shore above the sea, the fortifications here present a wall on the water side, but only a parapet on the land. Hence, from the sea, the towers look eminently lofty; & they are of all shapes; in some part their windows are formed by the open spaces of the battlements. In some part, there are balconies. Several gates & archway are to be seen walled up. Colonnades are disclosed, closed up. Pilasters. The fall, or rather crumbling away of the wall at one angle discloses a relating column of white marble, looking strange as the resurrection of a long mason up in a tomb. Reminded me of the Abbotsford walls — only on a grand scale. When long masses of the masonry have fallen, they lie like rocks, in confused heaps, the mortar as hard as the stone. — At dinner today the French attaché estimated

A PAGE FROM ONE OF MELVILLE'S JOURNALS

eternity." And the youthful pillar of the Juvenile Total Abstinence Association, growing in wisdom as he took on years, lived to do regal penance for his unholy childhood pledge. His avowed refusal to believe in a Temperance Heaven would seem to imply a conviction that it is only the damned who never drink. In his amazing novel *Mardi*—which won him acclaim in France as *"un Rabelais Americain"*—wine flows in ruddy and golden rivers. And the most brilliantly fantastic philosophising, the keenest wit of the demi-gods that lounge through this wild novel, are concomitant upon the heroic draining of beaded bumpers. In *Mardi*, Melville celebrates the civilising influences of wine with the same devout and urbane affection to be found in Horace and Meredith. On occasion, however, he seems to share Baudelaire's conviction that "one should be drunk always"—and drunk on wine in the manner of the best period. He quotes with approval the epitaph of Cyrus the Great: "I could drink a great deal of wine, and it did me a great deal of good." In *Clarel* he asks: "At Cana, who renewed the wine?" In the riotous chapter wherein "Taji sits down to Dinner with five-and-twenty Kings, and a royal Time they have," there is an exuberant tilting of calabashes that would have won the esteem even of Socrates and Pantagruel. One wonders if Rabelais, in his youth, did not belong to some Juvenile Total Abstinence Society, or if Socrates, who both lived and died over a cup, had not as a boy committed an equally heinous sacrilege to Dionysus.

On board the *Highlander* Melville was too young yet to have come to a sense of the iniquity of the deadly virtues. He was not thereby, however, tempted to the optimism of despair that preaches that because God is isolated in His Heaven, all is right with the world. Even at seventeen Melville had keenly felt that much in the world needs mending. And at seventeen—more than at any other period—he felt moved to exert himself to set the world aright. Ashipboard, the field of his operations being very limited, he cast a missionary eye upon the rum-soaked profanity and lechery of his ship-mates. "I called to mind a sermon I had once heard in a church in behalf of sailors," says Melville, "when the preacher called them strayed lambs from the fold, and compared them to poor lost children, babes in the wood, or orphans without fathers or mothers." Overflowing with the milk of human kindness at the sad condition of these amiable outcasts, Melville, during his first watch, made bold to ask one of them if he was in the habit of going to church. The sailor answered that "he had been in a church once, some ten or twelve years before, in London, and on a week-day had helped to move the Floating Chapel round the Battery from North River." This first and last effort of Melville's to evangelise a shipmate ended in winning Melville hearty ridicule. "If I had not felt so terribly angry," he says, "I should certainly have felt very much like a fool. But my being so angry prevented me from feeling foolish, which is very lucky for people in a passion." Though Melville made no further effort to save the souls of his shipmates, his own seems not to have been jeopardised by any hankering after the instruments of damnation.

As has been said, he was without friends, both ashipboard and later ashore; a complete absence of companionship that on occasion inspired him with a parched desire for some friend to whom to say "how sweet is solitude." He craved in his isolation, he says, "to give his whole soul to another; in its loneliness it was yearning to throw itself into the unbounded bosom of some immaculate friend." In *Redburn,* Melville spends a generous number of pages in celebrating his encounter with a good-for-nothing but courtly youth whom he calls Harry Bolton. "He was one of those small, but perfectly formed beings with curling hair, and silken muscles, who seem to have been born in cocoons. His complexion was a mantling brunette, feminine as a girl's; his feet were small; his hands were white; and his eyes were large, black and womanly: and, poetry aside, his voice was as the sound of a harp." How much of Harry Bolton is fact, how much fiction, is impossible to tell. The most significant thing about him is Melville's evident affection for him, no matter who made him. In *Redburn,* this engaging dandy kidnaps Melville, and takes him for a mysterious night up to London: a night spent, to Melville's consternation, in a gambling palace of the sort that exists only in the febrile and envious imagination of vitriolic puritans. In his description of this escapade, Melville owes more, perhaps, to his early spiritual guides than to any first-hand observation. This flight to London in *Redburn,* its abrupt reversal, and the escape to America of Harry Bolton, may, of course, all be founded on sober fact. But there is a lack of verisimilitude in the recounting that prompts to the suspicion that in this part of the narrative, Melville is making brave and unconvincing concessions to romance. Not, of course, that Melville in his youth was incapable of the wild impetuosity of suddenly leaving his ship and running up to London with an engagingly romantic stranger: he did more impulsive and far more surprising things than that before he died. But his account of this adventure in *Redburn* reads hollow and false. Harry Bolton must be discounted as myth until he is more cogently substantiated as history.

In Liverpool Melville seems to have spent his leisure in company with his thoughts, wandering along the docks and about the city. Each Sunday morning he went regularly to church; Sunday afternoons he spent walking in the neighbouring country. His most vivid impressions of Liverpool were of the terrible poverty he saw, and it is doubtful if there is a more ruthless piece of realism in the language than his account in *Redburn* of the slow death through starvation of the mother and children that Melville found lying in a cellar, and whose lives he tried in vain to save. The green cold bodies in the morgue, the ragpickers, the variety of criminals that haunt the shadows of the docks: these too came in for characterisation.

The noblest sight that Melville found in England, it would seem, was the truck-horses he saw round the docks. "So grave, dignified, gentlemanly and courteous did these fine truck horses look—so full of calm intelligence and sagacity, that often I endeavoured to get into conversation with them as they stood in contemplative attitudes while their loads were preparing." And Melville admired the truckmen also. "Their spending so much of their valuable lives in the high-bred company of their horses seems to have mended their manners and improved their taste; but it has also given to them a sort of refined and unconscious aversion to human society." Though Melville grew to a most uncomplimentary rating of the human biped, he always cherished a very deep reverence for some of his four-footed brothers. "There are unknown worlds of knowledge in brutes," he wrote; "and whenever you mark a horse, or a dog, with a peculiarly mild, calm, deep-seated eye, be sure he is an Aristotle or a Kant, tranquilly speculating upon the mysteries in man."

The trip back across the Atlantic, after six weeks in Liverpool, though longer than the out-bound passage, was for Melville less of an ordeal. He was no longer a bewildered stranger in the forecastle or in the riggings, so he turned his eye to other parts of the ship. It was the steerage of the *Highlander* packed with its four or five hundred emigrants, that gave him most bitter occasion to reflect on the criminal nature of the universe. Because of insufficient provisions in food for an unexpectedly prolonged voyage, the dirty weather, and the absence of the most indispensable conveniences, these emigrants suffered almost incredible hardships. Before they had been at sea a week, to hold one's head down the fore hatchway, Melville says, was like holding it down a suddenly opened cesspool. The noisome confinement in this close unventilated and crowded den, and the deprivation of sufficient food, helped by personal uncleanliness, brought on a malignant fever among the emigrants. The result was the death of some dozens of them, a panic throughout the ship, and a novel indulgence in spasmodic devotions. "Horrible as the sights of the steerage were, the cabin, perhaps, presented a scene equally despairing. Trunks were opened for Bibles; and at last, even prayer-meetings were held over the very tables across which the loud jest had been so often heard."

But with the coming of fair winds and fine weather the pestilence subsided, and the ship steered merrily towards New York. The steerage was cleaned thoroughly with sand and water. The place was then fumigated, and dried with pieces of coal from the gallery: so that when the *Highlander* streamed into New York harbour no stranger would have imagined, from her appearance, that the *Highlander* had made other than a tidy and prosperous voyage. "Thus, some sea-captains take good heed that benevolent citizens shall not get a glimpse of the true condition of the steerage while at sea."

As they came into the Narrows, "no more did we think of the gale and the plague; nor turn our eyes upward to the stains of blood still visible on the topsail, whence Jackson had fallen. Oh, he who has never been afar, let him once go from home, to know what home is. Hurra! Hurra! and ten thousand times hurra! down goes our anchor, fathoms down into the free and independent Yankee mud, one handful of which was now worth a broad manor in England."

Melville spent the greater part of the night "walking the deck and gazing at the thousand lights of the city." At sunrise, the *Highlander* warped into a berth at the foot of Wall street, and the old ship was knotted, stem and stern, to the pier. This knotting of the ship was the unknotting of the bonds of the sailors; for, the ship once fast to the wharf, Melville and his shipmates were free. So with a rush and a shout they bounded ashore—all but Melville. He went down into the forecastle and sat on a chest. The ship he had loathed, while he was imprisoned in it, grew lovely in his eyes when he was free to bid it forever farewell. In the tarry old den he sat, the only inhabitant of the deserted ship but for the mate and the rats. He sat there and let his eyes linger over every familiar old plank. "For the scene of suffering is a scene of joy when the suffering is past," he says, inverting the reflection of Dante; "and the silent reminiscence of hardship departed, is sweeter than the presence of delight." According to this philosophy, the more accumulated and overwhelming the hardships we survive, the richer and sweeter will be the ensuing hours of thoughtful recollection. For whom the Lord loveth He chasteneth. And pleasure's crown of pleasure is remembering sorrier things. So indoctrinated, Melville should have viewed the concluding scene with the captain of the *Highlander,* on the day the sailors drew their wages, with eternal thanksgiving.

"Seated in a sumptuous arm-chair, behind a lustrous inlaid desk, sat Captain Riga, arrayed in his City Hotel suit, looking magisterial as the Lord High Admiral of England. Hat in hand, the sailors stood deferentially in a semi-circle before him, while the captain held the ship-papers in his hand, and one by one called their names; and in mellow bank notes—beautiful sight!—paid them their wages. . . . The sailors, after counting their cash very carefully, and seeing all was right, and not a bank-note was dog-eared, in which case they would have demanded another, salaamed and withdrew, leaving me face to face with the Paymaster-general of the Forces."

Melville stood awhile, looking as polite as possible, he says, and expecting every moment to hear his name called. But no such name did he hear. "The captain, throwing aside his accounts, lighted a very fragrant cigar, took up the morning paper—I think it was the *Herald*—threw his leg over one arm of the chair, and plunged into the latest intelligence from all parts of the world."

Melville hemmed, and scraped his foot to increase the disturbance. The Paymaster-general looked up. Melville demanded his wages. The captain laughed, and taking a long inspiration of smoke, removed his cigar, and sat sideways looking at Melville, letting the vapour slowly wriggle and spiralise out of his mouth.

"Captain Riga," said Melville, "do you not remember that about four months ago, my friend Mr. Jones and myself had an interview with you in this very cabin; when it was agreed that I was to go out in your ship, and receive three dollars per month for my services? Well, Captain Riga, I have gone out with you, and returned; and now, sir, I'll thank you for my pay."

"Ah, yes, I remember," said the captain. *"Mr. Jones!* Ha! Ha! I remember Mr. Jones: a very gentlemanly gentleman; and stop—*you,* too, are the son of a wealthy French importer; and—let me think—was not your great-uncle a barber?"

"No!" thundered Melville, his Gansevoort temper up.

Captain Riga suavely turned over his accounts. "Hum, hum!—yes, here it is: Wellingborough Redburn, at three dollars a month. Say four months, that's twelve dollars: less three dollars advanced in Liverpool—that makes it nine dollars; less three hammers and two scrapers lost overboard—that brings it to four dollars and a quarter. I owe you four dollars and a quarter, I believe, young gentleman?"

"So it seems," said Melville with staring eyes.

"And now let me see what you owe me, and then we'll be able to square the yards, Monsieur Redburn."

"Owe him!"—Melville confesses to thinking; "what do I owe him but a grudge." But Melville concealed his resentment. Presently Captain Riga said: "By running away from the ship in Liverpool, you forfeited your wages, which amount to twelve dollars; and there has been advanced to you, in money, hammers and scrapers, seven dollars and seventy-five cents; you are therefore indebted to me for precisely that sum. I'll thank you for the money." He extended his open palm across the desk.

The precise nature of Melville's eloquence at this juncture of his career has not been recorded. Penniless, he left the ship, to trail after his shipmates as they withdrew along the wharf to stop at a sailors' retreat, poetically denominated "The Flashes." Here they all came to anchor before the bar.

"Well, maties," said one of them, at last—"I s'pose we shan't see each other again:—come, let's splice the mainbrace all round, and drink to *the last voyage*."

And so they did. Then they shook hands all round, three times three, and disappeared in couples through the several doorways.

Melville stood on the corner in front of "The Flashes" till the last of his shipmates was out of sight. Then he walked down to the Battery, and within a stone's throw of the place of his birth, sat on one of the benches, under the summer shade of the trees. It was a quiet, beautiful scene, he says; full of promenading ladies and gentlemen; and through the fresh and bright foliage he looked out over the bay, varied with glancing ships. "It would be a pretty fine world," he thought, "if I only had a little money to enjoy it." He leaves it ambiguous whether or not be imbibed his optimism at "The Flashes." Equally veiled does he leave the mystery by which he came by the money to pay his passage on the steamboat up to Albany: a trip he took that afternoon. "I pass over the reception I met with at home; how I plunged into embraces, long and loving," he says:—"I pass over this."

For the home we return to, is never the home that we leave, and the more desperate the leave-taking, the more bathetic the return.

CHAPTER VI

PEDAGOGY, PUGILISM AND LETTERS

"It is often to be observed, that as in digging for precious metals in the mines, much earthly rubbish has first to be troublesomely handled and thrown out; so, in digging in one's soul for the fine gold of genius, much dulness and common-place is first brought to light. Happy would it be, if the man possessed in himself some receptacle for his own rubbish of this sort: but he is like the occupant of a dwelling, whose refuse cannot be clapped into his own cellar, but must be deposited in the street before his own door, for the public functionaries to take care of."
—HERMAN MELVILLE: *Pierre.*

THE record of the next three and a half years of Melville's life is extremely scant. What he was doing and thinking and feeling must be left almost completely to surmise. In the brief record of his life preserved in the Commonplace Book of his wife, this period between Liverpool and the South Seas is dismissed in a single sentence: "Taught school at intervals in Pittsfield and in Greenbush (now East Albany) N. Y." Arthur Stedman (who got his facts largely from Mrs. Melville), in his "Biographical and Critical Introduction" to *Typee,* slightly enlarges upon this statement. "A good part of the succeeding three years, from 1837 to 1840," says Stedman, "was occupied with school teaching. While so engaged at Greenbush, now East Albany, N. Y., he received the munificent salary of 'six dollars a quarter and board.' He taught for one term at Pittsfield, Mass., 'boarding around' with the families of his pupils, in true American fashion, and early suppressing, on one memorable occasion, the efforts of his larger scholars to inaugurate a rebellion by physical force." J. E. A. Smith, in his *Biographical Sketch* already cited, dates this "memorable" mating of pedagogy and pugilism somewhat earlier.

Besides teaching during these years, Melville was engaged in another activity, which all of his biographers—if they knew of it at all—pass over in decent silence: an activity to which Melville devotes a whole book of *Pierre.*

"It still remains to be said," says Melville, "that Pierre himself had written many a fugitive thing, which had brought him not only vast credit and compliments from his more immediate acquaintances, but the less partial applauses of the always intelligent and extremely discriminating public. In short, Pierre had frequently done that which many other boys have done—published. Not in the imposing form of a book, but in the more modest and becoming way of occasional contributions to magazines and other polite periodicals. Not only the public had applauded his gemmed little sketches of thought and fancy; but the high and mighty Campbell clan of editors of all sorts had bestowed upon them those generous commendations which, with one instantaneous glance, they had immediately perceived was his due. . . . One, after endorsingly quoting that sapient, suppressed maxim of Dr. Goldsmith's, which asserts that whatever is new is false, went on to apply it to the excellent productions before him; concluding with this: 'He has translated the unruffled gentleman from the drawing-room into the general levee of letters; he never permits himself to astonish; is never betrayed into anything coarse or new; as assured that whatever astonishes is vulgar, and whatever is new must be crude. Yes, it is the glory of this admirable young author, that vulgarity and vigour—two inseparable adjuncts—are equally removed from him.' "

In *Pierre,* Melville spends more than twenty-five closely printed pages—half satirical, half of the utmost seriousness—discussing his own literary growth: a passage of the highest critical and biographical interest. In its satirical parts the passage is consistently double-edged; therein, Melville ironically praises his early writing for possessing those very defects which his maturer work was damned for not exhibiting. It is doubtless true that his juvenile works were "equally removed from vulgarity and vigour." They were "characterised throughout by Perfect Taste," as he makes one critic observe "in an ungovernable burst of admiring fury." But the Perfect Taste was the Perfect Taste of Hannah More, and Dr. Akenside, and *Lalla Rookh.* With the publication of *Typee,* Melville was charged not only with the crimes of vulgarity and vigour, but with the milder accompanying vices of indecency and irreverence. His earliest writings were untouched by any of these taints. In *Pierre,* Melville speaks of "a renowned clerical and philological conductor of a weekly religious periodical, whose surprising proficiency in the Greek, Hebrew and Chaldaic, to which he had devoted by far the greater part of his life, peculiarly fitting him to pronounce unerring judgment upon works of taste in the English." Melville makes this critic thus deliver himself on Pierre's early efforts in letters: "He is blameless in morals, and harmless throughout." Another "unhesitatingly recommended his effusions to the family circle." A third had no reserve in saying that "the predominant end and aim of this writer was evangelical piety." Melville is here patently satirising the vitriolic abuse which *Typee* and *Omoo* provoked.

Only two of Melville's earliest effusions, written before the world had "fairly Timonised him" are known to survive. These appeared in *The Democratic Press and Lansingburgh Advertiser* for May 4, and May 18, 1839. The first is signed "L. A. V."; the second, known to exist only in a single mutilated clipping, in lacking the closing paragraphs, can give no evidence as to concluding signature. Copies of these two articles are preserved among Melville's papers, each autographed by him in faded brown ink. The interest of the earlier paper is heightened by this inscription, in Melville's hand, boldly scrawled across the inner margin: "When I woke up this morning, what the Devil should I see but your cane along in bed with me. I shall keep it for you when you come up here again." It is more easy to imagine Melville's astonishment in waking to find such a stately novelty as a walking-stick for a bed-fellow, than to fancy how the walking-stick found itself in such an unusual environment. It is about as futile to inquire into the history and meaning of this incident as soberly to debate "what songs the sirens sang and what name Achilles bore among the daughters of the King of Scyros." It is certain, however, that the Sirens had little hand in Melville's juvenile effusions. And of this fact Melville grew to be keenly aware. "In sober earnest," he says in *Pierre,* "those papers contained nothing uncommon; indeed, those fugitive things were the veriest commonplace." Yet as the initial literary efforts of a man who wrote *Typee* and *Moby-Dick* they are intensely interesting: interesting, like the longer prayers of St. Augustine, less because of their content than because of the personality from which they were derived.

What would seem to be Melville's first published venture in letters is here given, nearly complete.

For the Democratic Press
FRAGMENTS FROM A WRITING DESK
No. 1

MY DEAR M———, I can imagine you seated on that dear, delightful, old-fashioned sofa; your head supported by its luxurious padding, and with feet perched aloft on the aspiring back of that straight limbed, stiff-necked, quaint old chair, which, as our facetious W——— assured me, was the identical seat in which old Burton composed his Anatomy of Melancholy. I see you reluctantly raise your optics from the huge-clasped quarto which encumbers your lap, to receive the package which the servant hands you, and can almost imagine that I see those beloved features illumined for a moment with an expression of joy, as you read the superscription of your gentle protégé. Lay down I beseech you that odious black-lettered volume and let not its musty and withered leaves sully the virgin purity and whiteness of the sheet which is the vehicle of so much good sense, sterling thought, and chaste and elegant sentiment.

You remember how you used to rate me for my hang-dog modesty, my *mauvaise honte,* as my Lord Chesterfield would style it. Well! I have determined that hereafter you shall not have occasion to inflict upon me those flattering appellations of "Fool!" "Dolt!" "Sheep!" which in your indignation you used to shower upon me, with a vigour and a facility which excited my wonder, while it provoked my resentment.

And how do you imagine that I rid myself of this annoying hindrance? Why, truly, by coming to the conclusion that in this pretty corpus of mine was lodged every manly grace;

that my limbs were modelled in the symmetry of the Phidian
Jupiter; my countenance radiant with the beams of wit and
intelligence, the envy of the beaux, the idol of the women and
the admiration of the tailor. And then my mind! why, sir, I
have discovered it to be endowed with the most rare and extraordinary powers, stored with universal knowledge, and embellished with every polite accomplishment.

Pollux! what a comfortable thing is a good opinion of one's
self when I walk the Broadway of our village with a certain
air, that puts me down at once in the estimation of any intelligent stranger who may chance to meet me, as a *distingué* of
the purest water, a blade of the true temper, a blood of the
first quality! Lord! how I despise the little sneaking vermin
who dodge along the street as though they were so many foot-
men or errand boys; who have never learned to carry the head
erect in conscious importance, but hang that noblest of the
human members as though it had been boxed by some virago
of an Amazon; who shuffle along the walk with a quick uneasy
step, a hasty clownish motion, which by the magnitude of the
contrast, set off to advantage my own slow and magisterial
gait, which I can at pleasure vary to an easy, abandoned sort
of carriage, or to the more engaging alert and lively walk, to
suit the varieties of time, occasion, and company.

And in society, too—how often have I commiserated the
poor wretches who stood aloof, in a corner, like a flock of
scared sheep; while myself, beautiful as Apollo, dressed in a
style which would extort admiration from a Brummel, and
belted round with self-esteem as with a girdle, sallied up to the
ladies—complimenting one, exchanging a repartee with another; tapping this one under the chin, and clasping this one
round the waist; and finally, winding up the operation by kiss-
ing round the whole circle to the great edification of the fair,
and to the unbounded horror, amazement and ill-suppressed
chagrin of the aforesaid sheepish multitude; who with eyes
wide open and mouths distended, afforded good subjects on
whom to exercise my polished wit, which like the glittering
edge of a Damascus sabre "dazzled all it shone upon."

.   .   .   .

By my halidome, sir, this same village of Lansingburgh contains within its pretty limits as fair a set of blushing damsels as one would wish to look upon on a dreamy summer day! —When I traverse the broad pavements of my own metropolis, my eyes are arrested by beautiful forms flitting hither and thither; and I pause to admire the elegance of their attire, the taste displayed in their embellishments; the rich mass of the material; and sometimes, it may be, at the loveliness of the features, which no art can heighten and no negligence conceal.

But here, sir, here—where woman seems to have erected her throne, and established her empire; here, where all feel and acknowledge her sway, she blooms in unborrowed charms; and the eye undazzled by the profusion of extraneous ornament, settles at once upon the loveliest faces which our clayey natures can assume.

.   .   .   .   .   .

Nor, my dear M., does there reign in all this bright display, that same monotony of feature, form, complexion, which elsewhere is beheld; no, here are all varieties, all the orders of Beauty's architecture; the Doric, the Ionic, the Corinthian, all are here.

I have in "my mind's eye, Horatio," three (the number of the Graces, you remember) who may stand, each at the head of their respective orders.

.   .   .   .

When I venture to describe the second of this beautiful trinity, I feel my powers of delineation inadequate to the task; but nevertheless I will try my hand at the matter, although like an unskilful limner, I am fearful I shall but scandalise the charms I endeavour to copy.

Come to my aid, ye guardian spirits of the Fair! Guide my awkward hand, and preserve from mutilation the features ye hover over and protect! Pour down whole floods of sparkling champagne, my dear M————, until your brain grows giddy with emotion; con over the latter portion of the first Canto of Childe Harold, and ransack your intellectual repository for the loveliest visions of the Fairy Land, and you will be in a measure prepared to relish the epicurean banquet I shall spread.

The stature of this beautiful mortal (if she be indeed of earth) is of that perfect height which, while it is freed from the charge of being low, cannot with propriety be denominated tall. Her figure is slender almost to fragility but strikingly modelled in spiritual elegance, and is the only form I ever saw which could bear the trial of a rigid criticism.

Every man who is gifted with the least particle of imagination, must in some of his reveries have conjured up from the realms of fancy, a being bright and beautiful beyond everything he had ever before apprehended, whose main and distinguishing attribute invariably proves to be a form the indescribable loveliness of which seems to

> "—Sail in liquid light,
> And float on seas of bliss."

The realisation of these seraphic visions is seldom permitted us; but I can truly say that when my eyes for the first time fell upon this lovely creature, I thought myself transported to the land of Dreams, where lay embodied, the most brilliant conceptions of the wildest fancy. Indeed, could the Promethean spark throw life and animation into the Venus de Medici, it would but present the counterpart of ———.

Her complexion has the delicate tinge of the Brunett, with a little of the roseate hue of the Circassian; and one would swear that none but the sunny skies of Spain had shone upon the infancy of the being, who looks so like her own "dark-glancing daughters."

.   .   .   .

And then her eyes! they open their dark, rich orbs upon you like the full moon of heaven, and blaze into your very soul the fires of day! Like the offerings laid upon the sacrificial altars of the Hebrew, when in an instant the divine spark falling from the propitiated God kindled them in flames; so, a single glance from that Oriental eye as quickly fires your soul, and leaves your bosom in a perfect conflagration! Odds Cupids and Darts! with one broad sweep of vision in a crowded ball-room, that splendid creature would lay around her like the two-handed sword of Minotti, hearts on hearts, piled round in semi-circles! But it is well for the more rugged sex that this glorious being can vary her proud dominion, and give to the expression of her eye a melting tenderness which dissolves the most frigid heart and heals the wounds she gave before.

If the devout and exemplary Mussulman who dying fast in the faith of his Prophet anticipates reclining on beds of roses, gloriously drunk through all the ages of eternity, is to be waited on by Houris such as these: waft me ye gentle gales beyond this lower world and

"Lap me in soft Lydian airs!"

But I am falling into I know not what extravagances, so I will briefly give you a portrait of the last of these three divinities, and will then terminate my tiresome lucubrations.

. . . .

Here, my dear M———, closes this catalogue of the Graces, this chapter of Beauties, and I should implore your pardon for trespassing so long on your attention. If you, yourself, in whose breast may possibly be extinguished the amatory flame, should not feel an interest in these three "counterfeit presentments," do not fail to show them to ——— and solicit her opinion as to their respective merits.

Tender my best acknowledgments to the Major for his prompt attention to my request, and, for yourself, accept the assurance of my undiminished regard; and hoping that the smiles of heaven may continue to illuminate your way,
I remain, ever yours,

L. A. V.

These "chaste and elegant sentiments" are, surely, "embellished with every polite accomplishment." Melville called down the Nine Gods, and a host of minor deities; he ransacked Athens, Rhodes, Cyprus, Circassia, Lydia, Lilliputia, Damascus, this world and the next, for geographical adornments; he called up Burton, Shakespeare, Scott, Byron, Milton, Coleridge and Chesterfield, as well as Prometheus and Cinderella, Mahomet and Cleopatra, Madonnas and Houris, Medici and Mussulman, to strew carelessly across his pages. "Not in vain," says Melville of the idealisation of himself in the character of Pierre, "had he spent long summer afternoons in the deep recesses of his father's fastidiously picked and decorous library."   Not in vain, either, had he been submitted to three years of elementary drill in the classics at the Albany Academy.   "Not that as yet his young and immature soul had been accosted by the wonderful Mutes, and through the vast halls of Silent Truth, had been ushered into the full, secret, eternally inviolable Sanhedrim, where the Poetic Magi discuss, in glorious gibberish, the Alpha and Omega of the Universe," says Melville; "but among the beautiful imaginings of the second and third degree of poets he freely and comprehendingly ranged."   Melville was always a wide if desultory reader, more and more interested after the manner of Sir Thomas Browne, and the Burton with reference to whom he began his career in letters, in "remote and curious illusions, wrecks of forgotten fables, antediluvian computations, obsolete and unfamiliar problems, riddles that no living Œdipus would care to solve."   And this preoccupation—first made manifest in *Mardi* (1849)—must always stand in the way of his most typical writings ever becoming widely popular.   His earliest known piece of juvenile composition is interesting as revealing the crude beginnings of one of the manners superbly mastered in parts of *Moby-Dick*.   This early effusion, by revealing so crudely the defects of his qualities, reads as a dull parody of one of his most typical later manners.

With a Miltonic confidence in his own gifts, Melville came to view these earlier pieces as the first "earthly rubbish" of his "immense quarries of fine marble."   Melville goes on to say that "no commonplace is ever effectually got rid of, except by essentially emptying one's self of it into a book; for once trapped into a book, then the book can be put into the fire and all will be well."   "But they are not always put into the fire," he said with regret.   And because of his own laxity in cremation, his crude first fruits stalk abroad to accuse him.

At this early period, Melville had nothing very significant to say; but he seems to have been urged to say it with remorseless pertinacity. In *Pierre,* he satirises his youthful and reckless prolixity where he speaks of his manuscripts as being of such flying multitudes that "they were to be found lying all round the house; gave a great deal of trouble to the housemaids in sweeping; went for kindlings to the fires; and forever flitting out of the windows, and under the doorsills, into the faces of people passing the manorial mansion."

Having nothing very particular to write about, he followed an ancient tradition, and wrote of love. In *Pierre,* which is Melville's spiritual autobiography, and in *Pierre* alone, does Melville elaborately busy himself with romantic affection. And in *Pierre,* his is no sugared and conventional preoccupation. He traces his own development through the love-friendship of boyhood, the miscellaneous susceptibility of adolescence, to a crucifixion in manhood between the images of his wife and his mother. His first *Fragment from a Writing Desk* seems to have been conceived at a time before his "innumerable wandering glances settled upon some one specific object."

His second *Fragment from a Writing Desk* concerns itself with an allegorical quest of elusive feminine loveliness: a kind of *Coelebs in Search of a Wife,* allegorised and crossed with *Lalla Rookh.* It survives, as has been said, only as a fragment of a Fragment. Its conclusion must remain a mystery until some old newspaper file disgorges its secrets. It begins as follows:

For the Democratic Press

FRAGMENTS FROM A WRITING DESK

No. 2

"Confusion seize the Greek!" exclaimed I, as wrathfully rising from my chair, I flung my ancient Lexicon across the room and seizing my hat and cane, and throwing on my cloak, I sallied out into the clearer air of heaven. The bracing coolness of an April evening calmed my aching temples, and I slowly wended my way to the river side. I had promenaded the bank for about half an hour, when flinging myself upon the grassy turf, I was soon lost in revery, and up to the lips in sentiment.

I had not lain more than five minutes, when a figure effectually concealed in the ample folds of a cloak, glided past me, and hastily dropping something at my feet, disappeared behind the angle of an adjoining house, ere I could recover from my astonishment at so singular an occurrence.

"Cerbes!" cried I, springing up, "here is a spice of the marvellous!" and stooping down, I picked up an elegant little, rose-coloured, lavender-scented billet-doux, and hurriedly breaking the seal (a heart, transfixed with an arrow) I read by the light of the moon, the following:—

"GENTLE SIR:
If my fancy has painted you in genuine colours, you will on the receipt of this, incontinently follow the bearer where she will lead you.

INAMORITA."

"The deuce I will!" exclaimed I,—"But soft!"—And I reperused this singular document, turned over the billet in my fingers, and examined the hand-writing, which was femininely delicate, and I could have sworn was a woman's. Is it possible, thought I, that the days of romance are revived?—No, "The days of chivalry are over!" says Burke.

As I made this reflection, I looked up, and beheld the same figure which had handed me this questionable missive, beckoning me forward. I started towards her; but, as I approached, she receded from me, and fled swiftly along the margin of the river at a pace which, encumbered as I was with my heavy cloak and boots, I was unable to follow; and which filled me with sundry misgivings, as to the nature of the being, who could travel with such amazing celerity. At last, perfectly breathless, I fell into a walk; which, my mysterious fugitive perceiving, she likewise lessened her pace, so as to keep herself still in sight, although at too great a distance to permit me to address her."

The hero hastens after his guide—but always she eludes him. Piqued by her repeated escapes, he stops in a rage, and relieves his feelings in "two or three expressions that savoured somewhat of the jolly days of the jolly cavaliers." And under the circumstances, he felt fully justified in his profanity. "What! to be thwarted by a woman! Peradventure; baffled by a girl? Confusion! It was too bad! To be outwitted, generaled, routed, defeated, by a mere rib of the earth? It could not be borne!" Recovering his temper, he followed his capricious guide out of the town, into a shadowy grove to "an edifice, which seated on a gentle eminence, and embowered amidst surrounding trees, bore the appearance of a country villa."

"The appearance of this spacious habitation was anything but inviting; it seemed to have been built with a jealous eye to concealment; and its few, but well-defended windows were sufficiently high from the ground, as effectually to baffle the prying curiosity of the inquisitive stranger. Not a single light shone from the narrow casement; but all was harsh, gloomy and forbidding. As my imagination, ever alert on such an occasion, was busily occupied in assigning some fearful motive for such unusual precautions, my leader suddenly halted beneath a lofty window, and making a low call, I perceived slowly descending therefrom, a thick silken cord, attached to an ample basket, which was silently deposited at our feet. Amazed at this apparition, I was about soliciting an explanation: when laying her fingers impressively upon her lips, and placing herself in the basket, my guide motioned me to seat myself beside her. I obeyed; but not without considerable trepidation: and in obedience to the same low call which had procured its descent, our curious vehicle, with sundry creakings, rose in air."

This airy jaunt terminated, of course, in an Arabian Nights exterior, which Melville particularises after the "voluptuous" traditions of *Vathek* and *Lalla Rookh*. "The grandeur of the room," of course, "served only to show to advantage the matchless beauty of its inmate." This matchless beauty was, after established tradition, "reclining on an ottoman; in one hand holding a lute." Her fingers, too, "were decorated with a variety of rings, which as she waved her hand to me as I entered, darted forth a thousand coruscations, and gleamed their brilliant splendours to the sight."

"As I entered the apartment, her eyes were downcast, and the expression of her face was mournfully interesting; she had apparently been lost in some melancholy revery. Upon my entrance, however, her countenance brightened, as with a queenly wave of the hand, she motioned my conductress from the room, and left me standing, mute, admiring and bewildered in her presence."

"For a moment my brain spun round, and I had not at command a single of my faculties. Recovering my self-possession, however, and with that, my good-breeding, I advanced en cavalier and, gracefully sinking on one knee, I bowed my head and exclaimed—'Here do I prostrate myself, thou sweet Divinity, and kneel at the shrine of thy—' "

But here, just at the climax of the quest, the clipping is abruptly torn, and the reader is left cruelly suspended.

From the publication of *Lalla Rookh,* in 1817, to the publication of Thackeray's *Our Street* in 1847, there settled upon letters and life in England an epidemic of hankering for the exotic. At the instigation of *Lalla Rookh,* England made a prim effort to be "purely and intensely Asiatic," and this while delicately avoiding "the childishness, cruelty, and profligacy of Asia." In the fashionable literature of the period, the harem and the slave-market unburdened its gazelles and its interior decorations, and by a resort to divans and coruscating rubies, and ottar of roses, and lutes, and warm panting maidens, the "principled goodness" of Anglo-Saxon self-righteousness was thrilled to a discreet voluptuousness.

In his second *Fragment,* Melville has caught at some of the drift-wood of this great tidal wave that was washed across the Atlantic. And in acknowledgment of this early indebtedness, he in *Pierre* speaks of Tom Moore with an especial burst of enthusiasm, mating him with Hafiz, Anacreon, Catullus and Ovid.

Reared in a New England environment that had been soberly tempered by Mrs. Chapone and Mrs. Barbauld, Melville had, under the goadings of poverty, the frustrations of his environment, and the teasing lure of some stupendous discovery awaiting him at the rainbow's end, plunged into the hideousness of life in the forecastle of a merchantman. At both extremes of his journey he reaped only disillusion. As a practically penniless sailor in Liverpool he enjoyed the freedom of the streets: and the architecture of the city impressed him less than did the sights of the poverty and viciousness to which he was especially exposed. Back he came to Lansingburg, to the old pump in the yard, the stiff-corseted decorum, and the threadbare and pretentious proprieties of his mother, to decline into the enforced drudgery of teaching school. The sights of Liverpool and the forecastle had given no permanent added beauty to home. He did not comfortably fit into any recognised socket of New England respectability. He sought escape in books, in amateur authorship. And Burton, and Anacreon, and Tom Moore are not guaranteed to reconcile a boy in ferment to a tame and repugnant environment. He was like a strong wine that clears with explosive violence. He had been to sea once, and there acquired some skill as a sailor. The excitement and hardship and downrightness of ocean life, when viewed through the drab of the ensuing years, treacherously suffered a sea-change. After three and a half years of mounting desperation, he was ripe for a transit clean beyond the pale of civilisation.

"I am tormented with an everlasting itch for things remote," he later wrote in an effort to explain his second hegira; "I love to sail forbidden seas, and land on barbarous coasts." The trip to Liverpool had slammed the sash on one magic casement; but the greater part of the watery world was still to be viewed. "Why," he asks himself perplexed at his own mystery, "is almost every healthy boy with a robust healthy soul, at some time or other crazy to go to sea? Why did the old Persians hold the sea holy? Why did the Greeks give it a separate deity, and own brother to Jove? Surely all this is not without meaning. And still deeper the story of Narcissus, who because he could not grasp the tormenting, mild image he saw in the fountain, plunged into it and was drowned. But that same image, we ourselves see in all rivers and oceans. It is the image of the ungraspable phantom of life; and this is the key to all." The key he here offers to the heart of his mystery is itself locked in mystery; though when he compared himself to Narcissus tormented by the irony of being two, Melville may have been hotter on the trail of the truth than he was aware. His deepest insight, perhaps, came to him one midnight, out on the Pacific, where in the glare and the wild Hindoo odour of the tryworks of a whaler in full operation, he fell asleep at the helm. "Starting from a brief standing sleep," he says, "I was horribly conscious of something fatally wrong. I thought my eyes were open; I was half conscious of putting my fingers to the lids and mechanically stretching them still further apart. But, spite of all this, I could see no compass before me to steer by. Nothing seemed before me but a jet of gloom, now and then made ghastly by flashes of redness. Uppermost was the impression, that whatever swift, rushing thing I stood on was not so much bound to any haven ahead as rushing from all havens astern."

In a headlong retreat from all havens astern, on January 3, 1841, Melville shipped on board the *Acushnet,* a whaler bound for the South Seas.

CHAPTER VII

BLUBBER AND MYSTICISM

"And, as for me, if, by any possibility, there be any as yet undiscovered prime thing in me; if I shall ever deserve any real repute in that small but high hushed world which I might not be unreasonably ambitious of; if hereafter I shall do anything that, upon the whole, a man might rather have done than to have left undone; if, at my death, my executors, or more properly my creditors, find any precious MSS. in my desk, then here I prospectively ascribe all the honour and the glory to whaling; for a whale-ship was my Yale College and my Harvard."
—HERMAN MELVILLE: *Moby-Dick.*

In 1892, the year after Melville's death, Arthur Stedman wrote a "Biographical and Critical Introduction" to *Typee.* During the final years of Melville's sedulous isolation, Arthur Stedman was—with the minor exception of the late Dr. Titus Munson Coan, whose Missionary parentage Melville seems never to have quite forgiven him—the single man who clung to Melville with any semblance of personal loyalty. Stedman was unwavering in his belief that in his earlier South Sea novels, Melville had attained to his highest achievement: an achievement that entitled Melville to more golden opinions, Stedman believed, than Melville ever reaped from a graceless generation. To Stedman—as to Dr. Coan—Melville's later development into mysticism and metaphysics was a melancholy perversity to be viewed with a charitable forbearance, and forgiven in the fair name of Fayaway. Dr. Coan repeatedly used to recount, with a sigh at his frustration, how he made persistent attempts to inveigle Melville into Polynesian reminiscences, always to be rebuffed by Melville's invariable rejoinder: "That reminds me of the eighth book of Plato's *Republic.*" This was a signal for silence and leave-taking. What was the staple of Stedman's conversation is not known. But despite the fact that Melville was to him a crabbed and darkly shadowed hieroglyph, he clung to Melville with a personal loyalty at once humorous and pathetic. Melville to him was

the "man who lived with the cannibals," and merited canonisation because of this intimacy with unholy flesh. Stedman
published in the New York *World* for October 11, 1891, a tribute to his dead friend, significantly headed: *"Marquesan" Melville. A South Sea Prospero who Lived and Died in New
York. The Island Nymphs of Nukuheva's Happy Valley.*
While Stedman was not necessarily responsible for this caption, it is, nevertheless, a just summary of the fullest insight
he ever got into Melville's life and works. The friendship between Petrarch and Boccaccio is hardly less humorous than
the relationship between Melville and Stedman; and surely
Melville has suffered more, in death, if not in life, from the
perils of friendship than did Petrarch: more even than did
Baudelaire from the damaging admiration of Gautier. When
one's enemy writes a book, one's reputation is less likely to be
jeopardised by literary animosity than it is by the best superlatives of self-appointed custodians of one's good name. But
as Francis Thompson has observed, it is a principle universally
conceded that, since the work of a great author is said to be a
monument, the true critic does best evince his taste and sense
by cutting his own name on it. Critical biographers have contrived a method to hand themselves down to posterity through
the gods of literature, as did the Roman emperors through the
gods of Olympus—by taking the heads off their statues, and
clapping on their own instead. Criticism is a perennial
decapitation.

"I have a fancy," says Stedman, in his *Biographical and
Critical Introduction,* "that it was the reading of Richard
Henry Dana's *Two Years Before the Mast* which revived the
spirit of adventure in Melville's breast. That book was published in 1840, and was at once talked of everywhere. Melville must have read it at the time, mindful of his own experience as a sailor. At any rate, he once more signed a ship's
articles, and on January 1, 1841, sailed from New Bedford
harbour in the whaler *Acushnet,* bound for the Pacific Ocean
and the sperm fishery."

In the second part of this statement, Stedman attempts to
stick to the letter: but there is a flaw in his text. That Mel-

ville sailed in the *Acushnet* is corroborated by a statement in the journal of Melville's wife; in the record surviving in Melville's handwriting, headed "what became of the ship's company on the whaleship *Acushnet,* according to Hubbard, who came back in her (more than a four years' voyage) and visited me in Pittsfield in 1850;" as well as by surviving letters written by Richard Tobias Greene, the Toby of *Typee.*

The roster of Melville's ship is preserved in Alexander Starbuck's bulky *History of the American Whale Fishery from its Earliest Inception to the Year 1876* (published by the author, Waltham, Mass., 1878). Starbuck rates the *Acushnet* as a ship of 359 tons, built in 1840. Her managing owners are reported as having been Bradford Fuller & Co. Under command of Captain Pease she sailed from Fairhaven, bound for the whaling grounds of the Pacific, on January 3, 1841, and returned to Fairhaven on May 13, 1845, laden with 850 barrels of sperm oil, 1350 barrels of whale oil, and 13500 pounds of whale-bone. On July 18, 1845, she started upon her second voyage, under command of Captain Rogers, to return June 7, 1848, stocked with 500 barrels of sperm oil, 800 barrels of whale oil, and 6000 pounds of whale-bone. On December 4, 1847, she had a boat stove by a whale, with the loss of the third mate and four of the crew. Her third voyage, begun August 31, 1848, under command of Captain Bradley, was her last. As by some malicious fatality, the *Acushnet* was lost on St. Lawrence Island on August 31, 1851, within a month of the time when Melville brought *Moby-Dick* to its tragic close.

Between Stedman's and Starbuck's accounts of the time and place of Melville's sailing there is a discrepancy of half a mile and two days. This discrepancy, however, does not necessarily impugn Stedman's accuracy. Fairhaven is just across the Acushnet river from New Bedford, and "sailing from New Bedford" may be like "sailing from New York"—which is often in reality "sailing from Hoboken."

Stedman dates Melville's sailing January 1; Starbuck, January 3. Melville launches the hero of *Moby-Dick* neither from New Bedford nor from Fairhaven, but from Nantucket.

Ishmael begins his fatal voyage aboard the *Pequod* on December 25; and there is a fitting irony in the fact that on the day that celebrates the birth of the Saviour of mankind, the *Pequod* should sail forth to slay Moby-Dick, the monstrous symbol and embodiment of unconquerable evil.

That Dana's book should have fired Melville to an impetuous and romantic jaunt to the South Seas, though an ill-favoured statement, is Stedman's very own. When a boy concludes the Christmas holidays by a mid-winter plunge into the filthy and shabby business of whaling; when a young man inaugurates the year not among the familiar associations of the gods of his hearth, but among semi-barbarous strangers of the forecastle of a whaler: to make such a shifting of whereabouts a sign of jolly romantic exuberance, is engagingly naïve in its perversity.

Just what specific circumstances were the occasion of Melville's escape into whaling will probably never be known: what burst of demoniac impulse, either of anger, or envy, or spite; what gnawing discontent; what passionate disappointment; what crucifixion of affection; what blind impetuosity; what sinister design. But in the light of his writings and the known facts of his life it seems likely that his desperate transit was made in the mid-winter of his discontent. That the reading of Dana's book should have filled his head with a mere adolescent longing for brine-drenched locomotion and sent him gallantly off to sea is a surmise more remarkable for simplicity than insight.

Melville never wearies of iterating his "itch for things remote." Like Thoreau, he had a "naturally roving disposition," and of the two men it is difficult to determine which achieved a wider peregrination. It was Thoreau's proud boast: "I have travelled extensively in Concord." He believed that Concord, with its sylvan environment, was a microcosm "by the study of which the whole world could be comprehended," and so, this wildest of civilised men seldom strayed beyond its familiar precincts. His was a heroic provincialism, that cost him little loss either in worldliness or in wisdom. Though his head went swimming in the Milky Way, his feet were well-rooted in New England sod. "One world at a time" was the programme he set himself for digesting the universe: and he looked into the eyes of this world with cold stoical serenity.

Melville made no such capitulation with reality. Between the obdurate world of facts and his ardent and unclarified desires there was always, to the end of his life, a blatant incompatibility. Alongside the hard and cramping world of reality, and in more or less sharp opposition to it, he set up a fictitious world, a world of heart's desire; and unlike Thoreau, he hugged his dream in jealous defiance of reality. It is, of course, an ineradicable longing of man to repudiate the inexorable restrictions of reality, and return to the happy delusion of omnipotence of early childhood, an escape into some land of heart's desire. Goethe compared the illusions that man nourishes in his breast to the population of statues in ancient Rome which were almost as numerous as the population of living men. Most men keep the boundaries between these two populations distinct: a separation facilitated by the usual dwindling of the ghostly population. Flaubert once observed that every tenth-rate provincial notary had in him the debris of a poet. As Wordsworth complains, as we grow away from childhood, the vision fades into the light of common day. Thoreau clung to his visions; but they were, after all, cold-blooded and well-behaved visions. And by restricting himself to "one world at a time," by mastering his dream, he mastered reality. Alcott declared that Thoreau thought he dwelt in the centre of the universe, and seriously contemplated annexing the rest of the planet to Concord. The delicacy of the compliment to the rest of the planet has never been adequately appreciated. Melville's more violent and restive impulses never permitted him to feel any such flattering attachment to his whereabouts, whether it was Albany, Liverpool, Lima, Tahiti or Constantinople. Like Rousseau, who confessed himself "burning with desire without any definite object," Melville always felt himself an exile from the seacoast of Bohemia. But his nostalgia, his indefinite longing for the unknown, was not, in any literal sense, "homesickness" at all. As Aldous Huxley has observed:

"Those find, who most delight to roam
  'Mid castles of remotest Spain
That there's, thank Heaven, no place like home
So they put out upon their travels again."

That Melville came to no very pleasant haven of refuge in
the forecastle of the *Acushnet* is borne out by his drastic preference to be eaten by cannibals rather than abide among the
sureties of the ship and her company.   That he "left the ship,
being oppressed with hard fare and hard usage, in the summer of 1842 with a companion, Richard T. Greene (Toby) at
the bay of Nukuheva in the Marquesas Islands" is the statement in the journal of his wife vividly elaborated in *Typee*.
Of Melville's history aboard the *Acushnet* there is no
straightforward account. *Redburn, Typee, Omoo* and *White-
Jacket* are transparent chapters in autobiography.   From his
experiences on board the *Acushnet* Melville draws generously
in *Moby-Dick*: but these experiences do not for one moment
pretend to be the whole of the literal truth.   Only an insanity
as lurid as Captain Ahab's would mistake *Moby-Dick* for a
similarly reliable report of personal experiences. *Moby-Dick*
is, indeed, an autobiography of adventure; but adventure upon
the highest plane of spiritual daring.   Incidentally, it also offers the fullest, and truest, and most readable history of an
actual whaling cruise ever written.   But it is not a "scientific"
history.   The "scientific" historian, proudly unreadable, thanks
God that he has no style to tempt him out of the strict weariness of counting-house inventories; and in despair of presenting the truth, he boasts a make-shift veracity.   The truest
historians are, of course, the poets—and their histories are
"feigned."   Melville, writing in the capacity of poet, was li-
censed in the best interests of truth to expurgate reality.   And
though Captain Ahab's hunt of the abhorred Moby-Dick belongs as essentially to the realm of poetry as does the quest of
the Holy Grail, it is, withal, in its lower reaches, so broadly
based on a foundation of solid reality that it is possible, by considering *Moby-Dick* in double conjunction with the few facts
explicitly known of Melville during the period of his whaling
cruise, and the wealth of facts known of whaling in general,

to block in, with a considerable degree of certainty, the contours of his experiences aboard the *Acushnet*.

By all odds, the chief chapter in the history of whaling is the story of its rise and practical extinction in the Southern New England States. In this limited geographical area, trade in "oil and bone" was pursued with an alacrity, an enterprise and a prosperity unparalleled in the world's history. When, in 1841, Melville boarded the *Acushnet,* American whaling, after a development through nearly two centuries, was within a decade of its highest development, within two decades of its precipitous decay. The doom of whale-oil lamps and sperm candles was ultimately decided in 1859 with the opening of the first oil well in Pennsylvania, and sealed by the Civil War. Melville knew American whaling at the prime of its golden age, and taking it at its crest, he raised it in fiction to a dignity and significance incomparably higher than it ever reached in literal fact.

At the beginning of *Moby-Dick,* Melville culls from the most incongruous volumes an anthology of comments upon Leviathan, beginning with the Mosaic comment "And God created great whales," and ending, after eclectic quotations from Pliny, Lucian, Rabelais, Sir Thomas Browne, Spenser, Hobbes, Bunyan, Milton, Dryden, Pope, Paley, Blackstone, Hawthorne, Daniel Webster, Darwin, and dozens of others (including an excerpt "From 'Something' Unpublished") ends on the old whale song:

> "Oh, the rare old whale, mid storm and gale
> In his ocean home will be
> A giant in might, where might is right,
> And King of the boundless sea."

Rather than conventionally distribute his quotations throughout the book as chapter headings, Melville offers them all in a block at the beginning of the volume, somewhat after the manner of Franklin's grace said over the pork barrel. And extraordinarily effective is this device of Melville's in stirring the reader's interest to a sense of the wonder and mystery of this largest of all created live things, of the wild and distant seas wherein he rolls his island bulk; of the undeliverable, nameless perils of the whale with all the attending marvels of a thousand Patagonian sights and sounds. Even before the reader comes to the superb opening paragraph of *Moby-Dick*, the great flood-gates of the wonder-world are swung open, and into his inmost soul, as into Melville's, "two by two there float endless processions of the whale, and midmost of them all, one grand hooded phantom, like a snow hill in the air."

The literature of whaling slopes down from *Moby-Dick*, both before and after, into a wilderness of several hundred volumes.

There is but one attempt at a comprehensive history of whaling: Walter S. Tower's *A History of the American Whale Fishery* (Philadelphia, 1907). This slender volume first makes a rapid survey of the sources and proceeds from these to a cautious selection of the outstanding documented facts which by "economic interpretation" it presents as a consecutive story. Devoid of literary pretension, it is admirable in accuracy, compactness and clarity. The most comprehensive popular treatment of American whaling is to be found in Hyatt Verrill's *The Real Story of the Whaler* (1916): a more exuberant but less workmanly book than Tower's. Representative shorter surveys are to be found both in Winthrop L. Martin's very able *The American Merchant Marine* (1902) and Willis J. Abbot's *American Merchant Ships and Sailors* (1902).

Although the literature of whaling extends by repeated dilutions from "economic interpretations" to infant books, the classical sources for this extended literature tally less than a score. The great work on the *Fisheries and Fishing Industries of the United States,* prepared under the direction of G. Brown Goode in 1884, contains two articles on whaling of the first magnitude of importance: *Whalemen, Vessels, Apparatus and Methods of the Whale Fishery* and a *History of the Present Condition of the Whale Fishery.* The facts presented in these last two encyclopædic treatments are drawn principally from Alexander Starbuck's *History of the American Whale Fishery from Its Earliest Inception to the Year 1874,* published in 1876, and C. M. Scammon's *Marine Mammals of the North Western Coast of North America, with an Account of the American Whale Fishery,* published in 1874. Lorenzo Sabine's *Report on the Principal Fisheries of the American Seas,* published in 1870, while prior to the monumental works of Starbuck and Scammon in date of publication, enjoys no other priority. The most complete and detailed treatment of the origin and early development of whaling is to be found in William Scoresby's *An Account of the Arctic Regions,* dated 1820. Scoresby—"the justly renowned," according to Melville; "the excellent voyager"—was an English naval officer, and in his discussion of the whale fishery he deals solely with the European and principally with the British industry. But Scoresby's book is principally a classic as regards the earlier history of whaling. Scoresby seems to have convinced all later historians in this field of the folly of further research. Melville knew Scoresby's book—"I honour him for a veteran," Melville confesses—and drew from its erudition in *Moby-Dick.* Obed Macy's *History of Nantucket,* published in 1836, is one of the few important original sources for the history of whaling, and the most readable. Melville expresses repeated indebtedness to Macy. Macy's record has the tang of first-hand experience, and the flavour of local records. Because of the fact that many of the records from which this fine old antiquary of whales drew have since been destroyed by fire, his book enjoys the heightened authority of being a unique source. According to Anatole France, the perplexities of historians begin where events are related by two or by several witnesses, "for their evidence is always contradictory and always irreconcilable." The fire at Nantucket blazed a royal road to truth. Daniel Ricketson, in his *History of New Bedford* (1850) attempted to emulate Macy. And though Ricketson's sources, as Macy's, have been largely destroyed by fire, his authority, though irrefutable in so far as it goes, is less detailed and comprehensive.

Of published personal narrative of whale-hunting, Owen Chase's *Narrative of the Most Extraordinary and Distressing Ship Wreck of the Whale Ship Essex of Nantucket,* published

THROWING THE HARPOON

SOUNDING

in 1821, as well as F. D. Bennett's two-volume *Narrative of a Voyage Round the World,* published 1833-36, were drawn from by Melville in *Moby-Dick.* The account of the sinking of the *Essex* is important as being the source from which Melville borrowed, with superb transformation, the catastrophe with which he closes *Moby-Dick.* The sinking of the *Essex* —recounted in *Moby-Dick*—is the first and best known instance of a ship being actually sent to the bottom by the ramming of an infuriated whale, and in its sequel it is one of the most dreadful chapters of human suffering in all the hideous annals of shipwreck. "I have seen Owen Chase," Melville says in *Moby-Dick,* "who was chief mate of the *Essex* at the time of the tragedy: I have read his plain and faithful narrative: I have conversed with his son; and all within a few miles of the scene of the tragedy." Melville may here be using a technique learned from Defoe.

Though in *Moby-Dick* Melville makes several references to J. Ross Browne's *Etchings of a Whaling Cruise, with Notes on a Sojourn on the Island of Zanzibar,* mildly praising some of his drawings while reprobating their reproduction, he owes no debt to J. Ross Browne. Melville and Browne wrote of whaling with purposes diametrically opposed. Melville gloried in the romance of whales, and horsed on Leviathan, through a briny sunset dove down through the nether-twilight into the blackest haunted caverns of the soul. Browne provokes no such rhetorical extravagance of characterisation. He sat soberly and firmly down on a four-legged chair before a four-legged desk and wrote up his travels. "My design," he says, "is simply to present to the public a faithful delineation of the life of a whaleman. In doing this, I deem it necessary that I should aim rather at the truth itself than at mere polish of style." So Browne made a virtue of necessity, and convinced that "history scarcely furnishes a parallel for the deeds of cruelty" then "prevalent in the whale fishery," he sent his book forth "to show in what manner the degraded condition of a portion of our fellow-creatures can be ameliorated." In a study of Melville's life, Browne is important as presenting an ungarnished account of typical conditions aboard a whaler at

the time Melville was cruising in the *Acushnet*. Useful in
the same way are R. Delano's *Wanderings and Adventures;
Being a Narrative of Twelve Years' Life in a Whaleship*
(1846) and Captain Davis' spirited overhauling of his journal kept during a whaling trip, published in 1872 under the
title *Nimrod of the Sea*.

Though whales and Pilgrim Fathers would, at first blush,
seem to belong to two mutually repugnant orders of nature, yet
were they, by force of circumstance, early thrown into a
warring intimacy. And strangely enough, in this armed
alliance, it was the whale who made the first advances. Richard Mather, who came to Massachusetts Bay colony in 1635,
records in his journal, according to Sabine, the presence off the
New England coast of "mighty whales spewing up water in
the air like the smoke of a chimney . . . of such incredible
bigness that I will never wonder that the body of Jonah could
be in the belly of a whale." From this and other evidence it
seems undoubted that in early colonial days whales were undaunted by the strict observances of the Pilgrims, and browsed
in great numbers, even on Sabbath, within the sight of land.
Yet, despite this open violation of Scripture, the resourceful
Puritan pressed .them into the service of true religion. Believing that

> Whales in the sea
> God's voice obey,

they tolerated leviathan as an emissary more worthy than
Elijah's raven. And whenever an obedient whale, harkening
to the voice of God in the wilderness, was cast ashore, a part
of his bulk was fittingly appropriated for the support of the
ministry.

Tower establishes the fact that among the first colonists
there were men at least acquainted with, if not actually experienced in whaling. And it is quite generally accepted that the
settlement of Massachusetts was prompted not only by a protestant determination to worship God after the dictates of a
rebellious conscience, but by a no less firm determination to

vary Sunday observances with the enjoyment on secular days
of unrestricted fishing. As a result of this double Puritan
interest in worship and whaling, the history of the American
whaling fishery begins almost with the settlement of the
New England colonies.

By the end of the seventeenth century, whaling was established as a regular business, if still on a comparatively small
scale, in the different Massachusetts colonies, especially from
Cape Cod; from the towns at the eastern end of Long Island,
and from Nantucket. With the very notable exceptions of
New London, Connecticut, and New Bedford and the neighbouring ports in Buzzard's Bay, every locality subsequently to
become important in its whaling interests was well launched
in this enterprise before 1700. New London did not begin
whaling until the middle of the eighteenth century. New Bedford, though almost the last place to appear as a whaling port
—and this immediately before the Revolution—was destined
to stand, within a century after its beginnings in whaling, the
greatest whaling port the world has ever known, the city which,
in the full glory of whaling prosperity, would send out more
vessels than all other American ports combined.

The earliest colonial adventurers in whaling were men who
by special appointment were engaged to be on the lookout for
whales cast ashore. Emboldened by commerce with drift-
whales, these Puritan whalemen soon took to boats to chase
and kill whales which came close in, but which were not actually stranded.

In 1712, through the instrumentality of Christopher Hussey, Providence utilised a hardship to His creature to work
a revolution in whaling. Hussey, while cruising along the
coast, was caught up by a strong northerly wind, and despite
his prayers and his seamanship was blown out to sea. When
the sky cleared, Hussey's craft was nowhere to be seen by the
anxious watchers on shore. After awaiting his return for a
decent number of days, his wife and neighbours at home gave
him up as lost. But in the middle of their tribulations, a
familiar sail dipped over the horizon, and Hussey slowly
headed landward, dragging a dead sperm whale in tow: the

first sperm whale known to have been taken by an American whaler.

Hussey's exploit marked a radical change in whaling methods. All Nantucket lusted after sperm whales. The indomitable islanders began immediately to fit vessels, usually sloops of about thirty tons, to whale out in the "deep." These little vessels were fitted out for cruises of about six weeks. On their narrow decks there was no room for the apparatus necessary to "try out" the oil. So the blubber stripped from the whale was cast into the hold, the oil awaiting extraction until the vessel returned. Then the reeking whale fat, its stench smiting the face of heaven, was transferred to the huge kettles of the "try houses." There is an old saying that a nose that is a nose at all can smell a whaler twenty miles to windward. The New England indifference to the stenches of whaling suggests that the Puritan contempt for the flesh was not a virtue but a deformity.

Other whaling communities ventured out after the sperm whale in the wake of Nantucket. Year after year the colonial whalemen pushed further and further out into the "deep" as their gigantic quarry retreated before them. In 1774, Captain Uriah Bunker, in the brig *Amazon* of Nantucket, made the first whaling voyage across the equinoctial line to the Brazil Banks and, according to local tradition, returned to port with a "full ship" on April 19, 1775, just as the redcoats were in full retreat from Concord Bridge.

The Revolutionary War dealt a terrific blow to American whaling. Massachusetts was regarded as the hotbed of the Revolutionary spirit, and that colony was also the centre of the fishing industries. Hence, in 1775, "to starve New England," Parliament passed the famous act restricting colonial trade to British ports, and placing an embargo on fishing on the Banks of Newfoundland or on any other part of the North American coast. It was this same measure which inspired Burke in his Speech on *Conciliation* to his superbly eloquent tribute to the exploits of the American whalemen. When the war began there were in the whole American fleet between three and four hundred vessels—of an aggregate of about thirty-three thousand tons.   The annual product of this fleet was, according to Starbuck's estimate, "probably at least 45,000 barrels of spermaceti oil, and 8,500 barrels of right whale oil, and of bone nearly or quite 75,000 pounds."   Of all whaling communities, the island of Nantucket held out most stoutly, —aided by Melville's grandfather, who was sent to Nantucket in command of a detachment to watch the movements of the British fleet.   Yet when the war ended in 1783, Macy says that of the one hundred and fifty Nantucket vessels, only two or three old hulks remained.   In Nantucket, the money loss exceeded one million dollars.   So many of the young and active men perished in the war that in the eight hundred Nantucket families there were two hundred and two widows and three hundred and forty-two orphan children.

But even in the face of such prodigal disaster, the fiery spirit of Nantucket was unquenchable.   When the news came of the peace of 1783, the *Bedford,* just returned to Nantucket from a voyage, was hastily laden with oil and cleared for London.   This was, as a contemporary London newspaper remarks, "the first vessel which displayed the thirteen rebellious stripes of America in any British port."

Through the four decades following the Revolutionary War, the American whale fishery lived a precarious existence of constant ups and downs.   The whaling voyages were greatly lengthened during this period, however.   In 1789 Nantucket whalemen first went hunting the sperm whale off Madagascar, and in 1791 six whaleships fitted out at Nantucket for the Pacific Ocean.

The years between 1820 and 1835 were marked mainly by stable conditions and by a steady but gradual growth.   In 1820 the Pacific whaling was extended to the coast of Japan, and within the next few years the whalers were going to all parts of the South Sea and Indian Ocean.   And these years marked, too, the falling of Nantucket from her hundred years of pre-eminence in whaling, and the emergence of New Bedford as incomparably the greatest whaling port in the history of the world.   It was a Nantucket whaler, however, who in 1835 captured the first right whale on the northwest coast of

America, thereby opening one of the most important grounds ever visited by the whaling fleet.

The Golden Age of whaling falls between 1835 and 1860. In 1846 the whaling fleet assumed the greatest proportions it was ever to know. In that year, the fleet numbered six hundred and eighty ships and barks, thirty-four brigs, and twenty-two schooners, with an aggregate of somewhat over two hundred and thirty thousand tons. The value of the fleet alone at that time exceeded twenty-one million dollars, while all the investments connected with the business are estimated, according to Tower, at seventy million dollars, furnishing the chief support of seventy thousand persons. This great industry, so widespread in its operation, emanated, at the time of its most extensive development, from a cluster of thirty-eight whaling ports distributed along the southern New England coast from Cape Cod to New York, and on the islands to the south. The greatest of all the whaling ports, from 1820 onward, was New Bedford.

During the really great days of the whale fishery, the Pacific was by all odds the chief fishing ground. During the early eighteen-thirties, the Nantucket fleet began cruising mainly in the Pacific, and after 1840, the Nantucket whalers hunted there almost exclusively. The Nantucket fleet was soon followed by the majority of the New Bedford fleet, and a large proportion of the New London and Sag Harbor vessels.

These vessels, manned by a mixed company of Quakers, farm boys, and a supplementary compound of the dredgings of the terrestrial globe, would usually be gone for three years, not infrequently for four or five. As long as the craft held, and the food lasted, and an empty barrel lay in the hold, the captain kept to the broad ocean, eschewing both the allurements of home and the seductions of tattooed Didoes. When at last they sailed into the harbour of their home ports, weed-grown, storm-beaten, patched and forlorn, they usually looked, as Verrill says, more like the ghosts of ancient wrecks than seaworthy carriers of precious cargo manned by crews of flesh and blood. After a few months of repair and overhauling in port, these vessels were refitted for another cruise, and off they sailed again for another space of years. It thus happened that the veteran whalers of Nantucket and New Bedford and the sister ports could look back upon whole decades of their lives spent cruising upon the high seas: a fact that Melville amplifies with a cadence he learned from the Psalms. Of the Nantucketer he says: "For the sea is his; he owns it, as Emperors own empires; other seamen having but a right of way through it. He alone resides and riots on the sea; he alone, in Bible language, goes down to it in ships; to and fro ploughing it as his own special plantation. *There* is his home; *there* lies his business, which a Noah's flood would not interrupt, though it overwhelmed all the millions in China. He lives on the sea, as prairie cocks on the prairie; he hides among the waves, he climbs them as chamois hunters climb the Alps. For years he knows not the land; so that when he comes to it at last, it smells like another world, more strangely than the moon would to an earthsman. With the landless gull, that at sunset folds her wings and is rocked to sleep between billows; so at nightfall, the Nantucketer, out of sight of land, furls his sails, and lays him to his rest, while under his very pillow rush herds of walruses and whales."

The number of supplies, and the variety of articles required in fitting out a whaling ship for a cruise, was, of course, prodigious. For aside from the articles required in whaling, it was necessary that a whaling vessel should sail prepared for any emergency, and equipped to be absolutely independent of the rest of the world for years at a time, housekeeping upon the wide ocean, far from all grocers, costermongers, doctors, bakers and bankers. Aside from the necessary whaling equipment, there were needed supplies for the men, ship's stores and a dizzy number of incidentals: "spare boats, spare spars, and spare lines and harpoons, and spare everythings, almost, but a spare, Captain and a duplicate ship. . . . While other hulls are loaded down with alien stuff, to be transferred to foreign wharves, the world-wandering whale-ship carries no cargo but herself and crew, their weapons and their wants. She has a whole lake's contents bottled in her ample hold. She is ballasted with utilities.   Hence it is, that, while other ships may have gone to China from New York, and back again, touching at a score of ports, the whale-ship, in all that interval, may not have sighted one grain of soil; her crew having seen no man but floating seamen like themselves.   So that did you carry them the news that another flood had come; they would answer—'Well, boys, here's the ark!'"   N. H. Nye, a New Bedford outfitter, published in 1858 an inventory of *Articles for a Whaling Voyage:* a shopping list totalling some 650 entries, useful once to whalers with fallible memories, useful now to landsmen with lame imaginations.

When, from such a port as Nantucket or New Bedford, a whaling vessel was preparing to sail, there would be no house, perhaps, without some interest in the cruise.   Each took a personal pride in the success of the whalers: a pride clinched by the economic dependence of nearly every soul in the community upon the whalemen's luck.   During the time of continual fetching and carrying preparatory to the sailing in *Moby-Dick,* no one was more active, it will be remembered, than Aunt Charity Bildad, that lean though kind-hearted old Quakeress of indefatigable spirit.   "At one time she would come on board with a jar of pickles for the steward's pantry; another time with a bunch of quills for the chief mate's desk, where he kept his log; a third time with a roll of flannel for the small of some one's rheumatic back."   Hither and thither she bustled about, "ready to turn her hand and her heart to anything that promised to yield safety, comfort and consolation to all on board a ship in which her beloved brother Bildad was concerned, and in which she herself owned a score or two of well-saved dollars."   Nor did she forsake the ship even after it had been hauled out from the wharf.   She came off in the whaleboat with a nightcap for the second mate, her brother-in-law, and a spare Bible for the steward.   Such were the conditions in whaling-towns like Nantucket or New Bedford that there was nothing remarkable in Aunt Charity's behaviour.   In such communities, "whale was King."   The talk of the street was, as Abbot observes, of big catches and the price of oil and bone.   The conversation in the shaded parlours, where sea-shell, coral, and the trophies of Pacific cruises were the chief ornaments, was, in an odd mixture of Quaker idiom, of prospective cruises or of past adventures, of distant husbands and sons, the perils they braved, and when they might be expected home. Col. Joseph C. Hart, in his *Miriam Coffin, or the Whale Fishermen: a Tale* (1834) offers perhaps the truest and most vivid picture of life in Nantucket when whaling was at its prime. Speaking of himself in the third person in the dedication, Hart describes his book as being "founded on facts, and illustrating some of the scenes with which he was conversant in his earlier days, together with occurrences with which he is familiar from tradition and association." Though reprinted in California in 1872, *Miriam Coffin* is now very difficult to come by. It should be better known.

The extended voyages of the American whaleman were made in heavy, bluff-bowed and "tubby" crafts that were designed with fine contempt for speed, comfort or appearance. In writing of Nantucket whaling during the period about 1750, Macy says: "They began now to employ vessels of larger size, some of 100 ton burden, and a few were square-rigged." For over a century thereafter the changes in whaling vessels were almost solely in size. With the opening of the Pacific, the longer voyages and the desire for larger cargoes led, as a necessary result, to the employment of larger vessels. The first Nantucket ship sailing to the Pacific in 1791 was of 240-ton burden. By 1826, Nantucket had seventy-two ships carrying over 280 tons each, and before 1850 whalers of 400 to 500 tons burden were not unusual. The *Acushnet,* it will be remembered, was rated as a ship of 359 tons.

The vessels used in whaling, built, as has been said, less with a view to speed than to carrying capacity, had a characteristic architecture. The bow was scarce distinguishable from the stern by its lines, and the masts stuck up straight, without that rake which adds so much to the trim appearance of a clipper. Three peculiarities chiefly distinguished the whalers from other ships of the same general character. (1) At each mast head was fixed the "crow's-nest"—in some vessels a heavy barrel lashed to the mast, in others merely a small platform laid on the cross-trees, with two hoops fixed to the mast above, within which the look-out could stand in safety. Throughout Melville's experiences at sea, in the merchant marines, in whalers, and in the navy, it appears that his happiest moments were spent on mast-heads. (2) On the deck, amidships, stood the "try-works," brick furnaces holding two or three great kettles, in which the blubber was reduced to odourless oil. (3) Along each rail were heavy, clumsy wooden cranes, or davits, from which hung the whale boats—never less than five, sometimes more—while still others were lashed to the deck. For these boats were the whales' sport and playthings, and seldom was a big "fish" made fast without there being work made for the ship's carpenter.

As for the crow's-nest, and the business of standing mast-heads, Melville has more than a word to say. As Sir Thomas Browne wrote in the *Garden of Cyrus* of "the Quincuncial Lozenge, or Net-Work Plantations of the Ancients, Artificially, Naturally, Mystically Considered," to find, as Coleridge remarks, "quincunxes in heaven above, quincunxes in earth below, quincunxes in the mind of man, quincunxes in tones, in optic nerves, in roots of trees, in leaves, in everything," so Melville finds the visible and invisible universe a symbolic prefiguring of all the detailed peculiarities of whaling. In the town of Babel he finds a great stone mast-head that went by the board in the dread gale of God's wrath; and in St. Simon Stylites, he discovers "a remarkable instance of a dauntless stander-of-mast-heads, who was not to be driven from his place by fogs or frosts, rain, hail, or sleet; but valiantly facing everything out to the last, literally died at his post." And in Napoleon upon the top of the column of Vendome, in Washington atop his pillar in Baltimore, as in many another man of stone or iron or bronze, he sees standers of mast-heads.

In most American whalemen, the mast-heads were manned almost simultaneously with the vessel's leaving her port; and this even though she often had fifteen thousand miles, and more, to sail before reaching her proper cruising ground. And if, after a three, four, or five years' voyage, she found herself drawing near home with empty casks, then her mast-

heads were frequently kept manned, even until her skysail-
poles sailed in among the spires of her home port.

The three mast-heads were kept manned from sunrise to
sunset, the seamen taking regular turns (as at the helm) and
relieving each other every two hours, watching to catch the
faint blur of vapour whose spouting marks the presence of
a whale. "There she blows! B-l-o-o-ws! Blo-o-ows!" was
then sung out from the mast-head: the signal for the chase.

As for Melville, he tries to convince us he kept very sorry
watch, as in the serene weather of the tropics, he perched "a
hundred feet above the silent decks, striding along the deep,
as if the masts were gigantic stilts, while beneath you and
between your legs, as it were, swim the huge monsters of
the deep, even as ships once sailed between the boots of the
famous Colossus of old Rhodes." There, through his watches,
he used to swing, he says, "lost in the infinite series of the sea,
with nothing ruffled but the waves. The tranced ship indo-
lently rolls; the drowsy trade winds blow; everything resolves
you into languor." "I used to lounge up the rigging very
leisurely, resting in the top to have a chat with Queequeg, or
any one else off duty whom I might find there; then ascending
a little way further, and throwing a lazy leg over the topsail
yard, take a preliminary view of the watery pastures, and so
at last mount to my ultimate destination." According to Melville's own representation, the *Acushnet* was not a pint of oil
richer for all his watching in the thought-engendering altitude
of the crow's-nest. He admonishes all ship-owners of Nantucket to eschew the bad business of shipping "romantic, melancholy, absent-minded young men, disgusted with the cankering
cares of earth": young men seeking sentiment—as did he—in
tar and blubber. "Childe Harold not infrequently perches himself upon the mast-head of some luckless disappointed whale-
ship," he warns prosaic ship-owners, "young men hopelessly
lost to all honourable ambition," and indifferent to the selling
qualities of "oil and bone." It is well both for Melville and
Captain Pease, the testy old skipper of the ship *Acushnet*, that
he could not see into the head of Melville as he hung silently
perched in his dizzy lookout. "Lulled into such an opium-

like listlessness of vacant, unconscious reverie is this absent-minded youth by the blending cadence of waves with thoughts, that at last he loses his identity; takes the mystic ocean at his feet for the visible image of that deep, blue, bottomless soul, pervading mankind and nature; and every strange, half-seen, gliding, beautiful thing that eludes him; every dimly-discovered, uprising fin of some undiscernible form, seems to him the embodiment of those elusive thoughts that only people the soul by continually flitting through it. In this enchanted mood, thy spirit ebbs away to whence it came; becomes diffused through time and space; like Cranmer's sprinkled Pantheistic ashes, forming at last a part of every shore the round globe over."

When, from the mast-head, eyes less abstracted than Melville's sighted a whale, the daring and excitement of the ensuing pursuit in the whale-boats left Melville less occasion, during such energetic intervals, to luxuriate in high mysteries. And it seems likely that Melville was of more value to the ship's owners when in a whale-boat than riding the mast-head.

Through long years of whaling these boats had been developed until practical perfection had been reached. Never has boat been built which for speed, staunchness, seaworthiness and hardiness excels the whaleboat of the Massachusetts whalemen. These mere cockleshells, sharp at both ends and clean-sided as a mackerel, were about twenty-seven feet long by six feet beam, with a depth of twenty-two inches amidships and thirty-seven inches at the bow and stern. These tiny clinker-built craft can ride the heaviest sea, withstand the highest wind, resist the heaviest gale. Incredible voyages have been made in these whaling boats, not the least remarkable being the three months' voyage of two boats that survived the wreck of the *Essex* in 1819, or the even more remarkable six months' voyage of the whaling boat separated from the *Janet* in 1849. In *Mardi* Melville describes a prolonged voyage in a whale-boat. In this account Melville takes one down to the very plane of the sea. He is speaking from experience when he says: "Unless the waves, in their gambols, toss you and your chip upon one of their lordly crests, your sphere of vision is little larger than it would be at the bottom of a well. At best, your most extended view in any one direction, at least, is in a high slow-rolling sea; when you descend into the dark misty spaces, between long and uniform swells. Then, for the moment, it is like looking up and down in a twilight glade, interminable; where two dawns, one on each hand, seem struggling through the semi-transparent tops of the fluid mountains."

Of his first lowering in pursuit of a whale, he says in *Moby-Dick:* "It was a sight full of quick wonder and awe! The vast swells of the omnipotent sea; the surging, hollow roar they made, as they rolled along the eight gunwales, like gigantic bowls in a boundless bowling-green; the brief suspended agony of the boat, as it would tip for an instant on the knife-like edge of the sharper waves, that seemed almost threatening to cut it in two; the sudden profound dip into the watery glens and hollows; the keen spurrings and goadings to gain the top of the opposite hill; the headlong, sled-like slide down its other side:—all these, with the cries of the headsmen and harpooners, and the shuddering gasps of the oarsmen, and wondrous sight of the ivory *Pequod* bearing down upon her boats with outstretched sails, like a wild hen after her screaming brood;—all this was thrilling. Not the raw recruit, marching from the bosom of his wife into the fever heat of his first battle; not the dead man's ghost encountering the first unknown phantom in the other world,—neither of these can feel stranger and stronger emotions than that man does, who for the first time finds himself pulling into the charmed, churned circle of the hunted sperm whale."

After this first lowering, Melville returned to the ship to indulge in the popular nautical diversion of making his will. This ceremony concluded, he says he looked round him "tranquilly and contentedly, like a quiet ghost with a clean conscience sitting inside the bars of a snug family vault. Now then, thought I, unconsciously rolling up the sleeves of my frock, here goes for a cool, collected dive at death and destruction, and the devil fetch the hindmost."

In *Moby-Dick,* whales are sighted, chased, and captured; nor does Melville fail to give detailed accounts of these activities or of the ensuing "cutting in" and the "trying" of the oil.

One of the most vivid scenes in *Moby-Dick* is the description of the "try-works" in operation.

"By midnight," says Melville, "the works were in full operation. We were clean from the carcass; sail had been made; the wind was freshening; the wild ocean darkness was intense. But that darkness was licked up by the fierce flames, which at intervals forked forth from the sooty flues, and illuminated every rope in the rigging, as with the famed Greek fire. . . . The hatch, removed from the top of the works, now afforded a wide hearth in front of them. Standing on this were the Tartarean shapes of the pagan harpooners, always the whaleship's stokers. With huge pronged poles they pitched hissing masses of blubber into the scalding pots, or stirred up the fires beneath, till the snaky flames darted, curling, out of the doors to catch them by the feet. The smoke rolled away in sullen heaps. To every pitch of the ship there was a pitch of the boiling oil, which seemed all eagerness to leap into their faces. Opposite the mouth of the works, on the further side of the wide wooden hearth, was the windlass. This served for a sea-sofa. Here lounged the watch, when not otherwise employed, looking into the red heat of the fire, their tawny features, now all begrimed with smoke and sweat, their matted beards, and the contrasting barbaric brilliancy of their teeth, all these strangely revealed in the capricious emblazonings of the works. As they narrated to each other their unholy adventures, their tales of terror told in words of mirth; their uncivilised laughter forked upwards out of them, like the flames from the furnace: to and fro, in their front, the harpooners wildly gesticulated with their huge pronged forks and dippers; the wind howled on, and the sea leaped, and the ship groaned and dived, yet steadfastly shot her red hell further and further into the blackness of the sea and the night; and scornfully champed, and viciously spat round her on all sides." During this scene Melville stood at the helm, "and for long silent hours guarded the way of this fire-ship on the sea. Wrapped, for that interval, in darkness myself, I but the better saw the redness, the madness, the ghastliness of others. The continual sight of the fiend shapes before me, capering half in smoke and half in fire

these at last begat kindred visions in my soul, so soon as I
began to yield to that unaccountable drowsiness which ever
would come over me at a midnight helm."

In a chapter on dreams, in *Mardi,* one of the wildest chapters Melville ever wrote, and the one in which he profoundly
searched into the heart of his mystery, he compares his dreams
to a vast herd of buffaloes, "browsing on to the horizon, and
browsing on round the world; and among them, I dash with
my lance, to spear one, ere they all flee." In this world of
dreams, "passing and repassing, like Oriental empires in history," Melville discerned, "far in the background, hazy and
blue, their steeps let down from the sky, Andes on Andes,
rooted on Alps; and all round me, long rolling oceans, roll
Amazons and Orinocos; waver, mounted Parthians; and to
and fro, toss the wide woodlands: all the world an elk, and
the forest its antlers. Beneath me, at the equator, the earth
pulses and beats like a warrior's heart, till I know not whether
it be not myself. And my soul sinks down to the depths, and
soars to the skies; and comet-like reels on through such boundless expanses, that methinks all the worlds are my kin, and I
invoke them to stay in their course. Yet, like a mighty three
decker, towing argosies by scores, I tremble, gasp, and strain
in my flight, and fain would cast off the cables that hamper."

On that night that Melville drowsed at the helm of the
Acushnet while she was "freighted with savages, and laden
with fire, and burning a corpse, and plunging into that blackness of blackness" his soul sank deep into itself, and he seems
to have awakened to recognise in the ship that he drowsily
steered, the material counterpart of the darkest mysteries of
his own soul. It was then that he awoke to be "horribly conscious" that "whatever swift rushing thing I stood on was not
so much bound to any haven ahead as rushing from all havens
astern." And in reflecting upon that insight Melville plunges
into the lowest abyss of disenchantment. "The truest of men
was the Man of Sorrows," he says, "and the truest of all books
is Solomon's, and Ecclesiastes is the fine hammered steel of
woe. All is vanity. ALL . . . He who . . . calls Cowper,
Young, Pascal, Rousseau, poor devils all of sick men; and

throughout a care-free lifetime swears by Rabelais as passing wise, and therefore jolly;—not that man is fitted to sit down on tombstones, and break the green damp mould with unfathomably wondrous Solomon."

The greatest of all dreamers conquer their dreams; others, who are great, but not of the greatest, are mastered by them, and Melville was one of these.   There is a passage in the works of Edgar Allan Poe that Melville may well have pondered when he awoke at the helm of the *Acushnet* after looking too long into the glare of the fire: "There are moments when, even to the sober eye of reason, the world of our sad humanity may assume the semblance of a hell; but the imagination of man is no Carathes to explore with impunity its every cavern.   All the grim legion of sepulchral terrors cannot be regarded as altogether fanciful; but, like the demons in whose company Afrasiab made his voyage down the Oxus, they must sleep or they will devour us—they must be suffered to slumber or we perish."

CHAPTER VIII

LEVIATHAN

"At the battle of Breviex in Flanders, my glorious old gossiping ancestor Froissart informs me, ten good knights, being suddenly unhorsed, fell stiff and powerless to the plain, fatally encumbered by their armour. Whereupon the rascally burglarious peasants, their foes, fell to picking their visors; as burglars, locks; as oystermen oysters; to get at their lives. But all to no purpose. And at last they were fain to ask aid of a blacksmith; and not till then were the inmates of the armour despatched. Days of chivalry these, when gallant chevaliers died chivalric deaths! Yes, they were glorious times. But no sensible man, given to quiet domestic delights, would exchange his warm fireside and muffins, for a heroic bivouac, in a wild beechen wood, of a raw gusty morning in Normandy; every knight blowing his steel-gloved fingers, and vainly striving to cool his cold coffee in his helmet."

HERMAN MELVILLE: *Mardi.*

It was the same Edmund Burke who movingly mourned the departure of the epic virtues of chivalry, who in swift generalities celebrated the heroic enterprise of the hunters of leviathan. But Burke viewed both whaling and knight-errantry from a safe remove of time or place, and the crude everyday realities of each he smothered beneath billows of gorgeous generalisation. Burke offers a notable instance wherein romance and rhetoric conspired to glorify two human activities that are glorious only in expurgation. Piracy is picturesque in its extinction, and to the snugly domesticated imagination there is both virtue and charm in cut-throats and highwaymen. Even the perennial newspaper accounts of massacre and rape doubtless serve to keep sweet the blood of many a benevolent pew-holder. The incorrigible tendency of the imagination to extract sweet from the bitter, honey from the carcass of the lion, makes an intimate consideration of the filthy soil from which some of its choicest illusions spring, downright repugnant to wholesomemindedness. Intimately considered, both whaling and knight-errantry were shabby forms of the butchering business. Their virtues were but the nobler vices of barbarism: vices that take on a semblance of nobility only

153

when measured against the deadly virtues of emasculated righteousness. In flight from the deadly virtues, Melville was precipitated into the reeking barbarism of the forecastle of a
whaling ship. Whaling he applied as a counter-irritant to
New England decorum, and he seems to have smarted much
during the application. He was blessed with a high degree of
the resilience of youthful animal vigour, it is true; and there
is solace for all suffering, the godly tell us—omitting the ungodly solaces of madness and suicide. It will be seen that
whaling prompted Melville to extreme measures. The full
hideousness of his life on board the *Acushnet* has not yet
transpired.

The chief whaling communities—those of Nantucket and
Buzzard's Bay—were originally settled by Quakers. The
inhabitants of these districts in general retained in an uncommon measure throughout the golden age of whaling, the peculiarities of the Quaker. Never perhaps in the history of the
world has there been mated two aspects of life more humor-
ously incompatible than whale-hunting and Quakerism. This
mating produced, however, a race of the most sanguinary of
all sailors; a race of fighting Quakers: in Melville's phrase,
"Quakers with a vengeance." Though refusing from conscientious scruples to bear arms against land invaders, yet these
same Quakers illimitably invaded the Atlantic and the Pacific;
and though sworn foes to human bloodshed, yet did they, in
their straight-bodied coats, spill tons and tons of leviathan
gore. And so, as Melville goes on to point out, "there are
instances among them of men who, named with Scripture
names, and in childhood naturally imbibing the stately dramatic
thee and thou of the Quaker idiom; still, from the audacious,
daring, and boundless adventure of their subsequent lives,
strangely blend with these unoutgrown peculiarities, a thousand bold dashes of character, not unworthy a Scandinavian
sea-king, or a poetical Pagan Roman."

The two old Quaker captains of *Moby-Dick,* Bildad and
Peleg, are typical of the race that made Nantucket and New
Bedford the greatest whaling ports in all history. Peleg sig-
nificantly divides all good men into two inclusive categories:

"pious good men, like Bildad," and "swearing good men—something like me." The "swearing good men," Melville would seem to imply, in sacrificing piety to humanity, while standing lower in the eyes of God, stood higher in the hearts of their crew. Though Bildad never swore at his men, so Melville remarks, "he somehow got an inordinate quantity of cruel, unmitigated hard work out of them."

Typical of the cast of mind of the whaling Quaker is Captain Bildad's farewell to ship's company on board the ship in which he was chief owner: "God bless ye, and have ye in His holy keeping. Be careful in the hunt, ye mates. Don't stave the boats needlessly, ye harpooners; good white cedar plank is raised full three per cent. within the year. Don't forget your prayers, either. Don't whale it too much a' Lord's day, men; but don't miss a fair chance either; that's rejecting Heaven's good gifts. Have an eye to the molasses tierce, Mr. Stubb; it was a little leaky, I thought. If ye touch at the islands, Mr. Flask, beware of fornication. Good-bye, good-bye!"

The old log-books most frequently begin: "A journal of an intended voyage from Nantucket by God's permission." And typical is the closing sentence of the entry in George Gardener's journal for Saturday, January 21, 1757: "So no more at Present all being in health by the Blessing of God but no whale yet."

At first, the New England vessels were manned almost entirely by American-born seamen, including a certain proportion of Indians and coast-bred negroes. But as the fishery grew, and the number of vessels increased, the supply of hands became inadequate. Macy says that as early as about 1750 the Nantucket fishery had attained such proportions that it was necessary to secure men from Cape Cod and Long Island to man the vessels. Goode says: "Captain Isaiah West, now eighty years of age (in 1880), tells me that he remembers when he picked his crew within a radius of sixty miles of New Bedford; oftentimes he was acquainted, either personally or through report, with the social standing or business qualifications of every man on his vessel; and also that he remembers the first foreigner—an Irishman—that shipped with him, the circumstance being commented on at that time as a remarkable one." Time was, however, when it was easy to gather at New Bedford or New London a prime crew of tall and stalwart lads from the fishing coast and from the farms of the interior of New England. Maine furnished a great many whalemen, and for a long time the romance of whaling held out a powerful fascination for adventurous farmer boys of New Hampshire, Vermont, and Upper New York. During Melville's time the farms of New England still supplied a contingent of whalers. In writing of New Bedford he says: "There weekly arrive in this town scores of green Vermonters and New Hampshire men, all athirst for gain and glory in the fishery. They are mostly young, of stalwart frames; fellows who have felled forests, and now seek to drop the axe and snatch the whale-lance. Many are as green as the Green Mountains whence they came. In some things you would think them but a few hours old. Look there! that chap strutting round the corner. He wears a beaver hat and swallow-tailed coat, girdled with a sailor-belt and a sheath-knife. Here comes another with a sou'-wester and a bombazine cloak." Of course, these farm-boys were of the verdant innocence Melville paints them when they signed the ship's papers, not knowing a harpoon from a handspike. It is a curious paradox in the history of whaling,—a paradox best elaborated by Verrill,—that the ship's crew were almost never sailors. The captain, of course, the officers and the harpooners were usually skilled and efficient hands. But so filthy was the work aboard the whaler, and so perilous; so brutal the treatment of the crew, and so hazardous the actual earnings, that competent deep-water sailors stuck to the navy or the merchant marine. When Melville shipped from Honolulu as an "ordinary seaman in the United States Navy," he soon found occasion "to offer up thanksgiving that in no evil hour had I divulged the fact of having served in a whaler; for having previously marked the prevailing prejudice of men-of-war's-men to that much maligned class of mariners, I had wisely held my peace concerning stove boats on the coast of Japan."

And in *Redburn* he says "that merchant seamen generally affect a certain superiority to 'blubber-boilers,' as they contemptuously style those who hunt the leviathan."

When the farmer lads came down to the sea no more in adequate numbers, the whaleships were forced to fill their crews far from home, and to take what material they could get. Shipping offices, with headquarters at the whaling ports, employed agents scattered here and there in the principal cities, especially in the Middle West and the interior of New England. These agents received ten dollars for each man they secured for the ship's crew. Besides this, each agent was paid for the incidental expenses of transportation, board, and outfit of every man shipped. By means of lurid advertisements and circulars, these agents with emancipated conscience, made glowing promises to the desperate and the ignorant. Each prospective whaleman was promised a "lay" of the ship's catch. For in the whaling business, no set wages were paid. All hands, including the captain, received certain shares of the profits called "lays." The size of the lay was proportioned to the degree of importance pertaining to the respective duties of the ship's company. The captain usually received a lay of from one-twelfth to one-eighteenth; green hands about the one-hundred-and-fiftieth. What lay Melville received is not known. Bildad is inclined to think that the seven hundred and seventy-seventh lay was not too much for Ishmael; but Bildad was a "pious good man." Peleg, the "swearing good man," after a volcanic eruption with Bildad, puts Ishmael down for the three hundredth lay. Though this may exemplify the relation that, in Melville's mind, existed between profanity and kindness, it tells us, unfortunately, nothing of the prospective earnings of Melville's whaling. Of one thing, however, we can be fairly certain: Melville did not drive a shrewd and highly profitable bargain. The details of his life bear out his boast: "I am one of those that never take on about princely fortunes, and am quite content if the world is ready to board and lodge me, while I put up at the grim sign of the Thunder Cloud."

Each prospective whaler, besides being assured a stated

fraction of the ship's earnings, was by the agents promised an advance of seventy-five dollars, an outfit of clothes, as well as board and lodging until aboard ship. From this imaginary seventy-five dollars were deducted all the expenses which the agent defrayed, as well as the ten dollars head payment. By a shameless perversion of exaggerated charges, a really competent outfitter managed to ship his embryo whalemen without a cent of the promised advance. The agent who shipped J. Ross Browne and his unfortunate friend, was a suave gentleman of easy promises. "Whaling, gentlemen, is tolerably hard at first," Browne makes him say, "but it's the finest business in the world for enterprising young men. Vigilance and activity will insure you rapid promotion. I haven't the least doubt but you'll come home boat steerers. I sent off six college students a few days ago, and a poor fellow who had been flogged away from home by a vicious wife. A whaler, gentlemen, is a place of refuge for the distressed and persecuted, a school for the dissipated, an asylum for the needy! There's nothing like it. You can see the world; you can see something of life."

The first half of one of the truest and most popular of whaling chanteys, a lyric which must have been sung with heartfelt conviction by thousands of whalemen, runs:

'Twas advertised in Boston,
  New York and Buffalo,
Five hundred brave Americans
  A-whaling for to go.

They send you to New Bedford,
  The famous whaling port;
They send you to a shark's store
  And board and fit you out.

They send you to a boarding-house
  For a time to dwell.
The thieves there, they are thicker
  Than the other side of Hell.

They tell you of the whaling ships
A-going in and out.
They swear you'll make your fortune
Before you're five months out.

The second half of this ballad celebrates the hardships of life aboard ship: the poor food and the brutality of the officers. With this side of whaling we know that Melville was familiar. But of the usual preliminaries of whaling recounted by Browne and summarised in the chantey, Melville says not a word, either in *Moby-Dick* or elsewhere. Nor does tradition or history supplement this autobiographical silence. On this point we know nothing. Surely it would be intensely interesting to know how far egotism conspired with art in guiding Melville in the writing of the masterful beginning of *Moby-Dick*.

No matter by what process Melville found his way to the *Acushnet,* the whaling fleet was, indeed, at the time of his addition to it, "a place of refuge for the distressed and persecuted, a school for the dissipated, an asylum for the needy." J. Ross Browne was warned before his sailing that New Bedford "was the sink-hole of iniquity; that the fitters were all blood-suckers, the owners cheats, and the captains tyrants."

Though the arraignment was incautiously comprehensive, Browne confesses to have looked back upon it as a sound warning. The boasted advantages of whaling were not self-ishly withheld from any man, no matter what the race, or the complexion of his hide or his morals. The Spanish, Portuguese, Dutch, Swedish, Norwegian, English, Scotch, Irish,— in fact, men of almost every country of Europe, and this with no jealous discrimination against Asia, Africa, or the Islands of the Pacific,—were drawn upon by the whale fleet during the days of its greatest prosperity. "And had I not been, from my birth, as it were, a cosmopolite," Melville remarks parenthetically in *Redburn*. It would have been difficult for him to find a more promising field for the exercise of this inherited characteristic, than was whaling in 1841: and this, indeed, without the nuisance of leaving New Bedford. "In thoroughfares nigh the docks," he says, "any considerable seaport will fre-

quently offer to view the queerest nondescripts from foreign
ports. Even in Broadway and Chestnut streets, Mediterranean
mariners will sometimes jostle the affrighted ladies. Regent
street is not unknown to Lascars and Malays; and in Bombay, in the Apollo Green, live Yankees have often scared the
natives. But New Bedford beats all Water street and Wapping. In these last-mentioned haunts you see only sailors;
but in New Bedford, actual cannibals stand chatting at street
corners; savages outright; many of whom yet carry on their
bones unholy flesh. It makes a stranger stare." It will be
remembered that Ishmael spends his first night in New Bedford in bed with one of these very cannibals; and on the following morning, in a spirit of amiable and transcendent charity, goes down on his knees with his tattooed bed-fellow before a portable wooden deity: an experience fantastic and
highly diverting, nor at all outside the bounds of possibility.

It is a fact to chasten the optimism of apostles of the promiscuous brotherhood of man, that as the whaling crews grew
in cosmopolitanism, they made no corresponding advances
towards the Millennium. Had Nantucket and New Bedford
but grown to the height of their whaling activities in the
fourth century, they might have sent enterprising agents to
the African desert to tempt ambitious cenobites with offers of
undreamed-of luxuries of mortification. These holy men
might have worked miracles in whaling, and transformed the
watery wilderness of the Pacific into a floating City of God.
But in the nineteenth century of grace, the kennel-like forecastle of the whaler was the refuge not of the athletic saint,
but of the offscourings of all races, the discards of humanity,
and of this fact there is no lack of evidence. Nor did Melville's ship-mates, on the whole, seem to have varied this monotony. There survives this record in his own hand:

*"What became of the ship's company on the whale-ship
'Acushnet,' according to Hubbard who came back home in her
(more than a four years' voyage) and visited me in Pittsfield
in 1850.*

SPERM WHALING.   THE CAPTURE.
Drawing by A. Van Beest, R. Swain Gifford and Benj. Russell, 1850.

ONE OF SIX WHALING PRINTS.   LONDON, 1750.

"*Captain Pease*—returned & lives in asylum at the Vineyard.

"*Raymond,* 1st Mate—had a fight with the Captain & went ashore at Payta.

"*Hall,* 2nd Mate—came home & went to California.

"*3rd Mate,* Portuguese, went ashore at Payta.

"*Boatswain,* either ran away or killed at Ropo one of the Marquesas.

Smith, went ashore at Santa, coast of Peru, afterwards committed suicide at Mobile.

"*Barney,* boatswain, came home.

"*Carpenter,* went ashore at Mowee half dead with disreputable disease.

"*The Czar.*

"*Tom Johnson,* black, went ashore at Mowee, half dead (ditto) & died at the hospital.

"*Reed,* mulatto—came home.

"*Blacksmith,* ran away at San Francisco.

"*Blackus,* little black, ditto.

"*Bill Green,* after several attempts to run away, came home in the end.

"*The Irishman,* ran away, coast of Colombia.

"*Wright,* went ashore half dead at the Marquesas.

"*Jack Adams* and *Jo Portuguese* came home.

"*The Old Cook,* came home.

"*Haynes,* ran away aboard of a Sidney ship.

"*Little Jack,* came home.

"*Grant,* young fellow, went ashore half dead, spitting blood, at Oahu.

"*Murray,* went ashore, shunning fight at Rio Janeiro.

"*The Cooper,* came home."

Of the twenty-seven men who went out with the ship, only the Captain, the Second Mate, a Boatswain, the Cook, the Cooper and six of the mongrel crew (one of which made several futile attempts to escape) came back home with her. The First Mate had a fight with the Captain and left the ship; the Carpenter and four of the crew went ashore to die, two at least with venereal diseases, another went ashore spitting blood, another to commit suicide.

With this company Melville was intimately imprisoned on board the *Acushnet* for fifteen months. Of the everyday life of Melville in this community we know little enough. In *Moby-Dick* Melville has left voluminous accounts of the typical occupations of whaling—but beyond this nothing certainly to be identified as derived from life on the *Acushnet*. The ship's company on board the *Pequod,* in so far as is known, belong as purely to romance as characters of fiction can. It doubtless abbreviates the responsibilities of the custodians of public morals, that the staple of conversation on board the *Acushnet,* the scenes enacted in the forecastle and elsewhere in the ship, shall probably never be known. In *Typee* Melville says of the crew of the *Acushnet,* however: "With a very few exceptions, our crew was composed of a parcel of dastardly and mean-spirited wretches, divided among themselves, and only united in enduring without resistance the unmitigated tyranny of the captain."

Of the "very few exceptions" that Melville spares the tribute of contemptuous damnation, one alone does he single out for portraiture. "He was a young fellow about my own age," says Melville in *Typee,* of a seventeen-year-old shipmate, "for whom I had all along entertained a great regard; and Toby, such was the name by which he went among us, for his real name he would never tell us, was every way worthy of it. He was active, ready, and obliging, of dauntless courage, and singularly open and fearless in the expression of his feelings. I had on more than one occasion got him out of scrapes into which this had led him; and I know not whether it was from this cause, or a certain congeniality of sentiment between us, that he had always shown a partiality for my society. We had battled out many a long watch together, beguiling the weary hours with chat, song, and story, mingled with a good many imprecations upon the hard destiny it seemed our common fortune to encounter."

Toby, like Melville, had evidently not been reared from the cradle to the life of the forecastle; a fact that, despite his anxious effort, Toby could not entirely conceal. "He was one of that class of rovers you sometimes meet at sea," says Melville, "who never reveal their origin, never allude to home, and go rambling over the world as if pursued by some mysterious fate they cannot possibly elude."

By the spell of the senses, too, Melville was attracted to Toby. "For while the greater part of the crew were as coarse in person as in mind," says Melville, "Toby was endowed with a remarkably prepossessing exterior. Arrayed in his blue frock and duck trousers, he was as smart a looking sailor as ever stepped upon a deck; he was singularly small and slightly made, with great flexibility of limb. His naturally dark complexion had been deepened by exposure to the tropical sun, and a mass of jetty locks clustered about his temples, and threw a darker shade into his large black eyes."

There is preserved among Melville's papers a lock of hair, unusually fine and soft in texture, but not so much "jetty" as of a rich red-black chestnut colour, and marked "a lock of Toby's hair," and dated 1846—the year of the publication of *Typee*. When Melville and Toby parted in the Marquesas, each came to think that the other had most likely been eaten by the cannibals. Upon the publication of *Typee*, Toby was startled into delight to learn of Melville's survival and to rub his eyes at the flattering portrayal of himself. In a letter of his to Melville, dated June 16, 1856, he says: "I am still proud of the immortality with which you have invested me." The extent of the first extremity of his pride is not recorded. But in his first flush of immortality he seems to have sent Melville a lock of his hair,—an amiable vanity, perhaps, at Melville's celebration of his personal charms.

There survives with the lock of hair a daguerreotype of Toby, also of 1846. There are also two other photographs: the three strewn over a period of thirty years. These three photographs make especially vivid the regret at the lack of any early picture of Melville. Melville's likeness is preserved only in bearded middle-age: and such portraiture gives no more idea of his youthful appearance than does Toby's washed-out maturity suggest his Byronic earlier manner. There is

every indication that Melville was a young man of a very conspicuous personal charm.   From his books one forms a vivid
image of him in the freshness and agility and full-bloodedness
of his youth.   To bring this face to face with the photographs
of his middle age is a challenge to the loyalty of the imagination.   All known pictures of Melville postdate his creative
period.   They are pictures of Melville the disenchanted philosopher.   As pictures of Melville the adventurer and artist,
they survive as misleading posthumous images.

Of Toby's character, Melville says : "He was a strange way-
ward being, moody, fitful, and melancholy—at times almost
morose.   He had a quick and fiery temper too, which, when
thoroughly roused, transported him into a state bordering on
delirium.   No one ever saw Toby laugh.   I mean in the hearty
abandonment of broad-mouthed mirth.   He did sometimes
smile, it is true; and there was a good deal of dry, sarcastic
humour about him, which told the more from the imperturbable
gravity of his tone and manner."

After escaping from the *Acushnet* with Melville into the
valley of Typee, Toby in course of time found himself back
to civilisation, where the history of his life that he kept so
secret aboard the *Acushnet* came more fully to be known.

Toby, or Richard Tobias Greene, was, according to notices
in Chicago papers at the time of his death on August 24, 1892,
born in Dublin, Ireland, in 1825.   He was as a child brought
to America by his father, who settled in Rochester, New
York, where Toby "took public school and academic courses."
Before he was seventeen he shipped aboard the *Acushnet,* there
to fall in with Melville and to accompany him into the uncorrupted heart of cannibalism.   Toby returned to civilisation to
study law with John C. Spencer, "the noted attorney whose
son was executed for mutiny at Canandaigua, New York," and
was, in time, admitted to the bar.   He relinquished jurispru-
dence for journalism, and was for some indefinite period editor
of the *Buffalo Courier*.   He restlessly varied his activities by
assisting in constructing the first telegraph line west of New
York State, and opened the first telegraph office in Ohio, at
Sandusky.   For some years he published the *Sandusky Mirror*.

In 1846

"TOBY"
RICHARD TOBIAS GREENE

In 1865

In 1857 he moved to Chicago and took a place on the *Times*. With the Civil War he enlisted in the 6th Infantry of Missouri and for three years was "trusted clerk at General Grant's headquarters." He was discharged June, 1864, to enlist again October 19, 1864, in the 1st Illinois Light Artillery. With the end of the war he returned to Chicago, ruined in health. Yet he continued to exert himself as a public-minded citizen, and at his funeral were "many fellow Masons, comrades from the G.A.R. and others who came to pay their respects to the late traveller, editor and soldier."

After the publication of *Typee* there were delighted exchanges of recognition and gratitude between him and Melville. And though these two men grew further and further apart with years, there continued between them an irregular correspondence and a pathetic loyalty to youthful associations: felicitations that grew to be as conscientious and hollow as the ghastly amiabilities of a college reunion. Toby's son, born in 1854, he named Herman Melville Greene (a compliment to Melville adopted by some of his later shipmates in the navy); and Melville presented his namesake with a spoon—the gift he always made to namesakes. Toby's nephew was named Richard Melville Hair, and another spoon was shipped west. In 1856 Toby wrote Melville he had read Melville's most recent book, *Piazza Tales*. Toby's critical efforts exhausted themselves in the comment: *"The Encantadas called up reminiscences of the Acushnet, and days gone by."* In 1858, when Melville was lecturing about the country, Toby addressed a dutiful letter to his "Dear Old Shipmate," asking that Melville visit him while in Cleveland. If the visit was ever made, it has not transpired. In 1860 Toby wrote to Melville: "Hope you enjoy good health and can yet stow away five shares of duff! I would be delighted to see you and 'freshen the nip' while you would be spinning a yarn as long as the main-top bowline." In acknowledgment Melville during the year following sent Toby the gift of a spoon. In reply Toby observes: "My mind often reverts to the many pleasant moonlight watches we passed together on the deck of the *Acushnet* as we whiled away the hours with yarn and song till eight bells." Even to the third generation Toby's descendants were "proud of the immortality" with which Melville had invested Toby. Miss Agnes Repplier has written on *The Perils of Immortality.* There are perils, too, in immortalisation.

But in the days of Toby's unredeemed immortality on board the *Acushnet* before he joined the Masons and the Grand Army of the Republic, Toby was to Melville a singularly grateful variation to the filth and hideousness and brutality of the human refuse with which he cruised the high seas in search of oil and bone.

Melville was fifteen months on board the *Acushnet;* and for the last six months of this period he was out of sight of land; cruising "some twenty degrees to the westward of the Gallipagos"—"cruising after the sperm-whale under the scorching sun of the Line, and tossed on the billows of the wide-rolling Pacific—the sky above, the sea around, and nothing else."

The ship itself was, at the expiration of this period, deplorable in appearance. The paint on her sides, burnt up by the scorching sun, was puffed up and cracked. She trailed weeds after her; about her stern-piece an unsightly bunch of barnacles had formed; and every time she rose on a sea, she showed her copper torn away, or hanging in jagged strips. The only green thing in sight aboard her was the green paint on the inside of the bulwarks, and that, to Melville, was of "a vile and sickly hue." The nearest suggestion of the grateful fragrance of the loamy earth, was the bark which clung to the wood used for fuel—bark gnawed off and devoured by the Captain's pig—and the mouldy corn and the brackish water in the little trough before which the solitary tenant of the chicken-coop stood "moping all day long on that everlasting one leg of his."

The usage on board in Melville's ship, as in that of J. Ross Browne and many another, had been tyrannical in the extreme. In *Typee* he says: "We had left both law and equity on the other side of the Cape." And Captain Pease, arbitrary and violent, promptly replied to all complaints and remonstrances with the butt-end of a hand-spike, "so convincingly administered as effectually to silence the aggrieved party."

"The sick had been inhumanly neglected; the provisions had been doled out in scanty allowance." The provisions on board the *Acushnet* had consisted chiefly of "delicate morsels of beef and pork, cut on scientific principles from every part of the animal and of all conceivable shapes and sizes, carefully packed in salt and stored away in barrels; affording a never-ending variety in their different degrees of toughness, and in the peculiarities of their saline properties. Choice old water, too, two pints of which were allowed every day to every soul on board; together with ample store of sea-bread, previously reduced to a state of petrification, with a view to preserve it either from decay or consumption in the ordinary mode, were likewise provided for the nourishment and gastronomic enjoyment of the crew." Captain Davis, in his *Nimrod of the Sea,* suggests that petrification is not the worst state of ship's-biscuits; he recounts how with mellower fare "epicures on board hesitate to bite the ship-bread in the dark, and the custom is to tap each piece as you break it off, to dislodge the large worms that breed there."

The itinerary of this fifteen months' cruise is not known. In *Moby-Dick* Melville says: "I stuffed a shirt or two into my carpet-bag, tucked it under my arm, and started for Cape Horn and the Pacific." In *Omoo,* Melville speaks óf "an old man-of-war's-man whose acquaintance I had made at Rio de Janeiro, at which place the ship touched in which I sailed from home." In *White-Jacket* and *Omoo* he speaks of whaling off the coast of Japan. And in *Moby-Dick,* in a passage that reads like an excerpt from the Book of Revelations, he indicates a more frigid whereabouts: "I remember the first albatross I ever saw. It was during a prolonged gale, in waters hard upon the Antarctic seas. From my forenoon watch below, I ascended to the overclouded deck; and there, dashed upọn the main hatches, I saw a regal, feathery thing of unspotted whiteness, and with a hooked, Roman bill sublime. At intervals, it arched forth its vast archangel wings, as if to embrace some holy ark. Wondrous flutterings and throbbings shook it. Though bodily unharmed, it uttered cries, as some king's ghost in supernatural distress. Through its inexpressible, strange eyes, methought I peeped to secrets which took hold of God. As Abraham before the angels, I bowed myself; the white thing was so white, its wings so wide, and in those for ever exiled waters, I had lost the miserable warping memories of traditions and of towns. Long I gazed at that prodigy of plumage. I cannot tell, can only hint, the things that darted through me then. But at last I awoke; when the white fowl flew to join the wing-folding, the invoking, and adoring cherubim!"

But what waters the *Acushnet* sailed, and what shores she touched before she dropped anchor in the Marquesas, little positively is known.

The last eighteen or twenty days, however, during which time the light trade winds silently swept the *Acushnet* towards the Marquesas, were to Melville, when viewed in retrospect, "delightful, lazy, languid." Land was ahead! And with the refreshing glimpse of one blade of grass in prospect, Melville and the whole ship's company resigned themselves to a disinclination to do anything, "and spreading an awning over the forecastle, slept, ate, and lounged under it the livelong day." The promise of the ship's at last breaking through the inexorable circle of the changeless horizon into the fragrance of firm and loamy earth, gave Melville an eye for the sea-scape he had formerly abhorred. "The sky presented a clear expanse of the most delicate blue, except along the skirts of the horizon, where you might see a thin drapery of pale clouds which never varied their form or colour. The long, measured, dirge-like swell of the Pacific came rolling along, with its surface broken by little tiny waves, sparkling in the sunshine. Every now and then a shoal of flying fish, scared from the water under the bows, would leap into the air, and fall the next moment like a shower of silver into the sea."

In later years, memory treacherously transformed this watery environment upon which Melville and Toby had vented their youthful and impotent imprecations. From his farm in the Berkshire Hills, he looked back regretfully upon his rovings over the Pacific, and by a pathetic fallacy, convinced himself that in them "the long supplication of my youth was answered." The spell of the Pacific descended upon him not while he was cruising the Pacific, however, but while he was busy upon his farm in Pittsfield, "building and patching and tinkering away in all directions," as he described his activities to Hawthorne.

Strangely jumbled anticipations haunted Melville, he says, as drowsing on the silent deck of the *Acushnet* he was being borne towards land: towards the Marquesas, one of the least known islands in the Pacific.

"The Marquesas! What strange visions of outlandish things does the very name spirit up!" exclaims Melville in excited prospect. "Naked houris—cannibal banquets—groves of cocoa-nut—coral reefs—tattooed chiefs—and bambo temples; sunny valleys planted with bread-fruit-trees—carved canoes dancing on the flashing blue waters—savage woodlands guarded by horrible idols—*heathenish rites and human sacrifices.*"

After fifteen months aboard the *Acushnet,* Melville was ripe to discover alluring Edenic beauties in tropical heathendom. And in the end, so intolerable was the prospect of dragging out added relentless days under the guardianship of Captain Pease, that as a last extremity, Melville preferred to risk the fate of Captain Cook, and find a strolling cenotaph in the bellies of a tribe of practising cannibals.

CHAPTER IX

THE PACIFIC

"There is, one knows not what sweet mystery about this sea, whose gentle awful stirrings seem to speak of some hidden soul beneath; like those fabled undulations of the Ephesian sod over the buried Evangelist St. John. And meet it is, that over these sea-pastures, wide-rolling watery prairies and Potters' Fields of all four continents, the waves should rise and fall, and ebb, and flow unceasingly; for here, millions of mixed shades and shadows, drowned dreams, somnambulisms, reveries; all that we call lives and souls, lie dreaming, dreaming, still; tossing like slumberers in their beds; the ever-rolling waves but made so by their restlessness."

—Herman Melville: *Moby-Dick.*

First sighted by Balboa in the year 1513, and for more than two centuries regarded by the Spaniards as their own possession, these midmost waters of the world lay locked behind one difficult and dangerous portal. During these centuries the Indian Ocean and the Atlantic—but arms of the Pacific—were gloomy with mysteries. The Spanish sailors used to chant a litany when they saw St. Elmo's Fire glittering on the mast-head, and exorcised the demon of the waterspout by elevating their swords in the form of crosses. Mermaids still lived in the tranquil blue waters. The darkness of the storm was thronged with gigantic shadowy figures. The pages of Purchas and Hackluyt offer no lack of supernatural visitations. Thus superstition joined with substantial danger to guard the entrance to the Pacific. Balboa himself was beheaded. Everybody who had to do with Magellan's first passage into the Pacific came to a bad end. The captain was murdered in a brawl by the natives of the Philippines; the sailor De Lepe, who first sighted the straits from the masthead, was taken prisoner by the Algerians, embraced the faith of the False Prophet, and so lost his everlasting soul; Ruy Falero died raving mad. There was a fatality upon the whole ship's company.

Two years before Magellan's memorable voyage, the western boundary of the Pacific had been approached by the Portuguese, Francisco Serrano having discovered the Molucca Islands immediately after the conquest of Malacca by the celebrated Albuquerque. To stimulate exertion, and to preclude contention in the rivalry of dominion between Portugal and Spain, Rodrigo Borgia, Pope Alexander the Sixth, drew a line down the map through the western limits of the Portuguese province of Brazil, and allotted to Portugal all heathen lands she should discover on the eastern half of this line; to Spain, all heathen lands to the west. So shadowy was the knowledge of geography at the time that this apportionment of His Holiness left it doubtful to which hemisphere the Moluccas belonged; and the precious spices peculiar to those islands rendered the decision important. To ascertain this was the purpose of Magellan's voyage across the Pacific. In this waste of waters Magellan made two discoveries: a range of small islands —including Guam among its number—which he named Ladrones, on account of the thievish disposition of the natives; and, at the cost of his life, one of the islands which has since been called the Philippines.

The voyage of Magellan proved that by the allotment of Alexander the Sixth, the Pacific belonged to Spain. And though for eight generations the Spaniards were hereditary lords of the Pacific, they soon grew greedy and jealous and lazy in their splendid and undisturbed monopoly. Once or twice, it is true, the English devils took the great galleon: but only once or twice in all these years. Lesser spoils occasionally fell into the hands of pirates; for did not Dampier take off Juan Fernandez a vessel laden with "a quantity of marmalade, a stately and handsome mule, and an immense wooden image of the Virgin Mary"? Towns, too, were occasionally sacked. But the Spaniards feared little danger, and ran few risks. They grew richer and lazier, and troubled themselves little in exploring the great expanse of the Pacific. They coasted the Americas as far north as California, which they half-suspected to be an island. The Galapagos, Juan Fernandez, and Masafuera they knew; a part of China, a part of Japan, the Philippines, Celebes, Timor, and the Ladrones. Voyages across the

Pacific between Manilla and Acapulco were not infrequent: but these voyages were sterile in discovery. The traditional route, once through the Straits of Magellan, was to touch at Juan Fernandez, coast South America, stand in at Panama, turn out to sea again, appear off Acapulco, and then sail in the parallel of 13° N. to the Ladrones. The Abbé Raynal states that the strictest orders were given by the Spanish Government prohibiting captains on any account to deviate from the track laid down on their charts during the voyage between these places.

In the darkness of this uncharted ocean there was believed to stretch a great southern continent of fabulous wealth and beauty: the Terra Australis Incognita that survived pertinaciously in the popular imagination until the time of Captain Cook. Members of the Royal Society had proved, beyond doubt, that the right balance of the earth required a southern continent; geographers pointed out how Quiros, Juan Fernandez and Tasman had touched at various points of this continent. Politicians and poets agreed that treasures of all kinds would be found there,—though they varied in their appropriation of these Utopian resources. The controversy over the existence of this continent was vehemently revived in 1770 by the appearance of Alexander Dalrymple's *An Historical Collection of the Several Voyages and Discoveries in the South Pacific Ocean.* Dalrymple was an ardent advocate of the reality of the Terra Australis Incognita, and to encourage an experimental confirmation of his faith, he dedicated his handsome quarto: "To the man who, emulous of Magellan and the heroes of former times, undeterred by difficulties and unseduced by pleasure, shall persist through every obstacle, and not by chance but by virtue and good conduct succeed in establishing an intercourse with a Southern Continent." Dr. Kippis, Captain Cook's biographer, writing in 1788, says he remembers how Cook's "imagination was captivated in the early part of his life with the hypothesis of a southern continent. He has often dwelt upon it with rapture." The year following Dalrymple's dedication, Captain Cook, back from his first voyage in the Pacific, was commissioned by the Earl of Sandwich, First Lord of the Admiralty, to go out and settle once and for all the mystery of the Southern Continent. So long as this mystery remained unsettled, the Pacific stretched a great limbo pregnant with the wildest fancies. Between the times of Magellan and Captain Cook there was no certainty as to what revelations it held to disgorge.

It was in 1575 that Drake climbed the hill and the tree upon its summit from which could be seen both the Atlantic and the Pacific oceans. "Almighty God," this devout pirate exclaimed, "of thy holiness give me life and leave to sail in an English ship upon that sea!" God heard his prayer, and blessed him with rich pirate spoils in the Pacific, and honoured him at home by a "stately visit" from the Queen. Yet he died at sea, and in a leaden coffin his body was dropped into the ocean slime. Cavendish continued the British tradition of lucrative piracy, and in 1586 captured the great plate galleon. This stimulated competition in high-sea robbery, until in 1594, the capture of Sir Richard Hawkins daunted even English courage.

In 1595, Alvaro Mendana de Neyra, departing from the beaten track across the Pacific on his way to occupy the Solomon Islands which he had discovered twenty-eight years earlier, chanced upon a new group of islands which he named Las Marquesas de Mendoca, in honour of his patron Mendoca, Marquis of Cenete, and viceroy of Peru. He had mass said on shore, refitted his vessels, planted a few crosses in devout memorial, to die before he accomplished the object of his voyage. and to leave the Marquesas unmolested by visitors until visited by Captain Cook in 1774. It was in the Marquesas, of course, that Melville lived with the cannibals.

The seventeenth century saw the Dutch upon the Pacific. During the greater part of the century, England was busy with troublesome affairs at home; the Spanish were too indolent to bestir themselves. Unmolested by competition, the great Dutch navigators, Joris Spilbergen, La Maire, Schouten, and,—most famous of all,—Tasman, drifted among the islands of the extreme southwest. It was not until 1664 that the French sailed upon the Pacific. To the end of the century belong the buccaneers—Morgan, Sawkin, Edward Cooke, Woodes, Rogers, Cowley, Clipperton, Shelvocke and Dampier. William Dampier, the greatest of these voyagers, crossed the Pacific, missing all islands but New Zealand. He added but little to the stock of knowledge that had been already collected from the narratives of Tasman, or Schouten. W. Clark Russell, in his life of Dampier, suggests it as probable "that his failure, coupled with the despondent tone that characterises his narrative, went far to retard further explorations of the South Seas. It was no longer disputed that a vast body of land stood in those waters. All that Dampier said in its favour was theoretical; all that he had to report as an eye-witness, all that he could speak to as facts, was extremely discouraging." The myth of the entrancing beauties and voluptuous charms of the South Seas owes nothing to Dampier—except, perhaps, a delayed inception. Of the inhabitants of the South Seas he reports that they had the most unpleasant looks and the worst features of any people he ever saw; and, says he: "I have seen a great variety of Savages." He speaks of them as "blinking Creatures," with "black skins and Hair frizzled, tall, thin, etc."

Russell considered the depressing influence of Dampier's recorded adventures manifested in the direction given to later navigators. Byron in 1764, Wallis, Mouat, and Cartaret in 1766, were despatched on voyages round the world to search the South Seas for new lands; but only one of them, Cartaret, deviated from Dampier's track, confining his explorations in this way to a glance at New Guinea and New Britain, to the discovery of New Ireland, lying adjacent to the island Dampier sailed around, and to giving names to the Solomon and other groups. Both Byron and Wallis, it is true, did enter the archipelago of the Society Islands, Wallis discovering island after island, until he reached Tahiti. Wallis's account of Otaheite—on the authority of the London Missionary Society "to be pronounced so as to rhyme with the adjective *mighty*"—and its people, occupies a great part of his narrative. Though his reception was not without a show of arms and bloodshed, the native women exerted themselves tirelessly to do unselfish penance for the hostile behaviour of the native males. Oammo, the ruling chief, retired from the scene, leaving the felicitation of the strangers in the hands of his consort, Oberea, "whose whole character," according to the observations of the London Missionary Society, "for sensuality exceeded even the usual standard of Otaheite." In the establishment of friendship that ensued, Wallis sent Lieutenant Furneaux ashore to erect a British pennant, and in defiance of the Pope, to take formal possession of the island in the name of King George the Third. Hopelessly unimpressed by the whole transaction, the natives took down the flag during the night, and for a long time afterwards the ruling chieftains wore it about their persons as a badge of royalty. Oberea's hospitality was requited by a parting gift of some turkeys, a gander, a goose, and a cat. Oberea's live stock figures repeatedly in the later annals of Tahiti.

Early in April, 1768, Tahiti was again visited by Europeans. Louis de Bougainville was in Tahiti only eight days. But, if Bougainville's account be not the bravado of patriotism, during that period his ship's company seem to have outdone their English predecessors in sensuality and open indecency. Several murders were committed more privately. And the natives, with an eye for the detection of such matters, exposed among the ship's crew a woman who had sailed from France disguised in man's apparel. Bougainville attached to himself a native youth, Outooroo, brother of a chieftain; Outooroo accompanied Bougainville to France. Within a few weeks after sailing from Tahiti, Bougainville discovered that Outooroo, as well as others aboard, were infected with venereal disease. Wallis very specifically asserts that his ship's company were untouched by disreputable symptoms six months before, and still longer after their visit at Tahiti. In any event, before the first year had elapsed after the discovery of Tahiti, its inhabitants were exhibiting unmistakable signs of their contact with civilisation. In 1799, the London Missionary Society gave warning to the world: "The present existence, and the general prevalence of the evil, is but too obvious; and it concurs with other dreadful effects of sensuality, to threaten

the entire population of this beautiful island, if it is not sea-
sonably averted by the happy influence of the gospel." The
steady extinction of the Polynesian races would seem to indicate that this happy influence has, to date, not been efficacious.
When Pope Alexander the Sixth gave to the indolent Spanish
the heathen for inheritance, His Holiness was being used by
a mysterious Providence as the guardian of heathendom. It
was not until he had been for over two centuries and a half
in his tomb, that the heretical and more enterprising English
came to dispel the Egyptian darkness that hung protectingly
over most of the islands of the Pacific, and to expose a competent barbarism to the devastating aggressions of civilisation.

Everybody knows how in 1769 the Royal Society, discovering that there would happen a transit of Venus, and that this
interesting astronomical event would be best observed from
some place in the Pacific, hit upon James Cook—Byron, Wallis and Cartaret all being in the Pacific at the time—master in
the Royal Navy, to command the expedition. The Marquesas
were chosen as the place for the observation; but while the
expedition was being fitted out, Captain Wallis returned to
England, bringing news of the discovery of Tahiti. So well
known is the story of Captain Cook that few can boast the
distinction of total ignorance of his three voyages to the
Pacific,—the first in command of an astronomical expedition,
the second in search of a Southern Continent, the third in
quest of a Northwest Passage; of his discoveries and adventures in every conceivable part of the Pacific; of his repeated
returns to Tahiti; of his finally being killed on the island called
by him Owhyhee, murdered despite the fact that he had shown
a power of conciliation granted to no other navigator in these
seas. For, a long time ago, there lived, on the island of
Hawaii, Lono the swine-god. He was jealous of his wife,
and killed her. Driven to frenzy by the act, he went about
boxing and wrestling with every man he met, crying, "I am
frantic with my great love." Then he sailed away for a foreign land, prophesying at his departure: "I shall return in
after times on an island bearing cocoa-nut trees, swine, and

dogs." When, after a year's absence, Cook returned to Hawaii, he arrived the day after a great battle, and the victorious natives were absolutely certain that Cook was the great swine-god, Lono, who long ages ago had departed mad with love, now, to add lustre to their triumph, returned on an island bearing cocoa-nut trees, swine, and dogs. This attribution of deity was hardly complimentary to Cook's crew. And in time the islanders tired of their enthusiasm and the expense of entertaining strolling deities. After sixteen days of prodigal hospitality, the natives began stroking the sides and patting the bellies of the sailors, telling them, partly by signs, partly by words, it was time to go. They went. But a week afterwards the ship returned. There was a quarrel. Among some people a quarrel leads to a fight. In a fight somebody naturally gets killed. Or, it may have been,—Walter Besant suggests,—that perhaps it may have occurred to some native humourist to wonder how a god would look and behave with a spear stuck right through him. Cook fell into the water, and spoke no more.

In his life, as in his death, Cook enjoyed all the successes. Boswell dined with him at Sir John Pringle's on April 2, 1776, and reported the glowing event to Dr. Johnson. A snuff-box was carved out of the planks of one of his vessels, and presented to James Fenimore Cooper. Fanny Burney records with pride her father's meeting the famous navigator, whom she herself met in society and in her own home. Joseph Priestly contemplated accompanying Cook to the South Seas. An artist—W. Hodges—was officially appointed to accompany him to perpetuate his exploits in oil. He read learned papers before the Royal Society, for one of which the counsel adjudged him the Copley Gold Medal. Six times was his portrait painted, and once was it seriously proposed that Dr. Johnson be appointed his official biographer. Not even by Omai, a native of Tahiti that Captain Furneaux brought to England, was Captain Cook's glory eclipsed. And Omai was received by the King, was painted by Sir Joshua Reynolds, and was laden with gifts when he was taken back to Tahiti by Captain Cook on his third voyage. Omai, too, attended meetings of the Royal Society, and it is to his credit that he behaved himself fairly well. It was regretted by the Directors of the London Missionary Society that though "great attention was paid to him by some of the nobility, it was chiefly directed to his amusement, and tended rather to augment than to diminish his habitual profligacy." In 1785-6, there was repeatedly performed at Covent Garden Theatre a pantomime named after him. The characters, besides Omai, were Towha, the Guardian Genius of Omai's Ancestors; Otoo, Father of Omai; Harlequin, Servant to Omai. To give a blend of edification to romance, the performance included, so a surviving play-bill announces, "a Procession exactly representing the dresses, weapons and manners of the Inhabitants of Otaheite, New Zealand, Tanna, Marquesas, Friendly, Sandwich and Easter Islands, and other countries visited by Captain Cook." In 1789, so vividly was the tragic end of Captain Cook still mourned, that at the Theatre-Royal, Covent Garden, was presented a spectacular tribute posted as *The Death of Captain.* It was "a Grand Serious Pantomimic Ballet, in Three Parts, as now exhibiting in Paris with uncommon applause, with the Original French Music, New Scenery, Machinery, and other Decorations." This performance may have been inspired by an *Ode on the Death of Captain Cook* penned by Miss Seward, the Swan of Lichfield: an ode praised by her fellow-townsman, Dr. Johnson. In 1774 there appeared in London "An Epistle from Oberea, Queen of Otaheite, to Joseph Banks, Esq., translated by T. Q. Z., Esq., Professor of the Otaheite Language in Dublin, and of all the Languages of the Undiscovered Islands in the South Seas, enriched with Historical and Explanatory Notes," and so novel and popular was the South Sea manner, that its author was mistaken for a wit, and his efforts at humour repeatedly and laboriously imitated. As a corrective to such levity, there appeared in 1779 an effusion in verse, adorned with vignette depicting Tahitian women dancing, entitled *The Injured Islanders; or, The Influence of Art upon the Happiness of Nature.* There is no lack of evidence to prove that the exploits of Captain Cook brought the South Seas, and especially Tahiti, into exuberant and irresponsible popularity. Nor did business enterprise nap during the festivities. Information which had been received of the great utility of the bread-fruit, induced the merchants and planters of the British West Indies to request that means might be used to transplant it thither. For this purpose a ship was benevolently commissioned by George the Third: the *Bounty*, commanded by Lieutenant Bligh. The voyage of the *Bounty* ended in a horrible tragedy and an intensely interesting romance. The story of the mutiny of the *Bounty*, and its astonishing sequels, joined further to vitalise the interest in the South Seas. A frigate, significantly called the *Pandora*, was sent out from England to Tahiti to seize the *Bounty* mutineers. Though the *Pandora* was despatched as a messenger of justice, the usual course of festivity, amusement and debaucheries was uninterrupted during the continuance of the ship at Tahiti. And the year following, with British doggedness, Captain Bligh returned to accomplish the purpose of his former voyage which had been frustrated by mutiny. In 1793, the *Daedalus*, Vancouver's storeship, stopped at Tahiti, leaving behind a Swedish sailor with a taste for savagery. The same year an American whaler, the *Matilda*, was wrecked off Tahiti, and the crew, delighted at their good fortune, betrayed no inclination for an immediate departure.

But while the frivolous, the sentimental, and the ungodly were busy converting Tahitian savagery into a Georgian idyll, the well-starched Wesleyan conscience crackled in horror at the black unredemption of the South Sea heathen. "The discoveries made in the great southern seas by the voyages undertaken at the command of his present majesty, George the Third," says a spokesman for the community, "excited wonderful attention, and brought, as it were, into light a world till then almost unknown. The perusal of the accounts of these repeated voyages could not but awaken, in such countries as our own, various speculations, according as men were differently affected. But when these islands were found to produce little that would excite the cupidity of ambition, or answer the speculations of the interested"—well, then it was that the protestant conscience bestirred itself, and on September 25, 1795, founded the London Missionary Society. It celebrated its first birthday by determining to begin work with the islands of the southern ocean, "as these, for a long time past, had excited peculiar attention. Their situation of mental ignorance and moral depravity strongly impressed on our minds the obligation we lay under to endeavour to call them from darkness into marvellous light. The miseries and diseases which their intercourse with Europeans had occasioned seemed to upbraid our neglect of repairing, if possible, these injuries; but above all, we longed to send to them the everlasting gospel, the first and most distinguished of blessings which Jehovah has bestowed upon the children of men."

A select committee of ministers, approved for evangelical principles and ability, was appointed to examine the candidates for the mission—who applied in great numbers—as to their views, capacity, and "knowledge in the mystery of godliness." Thirty missionaries were chosen: four ministers, six carpenters, two shoemakers, two bricklayers, two tailors (one of whom, "late of the royal artillery"), two smiths, two weavers, a surgeon, a hatter, a cotton manufacturer, a cabinet maker, a harness maker, a tinsmith, a cooper, and a butcher. There were three women and three children also in the party. On August 10, 1796, on the ship *Duff,* commanded by Captain Wilson, who had been wonderfully converted to God, this band, in chorus with a hundred voices, sang "Jesus, at thy command—we launch into the deep" as they sailed out of Spithead. The singing, it is said, produced "a pleasing and solemn sensation." On Sunday, March 5, 1797, after an uneventful voyage, the *Duff* dropped anchor at Tahiti. Seventy-four canoes came out to welcome the strangers and broke the Sabbath by crowding about the decks, "dancing and capering like frantic persons." Nor was the first impression made upon the Missionaries entirely favourable; "their wild disorderly behaviour, strong smell of cocoa-nut oil, together with the tricks of the arreoies, lessened the favourable impression we had formed of them; neither could we see aught of that elegance and beauty in their women for which they had been so greatly celebrated." Conversation with the natives was facilitated

by the presence of two tattooed Swedes—one formerly of the
crew of the *Matilda,* the other left by the *Daedalus.* During
sermon and prayer the natives were quiet and thoughtful,
"but when the singing struck up, they seemed charmed and
filled with amazement; sometimes they would talk and laugh,
but a nod of the head brought them to order." Next day,—for
they arrived on the Sabbath,—some of the missionaries landed
and were presented with the house King Pomare had built for
Captain Bligh. This important matter settled, the chief
thought it time to enquire after entertainment; "first sky-
rockets, next the violin and dancing, and lastly the bagpipe."
Lacking such diversions, the missionaries offered a few solos
on the German flute,—and "it plainly appeared that more lively
music would have pleased them better."

Domestic arrangements established, to the great diversion of
the natives, the missionaries tried to get some clothes on some
of them. The queen had to rip open the garments, it is true,
to get into them; but one Tanno Manoo, who was given a
warm week-day dress, and a showy morning gown and petti-
coat for the Sundays, "when dressed, made a very decent appearance; taking more pains to cover her breasts, and even to
keep her feet from being seen, than most of the ladies of
England have of late done." The natives were deeply perplexed by the proprieties of the Missionaries, and especially by
what to them seemed the unnatural chastity of the men.

Since the Missionaries had resolved to distribute their blessings, they sent a party of brethren to make investigations on
the Marquesas. The first visitors the ship received from the
shore were "seven beautiful young women, swimming quite
naked, except for a few green leaves tied round their middle;
nor did our mischievous goats even suffer them to keep their
green leaves, but as they turned to avoid them they were
attacked on each side alternately, and completely stripped
naked." Such, too, was their "symmetry of features, that as
models for the statuary and painter their equals can seldom be
found." As they danced about the deck, frequently bursting
out into mad fits of laughter, or talking as fast as their tongues
could go, surely they must have convinced more than one of

the meditative brethren of the total depravity of man. Nor
did these shameless savages confine their excursions to the
decks. "It was not a little affecting to see our own seamen
repairing the rigging, attended by a group of the most beautiful females, who were employed to pass the ball, or carry
the tar-bucket, etc.; and this they did with the greatest assidu-
ity, often besmearing themselves with the tar in the execu-
tion of their office. No ship's company, without great
restraints from God's grace, could ever have resisted such
temptations."

Harris and Crook, two of the brethren, daring temptation,
decided to stay at the Marquesas, and were moved ashore.
But before the *Duff* sailed back to Tahiti, Harris was found
on the shore about four o'clock one morning "in a most pitia-
ble plight, and like one out of his senses." It appears that
the Marquesan chief Tenae, taking Crook upon an inland jaunt,
had departed, conferring upon Harris all the privileges of
domesticity. Tenae's wife, sharing her husband's ideas of
hospitality, was troubled at Harris' reserve. So, "finding
herself treated with total neglect, became doubtful of his sex,"
says the London Missionary Society in a report dedicated to
George the Third, "and acquainted some of the other females
with her suspicion, who accordingly came in the night, when
he slept, and satisfied themselves concerning that point, but
not in such a peaceable way but that they awoke him. Discovering so many strangers, he was greatly terrified; and, perceiving what they had been doing, was determined to leave a
place where the people were so abandoned and given up to
wickedness; a cause which should have excited a contrary
resolution." Harris was forty years old at the time, and by
trade a cooper.

Crook, however, remained in the Marquesas for eighteen
months, where, alone, he tried to enlighten and improve the
natives. The Marquesas had a bad reputation among whalemen, and though they had been occasionally visited by enterprising voyagers—by Fanning, Krusenstern, Porter, and Finch
—they for long remained especially virulent in their native
depravity. It is true that Crook returned after many years

to place among the Marquesans four converted natives from the Society Islands. In 1834, two missionaries from England, accompanied by Darling from Tahiti and several converted natives, recommenced the arduous work of evangelising this ferocious people. During four years the faithful Stallworthy patiently toiled at his station, when in 1838 a French frigate landed two Catholic priests in the very and the only spot then cultivated by an English protestant labourer. These fellow-workers in Christ competed for the souls of heathens. Though, in 1839, to even the odds, Stallworthy received a reinforcement of one of his English brethren, after two years the English missionaries found it impossible "to maintain usefully their ground against the united influence of heathen barbarism, popish craft, French power, and French profligacy." Thus "ravished from the Protestant charity that had so long watched for its salvation," the Marquesans, when discovered by Melville, were in large part virgin in their barbarism.

At Tahiti, the brethren of the London Missionary Society continued to work unrestingly, and against incredible discouragement. The natives were, as Captain Cook discovered, "prodigious expert" as thieves. One snatcher-up of unconsidered trifles, when by way of punishment chained to a pillar with a padlock, not only contrived to get away, but to steal the padlock. Yet, by the representation of the London Missionary Society, "their honesty to one another seems unimpeachable," and they cultivated a Utopian sense of property: "They have no writing or records, but memory or landmarks. Every man knows his own; and he would be thought of all characters the basest, who should attempt to infringe on his neighbour, or claim a foot of land that did not belong to him, or his adopted friend." Indeed, despite the reprobation dealt out to them in tracts compiled for Sunday-school edification (Mrs. F. L. Mortimer's *The Night of Toil* being a typically diverting libel), the London Missionary Society, in its official reports, was—paradoxically enough —their most convincing apologist. The natural beauties of their country were again expatiated upon to the glory of the First Artist. So prodigal was the natural abundance of Tahiti that the brethren glorified it by converting it into a temptation. One of the brethren wrote in his journal: "O Lord, how greatly hast thou honoured me, that thousands of thy dear children should be praying for *me,* a wor ı! Lord, thou hast set me in a heathen land, but a land, if I may so speak, with milk and honey. O put more grace and gratitude into my poor cold heart, and grant that I may never with Jeshurun grow fat and kick." The natives themselves were untroubled by any such compunctions. "Their life is without toil," the brethren reported, "and every man is at liberty to do, go and act as he pleases, without the distress of care or apprehension of want: and as their leisure is great, their sports and amusements are various." Their personal beauty, their almost ostentatious cleanliness, their boundless generosity, were by the London Missionary Society insisted upon. The best of them, however, lived "in a fearfully promiscuous intercourse," and emulated the classical Greeks in infanticide and other reprehensible practices. Yet do the brethren allow that "in their dances alone is immodesty permitted; it may be affirmed, they have in many instances more refined ideas of decency than ourselves. They say that Englishmen are ashamed of nothing, and that we have led them to public acts of indecency never before practised among them." But then, as the London Missionary Society says in another place: "Their ideas, no doubt, of shame and delicacy are very different from ours; they are not yet advanced to any such state of civilisation and refinement." At their departure from native custom, however, they were untroubled by contrition. When asked "what is the true atonement for sin?" they answered, "Hogs and pearls." When the pleasant novelty of being exhorted and preached to wore off, they did not behave impeccably during the devotions of the brethren. They often cried out "lies" and "nonsense" during the sermon. At other times they tried to make each other laugh by repeating sentences after the brethren, or by playing antics, and making faces. Many of the natives used to lie down and sleep as soon as the sermon began, while "others were so trifling as to make remarks upon the missionaries' clothes, or upon their appearance.

"We are going to church, you see; and Kanoa, my Hawaiian associate, is blowing a shell to call the people to meeting, as we have no bell. Kanoa's wife, with one of her children is just behind us. Be sure to look at the king, son of the one who was killed, in his long shirt, and under his umbrella. The queen will come too, for both are very regular in their attendance; and, what is better still, we hope they are Christians.

"You may say, perhaps, that some things in this picture look more like breaking the Sabbath than keeping it; and you are quite right.

"The woman whom you see is a heathen, carrying her husband's skull as she goes on a visit to some other village. A party of the natives are pressing scraped cocoanuts in an oil-press, to get the oil to buy tobacco with. The dog is one of the many, as heathenish as their masters."

From *Story of the Morning Star,*
By Rev. Hiram Bingham.

Thus Satan filled their hearts with folly, lest they should believe and be saved." All the best inducements the brethren could hold out to tempt them into "the divine life" moved them not. "You talk to us of salvation, and we are dying," they said; "we want no other salvation than to be cured of our diseases and to live here always, and to eat and talk." So unappreciative were they of the efforts of the brethren that they explained the presence of the missionaries in Tahiti as growing out of a sensible desire to escape from the ugliness and worry and brutality of European civilisation. As for the lacerated solicitude and strange unselfishness of the brethren to confer upon each of them a soul with all of its pestering responsibilities : that, they found totally incomprehensible.

Excluding all considerations of intellect—in which both the Missionaries and the Polynesians seem to have been about equally endowed—the abyss between the brethren and the heathen was the abyss that separated John Knox from Aristophanes and the Greek Anthology: the abyss between the animal integrity of classical antiquity and the Hebraic heritage of the agonised conscience. Reason may pass back and forth over this chasm : but no man once touched by the traditions of Christianity can ever again sling his heart back across the abyss. If he attempt the feat—as witness the *Intimate Journals* of Paul Gauguin—he but adds corruption to crucifixion, and there is no doubt as to the last state of that man.

If the fall from innocence was begun in Eden, it was sealed beyond redemption in Bethlehem. For at the time of the inception of Christianity, the pagan world was going to its doom, and its death agonies were frightful in the extreme. Something had to be done to save humanity,—and something drastic. And humanity—which was at the same time the priest and the victim—found in the cross the justest symbol of its triumph in utter human defeat. More effectively to slander this world, Heaven was set up in libellous contrast; in order to heap debasement upon the flesh, the spirit was opposed to it as an infinitely precious eternal entity, tainted by contact with its mortal habitation. Blessedness lay not in harmony, but in division, and utter confusion was mistaken for total depravity. "For the flesh lusteth against the spirit, and the spirit against the flesh: and these are contrary the one to the other: so that ye cannot do the things that ye would." But these things classical antiquity did—being given over to a reprobate mind, so St. Paul tells us. The Wesleyan brethren found in Polynesia the same untroubled indulgence in "unrighteousness, fornication and wickedness," that had so troubled St. Paul. But in Tahiti there were no signs of the intellect that classical antiquity exhibited in the days of its reprobation. And though the Polynesians seemed to have thriven on unrighteousness, the brethren itched to infect them with misgivings, and this in a Holy Name. Melville was profoundly stirred to loathing at these efforts: a loathing heightened by the later contentions introduced into Tahiti by the rival proselyting of French Catholic missionaries. Lost in doubt and shame at such spectacles, in *Clarel* he thus invokes Christ:

> " By what art
> Of conjuration might the heart
> Of heavenly love, so sweet, so good,
> Corrupt into the creeds malign
> Begetting strife's pernicious brood,
> Which claimed for patron thee divine?
>   Anew, anew,
> For this thou bleedest, Anguished Face;
> Yea, thou through ages to accrue,
> Shall the Medusa shield replace:
> In beauty and in terror too
> Shall paralyse the nobler race—
> Smite or suspend, perplex, deter—
> Tortured, shall prove the torturer."

The brethren in Tahiti were without any of Melville's misgivings. Their faith was extraordinary. No less extraordinary was the native imperviousness to salvation. After the brethren had ceased to be an amusing novelty with gifts to bestow, the natives submitted them to neglect and mockery. Revolts against King Pomare and constant war kept the brethren in peril of their lives without releasing them to celestial jubilation. The Napoleonic wars cut them off from communication with England. During the first twelve years they heard from home only three times. These days of fruitless trial sifted the party. Many of the brethren seized any opportunity that offered to sail away on chance trading vessels. Of the seven who remained, two died. In 1801 eight new brethren came out to reinforce the number, then reduced to four. In 1804 old King Pomare died, and his son Oto became King under the title Pomare II. In the wars that followed, the mission seemed broken up: their house was burned, the printing press destroyed, and six of the brethren removed from Tahiti to Huahine. Two remained, however, to carry on the forlorn hope. But after all these years Pomare's heart began to soften. His gods seemed to be standing him in little stead. Defeated in battle, he escaped to Eimeo, and invited the missionaries to follow him. Here he ate a sacred turtle, and when no harm came to him he dared still further. Meanwhile it was proposed in England that proselyting in Polynesia be discontinued, since after sixteen years not one conversion had been effected. But those of undaunted faith protested. The ship bearing fresh supplies and news of the revived determination of those at home to prosecute the work was met in mid-ocean with the cargo of the rejected idols of the Tahitians. In a church seven hundred and twelve feet long, with twenty-nine doors and three pulpits, all paid for by himself,—the church in which Melville witnessed Sunday devotion—King Pomare had himself moistened on the forehead with the water of life.

Backed by their royal patron, the Missionaries undertook to convert Tahiti into a Polynesian Chautauqua. As Mrs. Helen Barrett Montgomery says, in her *Christus Redemptor*: "We cannot follow the glowing story of how the King had a code of laws made and read it to seven thousand of his people, who, by solemn vote, made these the law of the land." In 1839, Captain Hervey, in command of a whale-ship, reported of Tahiti: "It is the most civilised place I have been at in the South Seas. They have a good code of laws and no liquors are allowed to be landed on the island. It is one of the most gratifying sights the eye can witness to see, on Sunday, in their church, which holds about four thousand, the Queen near the pulpit with all her subjects about her, decently apparelled and seemingly in pure devotion." Three years later, Melville attended one of these services, and was less favourably impressed.

In 1823, the French establishment of the *Œuvre de la propagation de la Foi* formed at Lyons, and soon cast a beneficent eye upon North and South America and the islands of Oceania. In 1814, soon after the restoration of the Bourbons, the Abbé Coudrin had founded the Society of Picpus "to promote the revival of the Roman Catholic religion in France, and to propagate it by missions among unbelievers or pagans." This establishment received Papal sanction in 1817, and was placed under "the special protection of the Hearts of Jesus and Mary." In 1833, the Congregation of the Propaganda, with the confirmation of the Sovereign Pontiff, confided to the Society of Picpus the conversion of all the islands of the Pacific ocean. Two apostolic prefectures were established. M. E. Rouchouse was made bishop of Nilolopis, in partibus, and apostolic vicar of Eastern Oceania; M. C. Liansu was appointed as his prefect; two priests, Caret and Laval, and a catechist, Columban, or Murphy, were placed under his direction. In May, 1834, the Catholic missionaries arrived at Valparaiso, bound for the South Seas.

The benefits of the True Faith were not to advance into the Pacific unassisted by the secular arm. Two officers of the French Navy, Vincendon-Dumoulin and Desgraz, in their *Considerations générales sur la Colonisation Française dans l'Oceanie* thus speak for the less purely religious interests of France: "It is impossible for a traveller who may visit the islands of the Pacific, not to speculate on the destiny of the happy groups scattered over its bosom. The first thing that strikes him is the sight of men, consecrated to a religious work, meddling with the temporal affairs of these free people, whom they have brought under their domination, under pretence of directing their consciences. . . . When the rapid multiplication of the population of all European countries is considered, it is evident that before long a European colony will be formed in each of the innumerable islands of the Pacific, and mission-

ary efforts merit therefore all the attention of the government.
. . . On the signal from the first cannon that shall be fired
in Europe, a protecting flag will be seen to rise on each of
these islands now so peaceful. God grant that the tri-coloured flag of our nation may show itself with honour!"

At this time, it was a law of Tahiti that before a foreigner
could have leave to reside on the island, permission must be
granted by Queen Pomare and the chiefs. The Catholic missionaries, aware of this regulation, succeeded, however, in ef-
fecting a landing disguised as carpenters, and to this island,
partly idolatrous, partly heretic, they gave the salutation of
peace. Pomare, however, was unappreciative of their salute,
and refused to the disguised priests permission to remain.
This exclusion, in its sequel, raised the most delicate questions
of international diplomacy, and bestirred Pomare to scatter
anxious letters broadcast over the face of the earth. Her correspondence included a cosmopolitan company of Commodores
and Admirals, Queen Victoria, the President of the United
States, and Louis Philippe of France. Admiral Du Petit-
Thouars, in command of the *Venus,* was despatched to Tahiti
under special orders, "to make the Queen and the inhabitants
feel that France is a great and powerful nation." The *Venus*
arrived at Tahiti, August 27, 1838, and proceeded to summary
justice. Under the pressure of a broadside, Pomare was
obliged to beg pardon of the most Christian King. "I am
only," she wrote to Louis Philippe, "the sovereign of a little
insignificant island; may glory and power be with your majesty;—let your anger cease; and pardon me the mistake that
I have made."

It was further demanded of Pomare that she pay "a great
and powerful nation" the sum of two thousand dollars as a
more solid reparation for her bad behaviour. Pomare was
appalled at the magnitude of this sum: there was no such am-
plitude of wealth in her treasury. The missionaries were
moved in compassion to finance her political indiscretion. But
in the next humiliation dealt out to her, the brethren were unable to offer much assistance. The French Admiral bore instructions to require that the French flag be hoisted the day

following the receipt of the two thousand dollars, and that it be honoured by Pomare with a salute of twenty-one guns. The situation was awkward. Pomare was very short of powder. She assured the Admiral she had not enough for more than five shots. The Admiral paced the deck, and passed his fingers through his hair in considerable agitation. "What will they say in France," said the patriotic commander, "when they know that I furnished the powder to salute my own flag?" The difficulty was great. An expedient was necessary, and the Admiral hit upon one: "Mr. Consul," said he to the Rev. Pritchard, and British Consul, "I can give you some powder, and you can do with it as you please." According to the French report, Pritchard "himself loaded the bad cannon on the little island and directed the firing;" and soon after, the French observed Pritchard to look "thin and bilious, with an appearance of pride, and the cold dignity so natural to the English."

But the visiting Admiral had not yet completed his duty to "the justly irritated King of the French." He condescended to visit the Queen on purpose to introduce Moerenhaut as French consul. Moerenhaut had been American consul at Tahiti, but had been relieved of the responsibilities of that office at a request of Pomare to the President of the United States. Moerenhaut's life, in all of its varied and unsavoury details, has yet to be written: it would make an entertaining supplement to the *Police Gazette*. Moerenhaut himself adventured in letters, and in his *Voyages aux îles du Grand Ocean* he exposes many of the corrupt practices that he himself was instrumental in bringing about. The Admiral and Moerenhaut, in the name of Louis Philippe, drew up a convention with Pomare "to establish the right of French subjects to stay in the territory of the Tahitian sovereign."

During these proceedings, Captain Dumont D'Urville, cruising the Pacific, arrived at the Marquesas with two corvettes, the *Astrolabe* and the *Zélé*, hot from the Gambier islands, the seat of Bishop Rouchouse. At Gambier, when "all were gay and cheerful," D'Urville had been enlightened as to the true character of the heretical missionaries: "oppressors of the poor

Tahitians; in short, vampires, whose cruelties and inquisitorial tortures were as atrocious as their hypocrisy was disgusting." Before he left the jovial board, his indignation was so high that "he felt the honour of his flag" required that he sail to Tahiti and dispense "exemplary chastisement." Upon his arrival at the Marquesas he was surprised to find Du Petit-Thouars, who had been there, already departed. There was value to his visit, however, in giving to the pious efforts of Bishop Rouchouse the support of a few broadsides. But there were other scenes at the Marquesas of which Bishop Rouchouse, in good conscience, could not have approved. Melville asserts that while the *Acushnet* was at the Marquesas, "our ship was wholly given up to every species of riot and debauchery." In the official account of the voyages of Captain Dumont D'Urville is a more detailed account of a similar surrender. Melville says of the dances of the women of the Marquesas: "There is an abandoned voluptuousness in their character that I dare not attempt to describe." The French, in their official reports, exhibit a greater courage.

Captain Dumont D'Urville arrived in Tahiti nine days after the submission of Pomare, and the day following his arrival he accompanied Admiral Du Petit-Thouars on a visit to the Queen. He had not yet cooled in his patriotic indignation, so he addressed Pomare severely, and with gratifying results: "I perceived that Pomare was deeply affected, and that tears began to fall from her eyes, as she threw them on me with an evident expression of anger. At the same moment I also perceived that Captain Du Petit-Thouars endeavoured to diminish the effect of my words by some little liberties that he was taking with the Queen; such as pulling gently her hair, and patting her cheeks; he even added that she was foolish to be so much affected."

When her French visitors sailed away, Pomare on November 8, 1838, despatched a letter to her sister sovereign, Victoria, to implore "the shelter of her wing, the defence of her lion, and the protection of her flag." The Tahitians expressed their sense of the favours being forced upon them by the French by passing a law prohibiting "the propagation of any religious doctrines, or the celebration of any religious worship, opposed to that true gospel of old propagated in Tahiti by the missionaries from Britain; that is, these forty years past."

This breach of international courtesy brought Captain Laplace on the *Artémise* out to Tahiti "to obtain satisfaction from the Lutheran evangelists who had forced themselves on a simple and docile people." As the *Artemise* was off the coast, on April 22, 1839, she struck on a coral reef: an accident that resulted in the officers and crew being lodged on shore for two months. These two months must have given the brethren bitter fruit for reflection upon the ease with which their years of unselfish striving could be obliterated. According to the account of Louis Reybaud of the *Artémise*: "From the first, the most perfect harmony prevailed between the ship's company and the natives. Each of the latter chose his *tayo*,— that is, another self—among the sailors. Between *tayos* everything is common. At night, the *tayos*, French and Tahitian, went together to the common hut. Every sailor has thus a house, a wife, a complete domestic establishment. As jealousy is a passion unknown to these islanders, it may be imagined what resources and pleasures such an arrangement afforded our crew. The natives were delighted with the character of our people; they had never met with such gaiety, expansiveness, and kindness in any other foreigners. The beach presented the aspect of a continual holiday, to the great scandal of the missionaries. We have seen how the men managed, and what friends they found. The officers were not less fortunate. The island that Bougainville called the *New Cytherea* does not belie its name. When the evening set in, every tree along the coast shaded an impassioned pair; and the waters of the river afforded an asylum to a swarm of copper-coloured nymphs, who came to enjoy themselves with the young midshipmen. Wherever you walked you might hear the *oui! oui! oui!* the word that all the women have learnt with marvellous facility. It would have been far more difficult to teach them to say *non!*"

Among these relaxations, Captain Laplace found time publicly to declare to the islanders "how shameful and even dangerous it was to violate the faith of treaties, and how unjust and barbarous was intolerance." Before his sailing, Captain Laplace commanded Pomare to come aboard the *Artémise* to sign a treaty guaranteeing no discrimination against the French. Pomare's despondency at the beginning of the proceedings was solaced by champagne and brandy. Casimir Henricy, who accompanied the *Artémise* throughout her circumnavigatory voyage, says: "When the spirits of the party were sufficiently elevated to find everything good, and while the hands were yet sufficiently steady not to let the pen drop, the treaty was produced as the crowning act of the festivity. M. Laplace thought he had gained a great victory over Polynesian diplomacy; and, certainly, never was a political horizon more bright in flowers and bottles."

While Tahiti was the theatre of these religious and political cabals, more important and decisive measures occupied the mighty minds of Europe. The captains who had punished and conventionalised Pomare and her people had made their reports in person to their sovereign in Paris, and to the ministers of state, who had indicated their instructions. Honours and titles were awarded to the successful officers, and on their showing it was resolved that the Marquesas should first be taken possession of, and then Tahiti. Rear-Admiral Du Petit-Thouars was commissioned to execute the seizure. On board the *Reine Blanche,* accompanied by three frigates and three corvettes, he touched Fatu-Heva, the southernmost of the Marquesas, on April 26, 1842, and culminated his triumphant progress through the group in the bay of Tyohee at Nukuheva on May 31.

The *Acushnet* arrived at Nukuheva at a memorable time. "It was in the summer of 1842 that we arrived at the islands," says Melville; "the French had then held possession of them for several weeks."

CHAPTER X

MAN-EATING EPICURES—THE MARQUESAS

" 'Why, they are cannibals!' said Toby on one occasion when I eulogised
the tribe. 'Granted,' I replied, 'but a more humane, gentlemanly and
amiable set of epicures do not probably exist in the Pacific.' "
—HERMAN MELVILLE: *Typee*.

IT was sunset when the *Acushnet* came within sight of the
loom of the mountains of the Marquesas. Innumerable sea-
fowls, screaming and whirling in spiral tracts had, for some
days previous, been following the vessel as harbingers from
land. As the ship drew nearer to green earth, several of man-
of-war's-hawks, with their blood-red bills and raven plumage,
had circled round the ship in diminishing circles until Melville was able distinctly to mark the strange flashing of their
eyes; and then, as if satisfied by their observations, they would
sail up into the air as if to carry sinister warning on ahead.
Then,—driftwood on the oily swells; and finally had come the
glad announcement from aloft—given with that peculiar pro-
longation of sound that a sailor loves—"Land ho!"

After running all night with a light breeze straight for the
island, the *Acushnet* was in easy distance of the shore by
morning. But as the *Acushnet* had approached the island from
the side opposite to Tyohee—christened by Captain Porter,
Melville remembered, Massachusetts Bay,—they were obliged
to sail some distance along the shore. Melville was surprised
not to find "enamelled and softly swelling plains, shaded over
by delicious groves, and watered by purling brooks." Instead he found himself cruising along a bold rock-bound coast,
dashed high against by the beating surf, and broken here and
there into deep inlets that offered sudden glimpses of blooming
valleys, deep glens, waterfalls and waving groves. As the
ship sailed by the projecting and rocky headlands with their
short inland vistas of new and startling beauty, one of the
sailors exclaimed to Melville, pointing with his hand in the di-

rection of the treacherous valley: "There—there's Typee. Oh, the bloody cannibals, what a meal they'd make of us if we were to take it into our heads to land! but they say they don't like sailors' flesh, it's too salt. I say, matey, how should you like to be shoved ashore there, eh?" Melville shuddered at the question, he says, little thinking that within the space of a few weeks he would actually be a captive in that self-same valley.

Towards noon they swung abreast of their harbour. No description can do justice to its beauty, Melville tells us. But its beauty was to him not an immediate discovery. All that he saw was the tri-coloured flag of France trailing over the stern of six vessels, whose black hulls and bristling broadsides floated incongruously in that tranquil bay.

The first emissary from the shore to welcome the *Acushnet* was a visitor in that interesting state of intoxication when a man is amiable and helpless: a south-sea vagabond, once a lieutenant in the English navy, recently appointed pilot to the harbour by the invincible French. He was aided by some benevolent person out of his whale-boat into the *Acushnet,* and though utterly unable to stand erect or navigate his own body, he magnanimously proffered to steer the ship to a good anchorage: a feat Captain Pease did for himself, despite the amazing volubility of the visitor in contrary commands.

This renegade from Christendom and humanity was of a type not infrequently met with in accounts of the South Seas. At Hannamanoo, Melville came across another such—a white man in the South Sea girdle, and tattooed on the face, living among a tribe of savages and apparently settled for life, so perfectly satisfied seemed he with his circumstances. This man was an Englishman,—Lem Hardy he called himself,—who had deserted from a trading brig touching at Hannamanoo for wood and water some ten years previous. Aboard the *Acushnet* he told his history. "Thrown upon the world a foundling, his paternal origin was as much a mystery to him as the genealogy of Odin; and scorned by everybody, he fled the parish workhouse when a boy, and launched upon the sea. He had followed it for several years, a dog before the mast, and now

he had thrown it up forever." He had gone ashore as a
sovereign power, armed with a musket and a bag of ammuni-
tion, and soon became, what he was when Melville found him,
military leader of the tribe, war-god of the entire island, living under the sacred protection of an express edict of the taboo,
his person inviolable forever. In *Iles Marquises, ou Nouka-
Hiva, Histoire, Géographie, Mœurs et Considérations Générales* (Paris, 1843) by Vincendon-Dumoulin and Desgraz is
to be found (pages 356-359) a history of two more of these
vagabonds: one Joseph Cabri,·a Frenchman, and one E. Rob-
erts, an Englishman. Cabri returned to Europe, for a time,
to find the novelty of his tattooing both an embarrassment and
a source of livelihood. He was examined by grave learned
societies, was presented before several crowned heads, and submitted his person to intimate examination to any one who
would pay his fee. In 1818 he died in obscurity and poverty
in Valenciennes, his birth place. His historians regret that
his precious person was not preserved in alcohol to delight the
inquiring mind of later generations. The Pacific, it would
appear, was early a place of refuge for men with an insur-
mountable homesickness for the mud. Melville soon came to
believe that the gifts of civilisation to the South Seas were
without exception very doubtful blessings; he came to be a
special pleader for the barbaric virtues; when these virtues
were practised by legitimate barbarians; but the spectacle of
such men as Hardy fell beyond the pale of his unusually broad
sympathies. Though he was despairingly alert to the vices of
Christendom, never was he betrayed into a corrupt hankering
to recapitulate into savagery. Though he excused the cannibalism of the Marquesans as an amiable weakness, he gazed
upon Hardy "with a feeling akin to horror." Hardy's tattooing was to Melville the outward and visible sign of the
lowest degradation to which a mortal, nurtured in a civilisation
that had for thousands of years a pathetically imperfect
struggle striven to some significance above the beast, could
possibly descend. "What an impress!" Melville exclaimed in
superlative loathing. "Far worse than Cain's—*his* was perhaps a wrinkle, or a freckle, which some of our modern cos-

metics might have effaced." But Hardy's tattooing was to
Melville a mark indelible of the blackest of all betrayals.

More worthy emissaries than the pilot to the port of Tyohee
were to welcome Melville to the Marquesas. The entrance of
the *Acushnet* brought from the shore a flotilla of native canoes.
"Such strange outcries and passionate gesticulations I never
certainly heard or saw before," Melville says. "You would
have thought the islanders were on the point of flying at one
another's throats, whereas they were only amiably engaged in
disentangling their boats." Melville was surprised at the
strange absence of a single woman in the invading party, not
then knowing that canoes were "taboo" to women, and that
consequently, "whenever a Marquesan lady voyages by water,
she puts in requisition the paddles of her own fair body."

As the *Acushnet* approached within a mile and a half of the
foot of the bay, Melville noticed a singular commotion in the
water ahead of the vessel: the women, swimming out from
shore, eager to embrace the advantages of civilisation. "As
they drew nearer," Melville says, "and as I watched the rising
and sinking of their forms, and beheld the uplifted right arm
bearing above the water the girdle of tappa, and their long
dark hair trailing beside them as they swam, I almost fancied
they could be nothing else but so many mermaids. Under
slow headway we sailed right into the midst of these swimming nymphs, and they boarded us at every quarter; many
seizing hold of the chain-plates and springing into the chains;
others, at the peril of being run over by the vessel in her
course, catching at the bob-stays, and wreathing their slender
forms about the ropes, hung suspended in the air. All of them
at length succeeded in getting up the ship's side, where they
clung dripping with the brine and glowing with the bath, their
jet-black tresses streaming over their shoulders, and half en-
veloping their otherwise naked forms. There they hung,
sparkling with savage vivacity, laughing gaily at one another,
and chattering away with infinite glee. Nor were they idle the
while, for each performed the simple offices of the toilet for
the other. Their luxuriant locks, wound up and twisted into
the smallest possible compass, were freed from the briny ele-

ment; the whole person carefully dried, and from a small little round shell that passed from hand to hand, anointed with a fragrant oil: their adornments were completed by passing a few loose folds of white tappa, in a modest cincture, around the waist. Thus arrayed, they no longer hesitated, but flung themselves lightly over the bulwarks, and were quickly frolicking about the decks. Many of them went forward, perching upon the headrails or running out upon the bowsprit, while others seated themselves upon the taffrail, or reclined at full length upon the boats."

The ship was fairly captured, and it yielded itself willing prisoner. In the evening, after anchor had been struck, the deck was hung with lanterns, and the women, decked in flowers, danced with "an abandoned voluptuousness" that was a prelude "to every species of riot and debauchery." According to Melville's account, on board the *Acushnet* "the grossest licentiousness and the most shameful inebriety prevailed, with occasional and but short-lived interruptions, through the whole period of her stay."

Nor were the French at the Marquesas neglectful of their duties to the islanders. Admiral Du Petit-Thouars had stationed about one hundred soldiers ashore, according to Melville's account. Every other day the troops marched out in full regalia, and for hours went through all sorts of military evolutions to impress a congregation of naked cannibals with the superior sophistications of Christendom. "A regiment of the Old Guard, reviewed on a summer's day in the Champs Elysées," Melville vouches, "could not have made a more critically correct appearance." The French had also with them, to enrich their harvest of savage plaudits, a *puarkee nuee*, or "big hog"—in more cultivated language, a horse. One of the officers was commissioned to prance up and down the beach at full speed on this animal, with results that redounded to the glory of France. This horse "was unanimously pronounced by the islanders to be the most extraordinary specimen of zoology that had ever come under their observation."

It would be an ungracious presumption to contend that the French, while at the Marquesas, exhibited to the natives only the sterner side of civilisation. The behaviour of the French at Tahiti leaves room for the hope that they were no less gallant at the Marquesas. An officer of the *Reine Blanche,* writing at sea on October 10, 1842, of the exploits of his countrymen at Tahiti, says, in part: "In the evening, more than a hundred women came on board. At dinner time, the officers and midshipmen invited them gallantly to their tables; and the repasts, which were very gay, were prolonged sufficiently late at night, so that fear might keep on board those of the women who were afraid to sail home by the doubtful light of the stars." The last three lines of this letter were suppressed by the *Journal de Debats,* it is true, but given in the *National* and other journals. Three days later the letter was officially pronounced "inexact" by the *Moniteur,* which courageously asserted that "it is utterly false that a frigate has been the theatre of corruption, in any country whatever; and French mothers may continue to congratulate themselves that their sons serve in the navy of their country."

While the Frenchmen at the Marquesas—no less than the Americans, one hopes with pardonable patriotic jealousy—were giving their mothers at home cause for congratulation, Melville came to the determination to leave the ship; "to use the concise, point-blank phrase of the sailors, I had made up my mind to 'run away.'" And that his reasons for resolving to take this step were numerous and weighty, he says, may be inferred from the fact that he chose rather to risk his fortune among cannibals than to endure another voyage on board the *Acushnet.* In *Typee* he gives a general account of the captain's bad treatment of the crew, and his non-fulfilment of agreements. Life aboard the *Acushnet* has already been sufficiently expatiated upon.

Melville knew that immediately adjacent to Nukuheva, and only separated from it by the mountains seen from the harbour, lay the lovely valley of Happar, whose inmates cherished the most friendly relations with the inhabitants of Nukuheva. On the other side of Happar, and closely adjoining it, lay the magnificent valley of the dreaded Typee, the unappeasable enemies of both these tribes. These Typees enjoyed a

prodigious notoriety all over the islands. The natives of Nukuheva, Melville says, used to try to frighten the crew of the
Acushnet "by pointing to one of their own number and calling
him a Typee, manifesting no little surprise when we did not
take to our heels at so terrible an announcement." But having ascertained the fact that the tribes of the Marquesas dwell
isolated in the depths of the valleys, and avoided wandering
about the more elevated portions of the islands, Melville concluded that unperceived he might effect a passage to the mountains, where he might easily and safely remain, supporting
himself on such fruits as came in his way, until the sailing of
the ship. The idea pleased him greatly. He imagined himself seated beneath a cocoanut tree on the brow of the mountain, with a cluster of plantains within easy reach, criticising
the ship's nautical evolutions as she worked her way out of
the harbour, and contrasting the verdant scenery about him
with the recollections of narrow greasy decks and the vile
gloom of the forecastle.

Melville at first prided himself that he was the only person
on board the *Acushnet* sufficiently reckless to attempt an idyllic
sojourn on an island of irreclaimable cannibals. But Toby's
perennially hanging over the side of the ship, gazing wistfully
at the shore in moody isolation, coupled with Melville's knowledge of Toby's hearty detestation of the ship, of his dauntless
courage, and his other engaging traits as companion in high adventure, led Melville to share with Toby his schemes. A few
words won Toby's most impetuous co-operation. Plans were
rapidly made and ratified by an affectionate wedding of palms,
when, to elude suspicion, each repaired to his hammock to
spend a last night aboard the *Acushnet*.

On the morrow, with as much tobacco, ship's biscuit and
calico as they could stow in the front of their frocks, Melville
and Toby made off for the interior of Nukuheva,—but not
before Melville "lingered behind in the forecastle a moment
to take a parting glance at its familiar features." Their five
days of marvellous adventures that landed them finally in the
valley of Typee has abidingly tried the credulity of Melville's

In 1855

RICHARD TOBIAS GREENE
Editor of the *Sandusky Mirror*

readers—though never for an instant their patience. After reading these adventures, Stevenson expressed his slangy approval by hailing Melville as "a howling cheese." It has been questioned in passing whether or not the number of days that two strong male humans, going through incredible exertion, can support themselves upon a hunk of bread soaked in sweat and ingrained with shreds of tobacco, must not be fewer than Melville makes out. And did they, in sober verity, critics have asked, lower themselves down the cliff by swinging from creeper to creeper with horrid gaps between them—was it as steep as Melville says, and the creepers as far apart? And did they, on another occasion, as Melville asserts, break a second gigantic fall by pitching on the topmost branches of a very high palm tree? During these thrilling and terrible five days, hardship runs hard on the heels of hardship, and each obstacle as it presents itself, seems, if possible, more unsurmountable than the last. There is no way out of this, one says for the tenth time: but the sagacity and fearless confidence of Toby—to whom let glory be given—and the manful endurance of Melville through parching fever and agonising lameness, disappoint the lugubrious reader. On the third day after their escape, their ardour is cooled to a resolve to forego futile ramblings for a space. They crawled under a clump of thick bushes, and pulling up the long grass that grew around, covered themselves completely with it to endure another downpour. While the exhausted Toby slept through the violent rain, Melville tossed about in a raging fever, without the heart to wake Toby when the rain ceased. Chancing to push aside a branch, Melville was as transfixed with surprised delight as if he had opened a sudden vista into Paradise. He "looked straight down into the bosom of a valley, which swept away in long wavy undulations to the blue waters in the distance. Midway towards the sea, and peering here and there amidst the foliage, might be seen the palmetto-thatched houses of its inhabitants glistening in the sun that had bleached them to a dazzling whiteness. The vale was more than three leagues in length, and about a mile across its greatest width. Everywhere below me, from the base of the precipice upon whose very verge I had been unconsciously reposing, the surface of the vale presented a mass of foliage, spread with such rich profusion that it was impossible to determine of what description of trees it consisted. But perhaps there was nothing about the scenery I beheld more impressive than those silent cascades, whose slender threads of water, after leaping down the steep cliffs, were lost amidst the rich foliage of the valley. Over all the landscape there reigned the most hushed repose, which I almost feared to break, lest, like the enchanted gardens of the fairy tale, a single syllable might dissolve the spell." Toby was awakened and called into consultation. With his usual impetuosity, Toby wanted promptly to descend into the valley before them; but Melville restrained him, dwelling upon the perilous possibility of its inhabitants being Typees. Toby was with difficulty reined to circumspection, and off Melville and his companion started on a wild goose chase for a valley on the other side of the ridge. So fruitless and disheartening did this attempt prove, that Melville was reduced to the wan solace that it was, after all, better to die of starvation in Nukuheva than to be fed on salt beef, stale water and flinty bread in the forecastle of the *Acushnet.* Yet Toby was dauntless. Despite the defeats of the preceding day, Toby awoke on the following morning as blithe and joyous as a young bird. Melville's fever and his swollen leg, however, had left him not so exultant.

"What's to be done now?" Melville inquired, after their morning repast of a crumb of sweat-mixed biscuit and tobacco,—and rather doleful was his inquiry, he confesses.

"Descend into that same valley we descried yesterday," rejoined Toby, with a rapidity and loudness of utterance that led Melville to suspect almost that Toby had been slyly devouring the broadside of an ox in some of the adjoining thickets. "Come on, come on; shove ahead. There's a lively lad," shouted Toby as he led the way down a ravine that jagged steeply along boulders and tangled roots down into the valley; "never mind the rocks; kick them out of the way, as I do; and to-morrow, old fellow, take my word for it, we shall be in clover. Come on;" and so saying he dashed along the ravine like a madman.

Thus was piloted down into the heart of barbarism the man who was to emerge as the first Missionary Polynesia ever sent to Christendom. And on the chances of Toby's contagious impetuosity hung the annexation of a new realm to the king-dom of the imagination and the discovery of a new manner in the history of letters. For on that day, when Melville and Toby struggled down that ravine like Belzoni worming himself through the subterranean passages of the Egyptian catacombs, the Polynesians were without a competent apologist, and the literary possibilities of the South Seas were unsuspected.

Literature was, of course, already elaborated with fantas-tic patterns drawn from barbarism, and the Indians of Aphra Behn and Voltaire had given place to the redmen of Cooper. Earlier than this, however, the great discoverers, in their wealth of records, had given many an account of their con-tacts with savage peoples. But one searches in vain among these records for any very vivid sense that the savage and the Christian belong to the same order of nature. At best, one gathers the impression that in savagery God's image had been multiplied in an excess of contemptible counterfeits. Mel-ville reports that as late as his day "wanton acts of cruelty are not unusual on the part of sea captains landing at islands com-paratively unknown. Indeed, it is almost incredible, the light in which many sailors regard these naked heathens. They hardly consider them human. But it is a curious fact, that the more ignorant and degraded men are, the more contemptu-ously they look upon those whom they deem their inferiors." John G. Paton records in his *Autobiography* how, in 1860, three traders gleefully told him that to humble the natives of Tanna, and to diminish their numbers, they had let out on shore at different ports, four men ill with the measles—an ex-ceedingly virulent disease among savage peoples. "Our watch-words are," these jolly traders said, " 'sweep the creatures into the sea, and let white men occupy the soil.' " This senti-ment belongs more to a fixed human type, than to a period, of course: and that type has frequently taken to sailing strange seas. In treachery, cruelty, and profligacy, the exploits of European discoverers contain some of the rosiest pages in the history of villainy.

These sickening pages of civilised barbarism soon won to the savage ardent apologists, however, who applied an old technique of libel by imputing to the unbreeched heathen a touching array of the superior virtues. Montaigne was among the first to come forward in this capacity. "We may call them barbarous in regard to reasons rules," he said, "but not in respect to us that exceed them in all kinde of barbarisme. Their warres are noble and generous, and have as much excuse and beautie, as this humane infirmitie may admit: they ayme at nought so much, and have no other foundation amongst them, but the meere jelousie of vertue." Once in full current of idealisation Montaigne goes on to write as if he soberly believed that savage peoples were descended from a stock that Eve had conceived by an angel before the fall. In his dithyramb on the nobilities of savagery, Montaigne was unhampered by any first-hand dealings with savages, and he was far too wise ever to betray the remotest inclination to improve his state by migrating into the bosom of their uncorrupted nobility.

The myth of the "noble savage" was a taking conceit, however, and when Rousseau taught the world the art of reverie, he taught it also an easy vagabondage into the virgin forest and into the pure heart of the "natural man." In describing Rousseau's influence on the drawing rooms, Taine says that "The fops dreamed between two madrigals of the happiness of sleeping naked in the virgin forest." Rousseau's savage, "attached to no place, having no prescribed task, obeying no one, having no other law than his own will," was, of course, a wilful backward glance to the vanished paradise of childhood, not a finding of ethnology. Yet ethnology may prate as it will, the "noble savage" is a myth especially diverting to the oversophisticated, and like dreams of the virgin forest, thrives irrepressibly among the upholsterings of civilisation. The soft and ardent dreamer, no less than the sleek and parched imagination of Main Street, find compensation for the defeats of civilisation in dreams of a primitive Arcadia. While the kettle is boiling they relax into slippers and make the grand tour. Chateaubriand—whose life, according to Lemaître, was a "magnificent series of attitudes"—showed incredible hardihood of attitudinising in crossing the Atlantic in actual quest of the primitive. In the forest west of Albany he did pretend to find some satisfaction in wild landscape. He showed his "intoxication" at the beauties of wild nature by taking pains to do "various wilful things that made my guide furious." But Chateaubriand was less fortunate in his contact with savagery than he was with nature. His first savages he found under a shed taking dancing lessons from a little Frenchman, who, "bepowdered and befrizzled" was scraping on a pocket fiddle to the prancings of "ces messieurs sauvages et ces dames sauvagesses." Chateaubriand concludes with a reflection: "Was it not a crushing circumstance for a disciple of Rousseau?" And it is an indubitable fact that if the present-day disciples of the South Sea myth would show Chateaubriand's hardihood and migrate to Polynesia, they would find themselves in circumstances no less "crushing."

Melville was the first competent literary artist to write with authority about the South Seas. In his day, a voyage to those distant parts was a jaunt not lightly to be undertaken. In the Pacific there were islands to be discovered, islands to be annexed, and whales to be lanced. As for the incidental savage life encountered in such enterprise, that, in Montaigne's phrase, was there to be bastardised, by applying it to the pleasures of our corrupted taste. These attractions of whaling and patriotism—with incidental rites to Priapus—had tempted more than one man away from the comfort of his muffins, and more than one returned to give an inventory of the fruits of the temptation. The knowledge that these men had of Polynesia was ridiculously slight: the regular procedure was to shoot a few cannibals, to make several marriages after the manner of Loti. The result is a monotonous series of reports of the glorious accomplishments of Christians: varied on occasions with lengthy and learned dissertations on heathendom. But they are invariably writers with insular imagination, telling us much of the writer, but never violating the heart of Polynesia.

The Missionaries, discreetly scandalised at the exploitation of unholy flesh, went valiantly forth to fight the battle of righteousness in the midst of the enemy. The ·missionaries came to be qualified by long first-hand contact to write intimately of the heathen: but their records are redolent with sanctity, not sympathy. The South Sea vagabonds were the best hope of letters: but they all seem to have died without dictating their memoirs. William Mariner, it is true, thanks to a mutiny at the Tongo Islands in 1805, was "several years resident in those islands:" and upon Mariner's return, Dr. John Martin spent infinite patience in recording every detail of savage life he could draw from Mariner. Dr. Martin's book is still a classic in its way: detailed, sober, and naked of literary pretensions. This book is the nearest approach to *Typee* that came out of the South Seas before Melville's time. So numerous have been the imitators of Melville, so popular has been the manner that he originated, that it is difficult at the present day to appreciate the novelty of *Typee* at the time of its appearance. When we read Mr. Frederick O'Brien we do not always remember that Mr. O'Brien is playing "sedulous ape"—there is here intended no discourtesy to Mr. O'Brien— to Melville, but that in *Typee* and *Omoo* Melville was playing "sedulous ape" to nobody. Only when *Typee* is seen against the background of *A Missionary Voyage to the Southern Pacific Ocean performed in the years 1796, 1797, 1798 in the Ship Duff* (1799) and Mariner's *Tonga* (1816) (fittingly dedicated to Sir Joseph Banks, President of the Royal Society, and companion of Captain Cook in the South Seas) can Melville's originality begin to transpire.

This originality lies partly, of course, in the novelty of Melville's experience, partly in the temperament through which this experience was refracted. Melville himself believed his only originality was his loyalty to fact. He bows himself out of the Preface "trusting that his anxious desire to speak the ungarnished truth will gain him the confidence of his readers." When Melville's brother Gansevoort offered *Typee* for pub-

lication in England, it was accepted not as fiction but as ethnology, and was published as *Melville's Marquesas* only after
Melville had vouched for its entire veracity.

Though Melville published *Typee* upright in the conviction
that he had in its composition been loyal both to veracity and
truth, his critics were not prone to take him at his word. And
he was to learn, too, that veracity and truth are not interchangeable terms. Men do, in fact, believe pretty much what
they find it most advantageous to believe. We live by preju-
dices, not by syllogisms. In *Typee,* Melville undertook to show
from first-hand observation the obvious fact that there are two
sides both to civilisation and to savagery. He was among the
earliest of literary travellers to see in barbarians anything but
queer folk. He intuitively understood them, caught their
point of view, respected and often admired it. He measured
the life of the Marquesans against that of civilisation, and
wrote: "The term 'savage' is, I conceive, often misapplied,
and indeed when I consider the vices, cruelties, and enormities
of every kind that spring up in the tainted atmosphere of a
feverish civilisation, I am inclined to think that so far as the
relative wickedness of the parties is concerned, four or five
Marquesan Islanders sent to the United States as missionaries,
might be quite as useful as an equal number of Americans dispatched to the Islands in a similar capacity." Civilisation is
so inured to anathema,—so reassured by it, indeed,—that
Melville could write a vague and sentimental attack upon its
obvious imperfections with the cool assurance that each of his
readers, applying the charges to some neighbour, would ap-
prove in self-righteousness. But one ventures the "ungarnished truth" about any of the vested interests of civilisation
at the peril of his peace in this world and the next. It was
when Melville focussed his charge and wrote "a few passages
which may be thought to bear rather hard upon a reverend
order of men" with incidental reflections upon "that glorious
cause which has not always been served by the proceedings of
some of its advocates," that all the musketry of the soldiers of
the Prince of Peace was aimed at his head. Melville himself
was a man whose tolerance provoked those who sat in jealous

monopoly upon warring sureties to accuse him of license. He specifies his delight in finding in the valley of Typee that "an unbounded liberty of conscience seemed to prevail. Those who were pleased to do so were allowed to repose implicit faith in an ill-favoured god with a large bottle-nose and fat shapeless arms crossed upon his breast; whilst others worshipped an image which, having no likeness either in heaven or on earth, could hardly be called an idol. As the islanders always maintained a discrete reserve with regard to my own peculiar views on religion, I thought it would be excessively ill-bred in me to pry into theirs." This boast of delicacy did not pass unnoticed by "a reverend order of men." The vitriolic rejoinder of the London Missionary Society would seem to indicate that there may be two versions of "the ungarnished truth." It should be stated, however, that the English editions of *Typee* contain strictures against the Missionaries that were omitted in the American editions. But even Melville's unsanctified critics showed an anxiety to repudiate him. Both *Typee* and *Omoo* were scouted as impertinent inventions, defying belief in their "cool sneering wit and perfect want of heart." Melville's name was suspiciously examined as being a *nom de plume* used to cover a cowardly and supercilious libel. A gentleman signing himself G. W. P. and writing in the *American Review* (1847, Vol. IV, pp. 36-46) was scandalised by Melville's habit of presenting "voluptuous pictures, and with cool deliberate art breaking off always at the right point, so as without offending decency, he may excite unchaste desire." After discovering in Melville's writing a boastful lechery, this gentleman undertakes to discountenance Melville on three scores: (1) only the impotent make amorous boasts; (2) Melville had none of Sir Epicure Mammon's wished-for elixir; (3) the beauty of Polynesian women is all myth.

Unshaken in the conviction of his loyalty to fact, Melville discovered that the essence of originality lies in reporting "the ungarnished truth."

On the subject of "originality" in literature, Melville says in *Pierre:* "In the inferior instances of an immediate literary success, in very young writers, it would be almost invariably

observable, that for that instant success they were chiefly indebted to some rich and peculiar experience in life, embodied
in a book, which because, for that cause, containing original
matter, the author himself, forsooth, is to be considered
original; in this way, many very original books being the
product of very unoriginal minds." It is none the less true,
however, that though Melville and Toby both lived among the
cannibals, it was Melville, not Toby, who wrote *Typee*.

For four months Melville was held in friendly captivity by
the Typees. His swollen leg was healed by native doctors—
but not without prolonged pain and anxiety—he was fed, he
was amused, he was lionised by the valley. His hosts were
savages; they were idolaters, they were inhuman beasts who
licked their lips over the roasted thighs of their enemies; and
at the same time they were crowned with flowers, sometimes
exquisite in beauty, courteous in manners, and engaged all
day long in doing not only what they enjoyed doing, but what,
so far as Melville could judge, they had every right to enjoy
doing. With Toby, Melville was consigned to the household
of Kory-Kory. Kory-Kory, though a tried servitor and
faithful valet, was, Melville admits, in his shavings and tat-
toos, a hideous object to look upon—covered all over with
fish, fowl, and monster, like an illustrated copy of Goldsmith's
Animated Nature. Kory-Kory's father, Marheyo, a retired
gentleman of gigantic frame, was an eccentric old fellow, who
seems to have been governed by no fixed principles whatever.
He employed the greater part of his time in throwing up a
little shed just outside the house, tinkering away at it end-
lessly, without ever appearing to make any perceptible advance. He would eat, sleep, potter about, with fine contempt
for the proprieties of time or place. "Frequently he might
have been seen taking a nap in the sun at noonday, or a bath
in the stream at midnight. Once I beheld him eighty feet
from the ground, in the tuft of a cocoanut tree, smoking, and
often I saw him standing up to the waist in water, engaged
in plucking out the stray hairs of his beard, using a piece of
mussel-shell for tweezers. I remember in particular his having a choice pair of ear-ornaments, fabricated from the teeth

of some sea-monster. These he would alternately wear and take off at least fifty times in the course of a day, going and coming from his little hut on each occasion with all the tranquillity imaginable. Sometimes slipping them through the slits in his ears, he would seize his spear and go stalking beneath the shadows of the neighbouring groves, as if about to give a hostile meeting to some cannibal knight. But he would soon return again, and hiding his weapon under the projecting eaves of the house, and rolling his clumsy trinkets carefully in a piece of tappa, would resume his more pacific operations as quietly as if he had never interrupted them."

Kory-Kory's mother was, so Melville reports, the only industrious person in all the valley of Typee: "bustling about the house like a country landlady at an unexpected arrival: forever giving the young girls tasks to perform, which the little huzzies as often neglected; poking into every corner, and rummaging over bundles of old tappa, or making a prodigious clatter among the calabashes. She could not have employed her·elf more actively had she been left an exceedingly muscular and destitute widow, with an inordinate supply of young children, in the bleakest part of the civilised world." Yet was hers withal the kindliest heart imaginable. "Warm indeed," Melville says, "are my remembrances of the dear, good, affectionate old Tinor!"

There also belonged to the household, three young men, "dissipated, good-for-nothing, roystering blades of savages," and several girls. Of these, Melville has immortalised Fayaway, his most constant companion. He has anatomised her charms in the manner of his first *Fragment from a Writing-Desk*. But it is Fayaway in action, not Fayaway in still life, that survives in the imagination. At Melville's intercession, the taboo against women entering a boat was lifted. Many hours they spent together swimming, or floating in the canoe: diversions heightened in their heinousness by the fact that Fayaway for the most part clung to the primitive and summer garb of Eden—and the costume became her. Nor did Melville's depravity cease with his unblushing approval of nakedness. "Strange as it may seem," Melville writes in the

'40's, "there is nothing in which a young and beautiful female appears to more advantage than in the act of smoking." Fayaway not only smoked,—but she smoked a pipe, as they drifted in the canoe.   One day, as they were gliding along, Fayaway "seemed all at once to be struck with a happy idea. With a wild exclamation of delight, she disengaged from her person the ample robe of tappa which was knotted over her shoulder (for the purpose of shielding her from the sun), and spreading it out like a sail, stood erect with upraised arms in the head of the canoe.   We American sailors pride ourselves upon our straight clean spars, but a prettier mast than Fayaway made was never shipped aboard of any craft."   John La Farge has painted Fayaway in this attitude.

And the occupation of Toby during all this?   Soon after their arrival, Toby had been despatched to Nukuheva under pretence of procuring relief for Melville's swollen leg, actually to facilitate his and Melville's escape.   Toby never again returned to Typee.   He had been treacherously beguiled on board a whaler, unable to escape until he left his vessel at New Zealand.   "After some further adventures," says Melville in *The Story of Toby,* written in July, 1846, ten days after the two men discovered each other's existence through the instrumentality of *Typee,* and published as a "sequel" to that novel, "Toby arrived home in less than two years after leaving the Marquesas."

While Melville had the companionship of Toby in Typee, he was even then eager to get back to civilisation.   That savagery was good for savages he never wearied of contending.   But despite the idyllic delights of Typee—an idyll with a sombre background, however—Melville was never tempted to resign himself to its vacant animal felicity.   Melville, unlike Baudelaire and Whitman, was not stirred by the advantages of "living with the animals."   While among them, he evinced a desire neither to adopt their ways, nor to change them.   He made them pop-guns, he astonished them by exhibiting the miracle of sewing.   He tried to teach them to box.   "As not one of the natives had soul enough in him to stand up like a man, and allow me to hammer away at him, for my own personal satisfaction and that of the king, I was necessitated to fight with an imaginary enemy, whom I invariably made to knock under to my superior prowess."

Among the bachelors of the Ti, the men's club of the valley, he chatted, he smoked, he drowsed: he witnessed the Feast of the Calabashes when, for the livelong day "the drums sounded, the priests chanted, and the multitude roared and feasted"—a scene reminiscent of a University whole-heartedly given over to "campus activity." A mock battle was staged for his diversion. He entered the funeral fastnesses where the effigies of former heroes eternally paddled canoes adorned by the skulls of their enemies. He mused by pools, splashing with laughing bronze nymphs. Yet withal, Melville was a captive in the valley. His lameness, too, returned. His hosts began to make friendly but insistent suggestions that he be tattooed—a suggestion superlatively repugnant to him. He heard, moreover, the clamour of a cannibal feast, and lifted the cover of a tub under which lay a fresh human skeleton. Under these circumstances he taught old Marheyo two English words: *Home* and *Mother*. But he did not complete the trinity. *Forsan et haec olim meminisse juvabit.* It was time for him to depart.

One profoundly silent noon, as Melville lay lame and miserable under Kory-Kory's roof, Mow-Mow, the one-eyed chief, appeared at the door, and leaning forward towards Melville, whispered: *Toby pemi ena*—"Toby has arrived." That evening Mow-Mow's dead body floated on the Pacific, a boat-hook having been mortally hurled at his throat. And it was Melville who hurled the boat-hook.

An Australian whaler, touching at the harbour of Nuku-heva, had been informed of Melville's detention in Typee. Desirous of adding to his crew, the Captain had sailed round thither, and "hove to" off the mouth of the bay. Chary of the man-eating propensities of the Typees, the Captain sent in a boat-load of taboo natives from the other harbour, with an interpreter at their head, to procure Melville's release. Accompanied by a throng of armed natives, Melville was carried down to the shore—being too lame to walk the distance. A gun and an extravagant bounty of powder and calico were offered for Melville's release: but this bounty was clamorously and indignantly rejected. Karakoee, the head of the ransoming party, was menaced by furious gestures, and forced out into the sea, up to his waist in the surf. Blows were struck, wounds were given, and blood flowed. In the excitement of the fray, Melville was left to the guardianship of Marheyo, Kory-Kory, and Fayaway. Throwing to these three the articles that had been brought for his ransom, Melville bounded into the boat which was in immediate readiness to pull off towards the ship. It was not until the boat was about fifty yards from the shore that the savages recovered from their astonishment at Melville's alacrity in escape. Then Mow-Mow and six or seven warriors rushed into the sea and hurled their javelins at the retreating boat—and some of the weapons passed as close as was desirable. The wind was freshening every minute, and was right in the teeth of the retreating party. Karakoee, who was steering the boat, gave many a look towards a jutting point of the bay they had to pass. When they came within a hundred yards of the point, the savages on the shore dashed into the water, swimming out towards the boat: and by the time Melville's party reached the headland, the savages were spread right across the boat's course. The rowers got out their knives and held them ready between their teeth. Melville seized the boat-hook. Mow-Mow, with his tomahawk between his teeth, was nearest to the boat, ready the next instant to seize one of the oars. "Even at the moment I felt horror at the act I was to commit; but it was no time for pity or compunction, and with a true aim, and exerting all my strength, I dashed the boat-hook at him. I struck him below the throat, and forced him downward." Mow-Mow's body arose in the wake of the boat, but not to attack again. Another savage seized the gunwale, but the knives of the rowers so mauled his wrists, that before many moments the boat was past all the Typees, and in safety. In the closing tableau, Melville fell fainting into the arms of Karakoee.

Though later, when Melville was a sailor in the United

States Navy, he touched at the Marquesas, he never again set foot within the valley of Typee. Melville had known the Typees in their uncorrupted glory—strong, wicked, laughter-loving and clean. Mr. O'Brien visited Typee not many years ago, to find it pathetically fallen from its high estate. "I found myself," he says, "in a loneliness indescribable and terrible. No sound but that of a waterfall at a distance parted the sombre silence. . . . Humanity was not so much absent as gone, and a feeling of doom and death was in the motionless air, which lay like a weight, upon leaf and flower. The thin, sharp buzzing of the *nonos* was incessant." Mr. O'Brien discovered in the heart of the valley fewer than a dozen people who sat within the houses by cocoanut-husk fires, the acrid smoke of which daunted the *nonos*. "They have clung to their lonely *paepaes* despite their poverty of numbers and the ferocity of the *nonos*. They had clearings with cocoanuts and breadfruits, but they cared no longer to cultivate them, preferring rather to sit sadly in the curling fumes and dream of the past. One old man read aloud the *Gospel of St. John* in Marquesan, and the others listlessly listened, seeming to drink in little comfort from the verses, which he recited in the chanting monotone of their *uta*. . . . Nine miles in length is Typee, from a glorious cataract that leaps over the dark buttress wall where the mountain bounds the valley, to the blazing beach. And in all this extent of marvellously rich land, there are now this wretched dozen natives, too old or listless to gather their own food."

Thou hast conquered, O Galilean!

CHAPTER XI

"Ah, truant humour. But to me
That vine-wreathed urn of Ver, in sea
Of halcyons, where no tides do flow
Or ebb, but waves bide peacefully
At brim, by beach where palm trees grow
That sheltered Omai's olive race—
Tahiti should have been the place
For Christ in advent."
— HERMAN MELVILLE: *Clarel.*

IT was in the middle of a bright tropical afternoon that
Melville made good his escape from the valley of Typee. The
Australian whaler—called by Melville the *Julia*—which had
broken his four months' captivity, lay with her main-topsail
aback, about a league from the land. "She turned out to be
a small, slatternly looking craft, her hull and spars a dingy
black, rigging all slack and bleached nearly white, and everything denoting an ill state of affairs aboard. Leaning carelessly over the bulwarks were the sailors, wild, haggard-look-
ing fellows in Scotch caps and faded blue frocks; some of
them with cheeks of mottled bronze, to which sickness soon
changes the rich berry-brown of a seaman's complexion in the
tropics." So extraordinary was Melville's appearance—"a
robe of the native cloth was thrown over my shoulders, my
hair and beard were uncut, and I betrayed other evidences of
my recent adventure"—that as the boat came alongside, a low
cry ran fore and aft the deck. Immediately on gaining the
deck, Melville was beset on all sides by questions.

Indeed, never afterwards, it appears, could Melville escape
a like curiosity. Henceforth he was to be "the man who lived
among the cannibals." Nor does he always seem to have been
so uncommunicative as he grew in later years. In the Preface
to *Omoo,* after recording the fact that he kept no journal dur-

ing his wanderings in the South Seas, he says: "The frequency, however, with which these incidents have been verbally related, has tended to stamp them upon the memory." There is novelty in his logic: all twice-told tales are not always just-so stories. He says, too, in the Preface to *Typee:* "The incidents recorded in the following pages have often served, when 'spun as a yarn,' not only to relieve the weariness of many a night-watch at sea, but to excite the warmest sympathies of the author's shipmates."

Upon being taken aboard the *Julia,* Melville was almost immediately seen by the captain, a young, pale, slender, sickly looking creature, who signed Melville up for one cruise, engaging to discharge him at the next port.

Life on board the *Julia* was, if anything, worse than life on board the *Acushnet.* In the first place, Melville was ill. Not until three months after his escape from Typee did he regain his normal strength. And, as always, Melville looked back with regret upon leaving the life he had so wanted to escape from while he was in the midst of it. "As the land faded from my sight," he says, "I was all alive to the change in my condition. But how far short of our expectations is oftentimes the fulfilment of the most ardent hopes. Safe aboard of a ship—so long my earnest prayer—with home and friends once more in prospect, I nevertheless felt weighed down with a melancholy that could not be shaken off." Melville felt he was leaving cannibalism forever—and the departure shot a pang into his heart.

The ship's company were a sorry lot: reduced by desertion from thirty-two to twenty souls, and more than half of the remaining were more or less unwell from a long sojourn in a dissipated port. Some were wholly unfit for duty; one or two were dangerously ill. The rest managed to stand their watch, though they could do little. The crew was, for the most part, a typical whaling crew: "villains of all nations and dyes; picked up in the lawless Spanish Main, and among the savages of the islands." The provisions, too, on board the *Julia* were notoriously bad, even for a whaler. Melville's regret at leaving Typee was not mere wanton sentimentality.

The captain was despised by all aboard. He was commonly called "The Cabin Boy," "Paper Jack," "Miss Guy" and other descriptive titles. Though sheepish looking, he was a man of still, timid cunning that did not endear him to Melville.

The mate, John Jermin, was of the efficient race of short thick-set men: bullet headed, with a fierce little squint out of one eye, and a nose with a rakish tilt to one side. His was the art of knocking a man down with irresistible good humour, so the very men he flogged loved him like a brother. He had but one failing: he abhorred weak infusions, and cleaved manfully to strong drink. He was never completely sober: and when he was nearly drunk he was uncommonly obstreperous.

Jermin was master of every man aboard except the ship's carpenter,—a man so excessively ugly he went by the name of "Beauty." As ill-favoured as Beauty was in person, he was no less ugly in temper: his face had soured his heart. Melville witnessed an encounter between Jermin and Beauty: an encounter that showed up clearly the state of affairs on board. While Beauty was thrashing Jermin in the forecastle, the captain called down the scuttle: "Why, why, what's all this about? Mr. Jermin, Mr. Jermin—carpenter, carpenter: what are you doing down there? Come on deck; come on deck." In reply to this, Doctor Long Ghost cried out in a squeak, "Ah! Miss Guy, is that you? Now, my dear, go right home, or you'll get hurt." The captain dipped his head down the scuttle to make answer, to receive, full in the face, the contents of a tin of soaked biscuit and tea-leaves. Things were not well aboard the *Julia*.

But it was Doctor Long Ghost—he who so mocked the captain—who figures most largely in Melville's history: a man remarkable both in appearance and in personality. He was over six feet—a tower of bones, with a bloodless complexion, fair hair and a pale unscrupulous grey eye that twinkled occasionally with the very devil of mischief. At the beginning of the cruise of the *Julia*, as ship's doctor, he had lived in the cabin with the captain. But once on a time they had got into a dispute about politics, and the doctor, getting into a rage, had driven his argument home with his fist, and left the captain on the floor, literally silenced. The captain replied by shutting him up in his state-room for ten days on a diet of bread and water. Upon his release he went forward with his chests among the sailors where he was welcomed as a good fellow and an injured man.

The early history of Doctor Long Ghost he kept to himself; but it was Melville's conviction that he had certainly at some time or other spent money, drunk Burgundy, and associated with gentlemen. "He quoted Virgil, and talked of Hobbes of Malmsbury, besides repeating poetry by the canto, especially Hudibras." In the most casual manner, too, he could refer to an amour he had in Palermo, his lion hunting before breakfast among the Kaffirs, and the quality of coffee he had drunk in Muscat.

Melville was in no condition, physically, to engage in the ship's duties, so he and Doctor Long Ghost fraternised in the forecastle, where they were treated by the crew as distinguished guests. There they talked, played chess—with an outfit of their own manufacture—and there Melville read the books of the Long Doctor, over and over again, not omitting a long treatise on the scarlet fever.

At its best, the forecastle is never an ideal abode: but the forecastle of the *Julia*—its bunks half wrecked, its filthy sailors' pantry, and its plague of rats and cockroaches—must have made the *Highlander* seem as paradise in retrospect. The forecastle of the *Julia*, Melville says, "looked like the hollow of an old tree going to decay. In every direction the wood was damp and discoloured, and here and there soft and porous. Moreover, it was hacked and hewed without mercy, the cook frequently helping himself to splinters for kindling wood." The viciousness of the crew of the *Julia*, did not, of course, perceptibly enhance the charms of the forecastle. Nor was Melville's estate made more enviable when the man in the bunk next to his went wildly delirious. One night Melville was awakened from a vague dream of horrors by something clammy resting on him: his neighbour, with a stark stiff arm reached out into Melville's bunk, had during the night died. The crew rejoiced at his death.

For weeks the *Julia* tacked about among the islands of the South Seas. The captain was ill, and Jermin steered the *Julia,* to Tahiti, to arrive off the island the moment that Admiral Du Petit-Thouars was firing, from the *Reine Blanche,* a salute in honour of the treaty he had just forced Pomare to sign.

But to the astonishment of the crew, Jermin kept the ship at sea, fearing the desertion of all his men if he struck anchor. His purpose was to set the sick captain ashore, and to resume the voyage of the *Julia* at once, to return to Tahiti after a certain period agreed upon, to take the captain off. The crew were in no mood to view this manœuvre with indifference. Melville and Long Ghost cautioned them against the folly of immediate mutiny, and on the fly-leaf of an old musty copy of *A History of the Most Atrocious and Bloody Piracies,* a round-robin was indited, giving a statement of the crew's grievances, and concluding with the earnest hope that the consul would at once come off and see how matters stood. Pritchard, the missionary consul, was at that time in England; his place was temporarily filled by one Wilson, son of the well-known missionary of that name, and no honour to his ancestor. It did not promise well for the crew that Wilson was an old friend of Captain Guy's.

The round-robin was the prelude to iniquitous bullying and stupidity on the part of Wilson, Jermin, and Captain Guy. To the crew, it seemed that justice was poisoned at the fountain head. They gazed on the bitter waters, did a stout menagerie prance, and raged into mutiny. Then it was, after one of the men had all but succeeded in maliciously running the *Julia* straight upon a reef, that the good ship was piloted into the harbour of Papeetee, and the crew—including Melville and the Long Doctor, who were misjudged because of the company they kept—were for five days and nights held in chains on board the *Reine Blanche.* At the end of that time they were tried, one by one, before a tribunal composed of Wilson and two elderly European residents. Melville was examined last. One of the elderly gentlemen condescended to take a paternal interest in Melville. "Come here, my young friend," he said; "I'm extremely sorry to see you associated with these bad men; do you know what it will end in?" Melville was in no mood for smug and salvationly solicitations. He had already declared that his resolution with respect to the ship was unalterable: he stuck to this resolution. Wilson thereupon pronounced the whole crew clean gone in perversity, and steeped in abomination beyond the reach of clemency. He then summoned a fat old native, Captain Bob—and a hearty old Bob he proved—giving him directions to marshal the crew to a place of safe keeping.

Along the Broom Road they were led: and to Melville, escaped from the forecastle of the *Julia* and the confined decks of the frigate, the air breathed spices. "The tropical day was fast drawing to a close," he says; "and from where we were, the sun looked like a vast red fire burning in the woodlands—its rays falling aslant through the endless ranks of trees, and every leaf fringed with flame."

About a mile from the village they came to the *Calabooza Beretanee*—the English jail.

The jail was extremely romantic in appearance: a large oval native house, with a dazzling white thatch, situated near a mountain stream that, flowing from a verdant slope, spread itself upon a beach of small sparkling shells, and then trickled into the sea. But the jail was ill adapted for domestic comforts, the only piece of furniture being two stout pieces of timber, about twenty feet in length, gouged to serve as stocks. John La Farge, in his *Reminiscences of the South Seas,* says: "We try to find, by the little river that ends our walk, on this side of the old French fort, the calaboose where Melville was shut up. There is no one to help us in our search; no one remembers anything. Buildings occupy the spaces of woodland that Melville saw about him. Nothing remains but the same charm of light and air which he, like all others, has tried to describe and to bring back home in words. But the beach is still as beautiful as if composed by Claude Lorraine."

In this now-departed calaboose, Melville and the rest were kept in very lenient captivity by Captain Bob. Captain Bob's notion of discipline was delightfully vague. He insensibly remitted his watchfulness, and the prisoners were free to stroll further and further from the Calabooza. After about two weeks—for days melted deceptively into each other at Tahiti—the crew was again summoned before Wilson, again to declare themselves unshaken in their obstinate refusal to sail again with Captain Guy. So back to the Calabooza they were sent.

The English Missionaries left their cards at the Calabooza in the shape of a package of tracts; three of the French priests—whom the natives viewed, so Melville says, as "no better than diabolical sorcerers"—called in person. One of the priests—called by Melville, Father Murphy—discovered a compatriot among the crew, and celebrated the discovery by sending a present of a basket of bread. Such was the persuasion of the gift that, on Melville's count, "we all turned Catholics, and went to mass every morning, much to Captain Bob's consternation. He threatened to keep us in the stocks, if we did not desist."

After three weeks Wilson seems to have begun to suspect that it was not remotely impossible that he was making a laughing stock of himself in his futile attempt to break the mutineers into contrition. So off the *Julia* sailed, manned by a new crew. But before sailing, Jermin served his old crew the good turn of having their chests sent ashore. And when each was in possession of his sea-chest, the Calabooza was thronged with Polynesians, each eager to take a *tayo,* or bosom friend.

Though technically still prisoners, Melville and his former shipmates were allowed a long rope in their wanderings. Melville improved his leisure by attending, each Sunday, the services held in the great church which Pomare had built to be baptised in. In *Omoo,* Melville gives a detailed account of a typical Sabbath, and then launches into chapters of discussion upon the fruits of Christianity in Polynesia.

At church Melville had observed, among other puzzlingly incongruous performances, a young Polynesian blade standing up in the congregation in all the bravery of a striped calico shirt, with the skirts rakishly adjusted over a pair of white sailor trousers, and hair well anointed with cocoanut oil, ogling the girls with an air of supreme satisfaction. And of those who ate of the bread-fruit of the Eucharist in the morning, he knew several who were guilty of sad derelictions the same night. Desiring, if possible, to find out what ideas of religion were compatible with this behaviour, he and the Long Doctor called upon three sister communicants one evening. While the doctor engaged the two younger girls, Melville lounged on a mat with Ideea, the eldest, dallying with her grass fan, and improving his knowledge of Tahitian.

"The occasion was well adapted to my purpose, and I began.

" 'Ah, Ideea, mickonaree oee?' the same as drawling out— 'By the by, Miss Ideea, do you belong to the church?'

" 'Yes, me mickonaree,' was the reply.

"But the assertion was at once qualified by certain reservations; so curious that I cannot forbear their relation.

" 'Mickonaree *ena* (church member *here*), exclaimed she, laying her hand upon her mouth, and a strong emphasis on the adverb. In the same way, and with similar exclamations, she touched her eyes and hands. This done, her whole air changed in an instant; and she gave me to understand, by unmistakable gestures, that in certain other respects she was not exactly a 'mickonaree.' In short, Ideea was

> " 'A sad good Christian at the heart—
> A very heathen in the carnal part.' "

"The explanation terminated in a burst of laughter, in which all three sisters joined; and for fear of looking silly, the doctor and myself. As soon as good-breeding would permit, we took leave."

It is Melville's contention that the very traits in the Tahitians which induced the London Missionary Society to regard them as the most promising subjects for conversion, were, in fact, the most serious obstruction to their ever being Christians. "An air of softness in their manners, great apparent ingenuousness and docility, at first misled; but these were the mere accompaniments of an indolence, bodily and mental; a constitutional voluptuousness; and an aversion to the least restraint; which, however fitted for the luxurious state of nature, in the tropics, are the greatest possible hindrances to the strict moralities of Christianity." Of the Marquesans, Melville says in *Typee*: "Better it will be for them to remain the happy and innocent heathens and barbarians that they now are, than, like the wretched inhabitants of the Sandwich islands, to enjoy the mere· name of Christians without experiencing any of the vital operations of true religion, whilst, at the same time, they are made the victims of the worst vices and evils of civilised life."

Paul Gauguin, in his *Intimate Journals,* seems to share Melville's conviction that the Polynesians are disqualified by nature to experience "any of the vital operations of the spirit." In speaking of the attempts of the missionaries to introduce marriage into Polynesia he remarks cynically: "As they are going out of the church, the groom says to the maid of honour, 'How pretty you are!' And the bride says to the best man 'How handsome you are!' Very soon one couple moves off to the right and another to the left, deep into the underbrush where, in the shelter of the banana trees and before the Almighty, two marriages take place instead of one. Monseigneur is satisfied, and says, 'We are beginning to civilise them.' "

The good intentions of the Missionaries Melville does not question. But high faith and low intelligence is a dangerous if not uncommon mating of qualities. "It matters not," he says, "that the earlier labourers in the work, although strictly conscientious, were, as a class, ignorant, and in many cases, deplorably bigoted: such traits have, in some degree, characterised the pioneers of all faith. And although in zeal and disinterestedness, the missionaries now on the island are, perhaps, inferior to their predecessors, they have, nevertheless, in their own way, at least, laboured hard to make a Christian people of their charge."

As a result of this labour idolatry was done away with; the entire Bible was translated into Tahitian; the morality of the islanders was, on the whole, improved. These accomplishments Melville freely admits. But in temporal felicity, "the Tahitians are far worse off now than formerly; and although their circumstances, upon the whole, are bettered by the missionaries, the benefits conferred by the latter become utterly insignificant, when confronted with the vast preponderance of evil brought by other means." Melville found that there was still at Tahiti freedom and indolence; torches brandished in the woods at night; dances under the moon, and women decked with flowers. But he also found the Missionaries intent upon the abolition of the native amusements and customs—in their crowning efforts, decking the women out in hats "said to have been first contrived and recommended by the missionaries' wives; a report which, I really trust, is nothing but a scandal." To Melville's eyes, Tahiti was neither Pagan nor Christian, but a bedraggled bastard cross between the vices of two incompatible traditions. And in this blend he saw the promise of the certain extinction of the Polynesians. The Polynesians themselves were not blind to the doom upon them. Melville had heard the aged Tahitians singing in a low sad tone a song which ran: "The palm trees shall grow, the coral shall spread, but man shall cease."

Melville's plea was that Christendom treat Polynesia with reasonableness, and Christian charity: perhaps the two rarest qualities in the world. His plea was not without results; he unloosed upon himself exhibitions of venom of the wholehearted sort that enamour a misanthrope to life. The *Living Age* (Vol. XXVII) reprinted from the *Eclectic Review* a tribute which began: "Falsehood is a thing of almost invincible courage; overthrow it to-day, and with freshened vigour it will return to the lists to-morrow. *Omoo* illustrates this fact. We were under the illusion that the abettors of infidelity and the partisans of popery had been put to shame by the repeated refutation and exposure of their slanders against the Protestant Missions in Polynesia; but Mr. Melville's production proves that shame is a virtue with which these gentry are totally unacquainted, and that they are resharpening their missiles for another onset." This review then made it its object "to show that his statements respecting the Protestant

FIRST HOME OF THE PROTESTANT MISSIONARIES IN TAHITI
From a report of The London Missionary Society, published in 1799.

THE FLEET OF TAHITI
From an engraving after Hodges, the artist who accompanied
Captain Cook to the South Seas.

Mission in Tahiti are perversions of the truth—that he is guilty of deliberate and elaborate misrepresentation, and . . . that he is a prejudiced, incompetent, and truthless witness." It was taken for granted that Melville was guilty of the heinous crime of being a Catholic. From this presumption it was easy to understand that Melville's plea for sweetness and light was but the vicious ravings of a man "foiled and disappointed by the rejection of Mariolatry and the worship of wafers and of images, and of dead men by the Bible-reading Tahitians." By a convincing—if not cogent—technique of controversy, Melville's evidence was impugned by a discounting of the morals of the witness: a Catholic, and a disseminator of the "worst of European vices and the most dreadful of European diseases."

Melville was twenty-eight years old when he Quixotically championed the heathen in the name of a transcendental charity which he believed to be Christian. Amiable Protestant brethren undertook to disabuse him of his naive belief that the guardians of the faith of Christendom invariably regulate their conduct in the spirit of Christ. As Melville grew in wisdom he grew in disillusion: and his early tilt at the London Missionary Society contributed to his rapid growth. At the age of thirty-three he wrote in *Pierre*—a book planned to show the impracticability of virtue—that "God's truth is one thing, and man's truth another." He then maintained that the history of Christendom for the last 1800 years showed that "in spite of all the maxims of Christ, that history is as full of blood, violence, wrong, and iniquity of every kind, as any previous portion of the world's story." He says in *Clarel:*

> "The world is portioned out, believe:
> The good have but a patch at best,
> The wise their corner; for the rest—
> Malice divides with ignorance."

Melville points out that Christ's teachings seemed folly to the Jews because Christ carried Heaven's time in Jerusalem, while the Jews carried Jerusalem time there. "Did He not expressly say 'My wisdom is not of this world?' Whatever is really peculiar in the wisdom of Christ seems precisely the same folly to-day as it did 1850 years ago." In *Clarel,* he goes further, and calls the world

> "a den
> Worse for Christ's coming, since His love
> (Perverted) did but venom prove."

Though such a heretical idea was, to the Protestant brethren, of course, clean gone on the farthest side of damnation, yet were Melville and these same brethren working upon an identical major premise: each was righteously convinced that he was about his Father's business—each was attempting to rout the other in the name of Christ. The brethren rode forth in the surety of triumph; Melville retired within himself convinced that defeat was not refutation, and that his way had been, withal, the way of Heavenly Truth. And since his way bore but bitter fruit, he shook the dust of the earth from his feet, convinced that such soil was designed to nourish only iniquity. "Where is the earnest and righteous philosopher," he asks, framing his question to include himself in that glorious minority, "who looking right and left, and up and down through all the ages of the world, the present included; where is there such an one who has not a thousand times been struck with a sort of infidel idea, that whatever other worlds God may be Lord of, He is not Lord of this: for else this world would seem to give Him the lie; so utterly repugnant seem its ways to the instinctively known ways of Heaven." In this world, he grew to feel, a wise man resigns himself to the world's ways. "When we go to heaven," he taught, "it will be quite another thing. There, we can freely turn the left cheek, because the right cheek will never be smitten. There they can freely give all to the poor, for *there* there will be no poor to give to." And this, he contended, was a salutary doctrine: "I hold up a practical virtue to the vicious; and interfere not with the eternal truth, that, sooner or later, downright vice is downright woe." His milk of human kindness was not sweetened by the thunder of the Protestant brethren.

Resigned to the insight that while on earth no wise man aims at heaven except by a virtuous expediency, he accepted the London Missionary Society as one of the evils inherent in the universe, and leaving it to its own fate, looked prophetically forward to the Inter-Church World Movement. In *The Confidence Man* he makes one of the characters say: "Missions I would quicken with the Wall Street spirit. For if, confessedly, certain spiritual ends are to be gained but through the auxiliary agency of worldly means, then, to the surer gaining of such spiritual ends, the example of worldly policy in worldly projects should not by spiritual projectors be slighted. In brief, the conversion of the heathen, so far, at least, as depending on human effort, would, by the world's charity, be let out on contract. So much by bid for converting India, so much for Borneo, so much for Africa. You see, this doing good in the world by driblets is just nothing. I am for doing good in the world with a will. I am for doing good to the world once for all, and having done with it. Do but think of the eddies and maelstroms of pagans in China. People here have no conception of it. Of a frosty morning in Hong Kong, pauper pagans are found dead in the streets like so many nipped peas in a bin of peas. To be an immortal being in China is no more distinction than to be a snow-flake in a snow-squall. What are a score or two of missionaries to such a people? I am for sending ten thousand missionaries in a body and converting the Chinese *en masse* within six months of the debarkation. The thing is then done, and turn to something else." And in *Clarel*:

> "But preach and work:
> You'll civilise the barbarous Turk—
> Nay, all the East may reconcile:
> That done, let Mammon take the wings of even,
> And mount and civilise the saints in heaven."

But when Melville was in Tahiti he harboured less emancipated notions than he later achieved. He was then to all outward seeming little better than a beach-comber, disciplined for his participation in a mutiny he and the Long Doctor had ineffectively tried to prevent, and in the end abandoned by his ecclesiastical guardians to drift among the natives of Tahiti, and to find his way back home any way he could.

The authorities at Tahiti left the party at the Calabooza to its own disintegration: a sore on the island cured not by surgery but by neglect. Gradually the mutineers melted out of sight.

With the Long Doctor, Melville sailed across to the neighbouring island of Imeeo, there to hire themselves out as field-labourers to two South Sea planters: one a tall, robust Yankee, born in the backwoods of Maine, sallow, and with a long face; the other, a short florid little Cockney. This strange pair had cleared about thirty acres in the isolation of the wild valley of Martair, where they worked with invincible energy, and struggling against all odds to farm in Polynesia, and with Heaven knows what ideas of making a fortune on their crude plantation.

Melville had tried farming in Pittsfield, and he liked the labour even less in Polynesia than he did in Christendom. The Long Doctor throve not at all hoeing potatoes under a tropical sun, all the while saying masses as he watered the furrows with his sweat. Both Melville and the Long Doctor enjoyed the hunt they took in the wilds of the mountains: but back to the mosquitoes, the sweet-potatoes, and the hardships of agriculture, they decided to launch forth again upon the luck of the open road. What clothes they had were useless rags. So barefooted, and garbed like comic opera brigands or mendicant grandees, they started out on a tour of discovery around the island of Imeeo. After about ten days of pleasant adventure and hospitality from the natives they arrived at Partoo-wye to be accepted into the household of an aristocratic-looking islander named Jeremiah Po-Po, and his wife Arfretee. This was a household of converts: "Po-Po was, in truth, a Christian," Melville says: "the only one, Arfretee excepted, whom I personally knew to be such, among all the natives of Polynesia."

Arfretee fitted out Melville and the Doctor each with a new sailor frock and a pair of trousers: and after a bath, a pleasant dinner, and a nap, they came forth like a couple of bridegrooms.

Melville was in Partoowye, as guest of Po-Po, for about five weeks. At that time it was believed that Queen Pomare—who was then in poor health and spirits, and living in retirement in Partoowye—entertained some idea of making a stand against the French. In this event, she would, of course, be glad to enlist all the foreigners she could. Melville and the Long Doctor played with the idea of being used by Pomare as officers, should she take to warlike measures. But in this scheme they won little encouragement. For though Pomare had, previous to her misfortunes, admitted to her levees the humblest sailor who cared to attend upon Majesty, she was, in her eclipse, averse to receiving calls.

Shut off from an immediate prospect of interviewing Pomare, Melville improved his time by studying the native life, and by visiting a whaler in the harbour—the *Leviathan*—taking the precaution to secure himself a bunk in the forecastle should he fail of a four-poster at Court. His heart warmed to the *Leviathan* after his first visit of inspection on board. "Like all large, comfortable old whalers, she had a sort of motherly look:—broad in the beam, flush decks, and four chubby boats hanging at her breast." The food, too, was promising. "My sheath-knife never cut into better sea-beef. The bread, too, was hard, and dry, and brittle as glass; and there was plenty of both." The mate had a likeable voice: "hearing it was as good as a look at his face." But Melville still clung to the hope of winning the ear of Pomare. Although there was, Melville says, "a good deal of waggish comrades' nonsense" about his and Long Ghost's expectation of court preferment, "we nevertheless really thought that something to our advantage might turn up in that quarter."

Pomare was then upward of thirty years of age; twice stormily married; and a good sad Christian again,—after lapses into excommunication; she eked out her royal exchequer by going into the laundry business, publicly soliciting, by her agents, the washing of the linen belonging to the officers of ships touching in her harbours. Her English sister, Queen

Victoria, had sent her a very showy but uneasy headdress—
a crown. Having no idea of reserving so pretty a bauble for
coronation days, which came so seldom, her majesty sported it
whenever she appeared in public. To show her familiarity
with European customs, she touched it to all foreigners of
distinction—whaling captains and the like—whom she happened to meet in her evening walk on the Broom Road.

Melville discovered among Pomare's retinue a Marquesan
warrior, Marbonna,—a wild heathen who scorned the vices
and follies of the Christian court of Tahiti and the degeneracy of the people among whom fortune had thrown him.
Through the instrumentality of Marbonna, who officiated as
nurse of Pomare's children, Melville and the Doctor at last
found themselves admitted into the palace of Pomare.

"The whole scene was a strange one," Melville says; "but
what most excited our surprise was the incongruous assem-
blage of the most costly objects from all quarters of the globe.
Superb writing-desks of rosewood, inlaid with silver and
mother-of-pearl; decanters and goblets of cut glass; embossed
volumes of plates; gilded candelabras; sets of globes and
mathematical instruments; laced hats and sumptuous garments
of all sorts were strewn about among greasy calabashes half-
filled with *poee,* rolls of old tappa and matting, paddles and
fish-spears. A folio volume of Hogarth lay open, with a
cocoanut shell of some musty preparation capsized among
the miscellaneous furniture of the Rake's apartment."

While Melville and the Doctor were amusing themselves in
this museum of curiosities, Pomare entered, unconscious of
the presence of intruders.

"She wore a loose gown of blue silk, with two rich shawls,
one red, the other yellow, tied about her neck. Her royal
majesty was barefooted. She was about the ordinary size,
rather matronly; her features not very handsome; her mouth
voluptuous; but there was a care-worn expression in her
face, probably attributable to her late misfortunes. From
her appearance, one would judge her about forty; but she is
not so old. As the Queen approached one of the recesses, her
attendants hurried up, escorted her in, and smoothed the mats

on which she at last reclined. Two girls soon appeared, carrying their mistress' repast; and then, surrounded by cut glass and porcelain, and jars of sweetmeats and confections, Pomare Vahinee I., the titular Queen of Tahiti, ate fish and *poee* out of her native calabashes, disdaining either knife or spoon."

The interview between the Queen and her visitors was brief. Long Ghost strode up bravely to introduce himself. The natives surrounding the Queen screamed. Pomare looked up, surprised and offended, and waved the Long Doctor and Melville out of the house. Though Melville was later to view a South American King, was to win the smile of Victoria and meet Lincoln, Pomare was the first and only Polynesian Queen he ever saw.

Disappointed at going to court, feeling that they could no longer trespass on Po-Po's hospitality, "and then, weary somewhat of life in Imeeo, like all sailors ashore, I at last pined for the billows."

The Captain of the *Leviathan*—a native of Martha's Vineyard—was unwilling without persuasion to accept Melville, however. What with Melville's associations with Long Ghost, and the British sailor's frock Arfretee had given him, the Captain suspected Melville of being from Sydney: a suspicion not intended as flattery. Unaccompanied by Long Ghost, Melville finally interviewed the Captain, to find that worthy mellowed at the close of a spirituous dinner. "After looking me in the eye for some time, and by so doing, revealing an obvious unsteadiness in his own visual organs, he begged me to reach forth my arm. I did so; wondering what on earth that useful member had to do with the matter in hand. He placed his fingers on my wrist; and holding them there for a moment, sprang to his feet; and, with much enthusiasm, pronounced me a Yankee, every beat of my pulse." Another bottle was called, which the captain summarily beheaded with the stroke of a knife, commanding Melville to drain it to the bottom. "He then told me that if I would come on board his vessel the following morning, I would find the ship's articles on the cabin transom. . . . So, hurrah for the coast of Japan! Thither the ship was bound."

The Long Doctor, on second thought, decided to eschew the sea for a space. A last afternoon was spent with Po-Po and his family. "About nightfall, we broke away from the generous-hearted household and hurried down to the water. It was a mad, merry night among the sailors. An hour or two after midnight, everything was noiseless; but when the first streak of dawn showed itself over the mountains, a sharp voice hailed the forecastle, and ordered the ship unmoored. The anchors came up cheerily; the sails were soon set; and with the early breath of the tropical morning, fresh and fragrant from the hillsides, we slowly glided down the bay, and we swept through the opening in the reef."

Melville never saw or heard from Long Ghost after their parting on that morning.

CHAPTER XII

ON BOARD A MAN-OF-WAR

"Oh, give me the rover's life—the joy, the thrill, the whirl! Let me feel thee again, old sea! let me leap into the saddle once more. I am sick of these terra firma toils and cares; sick of the dust and reek of towns. Let me hear the clatter of hailstones on icebergs. Let me snuff thee up, sea-breeze! and whinny in thy spray. Forbid it, sea-gods! intercede for me with Neptune, O sweet Amphitrite, that no dull clod may fall on my coffin! Be mine the tomb that swallowed up Pharaoh and all his hosts; let me lie down with Drake, where he sleeps in the sea."
—HERMAN MELVILLE: *White-Jacket.*

In 1898, there appeared the *Memories of a Rear-Admiral Who Has Served for More Than Half a Century in the Navy of the United States.* S. R. Franklin, the author of this volume, had lived a long and useful life, with no design during his years of activity, it would seem, of bowing himself out of the world as a man-of-letters. But in the leisure of elderly retirement, he was persuaded by his friends to get rid of his reminiscences once for all by putting them into a book. Rear-Admiral Franklin took an inventory of his rich life, and accepted the challenge. Had he not roamed about the globe since he was sixteen years of age? And he had known a dozen famous Admirals, three Presidents, three Emperors, two Popes, five Christian Kings and a properly corresponding number of Queens, not to mention a whole army of lesser notables.

In 1842, as midshipman aboard the *United States* frigate, Franklin cruised the Pacific. The *United States* stopped at Honolulu, touched at the Marquesas. Franklin reports that the Bay of Nukuheva "makes one of the most beautiful harbours I have ever seen." But upon the natives he bestowed the contempt of a civilised man: "for the Marquesans were cannibals of the worst kind, and no one who desired to escape roasting ever ventured away from the coast." The *United States* did not remain long in these waters, "where there was nothing to do but look at a lot of half-naked savages." So off sailed the frigate to Tahiti, where a queen came aboard. But Franklin cannot remember whether it was Pomare or some other queen: "Ladies of that rank were not uncommon in those days in the South Seas."

Franklin had then been cruising among the islands of the Pacific for some months, and he was "not sorry when the time came to get under way for the coast." Men of Franklin's type are a credit to civilisation: men proud of their heritage, but unobtrusive in their pride. Franklin was unmoved by any sanctimonious hankering to improve the heathen, or by any romantic anxiety to ease into the mud of barbarism. "Savage and half-civilised life becomes very irksome," he says, "when the novelty is worn off."

"At Tahiti," he goes on to state, "we picked up some seamen who were on the Consul's hands. They were entered on the books of the ship, and became a portion of the crew. One of the number was Herman Melville, who became famous afterwards as a writer and an admiralty lawyer. He had gone to sea for his health, and found himself stranded in the South Pacific. I do not remember what the trouble was, but he and his comrades had left the ship of which they were a portion of the crew. Melville wrote a book, well known in its day, called *White-Jacket,* which had more influence in abolishing corporal punishment in the Navy than anything else. This book was placed on the desk of every member of Congress, and was a most eloquent appeal to the humane sentiment of the country. As an evidence of the good it did, a law was passed soon after the book appeared abolishing flogging in the Navy absolutely, without substituting any other mode of punishment in its stead; and this was exactly in accord with Melville's appeal."

"I do not think that I remember Melville at all," Franklin goes on to say; "occasionally will flash across my memory a maintop-man flitting across about the starboard gangway with a white jacket on, but there is not much reality in the picture which it presents to my mind. In his book he speaks of a certain seaman, Jack Chase, who was Captain of the maintop, of whom I have a very distinct recollection. He was about

as fine a specimen of seaman as I have ever seen in all my
cruising. He was not only that, but he was a man of intelligence, and a born leader. His top-mates adored him, although he kept them up to the mark, and made every man do
his share of work. Melville has given him considerable space
in his book, and seems to have had intense admiration for
him. He mentions also a number of officers whom it is not
difficult to recognise. The Commanding Officer, who had a
very red face, he called Captain Claret; a small but very energetic Midshipman, who made himself felt and heard about
the decks, he called Mr. Pert; the Gunner was 'Old Combustibles.' He gives no names, but to any one who served in
the Frigate *United States* it was easy to recognise the men by
their sobriquets. Melville certainly did a grand work in bringing his ability as a writer and his experience as a seaman to
bear upon the important matter—I mean corporal punishment
—which had been the subject of so much discussion in and
out of Congress."

The essential accuracy of Melville's account of life on board
the Frigate *United States* is thus, in the above as in other passages, vouched for by a Rear-Admiral. Franklin, himself,
however, is not exhaustively familiar with the life and works
of Melville, making him an "admiralty lawyer" who went to
sea for his health. And according to Franklin's account, Melville shipped on board the *United States* from Tahiti. According to Melville's own account, he left Eimeo—from the
harbour of Tamai—not on board a man-of-war, but on board
an American whaler bound for the fishing grounds off Japan.

The itinerary of Melville's rovings in the Pacific after he
left Tahiti cannot be stated with any detailed precision. In
an Appendix to the American edition of *Typee,* Melville says:
"During a residence of four months at Honolulu, the author
was in the confidence of an Englishman who was much employed by his lordship"—Sir George Paulet. In both *Typee*
and *Omoo* he speaks of conditions in the Sandwich Islands
with the familiarity of first-hand observation. The Frigate
United States sailed from Hampton Roads early in January,
1842. It doubled the Horn late in February, and joined the

Pacific squadron at Valparaiso. After spending the winter of 1842-3 off Monterey, the *United States* returned to Callao in the spring, and sailed for Honolulu, arriving in the early summer of 1843. According to his own account, Melville left Tahiti in the autumn of 1842. The *United States* left Tahiti in the summer of 1843. Melville speaks of revisiting the Marquesas and Tahiti after the experiences recorded in *Typee* and *Omoo*. In *Typee* he says: "Between two and three years after the adventures recorded in this volume, I chanced, while aboard a man-of-war, to touch at these islands"—the Marquesas. Though in this statement Melville is patently careless in his chronology, there is no reason to doubt his geography. According to the hypothesis that offers fewest difficulties—and none of these at all serious—it would appear that Melville left the Society Islands in the autumn of 1842, on board a whaler bound for the coast of Japan, to arrive in Honolulu some time in the early part of 1843, where, according to Arthur Stedman, he was "employed as a clerk." In the Introductory Note to *White-Jacket* he says: "In the year 1843 I shipped as 'ordinary seaman' on board a United States frigate, then lying in a harbour of the Pacific Ocean. After remaining in the frigate for more than a year, I was discharged from the service upon the vessel's arrival home." Melville was discharged in Boston, in October, 1844. It would appear that Melville shipped on board the *United States,* from Honolulu, in the summer of 1843, touching again at the Marquesas and at Tahiti, and returning home by way of the Peruvian ports.

Of Melville's experiences between the time of his leaving the Society Islands and that of his homeward cruise as a sailor in the United States Navy, nothing is known beyond the meagre details already stated.

In *White-Jacket; or, the World in a Man-of-War* (1850) Melville has left a fuller account, however, of his experiences on board the *United States*. The opening of *White-Jacket* finds Melville at Callao, on the coast of Peru—the last harbour he touched in the Pacific. In *Typee* and *Omoo* he had already recounted his adventures in the South Seas, with all the crispness and lucidity of fresh discovery. While on board the *United States* he returned to old harbours, and sailed past familiar islands. But *White-Jacket* is not a *Yarrow Revisited.* On the showing of *White-Jacket,* Melville's life in the navy was, perhaps, the happiest period in his life. It is true that in *Typee* he wrote: "I will frankly confess that after passing a few weeks in the valley of the Marquesas, I formed a higher estimate of human nature than I had ever before entertained. But, alas, since then I have been one of the crew of a man-of-war, and the pent-up wickedness of five hundred men has nearly overturned all my previous theories." And in *White-Jacket* he has many a very dark word to say for the navy. Sailors, as a class, do, of course, entertain liberal notions concerning the Decalogue; but in this they resemble landsmen, both Christian and cannibal. And in Melville's day—as before and after—from a frigate's crew might be culled out men of all callings and vocations, from a backslidden parson to a broken-down comedian. It is an old saying that "the sea and the gallows refuse nothing." But withal, more than one good man has been hanged. "The Navy," Melville says, "is the asylum for the perverse, the home of the unfortunate. Here the sons of adversity meet the children of calamity, and here the children of calamity meet the offspring of sin." According to this version, a typical man-of-war was a sort of State Prison afloat. "Wrecked on a desert shore," Melville says, "a man-of-war's crew could quickly found an Alexandria by themselves, and fill it with all the things which go to make up a capital." The *United States,* surely, lacked in none of the contradictions that go to make up a metropolis: "though boasting some fine fellows here and there, yet, on the whole, charged to the combings of hatchways with the spirit of Belial and unrighteousness." Or it was like a Parisian lodging house, turned upside down: the first floor, or deck, being rented by a lord; the second by a select club of gentlemen; the third, by crowds of artisans; and the fourth—on a man-of-war a basement of indefinite depth, with ugly-looking fellows gazing out at the windows—by a whole rabble of common people.

The good or bad temper, the vices and virtues of men-of-war's men were in a great degree attributable, Melville states, to their particular stations and duties aboard ship. Melville congratulated himself upon enjoying one of the most enviable posts aboard the frigate. It was Melville's office to loose the main-royal when all hands were called to make sail: besides his special offices in tacking ship, coming to anchor, and such like, he permanently belonged to the starboard watch, one of the two primary grand divisions of the ship's company. And in this watch he was a main-top-man; that is, he was stationed in the main-top, with a number of other seamen, always in readiness to execute any orders pertaining to the main-mast, from above the main-yard. In Melville's time, the tops of a frigate were spacious and cosy. They were railed in behind so as to form a kind of balcony, that looked airily down upon the blue, boundless, dimpled, laughing, sunny sea, and upon the landlopers below on the deck, sneaking about among the guns. It was a place, too, to test one's manhood in rough weather. From twenty to thirty loungers could agreeably recline there, cushioning themselves on old sails and jackets. In being a main-top-man, Melville prided himself that he belonged to a fraternity of the most liberal-hearted, lofty-minded, gay, elastic, and adventurous men on board ship. "The reason for their liberal-heartedness was, that they were daily called upon to expatiate themselves all over the rigging. The reason for their lofty-mindedness was, that they were high lifted above the petty tumults, carping cares, and paltrinesses of the decks below." And Melville attributed it to his having been a main-top-man, and that in the loftiest yard of the frigate, the main-royal-yard, "that I am now enabled to give such a free, broad, off-hand, bird's-eye, and more than all, impartial account of our man-of-war world; withholding nothing; inventing nothing; nor flattering, nor scandalising any; but meting out to all—commodore and messenger boy alike—their precise descriptions and deserts."

Melville says that the main-top-men, with amiable vanity, accounted themselves the best seamen in the ship; brothers one and all, held together by a strong feeling of *esprit de corps*. Their loyalty was especially centred in their captain, Jack Chase—a prime favourite and an oracle among the men.

Upon Jack Chase's instigation they all wore their hats at a peculiar angle; he instructed them in the tie of their neck handkerchiefs; he protested against their wearing vulgar *dungaree* trousers; he gave them lessons in seamanship. And he solemnly conjured them, with unmitigated detestation, to eschew the company of any sailor suspected of having served in a whaler.. On board the *United States,* Melville wisely held his peace "concerning stove boats on the coast of Japan."

Melville's admiration for Jack Chase was perhaps the happiest wholehearted surrender he ever gave to any human being. Jack Chase was "a Briton and a true-blue; tall and well-knit, with a clear open eye, a fine broad brow, and an abounding nut-brown beard. No man ever had a better heart or a bolder. He was loved by the seamen and admired by the officers; and even when the captain spoke to him, it was with a slight air of respect. No man told such stories, sang such songs, or with greater alacrity sprang to his duty. The main-top, over which he presided, was a sort of oracle of Delphi; to which many pilgrims ascended, to have their perplexities or difficulties settled." Jack was a gentleman. His manners were free and easy, but never boisterous; "he had a polite, courteous way of saluting you, if it were only to borrow a knife. He had read all the verses of Byron, all the romances of Scott; he talked of Macbeth and Ulysses; but above all things was he an ardent admirer of Camoen's *Lusiad,* part of which he could recite in the original." He spoke a variety of tongues, and was master of an incredible richness of Byronic adventure. "There was such an abounding air of good sense and good feeling about the man that he who could not love him, would thereby pronounce himself a knave. I thanked my sweet stars that kind fortune had placed me near him, though under him, in the frigate; and from the outset, Jack and I were fast friends. Wherever you may be now rolling over the blue billows, dear Jack, take my best love along with you," Melville wrote; "and God bless you, wherever you go." And this sentiment Melville cherished throughout his life. Almost the last thing Melville ever wrote was the dedication of his last novel, *Billy Budd*—existing only in manuscript, and completed three months before his death—to "Jack Chase, Englishman, wherever that great heart may now be, Here on earth or harboured in Paradise, Captain in the war-ship in the year 1843, In the U. S. Frigate *United States.*"

In *White-Jacket,* Melville glows with the same superlative admiration for Jack Chase that Ouida, or the Duchess, exhibit in portraying their most irresistible cavaliers; an enthusiasm similar to that of Nietzsche's for his Ubermensch. So contagious is Melville's love for his ship-mate that strange infections seem to have been caught therefrom. Though it is certainly not true that "all the world loves a lover," Melville's affection for Jack Chase won him at least one rather startling proof that Shakespeare's dictum is not absolutely false. The proof came in the following form:

"No 2 Guthuee Port, Arbrooth 13 May 1857
"Herman Melville Esquire
"Author of the white Jacket Mardi and others, Honour'd Sir Let it not displease you to be addressed by a stranger to your person not so to your merits, I have read the white jacket with much pleasure and delight 'I found it rich in wisdom and brilliant with beauty, ships and the sea and those who plow it with their belongings on shore—those subjects are idintified with Herman Melvil's name for he has most unquestioneably made them his own,, No writer not even Marryat himself has observed them more closely or pictured them more impressively, a delightful book it is. I long exceedingly to read Mardi, but how or where to obtain it is the task? I have just now received an invitation to cross the Atlantic from a Mr and Mrs Weed Malta between Bolston springs and saratoga Countie, ,, as also from Mr Alexer Muler my own Cousin, Rose bank Louistown

"I have for this many a day been wishing to see you 'to hear you speak to breath the same air in which you dwell' Are you the picture of him you so powerfully represent as the Master piece of all Gods works Jack Chase?—

"write me dear sir and say where Omidi 'sto be gote, I do much admire the American Authors Washington Irver **Mrs**

Stowe Allan Edgar Po the Late James Abbott and last though not least your good self— Did you ever read the history of Jeffery Rudel he was a young Noble man of Provence and reconed one of the handsomest and polite persons of his age. he lived in the time of Richard the first sir named cour de Lion who invited Jeffery to his court and it was there he first heard of the beauty wit, learning and virtue of the Countess of Tripoly by which he became so enamoured that he resolved upon seeing her purchased a vesel and in opesition to the King and the luxury of a Court set sail for Tripoly the obgect of his affections realised his most sanguine expectations.

"were you to cross the atlantic you should receive a cordeial reception from Mr George Gordon my-beloved & only brother & I'd bid you welcome to old s"t Thomas a Becket famed for kindness to strangers.—

"permite me Dear Sir to subskribe myself your friend although unseen and at a Distance   "Eliza Gordon

"Heaven first sent letters,
  For some wretches aid,
  Some banished Lover
  Or some Captive maid
            "Pope."

Besides the "Master piece of all Gods works Jack Chase" and his comrades of the main-top, Melville was fortunate in finding a few other ship-mates to admire. There was Lemsford, "a gentlemanly young member of the after-guard," a poet, to whose effusions Melville was happy to listen. "At the most unseasonable hours you would behold him, seated apart, in some corner among the guns—a shot-box before him, pen in hand, and eyes 'in a fine frenzy rolling.' Some deemed him a conjurer; others a lunatic. The knowing ones said that he must be a crazy Methodist." Another of Melville's friends was Nord. Before Melville knew him, he "saw in his eye that the man had been a reader of good books; I would have staked my life on it, that he had seized the right meaning of Montaigne." With Nord, Melville "scoured all the prairies of reading; dived into the bosoms of authors, and tore out their hearts." Melville's friend Williams "was a thorough-going Yankee from Maine, who had been both a pedlar and a pedagogue in his day. He was honest, acute, witty, full of mirth and good humour—a laughing philosopher." Beyond these, Melville was chary of his friendship, despite the personal intimacies imposed by the crowded conditions on shipboard. For living on board a man-of-war is like living in a market, where you dress on the doorsteps and sleep in the cellar.

Yet even on board the *United States* Melville did find it possible to get some solitude. "I am of a meditative humour," he says, "and at sea used often to mount aloft at night, and, seating myself on one of the upper yards, tuck my jacket about me and give loose to reflection. In some ships in which I have done this, the sailors used to fancy that I must be studying astronomy—which, indeed, to some extent, was the case. For to study the stars upon the wide, boundless ocean, is divine as it was to the Chaldean Magi, who observed their revolutions from the plain."

Melville was not only fortunate in his friends on the top, and above, but also in the mess to which he belonged: "a glorious set of fellows—Mess No. 1!—numbering, among the rest, my noble Captain Jack Chase. Out of a pardonable self-conceit they called themselves the *Forty-two-pounder Club;* meaning that they were, one and all, fellows of large intellectual and corporeal calibre."

In *White-Jacket,* Melville's purpose was to present the variegated life aboard a man-of-war; to give a vivid sense of the complexity of the typical daily existence aboard a floating armed city inhabited by five hundred male human beings. And no one else has ever done this so successfully as has Melville. "I let nothing slip, however small," he says; "and feel myself actuated by the same motive which has prompted many worthy old chroniclers to set down the merest trifles concerning things that are destined to pass entirely from the earth, and which, if not preserved in the nick of time, must infallibly perish from the memories of man. Who knows that this humble narrative may not hereafter prove the history of an obsolete barbarism?" For *White-Jacket* is, certainly, written with no intent to glorify

war. It is a book that a militaristic country would do well
to suppress. "Courage," Melville teaches therein, "is the most
common and vulgar of the virtues." Of a celebrated and
dauntless fighter he says: "a hero in this world;—but what
would they have called him in the next?" "As the whole matter of war is a thing that smites common sense and Christianity in the face," he contends, "so everything connected with
it is utterly foolish, unchristian, barbarous, brutal, and savour-
ing of the Feejee Islands, cannibalism, saltpetre, and the
devil."

But Melville's anti-militaristic convictions in no sense perverted his astonishingly vital presentation of life on board
the *United States*. Though in contemplation he despised war,
and was open-eyed to the abuses and iniquity on all sides of
him on board the frigate; in actual fact he seems to have been
unusually happy as a sailor in the navy, among his comrades
of the top. The predominant mood of the book is the rollick-
ing good-humour of high animal spirits.

There were black moments in his pleasant routine, however:
the terrible nipping cold, and blasting gales, and hurricanes of
sleet and hail in which he furled the main-sail in rounding Cape
Horn; the flogging he witnessed; his watches at the cot of his
mess-mate Shenley in the subterranean sick-bay, and Shenley's death and burial at sea; the barbarous amputation he
witnessed, and the death of the sick man at the hands of the
ship's surgeon—a scene that Flaubert might well have been
proud to have written.* And there were ugly experiences during the cruise that were among the most lurid in his life.

Throughout the cruise, it seems, for upward of a year he
had been an efficient sailor, alert in duties, circumspect in his
pleasures, liked and respected by his comrades. The ship
homeward bound, and he within a few weeks of being a free-
man, he heard the boatswain's mate bawling his name at all
the hatchways and along the furtherest recesses of the ship:
the Captain wanted him at the mast. Melville's heart jumped
to his throat at the summons, as he hurriedly asked Fluke, the
boatswain's mate at the fore-hatchway, what was wanted
of him.

"Captain wants you at the mast," Fluke replied. "Going to flog ye, I guess."

"For what?"

"My eyes! you've been chalking your face, hain't ye?"

Swallowing down his heart, he saw, as he passed through the gangway to the dread tribunal of the frigate, the quarter-master rigging the gratings; the boatswain with his green bag of scourges; the master-at-arms ready to help off some one's shirt. On the charge of a Lieutenant, Melville was accused by the Captain of failure in his duty at his station in the star-board main-lift: a post to which Melville had never known he was assigned. His solemn disclaimer was thrown in his teeth, and for a thing utterly unforeseen, and for a crime of which he was utterly innocent, he was about to be flogged.

"There are times when wild thoughts enter a man's breast, when he seems almost irresponsible for his act and his deed," writes the grandson of General Peter Gansevoort. "The Captain stood on the weather-side of the deck. Sideways, on an unobstructed line with him, was the opening of the lee-gangway, where the side-ladders are suspended in port. Nothing but a slight bit of sinnate-stuff served to rail in this opening, which was cut right to the level of the Captain's feet, showing the far sea beyond. I stood a little to windward of him, and, though he was a large, powerful man, it was certain that a sudden rush against him, along the slanting deck, would infallibly pitch him headforemost into the ocean, though he who so rushed must needs go over with him. My blood seemed clotting in my veins; I felt icy cold at the tips of my fingers, and a dimness was before my eyes. But through that dimness the boatswain's mate, scourge in hand, loomed like a giant, and Captain Claret, and the blue sea seen through the opening at the gangway, showed with an awful vividness. I cannot analyse my heart, though it then stood still within me. But the thing that swayed me to my purpose was not alto-gether the thought that Captain Claret was about to degrade me, and that I had taken an oath with my soul that he should not. No, I felt my man's manhood so bottomless within me, that no word, no blow, no scourge of Captain Claret could cut me deep enough for that. I but swung to an instinct within me—the instinct diffused through all animated nature, the same that prompts even a worm to turn under the heel. The privilege, inborn and inalienable, that every man has of dying himself, and inflicting death upon another, was not given to us without a purpose."

Captain Claret ordered Melville to the grating. The ghost of Peter Gansevoort, awakening in Melville, measured the distance between Captain Claret and the sea.

"Captain Claret," said a voice advancing from the crowd. Melville turned to see who this might be that audaciously interrupted at a juncture like this. It was a corporal of marines, who speaking in a mild, firm, but extremely deferential manner, said : "I know that man, and I know that he would not be found absent from his station if he knew where it was." This almost unprecedented speech inspired Jack Chase also to intercede in Melville's behalf. But for these timely intercessions, it is very likely that Melville would have ended that day as a suicide and a murderer. There is no lack of evidence, both in his writings and in the personal recollections of him that survive, that the headlong violence of his passion, when deeply stirred, balked at no extremity. And that day as the scourge hung over him for an offence he had not committed, he seems to have been as murderously roused as at any other known moment in his life. Though hating war, he boasted "the inalienable right to kill": and the ghost of Mow-Mow, at the day of final reckoning, can attest that this boast was not lightly given. Like the whaling Quakers that he so much admired, he was "a pacifist with a vengeance."

This scene happened during the run of the *United States* from Rio to the Line. At Rio, Melville had gone ashore with Jack Chase and a few other discreet and gentlemanly top-men. But of the dashing adventures—if any—that they had on land, Melville is silent : "my man-of-war alone must supply me with the staple of my matter " he says; "I have taken an oath to keep afloat to the last letter of my narrative."

In so far as fine weather and the ship's sailing were concerned, the whole run from Rio to the Line was one delightful yachting. Especially pleasant to Melville during this run were his quarter watches in the main-top. Removed from the immediate presence of the officers, he and his companions could there enjoy themselves more than in any other part of the ship. By day, many of them were industrious making hats or mending clothes. But by night they became more romantically inclined. Seen from this lofty perch, of moonlight nights, the frigate must have been a glorious sight. "She was going large before the wind, her stun'-sails set on both sides, so that the canvases on the main-mast and fore-mast presented the appearance of two majestic, tapering pyramids, more than a hundred feet broad at the base, and terminating in the clouds with the light cope-stone of the royals. That immense area of snow-white canvas sliding along the sea was indeed a magnificent spectacle. The three shrouded masts looked like the apparition of three gigantic Turkish Emirs striding over the ocean." From there, too, the band, playing on the poop, would tempt them to dance; Jack Chase would well up into song during silent intervals: songs varied by sundry yarns and twisters of the top-men.

One pleasant midnight, after the *United States* had crossed the Line and was running on bravely somewhere off the coast of Virginia, the breeze gradually died, and an order was given to set the main-top-gallant-stun'-sail. The halyards not being rove, Jack Chase assigned to Melville that eminently difficult task. That this was a business demanding unusual sharpsightedness, skill, and celerity is evident when it is remembered that the end of a line, some two hundred feet long, was to be carried aloft in one's teeth and dragged far out on the giddiest of yards, and after being wormed and twisted about through all sorts of intricacies, was to be dropped, clear of all obstructions, in a straight plumb-line right down to the deck.

"Having reeved the line through all the inferior blocks," Melville says, "I went out to the end of the weather-top-gallant-yard-arm, and was in the act of leaning over and passing it through the suspended jewel-block there, when the ship gave a plunge in the sudden swells of the calm sea, and pitching me still further over the yard, threw the heavy skirts of my jacket right over my head, completely muffling me. Somehow I thought it was the sail that had flapped, and under that impulse threw up my hands to drag it from my head, relying upon the sail itself to support me meanwhile. Just then the ship gave another jerk, and head foremost I pitched over the yard. I knew where I was, from the rush of air by my ears, but all else was a nightmare. A bloody film was before my eyes, through which, ghost-like, passed and repassed my father, mother, and sisters. An unutterable nausea oppressed me; I was conscious of groping; there seemed no breath in my body. It was over one hundred feet that I fell—down, down, with lungs collapsed as in death. Ten thousand pounds of shot seemed tied to my head, as the irresistible law of gravitation dragged me, head foremost and straight as a die, towards the infallible centre of the terrequeous globe. All I had seen, and read, and heard, and all that I had thought and felt in my life—seemed intensified in one fixed idea in my soul. But dense as this idea was, it was made up of atoms. Having fallen from the projecting yard-arm end, I was conscious of a collected satisfaction in feeling, that I should not be dashed on the deck, but would sink into the speechless profound of the sea.

"With the bloody, blind film before my eyes, there was a still stranger hum in my head, as if a hornet were there; and I thought to myself, Great God! this is Death! Yet these thoughts were unmixed with alarm. Like frost-work that flashes and shifts its scared hues in the sun, all my braided, blended emotions were in themselves icy cold and calm.

"So protracted did my fall seem, that I can even now recall the feeling of wondering how much longer it would be, ere all was over and I struck. Time seemed to stand still, and all the worlds seemed poised on their poles, as I fell, soul-becalmed, through the eddying whirl and swirl of the Maelstrom air.

"At first, as I have said, I must have been precipitated head foremost; but I was conscious, at length, of a swift, flinging motion of my limbs, which involuntarily threw themselves out, so that at last I must have fallen in a heap. This is more likely, from the circumstance that when I struck the sea, I felt as if some one had smote me slantingly across the shoulder and along part of my right side.

"As I gushed into the sea, a thunder-boom sounded in my ear; my soul seemed flying from my mouth. The feeling of death flooded over me with the billows. The blow from the sea must have turned me, so that I sank almost feet foremost through a soft, seething, foamy lull. Some current seemed hurrying me away; in a trance I yielded, and sank deeper and deeper into the glide. Purple and pathless was the deep calm now around me, flecked by summer lightnings in an azure afar. The horrible nausea was gone; the bloody, blind film turned a pale green; I wondered whether I was yet dead, or still dying. But of a sudden some fashionless form brushed my side—some inert, coiled fish of the sea; the thrill of being alive again tingled in my nerves, and the strong shunning of death shocked me through.

"For one instant an agonising revulsion came over me as I found myself utterly sinking. Next moment the force of my fall was expended; and there I hung, vibrating in the mid-deep. What wild sounds then rang in my ear! One was a soft moaning, as of low waves on the beach; the other wild and heartlessly jubilant, as of the sea in the height of a tempest. Oh soul! thou then heardest life and death: as he who stands upon the Corinthian shore hears both the Ionian and the Ægean waves. The life-and-death poise soon passed; and then I found myself slowly ascending, and caught a dim glimmering of light. Quicker and quicker I mounted; till at last I bounded up like a buoy, and my whole head was bathed in the blessed air."

With his knife, Melville ripped off his jacket, struck out boldly towards the elevated pole of one of the life-buoys which had been cut away, and was soon after picked up by one of the cutters from the frigate.

"Ten minutes after, I was safe on board, and, springing aloft, was ordered to reeve anew the stun'-sail-halyards, which, slipping through the blocks when I had let go the end, had unrove and fallen to the deck." Amphitrite had, indeed, interceded with Neptune, and the sea-gods strove to answer Melville's prayer. But Melville always, even in the lowest abyss of despair, clung passionately to life. And the night he was hurled from the mast he was hurled from among friends, and into waters that washed the neighbouring shores of his birth.

Melville's long wanderings were nearly at an end. With the home port believed to be broad on their bow, under the stars and a meagre moon in her last quarter, the main-top-men gathered aloft in the top, and round the mast they circled, "hand in hand, all spliced together. We had reefed the last top-sail; trained the last gun; blown the last match; bowed to the last blast; been tranced in the last calm. We had mustered our last round the capstan; been rolled to grog the last time; for the last time swung in our hammocks; for the last time turned out at the sea-gull call of the watch. We had seen our last man scourged at the gangway; our last man gasp out the ghost in the stifling sick-bay; our last man tossed to the sharks."

And there Melville has left this brother band—with the anchor still hanging from the bow—with the land still out of sight. "I love an indefinite infinite background," he says,— "a vast, heaving, rolling, mysterious rear!"

CHAPTER XIII

INTO THE RACING TIDE

"As the vine flourishes, and the grape empurples close up to the very walls and muzzles of cannoned Ehrenbreitstein; so do the sweetest joys of life grow in the very jaws of its peril."—HERMAN MELVILLE: *Pierre*.

"UNTIL I was twenty-five," Melville once wrote to Hawthorne, "I had no development at all." When the cable and anchor of the *United States* were all clear, and when he bounded ashore on his native soil, Melville was in his twenty-fifth year. "From my twenty-fifth year," he wrote Hawthorne, "I date my life."

His three years of wandering, crowded as they were with alienating experiences, had, of course, worked deep changes in him: changes more radical than in the dizzy whirl of strangely peopled adventures it was possible for him to gauge. In memory, the fitful fever of the past, deceitfully seems to strive not. But we delude ourselves when we fancy that it sleeps well. During his far driftings, Melville had clung reverently to thoughts of home, his imagination treacherously caressing those very scenes whose intimate contact had filled him with revulsion. "Do men ever hate the thing they love?" he asks in *White-Jacket*, perplexed at the paradox of this perpetual recoil. He was eternally looking both before and after, but never with the smug and genial after-dinner optimism of Rabbi Ben Ezra. The insufficient present was always poisoned, to him, by bitter margins of pining and regret. In headlong escape from his household gods he had been landed among South Sea islands that in retrospect he viewed as "authentic Edens." Yet even in Paradise did he feel himself an exile, teaching old Marheyo to say "Home" and "Mother," converting into sacred words the countersigns of a former Hell. He tells in *White-Jacket*, how, with the smell of tar in his nostrils, out of sight of land, with a stout ship under his

250

feet, and snuffing the ocean air, in the silence and solitude of
the deep, during the long night watches used to come throng-
ing about his heart "holy home associations." And he closes
White-Jacket with the reflection that "Life's a voyage that's
homeward-bound!" But he sailed with sealed orders.

Of Melville's impressions upon his return he has left no
record. During his three years of whaling and captivity
among cannibals, and mutiny, and South Sea driftings, and
adventures in the Navy, life at home had gone along in its
regular necessary way; and the scenes of his youth, despite
their transformation in his memory, lived on in solid fact un-
changed. The identical trees in the Boston Common blotted
out the same patterns against the New England stars; none
of the streets had swerved from off their prim and angular
respectability. His mother he found living in Lansingburg,
just out from Albany, N. Y. There was the same starched
calico smell to his sister's dresses, the same clang-tint to his
mother's voice. Such was the calibre of his imagination, that
he must have found life at Lansingburg unbelievably like he
knew it must be, yet very different from what he was prepared
to find.

His brothers must have first appeared intimate strangers
to him. His elder brother, Gansevoort, had given up his hat
and fur shop, was well established in law and had won a
creditable name for himself in politics. His younger brother,
Allan, was beginning a successful legal career, with his name
emblazoned on a door at 10 Wall Street. Maria was, after
all, a Gansevoort; she was not too proud to keep her brothers
reminded that she had borne sons. Melville's youngest
brother, Tom, had sprung from boyhood into the self-conscious
maturity of youth.

From vagabondage in Polynesia to the stern yoke of self-
supporting citizenship was a dizzy transition. But Melville
did not clear it at a bound. The very violence of the impact
between the two antipodal types of experience for a time must
have stunned Melville to their incompatibility. Tanned with
sea-faring, exuberant in health, rosy with the after-glow of
his proud companionship with Jack Chase, and the respect

and affection he had won from his associates on board the *United States,* he was effulgent with amazing tales—the enviable hero of endless incredible adventures. His home-coming may well have been not only a staggering, but a joyous adventure. For he entered Lansingburg trailing clouds of glory. He was panoplied in romance; and though bodily he was in a suburb of Albany, his companion image was the distant adventurer he saw mirrored in the admiring and jealous imagination of his friends. With what melancholy—if any—he viewed this reflected image, and to what degree he was, Narcissus-wise, conscious of its irony, we do not know. But if *Typee* and *Omoo* be any index of his mood, he returned home happier and wholesomer than at any other period of his life. Before many years, unsolved problems of his youth were to reassert themselves, heightened in difficulty and in pertinacity. Yet for a time, at least, so it would appear, he reaped very substantial benefits from his escape beyond civilisation.

According to J. E. A. Smith, Melville was soon beset by his enthralled and wide-eyed friends to put his experiences into a book. Even if such a challenge had never been made, it is difficult to see how Melville could have escaped plunging into literature. For the hankering for letters had earlier stirred in Melville's blood,—a hankering that he had before succumbed to, swathing a vacuity of experience in the grave-wrappings of rhetoric and prolixity. Now he was rich in matter; because of the very straitened circumstances of his family, he was faced again by the necessity of earning some money if he stayed at home; and in so far as we know, he was untempted to venture forth either as vagabond or efficiency expert.

Soon after his arrival home he must have settled down to composition. For the manuscript of *Typee* was bought in London by John Murray, by an agreement dated December, 1845.

At the time of the completion of *Typee,* Melville's brother, Gansevoort, was starting for London as Secretary to the American Legation under Minister McLane. Gansevoort threw *Typee* in among his luggage, to try its luck among British publishers. Whether *Typee* had previously been refused in the United States has not yet transpired. In any event, John Murray bought the English rights to print a thousand copies of *Typee*—a purchase that cost him £100. Murray did not close the sale, however, until he was assured that *Typee* was a sober account of actual experiences. *Typee* appeared in two parts in Murray's "Colonial and Home Library." Part I appeared on February 26, 1846; Part II on April 1 of the same year.

Encouraged by the temerity of John Murray, Wiley and Putnam of New York bought the American rights for *Typee*. And by an agreement made in England, *Typee* appeared simultaneously in New York and London: in America under the title, *Typee, a Peep at Polynesian Life During Four Months' Residence in a Valley of the Marquesas.* In 1849, Harper Brothers took over *Typee,* and issued it shorn of some of the passages the Missionaries had found most objectionable. Up to January 1, 1849, Wiley and Putnam had sold 6,392 copies of *Typee:* a sale upon which Melville gained $655.91. Up to April 29, 1851, 7,437 copies of *Typee* had been sold in England, netting Melville, if accounts surviving in Allan's hand be correct, $708.40.

Under the date of April 3, 1846—two days after the appearance in England of Part II of *Typee,* Gansevoort wrote Melville the following letter—the last letter, it appears, he ever wrote:

"MY DEAR HERMAN:

"Herewith you have copy of the arrangement with Wiley & Putnam for the publication in the U. S. of your work on the Marquesas. The letter of W. & P. under date of Jan. 13th is the result of a previous understanding between Mr. Putnam and myself. As the correspondence speaks for itself, it is quite unnecessary to add any comment. By the steamer of to-morrow I send to your address several newspaper comments and critiques of your book. The one in the *Sun* was written by a gentleman who is very friendly to myself, and who may possibly for that reason have made it unusually eulogistic.

"Yours of Feb. 28 was rec'd a few days ago by the daily packet from Joshua Bates. I am happy to learn by it that the previous intelligence transmitted by me was 'gratifying enough.' I am glad that you continue busy, and on my next or the after that will venture to make some suggestions about your next book. In a former letter you informed me that Allan had sent you $100 home, the fruit of my collection. (I refer to the money sent at your request). It appears that this was not so, for Allan informs me that the $100 was part of the £90 s 10—making £100 which I sent out by the Jan. 2 Steamer. Allan seems to find it entirely too much trouble to send me the monthly accounts of receipts and disbursements. I have received no accounts from him later than up to Nov. 30th and consequently am in a state of almost entire ignorance as to what is transpiring at No. 10, Wall Street. This is very unthinking in him, for my thoughts are so much at home that much of my time is spent in disquieting apprehensions as to matters & things there. I continue to live within my income, but to do so am forced to live a life of daily self-denial. I do not find my health improved by the sedentary life I have to lead here. The climate is too damp & moist for me. I sometimes fear I am gradually breaking up. If it be so—let it be—God's will be done. I have already seen about as much of London society as I care to see. It is becoming a toil to me to make the exertion necessary to dress to go out, and I am now leading a life really as quiet as your own in Lansingburg. —I think I am growing phlegmatic and cold. Man stirs me not, nor women either. My circulation is languid. My brain is dull. I neither seek to win pleasure or avoid pain. A degree of insensibility has been long stealing over me, & now seems completely established, which, to my understanding, is more akin to death than life. Selfishly speaking, I never valued life very much—it were impossible to value it less than I do now. The only personal desire I now have is to be out of debt. That desire waxes stronger within me as others fade. In consideration of the little egotism which my previous letters to you have contained, I hope that mother, brothers & sister will pardon this babbling about myself.

"Tom's matter has not been forgotten. You say there is a subject, etc., etc., 'on which I intended to write but will defer it.' What do you allude to? I am careful to procure all the critical notices of *Typee* which appear & transmit them to you. The steamer which left Boston on the 1st inst. will bring me tidings from the U. S. as to the success of *Typee* there. I am, with love and kisses to all,

> "Affectionately, Your brother,
> "GANSEVOORT MELVILLE."

With this letter, Gansevoort enclosed fourteen lines from Act III, Scene I of *Measure for Measure,* beginning "Ah, but to die." On May 12, he was dead. His countrymen celebrated his decease. *The Wisconsin,* a newspaper published in Milwaukee, for example, published, on July 1, a florid tribute to his memory, declaring him "dear to the people of the West." "And though he died young in years," the *Wisconsin* goes on to say, "for genius, thrilling eloquence and enlarged patriotism, he was known to the people from Maine to Louisiana."

But already had Melville achieved a wider, if less beatified, reputation. The notice that *Typee* attracted extended considerably beyond either Maine or Louisiana. And its success was none the less brilliant because it was in part a *succes de scandal.* Christendom has progressed since 1846, and *Typee* has, for present-day readers, lost its charm of indelicacy. Yet, despite the violation of the proprieties of which Melville was accused, Longfellow records in his journal for July 29, 1846: "In the even ng we finished the first volume of *Typee,* a curious and interesting book with glowing descriptions of life in the Marquesas." There is no indication that even Longfellow found it discreet to omit any passages as he read *Typee* to his family before the fire. It is to be remembered, however, that in 1851 the *Scarlet Letter* was attacked as being nothing but a deliberate attempt to attract readers by pandering to the basest taste: "Is the French era actually begun in our literature?" a shocked reviewer asked.

The appearance of *Omoo* on January 30, 1847, augmented Melville's notoriety, and contributed to his fame. Both *Typee* and *Omoo* stirred up a whole regiment of critics, at home, in England and in France. France was patronising, of course, after the manner of the period; but France flattered Melville by the prolixity of her patronage. The interest of France in Melville was not a merely literary absorption, however. Melville had arrived at the Marquesas in the wake of Admiral Du Petit-Thouars; and at Tahiti Melville had been a prisoner on board the *Reine Blanche*. In England, Melville was flattered not only by vitriolic evangelistical damnation, and the uncritical flatter of Gansevoort's friends, but even *Blackwood's*, the most anti-American of British journals, said of *Omoo:* "Musing the other day over our matutinal hyson, the volume itself was laid before us, and we found ourselves in the society of Marquesan Melville, the Phœnix of modern voyages—springing, it would seem, from the mingled ashes of Captain Cook and Robinson Crusoe." Writing of *Typee,* the insular *John Bull* said: "Since the joyous moment when we first read *Robinson Crusoe* and believed it, we have not met so bewitching a book as this narrative of Herman Melville's." The *London Times* descended to amiability and said: "That Mr. Melville will favour us with his further adventures in the South Seas, we have no doubt whatever. We shall expect them with impatience, and receive them with pleasure. He is a companion after our own hearts. His voice is pleasant, and we are sure that if we could see his face it would be a pleasant one." While such pronouncements were no earnest of fame, they may have contributed somewhat to augment Melville's royalties. And in *Mardi*—written before Melville's secular critics began to assail him—Melville took a violent fling at his reviewers. "True critics," he said, "are more rare than true poets. A great critic is a sultan among satraps; but pretenders are thick as ants striving to scale a palm after its aerial sweetness. Oh! that an eagle should be stabbed by a goose-quill!" Withal, when Melville wrote *Mardi.* he had spent some reflection on the nature of Fame, and mocked at those who console themselves for the neglect of their contemporaries by bethinking themselves of the glorious harvest of bravos their ghosts will reap. And time, he saw, was an undertaker, not a resurrectionist: "He who on all hands passes for a cipher to-day, if at all remembered, will be sure to pass to-morrow for the same. For there is more likelihood of being overrated while living than of being underrated when dead."

Noticed by reviewers, and encouraged by payments from his publishers, Melville began to look more hopefully at the world. In *Clarel* he later wrote: "The dagger-icicle draws blood; but give it sun." He seemed at last to have stepped decoratively and profitably into his assigned niche in the cosmic order. It was delightful to rehearse outlived pleasures and hardships; and it was a lucrative delight: by writing, too, some men had achieved fame. And so, undeterred by the wail of the Preacher of Jerusalem, Melville settled to the multiplication of books. He would perpetuate his reveries—and he doubted not that sparkling wines would crown his cup. Then it was that the beckoning image of an ultimate earthly felicity swam over the beaded brim.

Melville had dedicated *Typee* to Chief Justice Lemuel Shaw of Massachusetts. The Shaws and the Melvilles were friends of years' standing. When a student at Amherst, Lemuel Shaw had been engaged to Melville's aunt, Nancy. "To his death," says Frederic Hathway Chase in his *Lemuel Shaw*, "Shaw carefully preserved two tender notes written in the delicate hand of his first betrothed, timidly referring to their immature plans for the future and her admiration and love for him. The untimely death of the young lady, unhappily cut short their youthful dreams, and not until he was thirty-seven years of age were Shaw's affections again engaged. The intimacy between Shaw and the Melville family, however, continued after the young lady's death." Yet were the demands of Shaw's affections not satisfied by his intimacy with the Melvilles or by the two love-letters among his precious belongings. He married twice; the first time in 1818 to Elizabeth Knapp; the second time in 1827 to Hope Savage. By each wife he had two children. By Elizabeth, John Oakes, who died in 1902; and Elizabeth, who married Melville. By Hope, was born to him Lemuel, who lived till 1884, and Samuel Savage, born in 1833 in the Shaw home at 49 Mount Vernon Street,

Boston, where he lived till his death in 1915. Melville heartily detested his brothers-in-law.

On March 19, 1846, Melville wrote from Lansingburg to Chief Justice Shaw:

"MY DEAR SIR:

"Herewith you have one of the first bound copies of *Typee* I have been able to procure—the dedication is very simple, for the world would hardly have sympathised to the full extent of those feelings with which I regard my father's friend and the constant friend of all his family.

"I hope that the perusal of this little narrative of mine will afford you some entertainment, even if it should not possess much other merit. Your knowing the author so well, will impart some interest to it.—I intended to have sent at the same time with this copies of *Typee* for each of my aunts, but have been disappointed in not receiving as many as I expected.—I mention, however, in the accompanying letter to my Aunt Priscilla that they shall soon be forthcoming.

"Remember me most warmly to Mrs. Shaw & Miss Elizabeth, and to all your family, & tell them I shall not soon forget that agreeable visit to Boston.

"With sincere respect, Judge Shaw, I remain gratefully & truly yours,

"HERMAN MELVILLE.

"CHIEF JUSTICE SHAW,
    "Boston."

The Aunt Priscilla mentioned in this letter was a sister of Melville's father—fifth child of Major Thomas Melville. She was born in 1784, and upon her death in 1862, she showed that her appreciation of Melville's earlier solicitude had been substantial, by bequeathing him nine hundred dollars. The Miss Elizabeth of the letter, the only daughter of Chief Justice Shaw, and Melville were married on August 4, 1847.

On the evidence of surviving records, Melville's father had resigned himself to the institution of marriage as to one of the established conveniences of Christendom. Allan was a practical man, and he soberly saw that he gained more than he lost by generously sharing his bed and the fireside zone with a competent accessory to his domestic comforts. If he was ever a romantic lover, it was in the folly of his youth. Though romantic love be a tingling holiday extravagance, he mistrusted—and Allan never doubted his wisdom—its everyday useability for a cautious and peace-loving man. And since Dante had married Gemma Donati, since Petrarch had had children by an unknown concubine, Maria had reason to congratulate herself that Allan evinced for her no adoration of the kind lavished upon the sainted Beatrice or upon the unattainable Laura.

In his approach to marriage, Melville showed none of the prosaic circumspection of his father. From his idealisation of the proud cold purity of Maria, Melville built up a haloed image of the wonder and mystery of sanctified womanhood: without blemish, unclouded, snow-white, terrible, yet serene. And before this image Melville poured out the fulness of his most reverential thoughts and beliefs. The very profundity of his frustrated love for Maria, and the accusing incompatibility between the image and the fact, made his early life a futile and desperate attempt to escape from himself. The peace, and at the same time the stupendous discovery that he craved: that he found neither at home nor over the rim of the world. When with Maria, he had craved to put oceans between them; when so estranged, he was parched to return.

In his wanderings, he had seen sights, and lived through experiences to disabuse him of his fantastic idealisation of woman. In fact, however, such experiences may but tend to heighten idealisation. In the Middle Age, the Blessed Mother was celebrated in a duality of perplexing incompatibility: she was at once the Virgin Mother of the Son of God, and the patron of thieves, harlots and cutthroats. She was at once an object of worship and a subject of farce. She was woman. Protestantism, restoring woman to her original Hebraic dignity of a discarded rib, evinced in marriage an essentially biological interest, and regulated romantic love into uxoriousness. Allan was a good Protestant. But neither Mrs. Chapone nor

Fayaway were able to precipitate Melville into that form of heresy. Fayaway was Fayaway: and her father was a cannibal. Civilisation had given her no veils; Christianity had given her no compunctons. She was neither a mystery nor a sin. Untouched did she leave the sacred image in his heart.

To Elizabeth Shaw, Melville transferred his idealisation of his mother. In *Pierre* he says: "this softened spell which wheeled the mother and son in one orbit of joy seemed a glimpse of the glorious possibility, of the divinest of those emotions which are incident to the sweetest season of love." In *Pierre,* Melville declared that the ideal possibilities of the love between mother and son, seemed "almost to realise here below the sweet dreams of those religious enthusiasts, who paint to us a Paradise to come, when etherealised from all dross and stains, the holiest passion of man shall unite all kindreds and climes in one circle of pure and unimpaired delight." And in this "courteous lover-like adoration" of son for mother, Melville saw the "highest and airiest thing in the whole compass of the experience of our mortal life." And "this heavenly evanescence," Melville declares, "this nameless and infinitely delicate aroma of inexpressible tenderness and attentiveness," is, "in every refined and honourable attachment, contemporary with courtship." In *Pierre,* Melville spends a chapter of dithyramb in celebration of this sentiment which, inspired by one's mother, one transfers to all other women honourably loved. "Love may end in age, and pain and need, and all other modes of human mournfulness; but love begins in joy. Love's first sigh is never breathed, till after love hath laughed. Love has not hands, but cymbals; Love's mouth is chambered like a bugle, and the instinctive breathings of his life breathe jubilee notes of joy." And during his courtship of Elizabeth Shaw, it seems that in Melville were "the audacious immortalities of divinest love."

None of Melville's letters of courtship survive. There are more direct evidences of the fruits of his love, than of its early bloom. There are, however, two letters of his wife's, written during the month of the marriage. The first was written during the wedding trip.

"Center Harbor, Aug. 6th, 1847.

"My Dear Mother:

"You know I promised to write you whenever we came to a stopping place, and remained long enough. We are now at Center Harbor, a most lonely and romantic spot at the extremity of Winnipiscogee Lake, having arrived last evening from Concord—and we intend to remain until to-morrow. One object in stopping so long and indeed principal one was to visit 'Red Hill'—a mountain (commanding a most beautiful view of the lake) about four miles distant. But to-day it is so cloudy and dull, I am afraid we shall not be able to accomplish it—so you see I have a little spare time, and improve it by writing to relieve any anxiety you may feel. Though this is but the third day since our departure, it seems as if a long time had passed, we have seen so many places of novelty and interest. The stage ride yesterday from Franklin here, though rather fatiguing, was one of great attraction from the beautiful scenery. To-morrow we again intend to take the stage to Conway, and from there to the White Mountains. I will write again from there, and tell you more of what I have seen, but now I send this missive more to let you know of our safety and well-being than anything else.

"I hope by this time you have quite recovered from your indisposition, and that I shall soon hear from you to be assured of it—I hardly dare to trust myself to speak of what I felt in leaving home, but under the influence of such commingling thoughts, it entirely escaped me to tell you of any place to which you might address a letter to me so that I should be sure to get it. Now I am *very* anxious and impatient to hear from you, and I hope you will lose no time in writing if it be only a very few lines. Herman desires to add a postscript to my letter, and he will tell you when and where to write so that I may get it.

Remember me with affection to father and ask him to let me have a letter from him soon,—to all members of the family and to Mrs. Melville and the girls—my mother and sisters —how strangely it sounds. Accept a great deal of love for yourself, my dear mother, and believe me as ever, your affectionate daughter, Elizabeth—even though I add to it—Melville —for the first time.

                                    "Friday morning.
"MY DEAR SIR:
    "At my desire Lizzie has left a small space for a word or two.—We arrived here last evening after a pleasant ride from Franklin, the present terminus of the Northern Rail Road. The scenery was in many places very fine, & we caught some glimpses of the mountain region to which we are going. Center Harbor where we now are is a very attractive place for a tourist, having the lake for boating and trouting, and plenty of rides in the vicinity, besides Red-Hill, the view from which is said to be equal to anything of the kind in New England.' A rainy day, however, has thus far prevented us from taking our excursion, to enjoy the country.—To-morrow, I think we shall leave for Conway and thence to Mt. Washington & so to Canada. I trust in the course of some two weeks to bring Lizzie to Lansingburgh, quite refreshed and invigourated from her rambles.—Remember me to Mrs. Shaw & the family, and tell my mother that I will write to her in a day or two.
                    "Sincerely yours,
                        "HERMAN MELVILLE.
    "Letters directed within four or five days from now, will probably reach us at Montreal."

    The second letter explains itself:

                    "LANSINGBURGH, Aug. 28th, 1847.
"MY DEAR MOTHER:
    "We arrived here safe and well yesterday morning, and I intended to have written a few lines to you then, but I was so tired, and had so much to do to unpack and put away my things, I deferred it until to-day.
    "We left Montreal on Tuesday evening and the next day in the afternoon hailed Whitehall, at the foot of Lake Champlain, after a very pleasant sail on that beautiful piece of water. The next question was whether we should proceed to

Lansingburgh by stage or take the canal boat. We thought
stage riding would be rather tame after the beautiful scenery
of Vermont, and as I had never been in a canal boat in my
life, Herman thought we had better try it for the novelty.
This would expedite our journeying, too, and having once set
our faces homeward, we were not disposed to delay. Being
fully forewarned of the inconvenience we might expect in
passing a night on board a canal boat—a crowded canal boat,
too, and fully determined to meet them bravely, we stepped on
board—not without some misgivings, however, as we saw the
crowds of men, women and children come pouring in, with
trunks and handbags to match. Where so many people were
to store themselves at night was a mystery to be yet unravelled,
and what they all *did* do with themselves is something I have
not yet found out. Well, night drew on—and after sitting
on deck on trunks or anything we could find (and having to
bob our heads down every few minutes when the helmsman
sang out 'Bridge!' or 'Low Bridge!') it became so damp and
chilly that I was finally driven below.

"Here was a scene entirely passing description. The Ladies' 'Saloon!' they politely termed it so, so we were informed
by a red and gilt sign over it. A space about as large as my
room at home, was separated from the gentlemen's 'Saloon'
by a curtain only. About 20 or 25 women were huddled into
this. Each one having two children apiece of all ages, sexes,
and sizes, said children, as is usual on such occasions, lifting
up their respective voices, very loud indeed, in one united
chorus of lamentations.

"A narrow row of shelves was hooked up high on each side
and on these some & more fortunate mothers had closely
packed their sleeping babies while they sat by to prevent their
rolling out. I looked round in vain for a place to stretch my
limbs, but it was not to be thought of—but after a while by a
fortunate chance I got a *leaning* privilege, and fixing my
carpet-bag for a pillow, I made up my mind to pass the night
in this manner. One by one the wailing children dropped off
to sleep and I had actually lost myself in a sort of doze, when
a new feature in the case became apparent. Stepping carefully

over the outstretched forms on the floor came two men, each bearing a pile of boards or little shelves like those already suspended. These they hooked up against the sides in the smallest conceivable spaces, using every available inch of room—and were intended to sleep (!) upon. I immediately pounced upon one of them which I thought might be accessible, and was just consulting with myself as to the best means of getting onto it, when I was politely requested by one of the sufferers to take the shelf above from which she wished to remove her children to the one I thought to occupy—of course I complied, and after failing in several awkward attempts, I managed to climb and crawl into this narrow aperture like a bug forcing its way through the boards of a fence. Sweltering and smothering I watched the weary night hours pass away, for to sleep in such an atmosphere was impossible. I rose at 3 o'clock, thinking it was five, spent a couple of hours curled up on the floor, and was right glad when Herman came for me, with the joyful intelligence that we were actually approaching Whitehall—the place of our destination. He also passed a weary night, though his sufferings were of the opposite order—for while I was suffocating with the heat and bad atmosphere, he was on deck, chilled and half-frozen with the fog and penetrating dampness, for the gentlemen's apartment was even more crowded than the ladies'—so much so that they did not attempt to hang any shelves for them to lie upon. All they could do was to sit bolt upright firmly wedged in and if one of them presumed to *lean* at all or even to *nod* out of the perpendicular it was thought a great infringement of rights, and he was immediately called to order. So Herman preferred to remain on deck all night to being in this crowd. We left the boat and took the cars about an hour's ride from Lansingburgh, and surprised the family at 6 o'clock in the morning before they were up. We were very warmly welcomed and cared for and soon forgot our tribulations of the canal boat. I was much disappointed to miss the boys—they had only left the day before—it was too bad—I am looking forward with such impatience to see you and father, and sincerely hope nothing will happen to prevent your coming.

"I suppose we shall not be long here: Allan is looking out for a house in N. Y. and will be married next month.

"You know a proposition was made before I came here that I should furnish my own room, which for good reasons were then set aside—but if it is not too late now, I should like very much to do it if we go to N. Y.—but we can talk about that when I see you. I must bring my scribbling to a close, after I have begged you or somebody to write me. I have not received a single line since I left home. How did the dinner party go off? I want to hear about everything and everybody at home. Please give my warmest love to all and believe me your affectionate daughter,

"ELIZABETH S. M.

"Herman desires his kindest remembrances to all."

Soon after the marriage, Melville and his wife moved from Lansingburg to New York, where they lived with Melville's brother, Allan, and his household of sisters. The letters of Mrs. Melville's are the only surviving records of the intimate details of this domestic arrangement. They are interesting, too, as revelation of the character of Mrs. Melville. The three following are typical:

"NEW YORK, Dec. 23rd, 1847.

"Thank you, dear Mother, for your nice long letter. I was beginning to be afraid you had forgotten your part of the contract for that week, but Saturday brought me evidence to the contrary and made us even. And I should have written you earlier, but the days are so short, and I have so much to do, that they fly by without giving me half the time I want. Perhaps you will wonder what on earth I have to occupy me. Well in fact I hardly know exactly myself, but true it is little things constantly present themselves and dinner time comes before I am aware. We breakfast at 8 o'clock, then Herman goes to walk and I fly up to put his room to rights, so that he can sit down to his desk immediately on his return. Then I bid him good-bye, with many charges to be an industrious boy and not upset the inkstand and then flourish the duster,

make the bed, etc., in my own room. Then I go down-
stairs and read the papers a little while, and after that I am
ready to sit down to my work—whatever it may be—darning
stockings—making or mending for myself or Herman—at all
events, I haven't seen a day yet, without *some* sewing or other
to do. If I have letters to write, as is the case to-day, I usually do that first—but whatever I am about I do not much
more than get thoroughly engaged in it, than ding-dong goes
the bell for luncheon. This is half-past 12 o'clock—by this
time we must expect callers, and so must be dressed immediately after lunch. Then Herman insists upon taking a walk
of an hour's length at least. So unless I can have rain or
snow for an excuse, I usually sally out and make a pedestrian
tour a mile or two down Broadway. By the time I come
home it is two o'clock and after, and then I must make myself
look as bewitchingly as possible to meet Herman at dinner.
This being accomplished, I have only about an hour of available time left. At four we dine, and after dinner is over,
Herman and I come up to our room and enjoy a cosy chat
for an hour or so—or he reads me some of the chapters he
has been writing in the day. Then he goes down town for
a walk, looks at the papers in the reading room, etc., and
returns about half-past seven or eight. Then my work or
my book is laid aside, and as he does not use his eyes but very
little by candle light, I either read to him, or take a hand at
whist for his amusement, or he listens to our reading or conversation, as best pleases him. For we all collect in the parlour in the evening, and generally one of us reads aloud for the
benefit of the whole. Then we retire very early—at 10 o'clock
we all disperse. Indeed we think that quite a late hour to be
up. This is the general course of daily events—so you see
how my time is occupied; but sometime—dear me! we have to
go and make calls! and then good-bye to everything else for
that day! for upon my word, it takes the whole day, from 1
o'clock till four! and then perhaps we don't accomplish more
than two or three, if unluckily they chance to be in—for everybody lives so far from everybody else, and all Herman's and
Allan's friends are *so* polite, to say nothing of Mrs. M.'s old

acquaintances, that I am fairly sick and tired of returning calls. And no sooner do we do up a few, than they all come again, and so it has to be gone over again.

"You know ceremonious calls were always my abomination, and where they are all utter strangers and we have to send in our cards to show who we are, it is so much the worse. Excepting calls, I have scarcely visited at all. Herman is not fond of parties, and I don't care anything about them here. To-morrow night, for a great treat, we are going to the opera —Herman & Fanny and I—and this is the first place of public amusement I have attended since I have been here—but somehow or other I don't care much about them now.

"I am glad to hear that father and all are so well—except Sam—how is his cough now? don't forget to tell us when you write.

"If Susan Haywood and Fanny Clarke are at our house please give my love to them and ask Susan to answer my letter. How is Mrs. Marcus Morton and Mrs. Hawes? I hope you will be able to write me this week though I know *your* time is very much occupied—but then you know any letter—even the shortest and most hurried is acceptable and better than none— though I must confess my prejudice sins in favour of *long* ones—but I am glad to hear *anything* from home. You addressed my last letter just right and it came very straight— but Allan's name is spelt with an 'a' instead of an 'e'—as Allan —not Allen—different names, you see—I am hoping that sometime or other father will find time to write to me—though I know he is so much occupied with other matters.

"Thank you for your kindness about the picture box—as I do not need any article at present, I will keep the dollar till I do—it will be the same thing, you know, and I have already got such a New Year's present in the big box upstairs—by the way, in about a week more, it will be time to open it. Oh, what do you think about my calling on Mrs. Joe Henshaw and Josephine—they are living here and came here after I did, so perhaps I ought to call first if it is best for me to visit them —being connected with the Haywoods perhaps it would be better to renew the acquaintance. What do you think about it? Please tell me when you write, and get their address from Aunt Haywood, if you think I had better call. I am afraid you are tired of this long letter; but I have done now. Goodbye, and love to all.

"Affectionately yours,
"ELIZABETH S. MELVILLE.

"P. S. I have a letter from Mrs. Warpwell a few days since—I didn't know she had lost one of her twins before. Why didn't you tell me? My love to Mrs. Sullivan. I hope she is quite well again. Tell Lem we expect him next month in his mention to make us a visit."

"NEW YORK, Feb. 4th, 1848.
"103 Fourth Avenue.

"MY DEAR MOTHER:

"Every day for the last week I have been trying to write to you, but have been prevented. I received your letter by Lemuel with much pleasure and the next time you write I want you to tell me more about Carrie—how she and the small baby are getting along—and whether she took ether when she was sick and if so, with what effect. What they have decided to name the baby and all about it. Your presents were very acceptable—Herman was much gratified with your remembrance to him—and intends to make his acknowledgment for himself. You forgot Kate in the multitude of Melvilles—so I just gave her my share of the bill you enclosed without saying anything about it—knowing you would not intentionally leave her out—or rather I gave the bill to Helen for herself, Fanny and Kate, as she could get what they most wanted better than I—so it's all right now, and I will take the will for the deed and thank you all the same.

"The key of the basket that you wanted me to send—you know—I have *no bills* there whatever—you have them all. I only have an account of the expenditure and a memorandum of the bills that were paid—not the item of the bills. If you have an opportunity where it will come safe I should like to have you send me that basket very much.

"You speak of a Mr. Crocker whom you wish me to receive.

If he will call I shall be very happy to see him. You know we are recently renumbered and our address now is 'No. 103 Fourth Avenue', 'between 11th & 12th Streets'—it is safer to add for a time.

"Lem seems to be enjoying himself highly with the amusements out of doors, and the society within. Last night he went to a masked ball, under the auspices of Mrs. Elwell, through Aunt Marat's kindness, and a very fine appearance he presented, I can assure you, in an old French court dress—with a long curled horse-hair wig, chapeau bras—knee breeches, long stockings, buckles, snuff box and all—it was a very becoming dress to him, and exactly suited to his carriage and manners—I wish you could have seen him. We went to a party ourselves last evening, but we had a deal of fun helping him to dress—he went masked of course, but being introduced by Mrs. Elwell was very kindly received—taking Mrs. Dickinson (the hostess) down to supper, and doing the polite thing to the nine Misses Dickinson. He enjoyed it much, as you may suppose, and did not get home till four o'clock in the morning, and even then the ball had not broken up. At this present moment—11 o'clock—I believe he is dozing on the parlour sofa—to gain strength to go to the opera this evening.

"We have been very dissipated this week for us, for usually we are very quiet. Wednesday evening we passed at Mrs. Thurston's and were out quite late—last night at a party—a very pleasant one too, where by the way—I passed off for Miss Melville and as such was quite a belle!! And to-night in honour of our guest, we go to the Opera. We have resolved to stop after this though and not go out at all for while Herman is writing the effect of keeping late hours is very injurious to him—if he does not get a full night's rest or indulges in a late supper, he does not feel right for writing the next day. And the days are too precious to be thrown away. And to tell the truth I don't think he cares *very* much about parties either, and when he goes it is more on my account than his own. And it's no sacrifice to me, for I am quite as contented, and more—to stay at home so long as he will stay with me. He has had communications from London publishers with very liberal offers for the book in hand—and one from Berlin to translate from the first sheets into German—but as yet he has closed with none of them, and will not in a hurry.

"I believe I forgot in my last to acknowledge the receipt of a paper from father—I was very glad of it—please present my thanks—I have intended to write to father for a good while—but I like to have answers to my letters—so if father has not time to write in reply, you must write for him. Give my love to him and to all the family—and when you see Susan Morton ask her to write to me.

"Tell Aunt Lucretia I was delighted to get her note, and I will write to her.

"Now I have written you a famous long letter and I hope you will write me as long a one very soon, for I have not heard from home for more than a week now—not since Lem came.

"Give my love to Mrs. Sullivan, and believe me as ever truly yours,

"E. S. MELVILLE."

"NEW YORK, May 5th, 1848.

"MY DEAR MOTHER:

"I am very much occupied to-day but I snatch a few moments to reply to your letter which though rather tardy in forthcoming was very acceptable. But you did not tell me what I most wanted to know—about Sam. And your indefinite allusion to it, when we were all waiting to hear, was rather tantalising. Does 'this season' means *now* in his present vacation, or sometime in the course of the year? I suppose his vacation has already commenced if he is out at Milton, then why not let him come immediately and make his visit, because if he waits till warm weather it will not be nearly so pleasant or so beneficial for him. Maria Percival writes me that she is coming on soon and he might come with her. Please write me something *definite* about it, as soon as you can, and do let him come. We want him to very much, and the sooner the better.

"You ask about our coming to Boston but I guess the house will be ready to *clean again* by that time—for it will not be

before July, perhaps August. Herman of course will stick to
his work till 'the book' is published and his services are required till the last moment—correcting proof, etc. The book
is done now, in fact (you need not mention it) and the copy
for the press is in progress, but when it is published on both
sides of the water a great deal of delay is unavoidable and
though Herman will have some spare time after sending the
proof sheets to London which will be next month sometime
probably he will not want to leave New York till the book is
actually on the book-sellers' shelves. And then I don't care
about leaving home till my cold is over because I could not
enjoy my visit so much. So though I am very impatient for
the time to come I must e'en wait as best I may and enjoy the
anticipation.

"We are looking out for Tom to return every day, his ship
has been reported in the papers several times lately as homeward bound and Herman wrote to the owner at Westport
and received answer that he looked for the ship the first of
May. That has already past and we are daily expecting a
letter to announce her actual arrival. Then Herman will have
to go over to Westport for Tom and see that he is regularly
discharged and paid, and bring him home. As yet he, Tom,
is in entire ignorance of the changes that have taken place in
his family and of their removal to New York. So he will be
much surprised I think. As you may suppose, Mother is
watching and counting the days with great anxiety for he is the
baby of the family and his mother's pet.

"Augusta is going to Albany in a few days to visit the
Van Renssalaers. They have been at her all winter to go up
the river but she would not, and now Mr. Van Renssalaer is
in town and will not go back without her. And in a few
weeks Helen is going to Lansingburgh to visit Mrs. Jones.

"I should write you a longer letter but I am very busy to-day
copying and cannot spare the time so you must excuse it and
all mistakes. I tore my sheet in two by mistake thinking it
was my copying (for we only write on one side of the page)
and if there is no punctuation marks you must make them
yourself for when I copy I do not punctuate at all but leave

it for a final revision for Herman.   I have got so used to write without (.) I cannot always think of it.

"Please write me *very soon* this week—if only a few lines and tell me about Sam's coming.

"My love to all, to father when you write and to Sue Morton if she is at our house, Mrs. Hawes etc. and believe me as ever your affectionate

"E. S. MELVILLE.

"Miss Savage & Miss Lincoln called to see me a day or two ago.

"Please spell Allan's name with an A, not E.   *Allan,* not *Allen.*"

During this period, the household at 103 Fourth Avenue was busy getting *Redburn* and *Mardi* ready for the press. Melville's sister Augusta seems to have been exhaustless in copying manuscript.   Melville's mother-in-law reports "Miss Augusta is all energy, united with much kindness."   Augusta also evinced a strong religious bent, and during song services —which she loved to attend—she used to grip her hymnal athletically, and beat time with an aggressive rhythm.   Her Hymn Book survives, pasted up with dozens of clippings of hymns and prayers, a "selection" entitled *The Sinner's Friend,* and the vivacious couplet:

> "Jesus, mine's a pressing case.
> Oh, more grace, *more grace, MORE GRACE!*"

But song-services, and copying manuscript, were not enough to fill Augusta's busy days.   In January, 1848, she was commissioned to find a name satisfactory for Melville's first child. Mrs. Herman Melville was in Boston to be with her mother and family at the time of the childbirth.   On January 27, 1849, Augusta wrote from New York to "My dear Lizzie, My sweet Sister," reporting that she had been "searching the Genealogical Tree" with designs upon an ancestor with a choice name: and she spends two very diverting and animated pages recounting her adventures among the branches.   Her search was

ELIZABETH SHAW MELVILLE

rewarded to her satisfaction: *"Malcolm Melville!* how easily it runs from my pen; how sweetly it sounds to my ear; how musically it falls upon my heart. Malcolm Melville! Methinks I see him in his plaided kilts, with his soft blue eyes, & his long flaxen curls. How I long to press him to my heart. There! I can write no more. The last proof sheets are through. *Mardi's* a book." Augusta concludes with a quotation from *Mardi:* " 'Oh my own Kagtanza, child of my prayers. Oro's blessing on thee!' "

In her search of the Genealogical Tree, Augusta had contemptuously brushed by all female branches: she had determined that Melville's first child should be a son—and a son with blue eyes and blond hair—and in her choice of a name for the unborn infant, she contemptuously ignored the possibility of the child turning out to be a girl. On February 16, 1849, was born in Boston, to Melville and his wife, their first child. There was potency in Augusta's prayers. It was a boy.

On April 14, 1849, *Mardi* appeared, published, as was *Omoo,* by Harper and Brothers in America, by Richard Bentley in London. *Redburn* appeared on August 18 of the same year. By February 22, 1850 (the date of Melville's fifth royalty account from Harper and Brothers), 2,154 copies of *Mardi,* and 4,011 copies of *Redburn* had been sold. On February 1, 1848, Melville had overdrawn his account with Harper's to the extent of $256.03. On December 5, 1848, Harper's advanced Melville $500; on April 28, 1848, $300; on July 2, 1849, $300; on September 14, 1849, $500. Though *Mardi* and *Redburn* had had a fairly generous sale, the deduction of his royalties on February 22, 1850, left him in debt to Harper's $733.69. The outlook was not bright for the responsibilities of fatherhood.

On April 23, Melville sent to his father-in-law a note "conveying the intelligence of Lizzie's improving strength, and Malcolm's precocious growth. Both are well." Melville went on to say that Samuel, the brother-in-law for whom he felt not the most enthusiastic affection, was expected by all "to honour us with his presence during the approaching vacation:

and I have no doubt he will not find it difficult to spend his time pleasantly with so many companions." Does Melville here imply that for himself, as a sensible man, he would prefer more solitude? In conclusion, Melville says: "I see that *Mardi* has been cut into by the *London Atheneum*, and also burnt by the common hangman by the *Boston Post*. However, the *London Examiner* & *Literary Gazette* & other papers this side of the water have done differently. These attacks are matters of course, and are essential to the building up of any permanent reputation—if such should ever prove to be mine—'There's nothing in it!' cried the dunce when he threw down the 47th problem of the 1st Book of Euclid— 'There's nothing in it!'—Thus with the posed critic. But Time, which is the solver of all riddles, will solve *Mardi*."

The riddle of *Mardi* goes near to the heart of the riddle of Melville's life. "Not long ago," Melville says in the preface to *Mardi*, "having published two narratives of voyages in the Pacific, which, in many quarters, were received with incredulity, the thought occurred to me, of indeed writing a romance of Polynesian adventure, and publishing it as such; to see whether the fiction might not, possibly, be received for a verity: in some degree the reverse of my previous experience. This thought was the germ of others, which have resulted in *Mardi*."

Mardi, as *Moby-Dick*, starts off firmly footed in reality. The hero, discontented on board a whaler, hits upon the wild scheme of surreptitiously cutting loose one of the whale boats, and trusting to the chances of the open Pacific. It is sometimes the case that an old mariner will conceive a very strong attachment for some young sailor, his shipmate—a Fidus-Achates-ship, a league of offence and defence, a copartnership of chests and toilets, a bond of love and good-feeling. Such a relationship existed between the hero of *Mardi* and his Viking shipmate Jarl. Jarl was an old Norseman to behold: his hands as brawny as the paws of a bear; his voice as hoarse as a storm roaring round the peak of Mull; his long yellow hair waving about his head like a sunset. In the crow's-nest of the ship the project of escape was confided to Jarl. Jarl advised with elderly prudence, but seeing his chummy's resolution immovable, he changed his wrestling to a sympathetic hug, and bluntly swore he would follow through thick and thin. The escape was successfully made, and for days the two men drifted at sea: and it was an eventful if solitary drifting. After sixteen days in their open boat, "as the expanded sun touched the horizon's rim,·a ship's uppermost spars were observed, traced like a spider's web against its crimson disk. It looked like a far-off craft on fire." Bent upon shunning a meeting—though Jarl "kept looking wistfully over his shouler; doubtlessly praying Heaven that we might not escape"—they lowered sail. As the ship bore down towards them, they saw her to be no whaler —as they had feared—but a small, two-masted craft in unaccountable disarray. They lay on their oars, and watched her in the starlight. They hailed her loudly. No return. Again. But all was silent. So, armed with a harpoon, they eventually boarded the strange craft. The ship was in a complete litter; the deserted tiller they found lashed. Though it was a nervous sort of business, they explored her interior. Many were the puzzling sights they saw; but except for a supernatural sneeze from the riggings, there was no evidence of life aboard. At dawn, however, they discovered, in the maintop, a pair of South Sea Islanders: Samoa, and Annatoo. "To be short, Annatoo was a Tartar, a regular Calmuc; and Samoa— Heaven help him—her husband." Upon this pair, Melville has lavished chapter after chapter of the most finished and competent comedy. Annatoo is as perfect, in her way, as is Zuleika Dobson. And Samoa—well, Samoa, on occasion, thinks it discreet to amputate his wounded arm.

"Among savages, severe personal injuries are, for the most part, accounted but trifles. When a European would be taking to his couch in despair, the savage would disdain to recline.

"More yet. In Polynesia, every man is his own barber and surgeon, cutting off his beard or arm, as occasion demands. No unusual thing, for the warriors of Varvoo to saw off their own limbs, desperately wounded in battle. But owing to the clumsiness of the instrument employed—a flinty, serrated shell —the operation has been known to last several days. Nor will they suffer any friend to help them; maintaining, that a matter so nearly concerning a warrior is far better attended to by himself. Hence it may be said, that they amputate themselves at their leisure, and hang up their tools when tired. But, though thus beholden to no one for aught connected with the practice of surgery, they never cut off their own heads, that ever I heard; a species of amputation to which, metaphorically speaking, many would-be independent sort of people in civilised lands are addicted.

"Samoa's operation was very summary. A fire was kindled in the little caboose, or cook-house, and so made as to produce much smoke. He then placed his arm upon one of the windlass bitts (a short upright timber, breast-high), and seizing the blunt cook's axe would have struck the blow; but for some reason distrusting the precision of his aim, Annatoo was assigned to the task. Three strokes, and the limb, from just above the elbow, was no longer Samoa's; and he saw his own bones; which many a centenarian can not say. The very clumsiness of the operation was safety to the subject. The weight and bluntness of the instrument both deadened the pain and lessened the hemorrhage. The wound was then scorched, and held over the smoke of the fire, till all signs of blood vanished. From that day forward it healed, and troubled Samoa but little.

"But shall the sequel be told? How that, superstitiously averse to burying in the sea the dead limb of a body yet living; since in that case Samoa held, that he must very soon drown and follow it; and how, that equally dreading to keep the thing near him, he at last hung it aloft from the topmast-stay; where yet it was suspended, bandaged over and over in cerements. The hand that must have locked many others in friendly clasp, or smote a foe, was no food, thought Samoa, for fowls of the air nor fishes of the sea.

"Now, which was Samoa? The dead arm swinging high as Haman? Or the living trunk below? Was the arm severed from the body, or the body from the arm? The residual part of Samoa was alive, and therefore we say it was he. But which of the writhing sections of a ten times severed worm, is the worm proper?"

There are more cosy pleasures aboard the old ship, however, than amputation: "Every one knows what a fascination
there is in wandering up and down in a deserted old tenement
in some warm, dreamy country; where the vacant halls seem
echoing of silence, and the doors creak open like the footsteps
of strangers; and into every window the old garden trees
thrust their dark boughs, like the arms of night-burglars; and
ever and anon the nails start from the wainscot; while behind
it the mice rattle like dice. Up and down in such old spectre
houses one loves to wander; and so much the more, if the place
be haunted by some marvellous story.

"And during the drowsy stillness of the tropical sea-day,
very much such a fancy had I, for prying about our little
brigantine, whose tragic hull was haunted by the memory of
the massacre, of which it still bore innumerable traces."

After delightful and exciting, and irresponsible days spent
sailing without chart, they find the vessel unseaworthy, leak-
ing in every pore; so again they take to their whale boat
soon to fall in with strangers. With this meeting, *Mardi*
swings into allegory,—and then it is that Melville first tries
his hand at the orphic style.

This second part of *Mardi* in its manner defies simple characterisation, though its purpose is simple enough. It is a quest
after Yillah, a maiden from Oroolia, the Island of Delight.
A voyage is made through the civilised world for her: and
though they find occasion for much discourse on international
politics, and an array of other topics, Yillah is not found. And
in an astonishing variety of fantastic and symbolic scenes—
many conceived in the manner of the last three books of Rabelais—they go on in futile search for her. They search among
the Islands of "those Scamps the Plujii," where all evil which
the inhabitants could impute neither to the gods nor to themselves were blamed upon the Plujii. There they meet an "old
woman almost doubled together, both hands upon her ab-
domen; in that manner running about distracted." When
asked of the occasion of her distraction she screamed "The
Plujii! The Plujii!" affectionately caressing the field of their
operations.

"And why do they torment you?" she was soothingly asked.

"How should I know? and what good would it do me if I did?"

And on she ran.

"Hearing that an hour or two previous she had been partaking of some twenty unripe bananas, I rather fancied that that circumstance might have had something to do with her suffering. But whatever it was, all the herb-leeches on the island would not have been able to alter her own opinions on the subject."

They visit jolly old Borabolla, and discuss the hereafter of fish. "As for the possible hereafter of the whale," says Melville, "a creature eighty feet long without stockings, and thirty feet round the waist after dinner is not inconsiderably to be consigned to annihilation." They are entertained by the gentry of Pimminee, and their host, being told they were strolling divinities, demigods from the sun "manifested not the slightest surprise, observing incidentally, however, that the eclipses there must be a sad bore to endure." They are entertained by the pallid and beautiful youth Donjalolo, with wives thirty in number, corresponding in name to the nights of the moon: wives "blithe as larks, more playful than kittens," though "but supplied with the thirtieth part of all that Aspasia could desire." Over flowing calabashes they discourse of super-men, and vitalism, and toad-stools, and fame, and thieves, and teeth, and democracy, and an interminable variety of other irrelevant and diverting matters. Incredible is the rich variety of *Mardi*.

There is infinite laughter in the book—but the laughter is at bottom the laughter of despair. "It is more pleasing to laugh, than to weep," Montaigne has said. But Montaigne preferred laughter not for that reason, but because "it is more distainfull, and doth more condemne us than the other. And me thinkes we can never bee sufficiently despised according to our merit." Melville's laughter, however, grew out of a desolation less emancipated than Montaigne's. "Let us laugh: let us roar: let us yell." Melville makes the philosopher in *Mardi* say: "Weeds are torn off at a fair; no heart bursts but in

secret; it is good to laugh though the laugh be hollow. Women
sob, and are rid of their grief; men laugh and retain it. Ha!
ha! how demoniacs shout; how all skeletons grin; we all
die with a rattle. Humour, thy laugh is divine; hence mirth-
making idiots have been revered; and so may I." And one of
the ultimate discoveries of the book is: "Beatitude there is
none. And your only Mardian happiness is but exemption
from great woes—no more. Great Love is sad; and heaven is
Love. Sadness makes the silence throughout the realms of
space; sadness is universal and eternal."

For *Mardi,* in its intention to show the vanity of human
wishes, is a kind of *Rasselas;* but because of its "dangerous
predominance of imagination," it is a *Rasselas* Dr. Johnson
would have despised. And the happiness sought in *Mardi* is
of a brand of felicity unlike anything the Prince of Abyssinia
ever had any itching to enjoy. *Mardi* is a quest after some
total and undivined possession of that holy and mysterious
joy that touched Melville during the period of his courtship:
a joy he had felt in the crucifixion of his love for his mother;
a joy that had dazzled him in his love for Elizabeth Shaw.
When he wrote *Mardi* he was married, and his wife was with
child. And *Mardi* is a pilgrimage for a lost glamour.

In these wanderings in search of Yillah, the symbol of this
faded ecstasy, the hero of *Mardi* is pursued by three shadowy
messengers from the temptress Hautia; she who was descended
from the queen who had first incited Mardi to wage war
against beings with wings. Despairing of ever achieving Yillah, Melville in the end turned towards the island of Hautia,
called Flozella-a-Nina, or "The Last-Verse-of-the-Song."
"Yillah was all beauty, and innocence; my crown of felicity;
my heaven below:—and Hautia, my whole heart abhorred.
Yillah I sought; Hautia sought me. Yet now I was wildly
dreaming to find them together. In some mysterious way
seemed Hautia and Yillah connected."

They land on the shore of Hautia's bower of bliss, when
"all the sea, like a harvest plain, was stacked with glittering
sheaves of spray. And far down, fathoms on fathoms, flitted
rainbow hues:—as seines-full of mermaids; half-screening

the bower of the drowned." Hautia lavished him with flowers, and with wine, that like a blood-freshet ran through his veins, she the vortex that draws all in. "But as my hand touched Hautia's, down dropped a dead bird from the clouds." And at the end of the madness into which Hautia had betrayed him, he and she stood together—"snake and victim: life ebbing from out me, to her."

In *Pierre,* Melville sadly reflects upon "the inevitable evanescence of all earthly loveliness: which makes the sweetest things of life only food for ever-devouring and omnivorous melancholy." And the nuptial embrace, he says, breaks love's airy zone. The etherealisations of the filial breast, he wrote, while contemporary with courtship, *preceding* the final banns and the rites, "like the bouquet of the costliest German wines, too often evaporate upon pouring love out to drink in the disenchanting glasses of the matrimonial days and nights." "I am Pluto stealing Proserpine," says Pierre; "and every accepted lover is. I am of heavy earth, and she of airy light. By heaven, but marriage is an impious thing!"

Yillah was to Melville lost for ever; and in Hautia was a final disillusionment. And on the shore, awaiting to destroy, "stood the three pale sons of him I had slain to gain the lost maiden, sworn to hunt me round eternity."

" 'Hail! realm of shades!' "—so *Mardi* concludes—"and turning my prow into the racing tide, which seized me like a hand omnipotent, I darted through. Churned in foam, that outer ocean lashed the clouds; and straight in my white wake, headlong dashed a shallop, three fixed spectres leaning o'er its prow: three arrows poising. And thus, pursuers and pursued fled on, over an endless sea."

Within a week of the completion of *Mardi,* Melville's wife wrote to her mother:

"I suppose by this time that you have received Sam's letter and are relieved of anxiety concerning his safe arrival. I was very glad to see him at last & hope he will enjoy his vacation. You need not fear his getting too much excited—he will not take too much exercise, for he can always get in an omnibus when he feels tired of walking. Yesterday he went down town with Tom—to the Battery—and to a gallery of paintings —and in the afternoon took a short walk with the girls. We should have gone to Brooklyn, but it was very cloudy and looked like rain—but we are going to-day as soon as I get done my copying (by the way we are nearly through—shall finish this week). Sam is very well and finds much amusement, especially in the 'ad-i-s-h-e-e-e-s!' (radishes) screamed continually under our window in every variety of cracked voices.

"I was very much pleased with my presents especially the 'boots' which fit me admirably—but I meant that to be a business transaction—else I should not have sent. 'Tapes' are *always* useful, especially if one has a husband who is continually breaking strings off of drawers as mine is—the cuffs were very pretty also—Herman was very much pleased with his pocket-book & says 'he has long needed such an article, for his bank bills accumulate to such an extent he can find no place to put them.'

"Mother feels very uneasy because Tom wants to go to sea again—he has been trying for a place in some store ever since he came home but not succeeding, is discouraged and says he must go to sea immediately. Herman has written Mr. Parker (Daniel P.) to see if he can send him out in one of his ships. I hope he will, if Tom must go, for Mr. Parker would be likely to take an interest in him and promote him.

"And now for something which I hardly know whether to write you or not I feel so undecided about it. My cold is very bad indeed, perhaps worse than it has ever been so early, and I attribute it entirely to the warm dry atmosphere so different from the salt air I have been accustomed to. And Herman thinks I had better go back to Boston with Sam to see if the change of air will not benefit me. And he will come on for me in two or three weeks, if he can—and then in August when he takes his vacation he will take me there again. But I don't know as I can make up my mind to go and leave him here— and besides I'm afraid to trust him to finish up the book without me! That is, taking all things into consideration I'm afraid I should not feel at ease enough to enjoy my visit without him with me. But there is time enough to consider about it before Sam goes—and if my cold continues so bad I think I shall go. But I must go to my writing else I shall not get done in time to go to Brooklyn."

CHAPTER XIV

ACROSS THE ATLANTIC AGAIN

"You said you were married, I think? Well, I suppose it is wise, after
all. It settles, ceńtralises, and confirms a man, I have heard. Yes, it
makes the world definite to him; it removes his morbid subjectiveness,
and makes all things objective; nine small children, for instance, may be
considered objective. Marriage, hey!—A fine thing, no doubt, no doubt:—
domestic—pretty—nice, all round.—So you are married?"
—HERMAN MELVILLE: *Pierre.*

IN October, 1849, at the age of thirty, five years after his
return from the South Seas, and two years after his marriage,
Melville again left home. His departure was not prompted
by any lack of diversion at home: there had been plenty of it
at 103 Fourth Avenue. Melville's brothers Allan and Tom,
his sisters Augusta, Fanny and Helen, his mother, his wife,
and the visits from Boston of the Shaws, had been a sufficiently varied company to divert any lover of humanity, and
to enamour a misanthrope to the family hearth. Withal,
Melville was not only a husband, but a father: and duties towards the support of the company with whom he lived were
blatantly clear. For this support he depended solely upon the
earnings from his books. In three years he had published five
volumes: *Typee, Omoo, Mardi* (in two volumes) and *Redburn.*
Though he had attracted wide attention as a writer, he was,
nevertheless, in debt to his publishers. Despite sisters, and
brothers, and wives, and babies, and mothers, and callers, he
had stuck relentlessly to his desk, and another book—*White-
Jacket*—he had finished in manuscript. His, as well as his sister Augusta's, was "a pressing case." So he decided to go to
England, to make personal intercession with publishers, hoping thereby to improve his income from the other side of the
Atlantic.

On October 11, 1849, after a detention of three or four days,
owing to wind and weather, he went on board the tug *Goliath*

a little after noon. A violent storm was blowing from the west, and with some confusion the passengers were transferred to the *Southampton,* a regular London liner that lay in the North River. By half-past five, with yards square, and sailing in half a gale, Melville was again out of sight of land.

"As the ship dashed on," says Melville in his journal of the trip, "under double-reefed topsails, I walked the deck, thinking of what they might be doing at home, and of the last familiar faces I saw on the wharf—Allan was there, and George Duyckinck, and a Mr. McCurdy, a rich merchant of New York, who had seemed somewhat interested in the prospect of his son (a sickly youth of twenty, bound for the grand tour) being very romantic. But to my great delight, the promise that the Captain had given me at an early day, he now made good; and I find myself in the individual occupancy of a large state-room. It is as big almost as my own room at home; it has a spacious berth, a large wash-stand, a sofa, glass, etc., etc. I am the only person on board who is thus honoured with a room to himself. I have plenty of light, and a little thick glass window in the side, which in fine weather I may open to the air. I have looked out upon the sea from it, often, tho not yet 24 hours on board."

The George Duyckinck who was among the party that had waved him off was, of course, one of two Duyckinck brothers who published in 1855 the two volume *Cyclopædia of American Literature:* a work vituperated in its day for shocking omissions and inaccuracies. Both the work and its critics have now fallen into a decent oblivion. Withal, in this same antiquated *Cyclopædia* is to be found one of the best informed summaries of the first half of Melville's life ever printed.

On October 12, Melville records in his journal his impressions upon finding himself again on the ocean. "Walked the deck last night till about eight o'clock," he says, "then made up a whist party and played till one of the number had to visit his room from sickness. Retired early and had a sound sleep Was up betimes and aloft, to recall the old emotions of being at the mast-head. Found that the ocean looked the same as ever. Have tried to read but find it hard work. However, there are some very pleasant passengers on board, with whom to converse. Chief among these is a Mr. Adler, a German scholar, to whom Duyckinck introduced me. He is author of a formidable lexicon (German or English); in compiling which he almost ruined his health. He was almost crazy, he tells me, for a time. He is full of the German metaphysics and discourses of Kant, Swedenborg, etc. He has been my principal companion thus far. There is also a Mr. Taylor among the passengers, cousin of James Bayard Taylor, the pedestrian traveller. There is a Scotch artist on board, a painter, with a most unpoetical looking child, a young-one all cheeks and forehead, the former preponderating. Young Mc-Curdy I find to be a lisping youth of genteel capacity, but quite disposed to be sociable. We have several Frenchmen and Englishmen. One of the latter has been hunting, and carries over with him two glorious pairs of antlers (moose) as trophies of his prowess in the Woods of Maine. We have also a middle-aged English woman, who sturdily walks the decks and prides herself upon her sea-legs, and being an old tar." There was also aboard "a Miss Wilbur (I think) of New York." Melville reports of Miss Wilbur that she "is of a marriageable age, keeps a diary, and talks about 'winning souls to Christ.'" In the evening, Melville "walked the deck with the German, Mr. Adler, till a late hour, talking of 'Fixed Fate, Free-will, free-knowledge absolute' etc. His philosophy is *Coleridgean;* he accepts the Scriptures as divine, and yet leaves himself free to inquire into Nature. He does not take it, that the Bible is absolutely infallible, and that anything opposed to it in Science must be wrong. He believes that there are things not of God and independent of Him,—things that would have existed were there no God; such as that two and two make four; for it is not that God so decrees mathematically, but that in the very nature of things, the fact is thus."

On the following morning, Melville was up early. "Opened my bull's eye window, and looked out to the East. The sun was just rising—the horizon was red;—a familiar sight to me, reminding me of old times. Before breakfast, went up to the mast-head by way of gymnastics. About ten o'clock the wind rose, the sun fell, and the deck looked dismally empty. By dinner time, it blew half a gale, and the passengers mostly retired to their rooms, sea-sick. After dinner, the rain ceased, but it still blew stiffly, and we were slowly forging along under close-reefed top-sails—mainsail furled. I was walking the deck, when I perceived one of the steerage passengers looking over the side; I looked too, and saw a man in the water, his head completely lifted above the waves,—about twelve feet from the ship, right amast the gangway. For an instant, I thought I was dreaming; for no one else seemed to see what I did. Next moment, I shouted 'Man Overboard!' and turned to go aft. I dropped overboard the tackle-fall of the quarter-boat, and swung it toward the man, who was now drifting close to the ship. He did not get hold of it, and I got over the side, within a foot or two of the sea, and again swung the rope toward him. He now got hold of it. By this time, a crowd of people—sailors and others—were clustering about the bulwarks; but none seemed very anxious to save him. They warned *me,* however, not to fall overboard. After holding on to the rope, about a quarter of a minute, the man let go of it and dropped astern under the mizzen chains. Four or five of the seamen jumped over into the chains and swung him more ropes. But his conduct was unaccountable; he could have saved himself, had he been so minded. I was struck by the expression of his face in the water. It was merry. At last he dropped off under the ship's counter, and all hands cried 'He's gone!' Running to the taffrail we saw him again, floating off —saw a few bubbles, and never saw him again. No boat was lowered, no sail was shaken, hardly any noise was made. The man drowned like a bullock. It afterward turned out, that he was crazy, and had jumped overboard. He had declared he would do so, several times; and just before he did jump, he had tried to get possession of his child, in order to jump into the sea, with the child in his arms. His wife was miserably sick in her berth."

In the steerage another crazy man was reported. But his lunacy turned out to be delirium tremens, consequent upon "keeping drunk for the last two months."

Sunday the fourteenth was "a regular blue devil day; a gale of wind, and everybody sick. Saloons deserted, and all sorts of nausea heard from the state-rooms. Managed to get thro' the day somehow, by reading and walking the deck, tho' the last was almost as much as my neck was worth. Saw a lady with a copy of *Omoo* in her hand two days ago. Now and then she would look up at me, as if comparing notes. She turns out to be the wife of a young Scotchman, an artist, going out to Scotland to sketch scenes for his patrons in Albany, including Dr. Armsby. He introduced himself to me by mentioning the name of Mr. Twitchell who painted my portrait gratis. He is a very unpretending young man, and looks more like a tailor than an artist. But appearances are etc.—" The portrait painted by Mr. Twitchell is now not known to exist.

Monday broke fair. "By noon the passengers were pretty nearly all on deck, convalescent. They seem to regard me as a hero, proof against wind and weather. My occasional feats in the rigging are regarded as a species of tight-rope dancing. Poor Adler, however, is hardly himself again. He is an exceedingly amiable man, and a fine scholar whose society is improving in a high degree. This afternoon Dr. Taylor and I sketched a plan for going down the Danube from Vienna to Constantinople; thence to Athens on the steamer; to Beyrout and Jerusalem—Alexandria and the Pyramids. From what I learn, I have no doubt this can be done at a comparatively trifling expense. Taylor has had a good deal of experience in cheap European travel, and from his knowledge of German is well fitted for a travelling companion thro Austria and Turkey. I am full (just now) of this glorious Eastern jaunt. Think of it:—Jerusalem and the Pyramids—Constantinople, the Egean and also Athens!—The wind is not fair yet, and there is much growling consequently. Drank a small bottle of London stout to-day for dinner, and think it did me good. I wonder how much they charge for it? I must find out."

On the sixteenth his journal looks back towards home. "What's little Barney about?" he asks of his son Malcolm. And of his wife: "Where's Orianna?" Four days later, having been "annoyed towards morning by a crying baby adjoining" he repeats this simple catechism.

The entire morning of the eighteenth—the day delightful and the ship getting on famously—Melville spent "in the maintop with Adler and Dr. Taylor, discussing our plans for the grand circuit of Europe and the East. Taylor, however, has communicated to me a circumstance that may prevent him from accompanying us—something of a pecuniary nature. He reckons our expenses at $400." Though Melville played with this idea of the trip into the East for some days, he in the end was forced by lack of funds to give it up. Not until 1856 did he see Greece, and Constantinople, and the Holy Land, and then under tragic circumstances.

The rest of the week went by eventlessly. Melville read, lounged, played cards, went into the Ladies' Saloon for the first time, there to "hear Mrs. Gould, the opera lady, sing." When he comes to Sunday, October 21, he is unusually laconic: on ship board at least, Melville was in a mood to sympathise with Fielding's liberties with the calendar in *Tom Jones* in counting six secular days as a full week. "Cannot remember what happened to-day," he writes; "it came to an end somehow." But on the morrow, his memory cleared. "I forgot to mention that *last night* about 9:30 P. M., Adler and Taylor came into my room, and it was proposed to have whiskey punches, which we *did* have accordingly. Adler drank about three tablespoons full—Taylor four or five tumblers, etc. We had an extraordinary time and did not break up till after two in the morning. We talked metaphysics continually, and Hegel, Schlegel, Kant, etc., were discussed under the influence of the whiskey. I shall not forget Adler's look when he quoted La Place the French astronomer—'It is not necessary, gentlemen, to account for these worlds by the hypothesis', etc. After Adler retired, Taylor and I went out on the bowsprit—splendid spectacle." Three days later there was further inducement to metaphysical discussion. "By evening blew a very stiff breeze and we dashed on in magnificent style. Fine moonlight night, and we rushed on thro' snow-banks of foam. McCurdy invited Adler, the Doctor and I into his room and ordered champagne. Went on deck again and remained till near midnight. The scene was indescribable—I never saw such sailing before."

On Saturday, October 27: "Steered our course in a wind. I played shuffle-board for the first time. Ran about aloft a good deal. McCurdy invited Adler, Taylor and I to partake of some *mulled wine* with him, which we did, in my room. Got—all of us—riding on the German horse again. Taylor has not been in Germany in vain. We sat down to whist, and separated at about three in the morning."

On the morrow, "Decks very wet, and hard work to take exercise. ('Where dat old man?') Read a little, dozed a little and to bed early." So passed another vacant Sabbath. In the margin opposite "Where dat old man?" Melville's wife has added in pencil: "Macky's baby words." Melville thrice quotes this question of Malcolm's—and each time Mrs. Melville explains it in the margin, and initials her explanation each time. The third time she writes: "First words of baby Malcolm's. E.S.M."

Monday was wet and foggy. Some of the passengers were sick. "In the afternoon tried to create some amusement by arraigning Adler before the Captain in a criminal charge. In the evening put the Captain in the chains, and argued the question 'which was best, a monarchy or a republic?' Had some good sport during the debate—the Englishman wouldn't take part in it tho'.—After claret and stout with Monsieur Moran and Taylor, went on deck and found it a moonlight midnight. Wind astern. Retired at 1 A. M."

On November 1, Melville wrote: "Just three weeks from home, and made the land—Start Point—about 3 P. M.—well up channel—passed the Lizzard. Very fine day—great number of ships in sight. Thro' these waters Blake's and Nelson's ships once sailed. Taylor suggested that he and I should return McCurdy's civilities. We did, and Captain Griswold joined and ordered a pitcher of his own. The Captain is a very intelligent and gentlemanly man—converses well and understands himself. I never was more deceived in a person than I was in him. Retired about midnight. Taylor played a rare joke upon McCurdy this evening, passing himself off as Miss Wilbur, having borrowed her cloak, etc. They walked together. Shall see Portsmouth to-morrow morning."

Saturday, Nov. 3rd: "Woke about six o'clock with an insane idea that we were going before the wind, and would be in Portsmouth in an hour's time. Soon found out my mistake. About eight o'clock took a pilot, who brought some papers two weeks old. Made the Isle of Wight about 10 A. M. High land—the Needles—Wind ahead and tacking. Get in to-night or to-morrow—or next week or year. Devilish dull, and too bad altogether. Continued tacking all day with a light wind from West. Isle of Wight in sight all day and numerous ships. In the evening all hands in high spirits. Played chess in the ladies' saloon—another party at cards; good deal of singing in the gentlemen's cabin and drinking—very hilarious and noisy. Last night every one thought. Determined to go ashore at Portsmouth. Therefore prepared for it, arranged my trunk to be left behind—put up a shirt or two in Adler's carpet bag and retired pretty early.

Sunday, Nov. 4th: "Looked out of my window first thing upon rising and saw the Isle of Wight again—very near— ploughed fields, etc. Light head wind—expected to be in a little after breakfast time. About 10 A. M. rounded the Eastern end of the Isle, when it fell flat calm. The town in sight by telescope. Were becalmed about three or four hours. Foggy, drizzly; long faces at dinner—no porter bottles. Wind came from the West at last. Squared the yards and struck away from Dover—distant 60 miles. Close reefed the topsails so as not to run too fast. Expect now to go ashore to-morrow morning early at Dover—and get to London via Canterbury Cathedral. Mysterious hint dropped me about my green coat. It is now eight o'clock in the evening. I am alone in my state-room—lamp in tumbler. Spite of past disappointments, I *feel* that this is my last night aboard the *Southampton*. This time to-morrow I shall be on land, and press English earth after the lapse of ten years—*then a sailor,* now H. M. author of *Peedee, Hullabaloo* and *Pog-Dog.* For the last time I lay aside my 'log' to add a line or two to Lizzie's letter—the last I shall write aboard. ('Where dat old man?—Where looks?')"

The account of his experiences in England is preserved in a separate note-book, formally beginning: "Commenced this journal at 25 Craven Street at 6-½ P. M. on Wednesday, Nov. 7, 1849—being just arrived from dinner at a chop house, and feeling like it."

"*Mon. Nov. 5th, 1849:* Having at the invitation of Mc-Curdy cracked some champagne with him, I returned about midnight to my state-room, and at four in the morning was wakened by the Captain in person, saying we were off Dover. Dressed in a hurry, ran on deck, and saw the lights ashore. A cutter was alongside, and after some confusion in the dark, we got off in her for the shore. A comical scene ensued, the boatman saying we could not land at Dover, but only at Deal. So to Deal we went, and were beached there just at break of day. Some centuries ago a person called Julius Cæsar jumped ashore about in this place, and took possession. It was Guy Fawkes day also. Having left our baggage (that is, Taylor, Adler and myself) to go round by ship to London, we were wholly non-encumbered, and I proposed walking to Canterbury—distant 18 miles, for an appetite to breakfast. So we strode thru this quaint old town of Deal, one of the Cinque Ports, I believe, and soon were in the open country. A fine Autumnal morning and the change from ship to shore was delightful. Reached Sandwich (6 miles) and breakfasted at a tumble down old inn. Finished with ale and pipes, visited 'Richbors' Castle'—so called—a Roman fortification near the sea shore. An imposing ruin, the interior was planted with cabbages. The walls some ten feet thick grown over with ivy. Walked to where they were digging—and saw, defined by a trench, the exterior wall of a circus. Met the proprietor —an antiquary—who regaled me with the history of the place. Strolled about the town, on our return, and found it full of interest as a fine specimen of the old Elizabethan architecture. Kent abounds in such towns. At one o'clock took the 2nd class (no 3rd) cars for Canterbury. The cathedral is on many accounts the most remarkable in England. Henry II, his

wife, and the Black Prince are here—and Becket. Fine cloisters. There is a fine thought expressed in one of the inscriptions on a tomb in the nave. Dined at the Falstaff Inn
near the Westgate. Went to the theatre in the evening, & was
greatly amused at the performance: More people on the stage
than in the boxes. Ineffably funny, the whole affair. All
three of us slept in one room at the inn—odd hole.

"*Tuesday, Nov. 6th:* Swallowed a glass of ale and away
for the R. R. Station & off for London, distant some 80 miles.
Took the third class car—exposed to the air, devilish cold
riding against the wind. Fine day—people sociable. Passed
thro Penshurst (P. S.'s place & Tunbridge—fine old ruin
that). Arrived at London Bridge at noon. Crossed at once
over into the city and down at a chop-house in the Poulberry
—having eaten nothing since the previous afternoon dinner.
Went and passed St. Paul's to the Strand to find our house.
They referred us elsewhere. Very full. Secured room at
last (one for each) at a guinea and a half a week. Very
cheap. Went down to the Queen's Hotel to inquire after our
ship friends—(on the way green coat attracted attention)—
not in. Went to Drury Lane at Julien's Promenade Concerts
(admittance 1 s.) A great crowd and fine music. In the
reading room to see 'Bentley's Miscellany' with something
about *Redburn.* (By the way, stopped at a store in the Row
& inquired for the book, to see whether it had been published.
They offered it to me at a guinea). At Julien's also saw
Blackwoods' long story about a short book. It's very comical.
Seemed so, at least, as I had to hurry on it. But the wonder
is that the old Tory should waste so many papers upon a
thing which I, the author, know to be trash, and wrote it to buy
some tobacco with. A good wash & turned in early.

"*Thursday, Nov. 8th:* Dressed, after breakfast at a coffee-
house, and went to Mr. Bentley's. He was out of town at
Brighton. The notices of *Redburn* were shown me.—Laugh-
able. Staid awhile, and then to Mr. Murray's, out of town.
Strolled about and went into the National Gallery. Dined
with the Doctor & Adler, and after dark a ramble thro'

Chancery Lane and Lincoln's Inn Fields, we turned into Holborn & so to the Princess's Theatre in Oxford Street. Went into the pit at the hall price—one shilling. The part of a Frenchman was very well played. So also, skater on the ice.

"Friday, Nov. 9th: Breakfasted late and went into Cheapside to see the 'Lord Mayor's show' it being the day of the great civic feast & festivities. A most bloated pomp, to be sure. Went down to the bridge to see the people crowding there. Crossed by Westminster, thro' the Parks to the Edgeware Road, & found the walk delightful, the sun coming out a little, and the air not cold. While on one of the bridges, the thought struck me again that a fine story might be written about a Blue Monday in November London—a City of Dis (Dante's) Cloud of Smoke—the damned, etc., coal boxes, oily waters, etc.—its marks are left upon you, etc., etc., etc."

In *Israel Potter* (1855) Melville devoted one chapter to a description of London Bridge: a chapter entitled: "In the City of Dis." The description begins: "It was late on a Monday morning in November—a Blue Monday—a Fifth of November—Guy Fawkes' Day!—very blue, foggy, doleful and gunpowdery, indeed." Melville had been husbanding for six years the impressions gathered on November 9, 1849.

On November 10, Melville received a reply to the note he had sent to Bentley announcing his presence in London. Bentley expressed a willingness to come up from Brighton to see Melville at any time convenient to Melville. Melville appointed "Monday noon, in New Burlington Street," and went forth again to explore the city. He visited the Temple Courts. By way of Cock Lane—reflecting on Dr. Johnson's Ghost—he walked on to the Charter House, "where I had a sociable chat with an old pensioner who guided me through some fine old cloisters, kitchens, chapels." Saturday night, with Adler, he strolled over to Holborn "vagabonding thro' the courts and lanes and looking in at windows. Stopped at a penny theatre—very comical. Adler afraid. To bed early." On Sunday Melville went "down to Temple Church to hear the music," looked in at St. Paul's, and then, with Adler, took a bus for Hampton Court." They enjoyed the ride down, the pictures at Hampton Court, and then dinner at the Adelphi in the evening.

On Monday, Melville saw Bentley. "Very polite," says Melville. "Gave me his note for £100 at ten days for *Redburn*. Couldn't do better, he said. He expressed much anxiety and vexation at the state of the copyright question. Proposed my new book *White-Jacket* to him and showed him the table of contents. He was much pleased with it, and notwithstanding the vexatious and uncertain state of the copyright matter, he made me the following offer: To pay me £200 for the first thousand copies of the book (the privilege of publishing that number) and as we might afterwards arrange concerning subsequent editions. A liberal offer. But he could make no advance—left him and called upon Mr. Murray. Not in. Out of town. . . . Walked to St. Paul's and sat over an hour in a dozy state listening to the chanting of the choir. Felt homesick and sentimentally unhappy."

To sweeten his blood, he sallied forth, with Adler, early on the morrow, "to see the last end of the Mannings. An innumerable crowd in all the streets. Police by hundreds. Men and women fainting. The man and wife were hung side by side—still unreconciled to each other—what a change from the time they stood up to be married together! The mob was brutish. All in all, a most wonderful, horrible, and unspeakable scene.—Breakfasted about 11 A. M. and went to the Zoological Gardens, Regent's Park. Very pretty. Fine giraffes. Dreary and rainy day."

On the morrow "Rigged up again, and in my *green* jacket called upon Mr. Murray in Albemarle Street. He was very civil, much vexed about copyright matters. I proposed *White-Jacket* to him—he seemed decidedly pleased and has since sent for the proof sheets, according to agreement. That evening we went to the New Strand Theatre, to see Coleman's *The Clandestine Marriage*. Melville's comment upon Leigh Murray, who played Melvil, would do credit to the lost diary of Mrs. Pepys: "the finest leg I ever saw on a man—a devilishly well turned-out man, upon my soul."

The day following—November 15—was by the Queen appointed as a day of special thanksgiving. Melville again sallied forth sight-seeing. On the morrow he made two attempts to see Murray; the second found him in. "Very polite—but would not be in his line to publish my book." On November 17, Colbour declined Melville's offer of £200 for a thousand copies of *White-Jacket*, "and principally because of the cussed state of the copyright. Bad news enough—I shall not see Rome—I'm floored—appetite unimpaired, however." On the 19th, he saw Longman, to be told "they bided by the original terms." On the twentieth, he saw Moxen, the publisher. "Found him in—sitting alone in a back room. He was at first very stiff, cold, clammy and clumsy. Managed to bring him to, tho, by clever speeches. Talked of Charles Lamb—he warmed up and ended by saying he would send me a copy of his works. He said he had often put Lamb to bed—drunk. He spoke of Dana—he published D's book here." Moxen sent Melville copies of Lamb's works: but Moxen did not accept Melville's invitation to publish *White-Jacket*.

On November 22—after a jovial evening spent over porter, gin, brandy, whiskey, and cigars—Melville rose late, and with a headache. So he rode out to Windsor, to inspect the state apartments,—which he found "cheerlessly damned fine"—and to view the Royal Stables. "On the way down from the town, met the Queen coming from visiting the sick Queen Dowager. Carriage and four going past with outriders. ˙ The Prince with her. My English friend bowed, so did I—salute returned by the Queen but not by the Prince. I would commend to the Queen, Rowland's Kalydon for clarifying the complexion. She is an amiable domestic woman though, I doubt not, and God bless her, say I, and long live the 'Prince of Whales'— The stables were splendid."

On Friday, November 23, at quarter to eleven, Melville "had just returned from Mr. Murray's where I dined agreeable to invitation. It was a most amusing affair. Mr. Murray was there in a short vest and dress coat, looking quizzical enough; his footman was there also, habited in small clothes and breeches, revealing a despicable pair of sheepshanks. The impudence of the fellow in showing his legs, and such a pair of legs too! in public, I thought extraordinary. The ladies should have blushed, one would have thought, but they did not. Lockhart was there also, in a prodigious white cravat (made from Walter Scott's shroud, I suppose). He stalked about like a half galvanised ghost,—gave me the tips of two skinny fingers, when introduced to me, or rather, I to him. Then there was a round faced chap by the name of Cook— who seemed to be Murray's factotum. His duty consisted in pointing out the portraits on the wall and saying that this or that one was esteemed a good likeness of the high and mighty ghost Lockhart. There were four or five others present, nameless, fifth-rate looking varlets and four lean women. One of them proved agreeable in the end. She had visited some time in China. I talked with her some time. Besides these there was a footman or boy in a light jacket with bell-buttons."

The lines following, Melville has heavily crossed out. They are, in most part, decipherable, however, and they are not excessively complimentary either to his host or the guest of honour. . "I managed to get through, though, somehow," Melville continues after this blotted abuse, "by conversing with Dr. Holland, a very eminent physician, it seems,—and a very affable, intelligent man who has travelled immensely. After the ladies withdrew, the three decanters, port, sherry and claret, were kept going the rounds with great regularity. I sat next to Lockhart and seeing that he was a customer who was full of himself and expected great homage, and knowing him to be a thoroughgoing Tory and fish-blooded Churchman and conservative, and withal editor of the *Quarterly*—I refrained from playing the snob to him like the rest—and the consequence was he grinned at me his ghastly smiles. After returning to the drawing-room coffee and tea were served. I soon after came away. After two more blotted lines, Melville concludes: "Oh, Conventionalism, what a ninny thou art, to be sure. And now I must turn in."

Melville continued to interview publishers, and publishers continued to chasten him with reflections on the state of the copyright laws. Between times he amused himself as best he could; but there was little novelty, brilliancy or excitement in the amusement. He was once entertained very formally at dinner, however: a Baroness Somebody on his left, an anonymous Baron opposite him, and near him at table "a most lovely young girl, a daughter of Captain Chamier, the sea novelist." And in these brilliant surroundings, he saw a copy of *Typee* on a table in the drawing room. He ran upon an old friend of Gansevoort's, too, and as a result was betrayed into sober and sentimental reflections. "No doubt, two years ago, or three, Gansevoort was writing here in London, about the same hour as this—alone in his chamber, in profound silence, as I am now. This silence, is a strange thing. No wonder the Greeks deemed it the vestibule to the higher mysteries."

He paid for his sentimentality, however, by passing "a most extraordinary night—one continuous nightmare—till daybreak. Hereafter, if I should be condemned to purgatory, I shall plead the night of November 25, 1849, in extenuation of the sentence."

On November 27, he abruptly left England, to find himself, two days following, "right snugly roomed in the fifth story of a lodging house No. 12 & 14 Rue de Bussy, Paris. It is the first night I have taken possession," he says, "and the chambermaid has lighted a fire of wood, lit the candle and left me alone, at 11 o'clock P. M. On first gazing round, I was struck by the apparition of a bottle containing a dark fluid, a glass, a decanter of water, and a paper package of sugar (loaf) with a glass basin next to it. I protest all this was not in the bond. But tho if I use these things they will doubtless be charged to me, yet let us be charitable, so I ascribe all this to the benevolence of Madame Capelle, my most polite, pleasant and Frenchified landlady below. I shall try the brandy before writing more—and now to resume my Journal." The account of Israel Potter's first night in Paris, after Benjamin Franklin shows him into lodgings in the Latin Quarter, is certainly built upon Melville's experience on this occasion. Israel finds in his room a heavy plate glass mirror; and among the articles genially reflected therein, he notes: "seventh, one paper of loaf sugar, nicely broken into sugar-bowl size; eighth, one silver teaspoon; ninth, one glass tumbler; tenth, one glass decanter of cool pure water; eleventh, one sealed bottle containing a richly hued liquid, and marked 'Otard.'" Melville makes a chapter out of Israel's adventures with this bottle of Otard,— a chapter in which Benjamin Franklin unburdens himself of much almanac moralising upon the almanac virtues.

Despite the Otard, and the snug quarters, and the diversions of Paris—diversions somewhat restricted by Melville's complete inability to speak French—Melville was not happy every moment he was in France. "Fire made, and tried to be comfortable. But this is not home and—but no repinings." Adler was in Paris at the time, however, and this somewhat cheered his solitude. Yet on December 2, when Melville left Adler after an evening of eau de vie and cigars, he "strolled out into a dark rainy night and made my melancholy way across the Pont (rather a biscuit's toss of the Morgue) to my sixth story apartment." And once safely in his room, he complained: "I don't like that mystic door tapestry leading out of the closet." On the following day he "looked in at the Morgue," and "bought two pair of gloves and one pair of shoes for Lizzie." That night, he dined with Adler, and "talked high German metaphysics till ten o'clock."

He visited the Hotel de Cluny, and found "the house just the house I'd like to live in." He made a half-hearted effort to see Rachel at the Theatre Française, but failed. He saw the obvious sights and on December 6 hurried away from Paris. He closes the record of his departure with a "Selah!" Even in Paris, he speaks of taking his "usual bath" upon getting up in the morning.

He touched at Brussels: and despite its architecture, "a more dull, humdrum place I never saw:" he hurried through Cologne, where he found "much to interest a pondering man like me." From Cologne he was headed for Coblenz: but he looked forward to the voyage with little eagerness: "I feel homesick to be sure—being all alone with not a soul to talk to—but the Rhine is before me, and I must on." Of Coblenz he wrote: "Most curious that the finest wine of all the Rhine is grown right under the guns of Ehrenbreitstein." "Opposite is this frowning fortress—and some 4000 miles away is America and Lizzie. To-morrow I am *homeward*-bound! Hurrah and three cheers!" "In the horrible long dreary cold ride to Ostend on the coach, in a fit of the nightmare was going to stop at a way-place, taking it for the place of my destination.

By December 13, he was back to his old chamber overlooking the Thames. Upon his arrival he was vaguely told "a gentleman from St. James called in his coach," and "was handed, with a meaning flourish, a note sealed with a coronet." The note was from the Duke of Rutland,—perversely called at times by Melville, *Mr.* Rutland—inviting Melville to visit Belvoir Castle "at any time after a certain day in January." "Cannot go," Melville writes—"I am homeward bound, and Malcolm is growing all the time." He called at Bentley's for letters. "Found one from Lizzie and Allan. Most welcome but gave me the blues most horribly. Felt like chartering a small boat and starting down the Thames embarked for New York." So he drank some punch to cheer him, and walked down the Strand to buy a new coat, "so as to look decent—for I found my green coat plays the devil with my respectability here." He haunted the bookshops, and "at last succeeded in getting the much desired copy of Rousseau's *Confessions,*" as well as an 1686 folio of Sir Thomas Browne.

On December 15, Melville "rigged for Bentley, whom I expect to meet at 1 P. M. about *White-Jacket.* Called but had not arrived from Brighton. Walked about a little and bought a cigar case for Allan in Burlington Arcade. Saw some pretty things for presents—but could not afford to buy." So back to his room he came, and filled up the time before four o'clock, when he was to call again at Bentley's, by writing up his journal. "He does not know that I am in town," Melville writes— "I earnestly hope that I shall be able to see him and I shall be able to do something about that 'pesky' book."

At six o'clock, Melville was back again in his room. "Hurrah and three cheers! I have just returned from Mr. Bentley's and have concluded an arrangement with him that gives me to-morrow his note for two hundred pounds (sterling). It is to be at 6 months and I am almost certain I shall be able to get it cashed at once. This takes a load off my heart. The two hundred pounds is in anticipiation, for the book is not to be published till the last of March next. Hence the long time of the note. The above mentioned sum is for the first 1000 copies, subsequent editions (if any) to be jointly divided between us. At eight to-night I am going to Mrs. Daniels'. What sort of an evening is it going to be? Mr. Bentley invited me to dinner for Wednesday at 6 P. M. This will do for a memorandum of the enjoyment. I have just read over the Duke of Rutland's note, which I had not fully perused before. It seems very cordial. I wish the invitation was for next week, instead of being so long ahead, but this I believe is the mode here for these sort of invitations into the country. (Memo. At 1 P. M. on Monday am to call at Mr. Bentley's.)"

· Under Sunday, December 16, Melville wrote: "Last night went in a cab to Lincoln's Inn Fields and found Mrs. Daniel and daughters. Very cordial. The elder 'daught' remarkably sprightly and the mother as nice an old body as any one could desire. Presently there came in several 'young gents' of various complexions. We had some coffee, music, dancing, and after an agreeable evening I came away at 11 o'clock, and walking to the Cock near Temple Bar, drank a glass of stout and home to bed after reading a few chapters in *Tristram Shandy*, which I have never yet read. This morning breakfasted at 10 at the Hotel De Sabloneue (very nice cheap little snuggery being closed on Sundays). Had a sweet omelette which was delicious. Thence walked to St. Thomas's Church, Charter House, to hear my famed namesake (almost) 'The Reverend H. Melvill.' I had seen him placarded as to deliver a charity sermon. The church was crowded—the sermon admirable (granting the Rev. gentleman's premises). Indeed he deserves his reputation. I do not think that I hardly ever heard so good a discourse before—that is for an 'orthodox' divine. It is now 3 P. M. I have had a fire made and am smoking a cigar. Would that one I knew were here. Would that the Little One too were here,—I am in a very painful state of uncertainty. I am all eagerness to get home— I ought to be home. My absence occasions uneasiness in a quarter where I most beseech heaven to grant repose. Yet here I have before me an open prospect to get some curious ideas of a style of life which in all probability I shall never have again. I should much like to know what the highest English aristocracy really and practically is. And the Duke of Rutland's cordial invitation to visit him at the castle furnishes me with just the thing I want. If I do not go, I am confident that hereafter I shall reprimand myself for neglecting such an opportunity of procuring 'material.' And Allan and others will account me a ninny.—I would not debate the matter a moment were it not that at least three whole weeks must elapse ere I start for Belvoir Castle—three weeks! If I could but get over them! And if the two images would only down for that space of time. I must light a second cigar and resolve it over again. (½ past 6 P. M.) My mind is made, rather is irrevocably resolved upon my first determination. A visit into Leicester would be very agreeable—at least very valuable, and in one respect, to me—but the three weeks are intolerable. To-morrow I shall go down to London Dock and book myself a state-room on board the good ship *Independence*. I have just returned from a lonely dinner at the Adelphi, where I read the Sunday papers. An article upon the 'Sunday School Union' particularly struck me. Would that I could go home in a steamer—but it would take an extra $100 out of my pocket. Well, it's only thirty days—one month—and I can weather it somehow."

On Monday, Melville concluded his arrangements with Bentley, who gave him a note for two hundred pounds sterling at six months. Melville also walked down to the London Docks to inspect the *Independence*. "She looks small and smells ancient," Melville writes. "Only two or three passengers engaged. I liked Captain Fletcher, however. He enquired whether I was a relative of Gansevoort Melville and of Herman Melville. I told him I was. I engaged my passage and paid ten pounds down. . . . Thence home; and out again, and took a letter for a Duke to the post office and a pair of pants to be altered to a tailor."

On Tuesday, Melville made another of his many pilgrimages

to the old book stores about Great Green Street and Lincoln's Inn. "Looked over a lot of ancient books of London. Bought one (A. D. 1766) for 3 and 2 pence. I want to use it in case I serve up the Revolutionary narrative of the beggar." What was the title of this "ancient book of London" is not known, and hence it is impossible to know what use he put it to, when in *Israel Potter* he did finally "serve up the Revolutionary narrative of the beggar." The same day he "stopped at a silversmith's (corner of Craven St. & Strand) and bought a solid spoon for the boy Malcolm—a fork, I mean. When he arrives to years of mastication I shall invest him with this fork —as in yore they did a young knight, with his good sword. Spent an hour or so looking over *White-Jacket* preparatory to sending it finally to Bentley—who, tho he has paid his money has not received his wares. At 6 I dine with him."

The dinner with Bentley went off well. Melville "had a very pleasant evening indeed" and "began to like" his publisher "very much." Melville reported that "He seems a very fine, frank, off-handed old gentleman. We sat down in a fine old room hung round with paintings (dark walls). A party of fourteen or so. There was a Mr. Bell there—connected with literature in some way or other. At all events an entertaining man and a scholar—but looks as if he loved old Pat. Also Alfred Henry Forester ('Alfred Crowquill')—the comic man. He proved a good fellow—free and easy and no damned nonsense, as there is about so many of these English. Mr. Bentley has one daughter, a fine woman of 25 and married, and four sons—young men. They were all at table. Some time after 11, went home with Crowquill, who invites me to go with him Thursday and see the Pantomime rehearsal at the Surrey Theatre."

The following evening Melville dined with Mr. Cook— whom he had despised, at first meeting, as Murray's factotum— in Elm Court, Temple, "and had a glorious time till noon of night. It recalled poor Lamb's 'Old Benchers.' Cunningham the author of *Murray's London Guide* was there and was very friendly. Mr. Rainbow also, and a grandson Woodfall, the printer of Junius, and a brother-in-law of Leslie the printer.

Leslie was prevented from coming. Up in the 5th story we dined." With a typical departure from the conventional orthography, Melville pronounced the evening, "The Paradise of Batchelors."

In *Harper's New Monthly Magazine* for April, 1854, Melville published a sketch entitled *Paradise of Bachelors and Tartarus of Maids.*" In 1854 he was living in Pittsfield, Massachusetts, in a household of women and young children— three of his sisters, his mother, his wife, and three of his own children. So surrounded, he had relinquished none of the pleasant memories of that December evening, in 1849, in those high chambers near Temple-Bar. "It was the very perfection of quiet absorption of good living, good drinking, good feeling, and good talk," Melville wrote in 1854. "We were a band of brothers. Comfort—fraternal, household comfort, was the grand trait of the affair. Also, you could plainly see that these easy-hearted men had no wives or children to give an anxious thought. Almost all of them were travellers, too; for bachelors alone can travel freely, and without any twinges of their conscience touching desertion of the fireside." The antithesis of this, Melville pictures in the second part of his account—*The Tartarus of Maids.*

Yet just on the eve of his going to these high festivities in the Temple, a letter was left him—"from home!" The letter reported: "All well and Barney ("Baby boy," Mrs. Melville has written in annotation on the margin of the journal) more bouncing than ever, thank heaven." On the following day, Melville began and finished the *Opium Eater,* and pronounced it "a most wonderful book."

On December 24, Melville was in Portsmouth. On Christmas morning he jumped into a small boat with the Captain and a meagre company of passengers, and "pulled off for the ship about a mile and a half distant. Upon boarding her we at once set sail with a fair wind, and in less than 24 hours passed the Land's End and the Scilly Isle—and standing boldly out on the ocean stretched away for New York. I shall keep no further diary. I here close it, with my departure from England, and my pointing for home."

On a blank page at end of his journal, he jotted some brief "Memoranda of things on the voyage." He noted Sir Thomas Browne's reference to cannibals in *Vulgar Errors,* and the fact that Rousseau, as a school master "could have killed his scholars sometimes." He observed that "a Dandy is a good fellow to scout and room with;" and copied out from Ben Jonson "Talk as much folly as you please—so long as you do it without blushing, you may do it with impunity." He itemised in his journal, too, the books obtained while abroad: a 1692 folio of Ben Jonson; a 1673 folio of Davenant; a folio of Beaumont and Fletcher; a 1686 folio of Sir Thomas Browne, and a folio of Marlowe's plays. He brought with him, also, a *Hudibras,* a *Castle of Otranto,* a *Vathek,* a *Corinne,* besides the confessions of Rousseau and of DeQuincey, and the autobiography of Goethe. The other books were guides, old maps, and other material for *Israel Potter.*

Melville arrived at 103 Fourth Avenue, on February 2, 1850. Mrs. Melville, in her journal, thus summarises her husband's trip. "Summer of 1849 we remained in New York. He wrote *Redburn* and *White-Jacket.* Same fall went to England and published the above. Stayed eleven weeks. Took little satisfaction in it from mere homesickness, and hurried home, leaving attractive invitations to visit distinguished people —one from the Duke of Rutland to pass a week at Belvoir Castle—see his journal."

Of his life after his return home, she says: "We went to Pittsfield and boarded in the summer of 1850. Moved to Arrowhead in fall—October, 1850."

On September 27, 1850, Bayard Taylor dispatched from the Tribune Office, New York, a note to Mary Angew. "Scarcely a day passes," Taylor wrote, "but some pleasant recognition is given me. I was invited last Friday to dine with Bancroft and Cooper; on Saturday with Sir Edward Belcher and Herman Melville. These things seem like mockeries, sent to increase the bitterness of my heart." It is not unlikely that Melville and Taylor fed and drank and smoked together on that Saturday evening, and that they parted, each envying the other as a happy and successful man.

CHAPTER XV

"And here again, not unreasonably, might invocation go up to those three Weird Ones, that tend Life's loom. Again we might ask them, what threads are these, oh, ye Weird Ones, that ye wove in the years foregone?"

—HERMAN MELVILLE: *Pierre.*

AT the time when Melville moved into the Berkshire Hills, the region around Lenox boasted the descriptive title: "a jungle of literary lions"—a title amiably ferocious in its provincial vanity. In this region, it is true, Jonathan Edwards had written his treatises on predestination, and with sardonic optimism had gloated over the beauties of hell; here Catherine Sedgewick wrote her amiable insipidities; here Elihu Burritt, "the learned Blacksmith" wrote out his *Sparks;* here Bryant composed; here Henry Ward Beecher indited many *Star-Papers;* here Headley and Holmes, Lowell and Longfellow, Curtis and G. P. R. James, Audubon and Whipple, Mrs. Sigourney and Martineau, Fanny Kemble and Frederick Bremer and the Goodale sisters either visited or lived. Impressed by this array of names—an array deceptively impressive to the New England imagination,—local pride has not blushed to explain: "By the river Arno, in the 'lake region' of Cumberland and Westmoreland, or on the placid river which flows through the Concord meadows, what congestion of literary associations! Like the instinct of the bee which, separated by great distances from the hive, possesses the infallible sense of direction for its return, so, too, the lovely 'nooks and corners' on the earth's surface are irresistibly and unerringly attracting choice spirits, which some way are sure to find them out and pre-empt them in the interests of their craft or clan. Berkshire is no exception to this."

When, in 1850, both Melville and Hawthorne moved into the Berkshires, these literary wilds were tamely domesticated, and sadly thinned of prowling genius. The coming of Melville and Hawthorne, however, marked the most important advent ever made into these regions. For there Melville wrote *Moby-Dick;* and there Melville and Hawthorne were to be thrown into an ironical intimacy.

In the autumn of 1850, Melville bought a spacious gambrel-roofed farmhouse at Pittsfield, situated along Holmes Road and not far from Broadhall, formerly the home of his uncle, and familiar to Melville's youth. Melville named the place Arrowhead. To Arrowhead he brought his retinue of female relatives, and set about to alternate farming with literature.

In the first of the *Piazza Tales* (1856), in *I and My Chimney* (*Putnam's Magazine,* March, 1856), and in *The Rose-wood Table* (*Putnam's Magazine,* May, 1856), Melville has left descriptions of Arrowhead, its inmates, and the surrounding country.

"When I removed into the country," Melville says in the *Piazza Tales,* "it was to occupy an old-fashioned farmhouse which had no piazza—a deficiency the more regretted because not only did I like piazzas, as somehow combining the cosiness of indoors with the freedom of outdoors, and it is so pleasant to inspect your thermometer there, but the country round about was such a picture, that in berry time no boy climbs hill or crosses vale without coming upon easels planted in every nook, and sunburned painters painting there. A very paradise of painters. The circle of the stars cut by the circle of the mountains. At least, so it looks from the house; though once upon the mountains, no circle of them can you see. Had the site been chosen five rods off, this charmed circle would not have been.

"The house is old. Seventy years since, from the heart of the Hearth Stone Hill, they quarried the Kaaba, or Holy Stone, to which, each Thanksgiving, the social pilgrims used to come. So long ago that in digging for the foundation, the workmen used both spade and axe fighting the Troglodytes of those subterranean parts—sturdy roots of a sturdy wood, encamped upon what is now a long landslide of sleeping meadow, sloping away off from my poppy bed. Of that knit

wood but one survivor stands—an elm, lonely through stead·
fastness.

"Whoever built the house, he builded better than he knew;
or else Orion in the zenith flashed down his Damocles' sword
to him some starry night, and said: 'Build there.' For how,
otherwise, could it have entered the builder's mind that, upon
the clearing being made, such a purple prospect would be his?
Nothing less than Greylock, with all his hills about him, like
Charlemagne among his peers.

"A piazza must be had.

"The house was wide—my fortune narrow . . . upon but
one of the four sides would prudence grant me what I wanted.
Now which side? Charlemagne, he carried it.

"No sooner was ground broken than all the neighbourhood,
neighbour Dives in particular, broke too—into a laugh. Piazza
to the north! Winter piazza! Wants, of winter midnights,
to watch the Aurora Borealis, I suppose; hope he's laid in a
good store of polar muffs and mittens.

"That was in the lion month of March. Not forgotten are
some of the blue noses of the carpenters and how they scouted
at the greenness of the cit, who would build his sole piazza to
the north. But March don't last forever; patience, and
August comes. And then, in the cool elysium of my northern
bower, I, Lazarus in Abraham's bosom, cast down the hill a
pitying glance on poor old Dives, tormented in the purgatory
of his piazza to the south.

"But, even in December, this northern piazza does not repel
—nipping cold and gusty though it be, and the north wind,
like any miller, bolting by the snow in finest flour—for then,
once more, with frosted beard, I pace the sleety deck, weather-
ing Cape Horn.

"In summer, too, Canute-like, sitting here, one is often reminded of the sea. For not only do long ground-swells roll
the slanting grain, and little wavelets of the grass ripple over
upon the low piazza, as their beach, and the blown down of
dandelions is wafted like the spray, and the purple of the
mountains is just the purple of the billows, and a still August
noon broods over the deep meadows, as a calm upon the Line;

but the vastness and the lonesomeness are so oceanic, and the silence and the sameness, too, that the first peep of a strange house, rising beyond the trees, is for all the world like spying, on the Barbary coast, an unknown sail."

In *I and My Chimney* Melville makes the old chimney at Arrowhead the chief character in a sketch of his domestic life at Pittsfield: himself and his wife, both freely idealised, are the other actors. This chimney, twelve feet square at the base, was built by Capt. David Bush who erected the house in 1780. It has three fireplaces on the first floor and the one formerly used for the kitchen fireplace is large enough for a log four feet long. This fireplace is panelled in pine, and above it hangs an Indian tomahawk, found and hung there by Melville. Around it are many nooks and cupboards. In *I and My Chimney* Melville wrote: "And here I keep mysterious cordials of a choice, mysterious flavour, made so by the constant naturing and subtle ripening of the chimney's gentle heat, distilled through that warm mass of masonry. Better for wines it is than voyages to the Indies; my chimney itself is a tropic. A chair by my chimney in a November day is as good for an invalid as a long season spent in Cuba. Often I think how grapes might ripen against my chimney. How my wife's geraniums bud there! But in December. Her eggs too—can't keep them near the chimney on account of hatching. Ah, a warm heart has my chimney."

Col. Richard Lathers, in his reminiscences of his Pittsfield residence, writes: "One of my nearest neighbours at Pittsfield was Herman Melville, author of the interesting and very original sea tales, *Typee* and *Omoo* (which were among the first books to be published simultaneously in London and New York), and of various other volumes of prose and verse. I visited him often in his well-stocked library, where I listened with intense pleasure to his highly individual views of society and politics. He always provided a bountiful supply of good cider—the product of his own orchard—and of tobacco, in the virtues of which he was a firm believer. Indeed, he prided himself on the inscription painted over his capacious fireplace: 'I and my chimney smoke together,' an inscription I have seen strikingly verified more than once when the atmosphere was heavy and the wind was east."

When Melville set up his family at Arrowhead, Hawthorne had already been settled at Lenox, some miles away, for a number of months. "I have taken a house in Lenox"—so he announced his removal—"I long to get into the country, for my health is not what it has been. An hour or two in a garden and a daily ramble in country air would keep me all right."

Though Melville and Hawthorne were at this time neither in very affluent circumstances, Hawthorne was, to all outward appearances, the more straitened of the two. He described his new home as "the very ugliest little bit of an old red farmhouse you ever saw," "the most inconvenient and wretched house I ever put my head in." His wife, however, was not so precipitous in her damnation, and writing to her mother on June 23, 1850, said: "We are so beautifully arranged (excepting the guest-chamber), and we seem to have such a large house *inside,* though outside the little reddest thing looks like the smallest of ten-feet houses. Enter our old black tumble-down gate,—no matter for that,—and you behold a nice yard, with an oval grass-plot and a gravel walk all round the borders, a flower-bed, some rose-bushes, a raspberry-bush, and I believe a syringa, and also a few tiger-lilies; quite a fine bunch of peonies, a stately double rose-columbine, and one beautiful Balsam Fir tree, of perfect pyramidal form, and full of a thousand melodies. The front door is wide open. Enter and welcome." Mrs. Hawthorne then elaborates upon the wealth of beauty she finds in her tactful disposition of the pictures, the furniture, and flowers, in the cramped interior. In this tabernacle she enshrined her two small children; and in the "immortal endowments" of her husband, she was inarticulate in felicity. "I cannot possibly conceive of my happiness," she wrote, "but, in a blissful kind of confusion, live on. If I can only be so great, so high, so noble, so sweet, as he in any phase of my being, I shall be glad. I am not deluded nor mistaken, as the angels know now, and as all my friends well know, in open vision!"

Of the actual daily events at Arrowhead and the Red House there is a great inequality in the wealth of records. Of the Red House we know much; of Arrowhead we know only too little. Though Mrs. Hawthorne was always childlike in her modesty and simplicity, "her learning and her accomplishments were rare and varied." She not only read Latin, Greek and Hebrew, but she kept an invaluable journal of the momentous trifles of her husband's life; and she wrote letters home that her Mother very properly preserved for posterity. Mrs. Melville positively knew no Hebrew; and what accounts of her husband she wrote have all disappeared. Only one letter of hers of this period survives:

"ARROWHEAD, Aug. 3, 1851.

"MY DEAR MOTHER:

"I have been trying to write to you ever since Sam came, but could not well find a chance. As it proved, I was not mistaken in supposing the little parcel he brought was a present from you, though I had no letter. The contents were beautiful and very acceptable. Do accept my best thanks for them. We were delighted to see Sam Savage on Tuesday, but as he did not notify us of the day we were not in waiting for him at the depot. However, he found his way out to us. To-day he and Sam have gone over to Lebanon to see the Shakers. The girls were much pleased with the collars, and Mother M. with her remembrance. The scarf you sent me was very handsome, but I am almost sorry you did not keep it for yourself, for it does not seem to me as if I should ever wear it—and certainly not this summer as I go nowhere not even to church. It will look very handsome with my new shawl, if ever I do wear it, though.

"You need not be afraid of the boys staying too long—I am only sorry that they cannot stay longer, but they think or rather Sam Savage thinks he must go to Red Hook this week. You know we do not make any difference for them and let them do just as they please and take care of themselves. Yesterday they went with Herman and explored a neighbouring mountain.

"Oh, you will be glad to hear, and I meant to have written it to father the other day, that in consideration of the recent decisions with regard to the copyright question, Mr. Bentley is to give Herman £150 and half profits after, for his new book—a much smaller sum than before, to be sure, but certainly worth waiting for—and quite generous on Mr. Bentley's part considering the unsettled state of things.

"I cannot write any more—it makes me terribly nervous— I don't know as you can read this I have scribbled it so."

At the time of Melville's moving to Arrowhead he was writing *Moby-Dick*. In the brief life of Melville in her journal, Mrs. Melville says: "Wrote *White-Whale* or *Moby-Dick* under unfavourable circumstances—would sit at his desk all day not writing anything till four or five o'clock—then ride to the village after dark—would be up early and out walking before breakfast—sometimes splitting wood for exercise. Published *White-Whale* in 1851—wrote *Pierre,* published 1852. We all felt anxious about the strain on his health in the spring of 1853."

When Hawthorne moved to Lenox he was forty-six years old—Melville's senior by fifteen years. "Bidding good-bye for ever to literary obscurity and to Salem," Mr. Julian Hawthorne says in his *Nathaniel Hawthorne and His Wife,* "Hawthorne now turned his face towards the mountains. The preceding nine months had told upon his health and spirits: and, had *The Scarlet Letter* not achieved so fair a success, he might have been long in recovering his normal frame of mind. But the broad murmur of popular applause, coming to his unaccustomed ears from all parts of his native country, and rolling in across the sea from academic England, gave him the spiritual refreshment born of the assurance that our fellow-creatures think well of the work we have striven to make good. Such assurance is essential, sooner or later, to soundness and serenity of mind. No man can attain secure repose and happiness who has never found that what moves and interests him has power over others likewise. Sooner or later he will begin to doubt either his own sanity or that of all the rest

of the world." Melville was never to know any such repose
and happiness.

Within the sanctities of the Red House, and among the solitudes of the surrounding country, Hawthorne enjoyed all the
companionship he desired. In 1842, Mrs. Hawthorne had
written to her mother: "Mr. Hawthorne's abomination of visiting still holds strong, be it to see no matter what angel;" and
in 1850, Hawthorne was no more eager for alliances even
with celestials. Not, indeed, that he was indifferent to his
fellowmen: that, his literary vocation would not permit. In
Sights from a Steeple he states: "The most desirable mode of
existence might be that of a spiritualised Paul Pry, hovering
invisible round men and women, witnessing their deeds, searching into their hearts, borrowing brightness from their felicity,
and shade from their sorrow, and retaining no emotion peculiar to himself." Hawthorne's son writes: "Now Hawthorne,
both by nature and by training, was of a disposition to throw
himself imaginatively into the shoes (as the phrase is) of
whatever person happened to his companion. For the time
being, he would seem to take their point of view and to
speak their language; it was the result partly of a subtle sympathy and partly of a cold intellectual insight, which led him
half consciously to reflect what he so clearly perceived. Thus,
if he chatted with a group of rude sea-captains in the smoking-
room of Mrs. Blodgett's boarding-house, or joined a knot of
boon companions in a Boston bar-room, or talked metaphysics
with Herman Melville on the hills of Berkshire, he would aim
to appear in each instance a man like as they were; he would
have the air of being interested in their interests and viewing
life by their standards. Of course, this was only apparent;
the real man stood aloof and observant." "Seeing his con-
genial aspect towards their little round of habits and beliefs,
they would leap to the conclusion that he was no more and
no less than one of themselves; whereas they formed but a
tiny arc in the great circle of his comprehension." Yet even
when not in the rôle of unimpassioned spectator, Hawthorne
was not the man to sit in pharisaical judgment upon his fellows. In *Fancy's Show-Box* he wrote: "Man must not dis-

ARROWHEAD

THE FIREPLACE
ARROWHEAD

claim his brotherhood, even with the guiltiest, since, though his hand be clean, his heart has surely been polluted by the flitting phantoms of iniquity." Emerson once said that there was no crime he could not commit: an amiable vanity he shared with many a more prosaic fellow. Hawthorne studied his own pure heart and learned that "men often over-estimate their capacity for evil." "I used to think," he wrote, "that I could imagine all feelings, all passions, and states of the heart and mind." Again: "Living in solitude till the fulness of time was come, I still kept the dew of my youth and the freshness of my heart. Had I sooner made my escape into the world, I should have grown hard and rough, and been covered with earthly dust, and my heart might have become callous by rude encounters with the multitude." G. P. Lathrop, in his *Study of Hawthorne,* says: "The visible pageant is only of value to him as it suggests the viewless host of heavenly shapes that hang above it like an idealising mirage." Yet never for a second did he lose himself among these heavenly visitations. He was eminently a man of sound sense: as W. C. Brownell has pointed out, he was "distinctly the most hard-headed of our men of genius." His son said of him: "He was the slave of no theory and no emotion; he always knew, so to speak, where he was and what he was about." His nature clearly was self-sustaining. He never felt the need of the support that in the realm of the affections is the reward of self-surrender. "He had no doubt an ideal family life," W. C. Brownell points out—"that is to say, ideal in a peculiar way, for he had it on rather peculiar terms, one suspects. These were, in brief, his own terms. He was worshipped, idolised, canonised, and on his side it probably required small effort worthily to fill the role a more ardent nature would have either merited less or found more irksome. He responded at any rate with absolute devotion. His domestic periphery bounded his vital interests."

J. E. A. Smith, however, who knew Hawthorne in the flesh, undertakes to portray Hawthorne in less austere outline. In his book *Taghconic: The Romance and Beauty of the Hills* (Boston, 1879) J. E. A. Smith, writing under the pseu-

donym "Godfrey Greylock," says: "But that Mr. Hawthorne's heart was warm and tender, I am well assured by
more than one circumstance, which I do not know that I am
at liberty to recall here. But there can be no wrong in mentioning the origin, as I have heard it, of the brotherly friendship between him and Herman Melville. As the story was told
me, Mr. Hawthorne was aware that Melville was the author of
a very appreciative review of the *Scarlet Letter* which appeared in the *Literary World,* edited by their common friends,
the Duyckincks; but this very knowledge, perhaps, kept two
very sensitive men shy of each other, although thrown into
company. But one day it chanced that when they were out
on a picnic excursion, the two were compelled by a thunder-
shower to take shelter in a narrow recess of the rocks of Monument Mountain. Two hours of enforced intercourse settled
the matter. They learned so much of each other's character,
and found that they held so much of thought, feeling and
opinion in common, that the most intimate friendship for the
future was inevitable."

Mr. Julian Hawthorne reports that Herman Melville—or
Omoo, as they called him,—soon became familiar and welcome
at the Red House. In a letter dated September 4, 1850, Mrs.
Hawthorne reported to her mother: "To-day, Mr. Hawthorne
and Mr. Melville have gone to dine at Pittsfield." It is in this
letter that Mrs. Hawthorne wrote the characterisation of Melville quoted in Chapter I.

Hawthorne finished *The House of the Seven Gables* on
January 27, 1851. The four months following Hawthorne
gave over to a vacation. "He had recovered his health," his
son says, "he had done his work, he was famous, and the
region in which he dwelt was beautiful and inspiriting. At
all events, he made those spring days memorable to his children. He made them boats to sail on the lake, and kites to
fly in the air; he took them fishing and flower-gathering, and
tried (unsuccessfully for the present) to teach them swimming. Mr. Melville used to ride or drive up, in the evenings,
with his great dog, and the children used to ride on the dog's

back." . . . "It was with Herman Melville that Hawthorne held the most familiar intercourse at this time, both personally and by letter." Hawthorne's son quotes "characteristic disquisitions" by Melville; "but Hawthorne's answers, if he wrote any," Mr. Julian Hawthorne goes on to say, entertaining a philosophical doubt in the face of Melville's specific mention of letters from Hawthorne, "were unfortunately destroyed by fire."

What would appear to be the earliest of the surviving letters of Melville to Hawthorne follows:

"PITTSFIELD, Wednesday morning.

"MY DEAR HAWTHORNE,—

"Concerning the young gentleman's shoes, I desire to say that a pair to fit him, of the desired pattern, cannot be had in all Pittsfield,—a fact which sadly impairs that metropolitan pride I formerly took in the capital of Berkshire. Henceforth Pittsfield must hide its head. However, if a pair of *bootees* will at all answer, Pittsfield will be very happy to provide them. Pray mention all this to Mrs. Hawthorne, and command me.

"'*The House of the Seven Gables: A* Romance. By Nathaniel Hawthorne. One vol. 16mo, pp. 344.' The contents of this book do not belie its rich, clustering, romantic title. With great enjoyment we spent almost an hour in each separate gable. This book is like a fine old chamber, abundantly, but still judiciously, furnished with precisely that sort of furniture best fitted to furnish it. There are rich hangings, wherein are braided scenes from tragedies! There is old china with rare devices, set out on the carved buffet; there are long and indolent lounges to throw yourself upon; there is an admirable sideboard, plentifully stored with good viands; there is a smell as of old wine in the pantry; and finally, in one corner, there is a dark little black-letter volume in golden clasps, entitled *Hawthorne: A Problem*. It has delighted us; it has piqued a re-perusal; it has robbed us of a day, and made us a present of a whole year of thoughtfulness; it has bred great exhilaration and exultation with the remembrance that the architect of the Gables resides only six miles off, and not three thousand miles away, in England, say. We think the book, for pleasantness of running interest, surpasses the other works of the author. The curtains are more drawn; the sun comes in more; genialities peep out more. Were we to particularise what most struck us in the deeper passages, we would point out the scene where Clifford, for a moment, would fain throw himself forth from the window to join the procession; or the scene where the judge is left seated in his ancestral chair. Clifford is full of an awful truth throughout. He is conceived in the finest, truest spirit. He is no caricature. He is Clifford. And here we would say that, did circumstances permit, we should like nothing better than to devote an elaborate and careful paper to the full consideration and analysis of the purport and significance of what so strongly characterises all of this author's writings. There is a certain tragic phase of humanity which, in our opinion, was never more powerfully embodied than by Hawthorne. We mean the tragedies of human thought in its own unbiassed, native, and profounder workings. We think that into no recorded mind has the intense feeling of the usable truth ever entered more deeply than into this man's. By usable truth, we mean the apprehension of the absolute condition of present things as they strike the eye of the man who fears them not, though they do their worst to him,—the man who, like Russia or the British Empire, declares himself a sovereign nature (in himself) amid the powers of heaven, hell, and earth. He may perish; but so long as he exists he insists upon treating with all Powers upon an equal basis. If any of those other Powers choose to withhold certain secrets, let them; that does not impair my sovereignty in myself; that does not make me tributary. And perhaps, after all, there is *no* secret. We incline to think that the Problem of the Universe is like the Freemason's mighty secret, so terrible to all children. It turns out, at last, to consist in a triangle, a mallet, and an apron,—nothing more! We incline to think that God cannot explain His own secrets, and that He would like a little information upon certain points Himself. We mortals astonish Him as much as He us. But it is this *Being* of the matter; there lies the knot with which we choke ourselves. As soon as you say *Me,* a *God,* a *Nature,* so soon you jump off from your stool and hang from the beam. Yes, that word is the hangman. Take God out of the dictionary, and you would have Him in the street.

"There is the grand truth about Nathaniel Hawthorne. He says NO! in thunder; but the Devil himself cannot make him say *yes.* For all men who say *yes,* lie; and all men who say *no,*—why, they are in the happy condition of judicious, unincumbered travellers in Europe; they cross the frontiers into Eternity with nothing but a carpet-bag,—that is to say, the Ego. Whereas those *yes*-gentry, they travel with heaps of baggage, and, damn them! they will never get through the Custom House. What's the reason, Mr. Hawthorne, that in the last stages of metaphysics a fellow always falls to *swearing* so? I could rip an hour. You see, I began with a little criticism extracted for your benefit from the *Pittsfield Secret Review,* and here I have landed in Africa.

"Walk down one of these mornings and see me. No nonsense; come. Remember me to Mrs. Hawthorne and the children.

"H. MELVILLE.

"P. S. The marriage of Phœbe with the daguerreotypist is a fine stroke, because of his turning out to be a *Maule.* If you pass Hepzibah's cent-shop, buy me a Jim Crow (fresh) and send it to me by Ned Higgins."

When, at the end of this letter, Melville found himself in Africa, he mistook gravely if he imagined he occupied the same continent with Hawthorne. Emile Montégut, it is true, has described Hawthorne as a "romancier pessimiste." Pessimist Hawthorne doubtless was,—a pessimist being precisely a nature without illusions. Hawthorne of course had, as Brownell has sufficiently taken pains to show, "the good sense, the lack of enthusiasm, the disillusioned pessimism of the man of the world." Hawthorne did say "No!" to life: but never, as Melville deceived himself into believing, "in thunder." Such an emphatic denial would have been an expression of ardour:

and Hawthorne was as without ardour as he was without illusion. Both Melville and Hawthorne were, in a sense, pessimists. Both were repelled by reality; both were quite out of sympathy with their time and its tendencies. But they had arrived at this centre of meeting from opposite points of the compass. Hawthorne was a pessimist from lack of illusions; the ardour of illusion, because of its exuberance in Melville, was at the basis of Melville's despair. Hawthorne took the same severely fatalistic view of himself and the life about him, as he did of life in his books. He accepted the universe as being unalterable, and towards his own destiny he felt satisfaction without elation. Like the Mohammedans who believe that they are preordained—but preordained to conquer,—so Hawthorne in his Calvinism, despite his depressed moods, had no serious doubts as to his election. Melville's endless questioning of "Providence and futurity, and of everything else that lies beyond human ken" were to Hawthorne merely a weariness of the flesh: he was satisfied in his fatalism, and without interest in speculation.

The next two letters announce that *Moby-Dick* is going through the press,—but they contain other incidental matter that must have been interesting—as a "human document" at least—even to Hawthorne. It is true that at this time, so his own son says, "Hawthorne became a sort of Mecca of pilgrims with Christian's burden upon their backs. Secret criminals of all kinds came to him for counsel and relief." He was weary, perhaps, of human documents: and Melville came to him, not for counsel, but in the intimate fraternity of the disenchanted.

"PITTSFIELD, June 29, 1851.

"MY DEAR HAWTHORNE,—

"The clear air and open window invite me to write to you. For some time past I have been so busy with a thousand things that I have almost forgotten when I wrote you last, and whether I received an answer. This most persuasive season has now for weeks recalled me from certain crotchety and over-doleful chimeras, the like of which men like you and me, and some others, forming a chain of God's posts round the world, must be content to encounter now and then, and fight them the best way we can. But come they will,—for in the boundless, trackless, but still glorious wild wilderness through which these outposts run, the Indians do sorely abound, as well as the insignificant but still stinging mosquitoes. Since you have been here, I have been building some shanties of houses (connected with the old one) and likewise some shanties of chapters and essays. I have been ploughing and sowing and raising and printing and praying, and now begin to come out upon a less bristling time, and to enjoy the calm prospect of things from a fair piazza at the north of the old farmhouse here.

"Not entirely yet, though, am I without something to be urgent with. The *Whale* is only half through the press; for, wearied with the long delays of the printers, and disgusted with the heat and dust of the Babylonish brick-kiln of New York, I came back to the country to feel the grass, and end the book reclining on it, if I may. I am sure you will pardon this speaking all about myself; for if I *say* so much on that head, be sure all the rest of the world are thinking about themselves ten times as much. Let us speak, though we show all our faults and weaknesses,—for it is a sign of strength to be weak, to know it, and out with it; not in set way and ostentatiously, though, but incidentally and without premeditation. But I am falling into my old foible,—preaching. I am busy, but shall not be very long. Come and spend a day here, if you can and want to; if not, stay in Lenox, and God give you long life. When I am quite free of my present engagements, I am going to treat myself to a ride and a visit to you. Have ready a bottle of brandy, because I always feel like drinking that heroic drink when we talk ontological heroics together. This is rather a crazy letter in some respects, I apprehend. If so, ascribe it to the intoxicating effects of the latter end of June operating upon a very susceptible and peradventure feeble temperament. Shall I send you a fin of the *Whale* by way of a specimen mouthful? The tail is not yet cooked, though the hell-fire in which the whole book is broiled might not unreasonably have cooked it ere this. This is the book's motto (the secret one), *Ego non baptiso te in nomine*—but make out the rest yourself.

"H. M."

"MY DEAR HAWTHORNE,—

"I should have been rumbling down to you in my pine-board chariot a long time ago, were it not that for some weeks past I have been more busy than you can well imagine,—out of doors,—building and patching and tinkering away in all directions. Besides, I had my crops to get in,—corn and potatoes (I hope to show you some famous ones by and by),—and many other things to attend to, all accumulating upon this one particular season. I work myself; and at night my bodily sensations are akin to those I have so often felt before, when a hired man, doing my day's work from sun to sun. But I mean to continue visiting you until you tell me that my visits are both supererogatory and superfluous. With no son of man do I stand upon any etiquette or ceremony, except the Christian ones of charity and honesty. I am told, my fellow-man, that there is an aristocracy of the brain. Some men have boldly advocated and asserted it. Schiller seems to have done so, though I don't know much about him. At any rate, it is true that there have been those who, while earnest in behalf of political equality, still accept the intellectual estates. And I can well perceive, I think, how a man of superior mind can, by its intense cultivation, bring himself, as it were, into a certain spontaneous aristocracy of feeling,—exceedingly nice and fastidious,—similar to that which, in an English Howard, conveys a torpedo-fish thrill at the slightest contact with a social plebeian. So, when you see or hear of my ruthless democracy on all sides, you may possibly feel a touch of a shrink, or something of that sort. It is but nature to be shy of a mortal who boldly declares that a thief in jail is as honourable a personage as Gen. George Washington. This is ludicrous. But Truth is the silliest thing under the sun. Try to get a living by Truth—and go to the Soup Societies. Heavens! Let any clergyman try to preach the Truth from its very stronghold, the pulpit, and they would ride him out of his church on his own pulpit bannister. It can hardly be doubted that all Reformers are bottomed upon the truth, more or less; and to the world at large are not reformers almost universally laughing-stocks? Why so? Truth is ridiculous to men. Thus easily in my room here do I, conceited and garrulous, revere the test of my Lord Shaftesbury.

"It seems an inconsistency to assert unconditional democracy in all things, and yet confess a dislike to all mankind—in the mass. But not so.—But it's an endless sermon,—no more of it. I began by saying that the reason I have not been to Lenox is this,—in the evening I feel completely done up, as the phrase is, and incapable of the long jolting to get to your house and back. In a week or so, I go to New York, to bury myself in a third-story room, and work and slave on my *Whale* while it is driving through the press. *That* is the only way I can finish it now,—I am so pulled hither and thither by circumstances. The calm, the coolness, the silent grass-growing mood in which a man *ought* always to compose,—that, I fear, can seldom be mine. Dollars damn me; and the malicious Devil is for ever grinning in upon me, holding the door ajar. My dear Sir, a presentiment is on me,—I shall at last be worn out and perish, like an old nutmeg-grater, grated to pieces by the constant attrition of the wood, that is, the nutmeg. What I feel most moved to write, that is banned,—it will not pay. Yet, altogether, write the *other* way I cannot. So the product is a final hash, and all my books are botches. I'm rather sore, perhaps, in this letter; but see my hand!—four blisters on this palm, made by hoes and hammers within the last few days. It is a rainy morning; so I am indoors, and all work suspended. I feel cheerfully disposed, and therefore I write a little bluely. Would the Gin were here! If ever, my dear Hawthorne, in the eternal times that are to come, you and I shall sit down in Paradise, in some little shady corner by ourselves; and if we shall by any means be able to smuggle a basket of champagne there (I won't believe in a Temperance Heaven), and if we shall then cross our celestial legs in the celestial grass that is forever tropical, and strike our glasses and our heads together, till both musically ring in concert,—then, O my dear fellow-mortal, how shall we pleasantly discourse of all the things manifold which now so distress us,—when all the earth shall be but a reminiscence, yea, its final dissolution an antiquity. Then shall songs be composed as when wars are over; humorous, comic songs,—'Oh, when I lived in that queer little hole called the world,' or, 'Oh, when I toiled and sweated below,' or, 'Oh, when I knocked and was knocked in the fight'—yes, let us look forward to such things. Let us swear that, though now we sweat, yet it is because of the dry heat which is indispensable to the nourishment of the vine which is to bear the grapes that are to give us the champagne hereafter.

"But I was talking about the *Whale*. As the fishermen say, 'he's in his flurry' when I left him some three weeks ago. I'm going to take him by his jaw, however, before long, and finish him up in some fashion or other. What's the use of elaborating what, in its very essence, is so short-lived as a modern book? Though I wrote the Gospels in this century, I should die in the gutter.—I talk all about myself, and this is selfishness and egotism. Granted. But how help it? I am writing to you; I know little about you, but something about myself. So I write about myself,—at least, to you. Don't trouble yourself, though, about writing; and don't trouble yourself about visiting; and when you *do* visit, don't trouble yourself about talking. I will do all the writing and visiting and talking myself.—By the way, in the last *Dollar Magazine* I read 'The Unpardonable Sin.' He was a sad fellow, that Ethan Brand. I have no doubt you are by this time responsible for many a shake and tremour of the tribe of 'general readers.' It is a frightful poetical creed that the cultivation of the brain eats out the heart. But it's my *prose* opinion that in most cases, in those men who have fine brains and work them well, the heart extends down to hams. And though you smoke them with the fire of tribulation, yet, like veritable hams, the head only gives the richer and the better flavour. I stand for the heart. To the dogs with the head! I had rather be a fool with a heart, than Jupiter Olympus with his head. The reason the mass of men fear God, and *at bottom dislike*

Him, is because they rather distrust His heart, and fancy Him all brain like a watch. (You perceive I employ a capital initial in the pronoun referring to the Deity; don't you think there is a slight dash of flunkeyism in that usage?) Another thing. I was in New York for four-and-twenty hours the other day, and saw a portrait of N. H. And I have seen and heard many flattering (in a publisher's point of view) allusions to the *Seven Gables.* And I have seen *Tales* and *A New Volume* announced, by N. H. So upon the whole, I say to myself, this N. H. is in the ascendant. My dear Sir, they begin to patronise. All Fame is patronage. Let me be infamous: there is no patronage in *that.* What 'reputation' H. M. has is horrible. Think of it! To go down to posterity is bad enough, any way; but to go down as a 'man who lived among the cannibals'! When I speak of posterity, in reference to myself, I only mean the babies who will probably be born in the moment immediately ensuing upon my giving up the ghost. I shall go down to some of them, in all likelihood. *Typee* will be given to them, perhaps, with their gingerbread. I have come to regard this matter of Fame as the most transparent of all vanities. I read Solomon more and more, and every time see deeper and deeper and unspeakable meanings in him. I did not think of Fame, a year ago, as I do now. My development has been all within a few years past. I am like one of those seeds taken out of the Egyptian Pyramids, which, after being three thousand years a seed and nothing but a seed, being planted in English soil, it developed itself, grew to greenness, and then fell to mould. So I. Until I was twenty-five, I had no development at all. From my twenty-fifth year I date my life. Three weeks have scarcely passed, at any time between then and now, that I have not unfolded within myself. But I feel that I am now come to the inmost leaf of the bulb, and that shortly the flower must fall to the mould. It seems to me now that Solomon was the truest man who ever spoke, and yet that he a little *managed* the truth with a view to popular conservatism; or else there have been many corruptions and interpolations of the text—In reading some of Goethe's sayings, so worshipped by his votaries, I came across this, '*Live in the all.*' That is to say, your separate identity is but a wretched one,—good; but get out of yourself, spread and expand yourself, and bring to yourself the tinglings of life that are felt in the flowers and the woods, that are felt in the planets Saturn and Venus, and the Fixed Stars. What nonsense! Here is a fellow with a raging toothache. 'My dear boy,' Goethe says to him, 'you are sorely afflicted with that tooth; but you must *live in the all,* and then you will be happy!' As with all great genius, there is an immense deal of flummery in Goethe, and in proportion to my own contact with him, a monstrous deal of it in me.

"H. MELVILLE.

"P. S. 'Amen!' saith Hawthorne.

"N. B. This 'all' feeling, though, there is some truth in. You must often have felt it, lying on the grass on a warm summer's day. Your legs seem to send out shoots into the earth. Your hair feels like leaves upon your head. This is the *all* feeling. But what plays the mischief with the truth is that men will insist upon the universal application of a temporary feeling or opinion.

"P. S. You must not fail to admire my discretion in paying the postage on this letter."

When Melville speaks of "the calm, the coolness, the silent grass-growing mood in which a man *ought* to compose," he has caught a demoralisation from Hawthorne. *Moby-Dick,* he says, was "broiled in hell-fire"; and the complete "possession" that mastered Hawthorne during the composition of *The Scarlet Letter* has been amply attested. Each man once, and once only, wrestled with the angel of his inspiration gloriously to conquer. But Hawthorne had little relish for such athletics: he preferred the relaxation of painstaking placidity. He said of *The Scarlet Letter* that "he did not think it a book natural for him to write." The pity of it is that he was not more frequently so unnatural. As an old man, Melville looked back upon his achievement, and recanted the corruption he had learned from Hawthorne:

ART

In placid hours well-pleased we dream
Of many a brave unbodied scheme.
But form to lend, pulsed life create,
What unlike things must meet and mate;
A flame to melt—a wind to freeze;
Sad patience—joyous energies;
Humility—yet pride and scorn;
Instinct and study;—love and hate:
Audacity—reverence. These must mate,
And fuse with Jacob's mystic heart,
To wrestle with the angel—art.

Apropos of the two letters last quoted, Mr. Julian Hawthorne says: "Mr. Melville was probably quite as entertaining and somewhat less abstruse, when his communications were by word of mouth. Mrs. Hawthorne used to tell of one evening when he came in, and presently began to relate the story of a fight which he had seen on an island in the Pacific, between some savages, and of the prodigies of valour one of them performed with a heavy club. The narrative was extremely graphic; and when Melville had gone, and Mr. and Mrs. Hawthorne were talking over his visit, the latter said, 'Where is that club with which Mr. Melville was laying about him so?' Mr. Hawthorne thought he must have taken it with him; Mrs. Hawthorne thought he had put it in the corner; but it was not to be found. The next time Melville came, they asked him about it; whereupon it appeared that the club was still in the Pacific island, if it were anywhere."

In the entry in his journal for July 30, 1851, Hawthorne wrote: "Proceeding homeward, we were overtaken by a cavalier on horseback, who saluted me in Spanish, to which I replied by touching my hat. But, the cavalier renewing his salutation, I regarded him more attentively, and saw that it was Herman Melville! So we all went homeward together, talking as we went. Soon Mr. Melville alighted, and put Julian in the saddle; and the little man was highly pleased, and sat on the horse with the freedom and fearlessness of an old equestrian, and had a ride of at least a mile homeward. I asked Mrs. Peters to make some tea for Herman Melville, and so she did; and after supper I put Julian to bed, and Melville and I had a talk about time and eternity, things of this world and of the next, and books, and publishers, and all possible and impossible matters, that lasted pretty deep into the night. At last he rose, and saddled his horse and rode off to his own domicile, and I went to bed. . . ."

On August 8, 1851, Hawthorne reports in his journal: "To-day Herman Melville and the two Duyckincks came in a barouche, and we all went to visit the Shaker establishment at Hancock." Of the Shakers, Hawthorne wrote: "They are certainly the most singular and bedevilled set of people that ever existed in a civilised land." One wonders what would have been Hawthorne's report of the valley of Typee.

The next letter acknowledges a lost communication from Hawthorne. It is dated, in Hawthorne's writing: "received July 24, 1851."

"My Dear Hawthorne: This is not a letter, or even a note, but merely a passing word to you said over your garden gate. I thank you for your easy flowing long letter (received yesterday), which flowed through me, and refreshed all my meadows, as the Housatonic—opposite me—does in reality. I am now busy with various things, not incessantly though; but enough to require my frequent tinkering; and this is the height of the haying season, and my nag is dragging home his winter's dinners all the time. And so, one way and another, I am not a disengaged man, but shall be very soon. Meanwhile, the earliest good chance I get, I shall roll down to you, my good fellow, seeing we—that is, you and I— must hit upon some little bit of vagabondage before autumn comes. Greylock—we must go and vagabondise there. But ere we start, we must dig a deep hole, and bury all Blue Devils, there to abide till the last Day. . . . Good-bye."

His X Mark.

And the last letter is a dithyramb of gratitude to Hawthorne for a letter of Hawthorne's (would that it survived!) in appreciation of *Moby-Dick*.

"PITTSFIELD, Monday Afternoon.

"MY DEAR HAWTHORNE:

"People think that if a man has undergone any hardship he should have a reward; but for my part, I have done the hardest possible day's work, and then come to sit down in a corner and eat my supper comfortably—why, then I don't think I deserve any reward for my hard day's work—for am I not at peace? Is not my supper good? My peace and my supper are my rewards, my dear Hawthorne. So your joy-giving and exultation-breeding letter is not my reward for my ditcher's work with that book, but is the good goddess's bonus over and above what was stipulated for—for not one man in five cycles, who is wise, will expect appreciative recognition from his fellows, or any one of them. Appreciation! Recognition! Is love appreciated? Why, ever since Adam, who has got to the meaning of this great allegory—the world? Then we pigmies must be content to have our paper allegories but ill comprehended. I say your appreciation is my glorious gratuity. In my proud, humble way,—a shepherd-king,—I was lord of a little vale in the solitary Crimea; but you have now given me the crown of India. But on trying it on my head, I found it fell down on my ears, notwithstanding their asinine length—for it's only such ears that sustain such crowns.

"Your letter was handed to me last night on the road going to Mr. Morewood's, and I read it there. Had I been at home, I would have sat down at once and answered it. In me divine magnanimities are spontaneous and instantaneous—catch them while you can. The world goes round, and the other side comes up. So now I can't write what I felt. But I felt pantheistic then—your heart beat in my ribs and mine in yours, and both in God's. A sense of unspeakable security is in me this moment, on account of your having understood the book. I have written a wicked book, and feel spotless as the lamb. Ineffable socialities are in me. I would sit down and dine with you and all the Gods in old Rome's Pantheon. It is a strange feeling—no hopelessness is in it, no despair. Content—that is it; and irresponsibility; but without licentious inclination.   I speak now of my profoundest sense of being, not of an incidental feeling.

"Whence came you, Hawthorne?   By what right do you drink from my flagon of life?   And when I put it to my lips—lo, they are yours and not mine.   I feel that the God-head is broken up like the bread at the Supper, and that we are the pieces.   Hence this infinite fraternity of feeling.   Now, sympathising with the paper, my angel turns over another leaf.   You did not care a penny for the book.   But, now and then as you read, you understood the pervading thought that impelled the book—and that you praised.   Was it not so? You were archangel enough to praise the imperfect body, and embrace the soul.   Once you hugged the ugly Socrates be-cause you saw the flame in the mouth, and heard the rushing of the demon,—the familiar,—and recognised the sound; for you have heard it in your own solitudes.

"My dear Hawthorne, the atmospheric scepticisms steal over me now, and make me doubtful of my sanity in writing you thus.   But, believe me, I am not mad, most noble Festus!   But truth is ever incoherent, and when the big hearts strike to-gether, the concussion is a little stunning.   Farewell.   Don't write me a word about the book.   That would be robbing me of my miserable delight.   I am heartily sorry I ever wrote anything about you—it was paltry.   Lord, when shall we be done growing?   As long as we have anything more to do, we have done nothing.   So, now, let us add *Moby-Dick* to our blessing, and step from that.   Leviathan is not the biggest fish;—I have heard of Krakens.

"This is a long letter, but you are not at all bound to answer it.   Possibly if you do answer it, and direct it to Herman Melville, you will missend it—for the very fingers that now guide this pen are not precisely the same that just took it up and put it to the paper.   Lord, when shall we be done changing? Ah! it is a long stage, and no inn in sight, and night coming, and the body cold.   But with you for a passenger, I am content and can be happy. I shall leave the world, I feel, with more satisfaction for having come to know you. Knowing you persuades me more than the Bible of our immortality.

"What a pity that, for your plain, bluff letter, you should get such gibberish! Mention me to Mrs. Hawthorne and to the children, and so, good-bye to you, with my blessing.

"HERMAN.

"P. S. I can't stop yet. If the world was entirely made up of Magians, I'll tell you what I should do. I should have a paper-mill established at one end of the house, and so have an extra riband for foolscap rolling in upon my desk; and upon that endless riband I should write a thousand—a million—a billion thoughts, all under the form of a letter to you. The divine magnet is on you, and my magnet responds. Which is the bigger? A foolish question—they are *one*.

"H.

"P. P. S. Don't think that by writing me a letter, you shall always be bored with an immediate reply to it—and so keep both of us delving over a writing-desk eternally. No such thing! I sha'n't always answer your letters and you may do just as you please."

Hawthorne had written Melville a "plain, bluff letter," and in reply was to be told, with "infinite fraternity," that "the god-head is broken up like the bread at the Supper" and that he was one of the pieces. Melville had dedicated *Moby-Dick* to Hawthorne, and Hawthorne made some sort of acknowledgment of the tribute. Melville, shrewdly suspected him, however, of caring "not a penny" for the book, but in archangelical charity praising less the "imperfect body" than the "pervading thought" which "now and then" he understood.

Moby-Dick was an allegory, of course—but withal an allegory of a solidity and substance that must have appeared to Hawthorne little short of grossly shocking. Hawthorne had been praised from his "airy and charming insubstantiality." And of himself he wrote, with engaging candour: "Whether from lack of power, or an unconquerable reserve, the Author's touches have often an effect of tameness." Hawthorne's "re-

serve" is, of course, all myth. Both Hawthorne and Melville, though each a recluse in life, overflow to the reader.
And as Brownell says of Hawthorne: "He does not tell very
much, but apparently he tells everything." But to Hawthorne,
Melville's overflowing, like a spring freshet, or a tidal wave,
must have been little less than appalling. Hawthorne's was
eminently a neat, fastidious style, as free from any eccen-
tricity or excess as from any particular pungency or colour.
Melville's was extravagant, capricious, vigorous, and "un-
literary": the energy of his undisciplined genius is its most
significant qualty. After all, was it possible for Hawthorne
to feel any deep sympathy for Melville's passionate enthusi-
asms, for Melville's catholic toleration, for Melville's quenchless curiosity, for Melville's varied laughter, for Melville's
spiritual daring? It is true that Hawthorne found Story's
"Cleopatra"—inspired, it might appear, by a fancy of the
young Victoria in discreet negligée—"a terrible, dangerous
woman, quite enough for the moment, but very like to spring
upon you like a tigress." He never visited George Eliot because there was another Mrs. Lewes. He was much troubled
by the nude in art. He pronounced Margaret Fuller's "in
many respects," a "defective and evil nature," and "Providence was kind in putting her and her clownish husband
and their child on board that fated ship." It is true that he
wrote a graceful if not very genial introductory essay—once
mistaken for a marvel quite eclipsing "Elia"—to relieve the
dark tone of *The Scarlet Letter*. And it is also true that he
accepted the adoration of his wife with the utmost gravity
and appreciation. Mrs. Hawthorne, in one of her letters to
her mother, by a transition in praise of Hawthorne's eyes—
"They give, but receive not"—comments at some length, on
her husband's "mighty heart," that "opens the bosom of men."
"So Mr. Melville," she says, "generally silent and incommuni-
cative, pours out the rich floods of his mind and experience
to him, so sure of appreciation, so sure of a large and generous
interpretation."

What interpretation Hawthorne gave to *Moby-Dick* has not
transpired. Hawthorne mentions *Moby-Dick* once in his pub-

lished works. In the *Wonder Book* he says: "On the hither side of Pittsfield sits Herman Melville, shaping out the gigantic conception of his white whale, while the gigantic shape of Greylock looms upon him from his study window." Only one available Hawthorne-Melville document is still unprinted: the "Agatha" letter, mentioned by Mr. Julian Hawthorne. But the "Agatha" letter says nothing of *Moby-Dick;* and though of impressive bulk, its biographical interest is too slight to merit its publication.

Born in hell-fire, and baptised in an unspeakable name, *Moby-Dick* is, with *The Scarlet Letter,* among the few very notable literary achievements of American literature. There has been published no criticism of Melville more beautiful or more profound than the essay of E. L. Grant Watson on *Moby-Dick* (*London Mercury,* December, 1920). It is Mr. Watson's contention in this essay, that the *Pequod,* with her monomaniac captain and all her crew, is representative of Melville's own genius, and in the particular sense that each character is deliberately symbolic of a complete and separate element. Because of the prodigal richness of material in *Moby-Dick,* the breadth and vitality and solid substance of the setting of the allegory, the high quality of *Moby-Dick* as a psychological synthesis has very generally been lost sight of. Like Bunyan, or Swift, Melville has enforced his moral by giving an independent and ideal verisimilitude to its innocent and unconscious exponents. The self-sustaining vitality of Melville's symbols has been magnificently vouched for by Mr. Masefield in his vision of the final resurrection. And the superb irony—whether unconscious or intended—of *Moby-Dick's* "towing the ship our Lord was in, with all the sweet apostles aboard of her," would surely have delighted Melville. *Pilgrim's Progress* is undoubtedly a tract; but, as Brownell observes, if it had been only a tract, it would never have achieved universal canonisation. Both *Pilgrim's Progress* and *Moby-Dick* are works of art in themselves, each leaning lightly —though of course to all the more purpose—on its moral. Most persons probably read *Gulliver* for the story, and miss the satire. In the same way, a casual reader of *Moby-Dick* may skip the more transcendental passages and classify it as a book of adventure. It is indeed a book of adventure, but upon the highest plane of spiritual daring. Ahab is, of course, the atheistical captain of the tormented soul; and his crew, so Melville says, is "chiefly made of mongrel renegades, and cast-aways and cannibals." And Ahab is "morally enfeebled, also, by the incompetence of mere unaided virtue or rightmindedness in Starbuck, the invulnerable jollitry of indifference or recklessness of Stubb, and the pervading mediocrity of Flash." But Ahab is Captain; and his madness is of such a quality that the white whale and all that is there symbolised, needs must render its consummation, or its ex.tinction. On the waste of the Pacific, ship after ship passes the *Pequod,* some well laden, others bearing awful tidings: yet all are sane. The *Pequod* alone, against contrary winds, sails on into that amazing calm, that extraordinary mildness, in which she is destroyed by *Moby-Dick.* "There is a wisdom that is woe, and there is a woe that is madness." And in *Moby-Dick,* the woe and the wisdom are mingled in the history of a soul's adventure.

Though *Moby-Dick* is not only an allegory, but an allegory designed to teach woeful wisdom, nowhere in literature, perhaps, can one find such uncompromising despair so genially and painlessly administered. Indeed, the despair of *Moby-Dick* is as popularly missed as is the vitriolic bitterness of *Gulliver.* There is an abundance of humour in *Moby-Dick,* of course: and there is mirth in much of the laughter. In *Moby-Dick,* it would appear, Melville has made pessimism a gay science. "Learn to laugh, my young friends," Nietzsche counsels, "if you are at all determined to remain pessimists." If there are tears, he smiles gallantly as he brushes them aside. "There are certain queer times and occasions in this strange mixed affair we call life," Melville says, "when a man takes this whole universe for a vast practical joke, though the wit thereof he but dimly discovers, and more than suspects that the joke is at nobody's expense but his own. There is nothing like the perils of whaling to breed this free and easy sort of genial, desperado philosophy; and with it I regard this whole voyage of the *Pequod,* and the great white whale its object." And for the most part, he does. But he declares, withal, that "the truest of all men was the Man of Sorrows, and the truest of all books is Solomon's, and Ecclesiastes is the fine hammered steel of woe. All is vanity. ALL." *Moby-Dick* was built upon a foundation of this wisdom, and this woe; and so keenly did Melville feel the poignancy of this woe, so isolated was he in his surrender to this wisdom, that this wisdom and this woe, which he had learned from Solomon and from Christ, he felt to be of that quality which in our cowardice we call madness.

CHAPTER XVI

THE GREAT REFUSAL

"My towers at last! These rovings end,
Their thirst is slacked in larger dearth:
The yearning infinite recoils,
    For terrible is earth."
                    —HERMAN MELVILLE: *L'Envoi.*

ON a bleak and snowy November day in 1851, the Hawthorne family, with their trunks, got into a large farm wagon and drove away from the little red house. And with the departure of Hawthorne, Melville had dreamed the last of his avenging dreams. There may have been some association between the two men while Hawthorne was in West Newton, and later in Concord, but no records survive. In 1856, on his way to the Holy Land, Melville visited Hawthorne at Southport two days after arriving in Liverpool. Melville's account of the meeting is thus recorded in his journal:

"*Sunday, Nov. 9:* Stayed home till dinner. After dinner took steamboat for Rock Ferry to find Mr. Hawthorne. On getting to R. F. learned he had removed thence 18 months previous and was now residing out of town.

"*Monday, Nov. 10:* Went among the docks to see the Mediterranean steamers. Saw Mr. Hawthorne at Consulate. Invited me to stay with him during my sojourn at Liverpool. Dined at Anderson's, a very nice place, and charges moderate.

"*Tuesday, Nov. 11:* Hawthorne for Southport, 20 miles distant on the seashore, a watering place. Found Mrs. Hawthorne & the rest awaiting tea for us.

"*Wednesday, Nov. 12:* At Southport, an agreeable day. Took a long walk by the sea. Sand & grass. Wild & desolate. A strong wind. Good talk. In the evening stout & fox & geese. Julian grown into a fine lad. Una taller than her

brother.   Mrs. Hawthorne not in good health.   Mr. Hawthorne stayed home with me.

"*Thursday, Nov. 13:* At Southport till noon.   Mr. H. & I
took train then for Liverpool.   Spent rest of day putting en-
quiries among steamers.

"*Friday. Nov. 14:* Took bus for London Road.   Called at
Mr. Hawthorne's.   Met a Mr. Bright.   Took me to his club
and luncheoned me there.

"*Sunday, Nov. 16:* Rode in the omnibus.   Went out to Fox-
hill Park, &c.   Grand organ at St. George's Hall."

Three days later, Melville was off for Constantinople.

In his *English Note-book,* under November 30th, 1856,
Hawthorne wrote:

"*November 30:* A week ago last Monday, Herman Melville
came to see me at the Consulate, looking much as he used to
do, and with his characteristic gravity and reserve of manner.
. . . We soon found ourselves on pretty much our former
terms of sociability and confidence. . . . He is thus far on
his way to Constantinople.   I do not wonder that he found
it necessary to take an airing through the world, after so many
years of toilsome pen-labour, following upon so wild and
adventurous a youth as his was.   I invited him to come and
stay with us at Southport, as long as he might remain in
this vicinity, and accordingly he did come the next day. . . .
On Wednesday we took a pretty long walk together, and sat
down in a hollow among the sand-hills, sheltering ourselves
from the high cool wind.   Melville, as he always does, began
to reason of Providence and futurity, and of everything else
that lies beyond human ken. . . . He has a very high and
noble nature, and is better worth immortality than the most
of us. . . . On Saturday we went to Chester together.   I
love to take every opportunity of going to Chester; it being
the one only place, within easy reach of Liverpool, which
possesses any old English interest.   We went to the Cathedral."—And then architecture gives place to personal comment.

Mr. Julian Hawthorne reports of this meeting: "At Southport the chief event of interest during the winter was a visit from Herman Melville, who turned up at Liverpool on his way to Constantinople, and whom Hawthorne brought out to spend a night or two with us. 'He looked much the same as he used to do; a little paler, perhaps, and a little sadder, and with his characteristic gravity and reserve of manner. I felt rather awkward at first, for this is the first time I have met him since my ineffectual attempt to get him a consular appointment from General Pierce. However, I failed only from real lack of power to serve him; so there was no reason to be ashamed, and we soon found ourselves on pretty much the former terms of sociability and confidence. Melville has not been well, of late; he has been affected with neuralgic complaints, and no doubt has suffered from too constant literary occupation, pursued without much success latterly; and his writings, for a long while past, have indicated a morbid state of mind. So he left his place in Pittsfield, and has come to the Old World. He informed me that he had "pretty much made up his mind to be annihilated"; but still he does not seem to rest in that anticipation, and I think will never rest until he gets hold of some definite belief. It is strange how he persists—and has persisted ever since I knew him, and probably long before—in wandering to and fro over these deserts, as dismal and monotonous as the sandhills amidst which we were sitting. He can neither believe, nor be comfortable in his unbelief; and he is too honest and courageous not to try to do one or the other. If he were a religious man, he would be one of the most truly religious and reverential; he has a very high and noble nature, and better worth immortality than most of us.'

"Melville made the rounds of Liverpool under the guidance of Henry Bright; and afterwards Hawthorne took him to Chester; and they parted the same evening, 'at a street corner, in the rainy evening. I saw him again on Monday, however. He said that he already felt much better than in America; but observed that he did not anticipate much pleasure in his rambles, for that the spirit of adventure is gone out of him.

He certainly is much overshadowed since I saw him last; but
I hope he will brighten as he goes onward. He sailed on
Tuesday, leaving a trunk behind him, and taking only a carpet-
bag to hold all his travelling-gear. This is the next best thing
to going naked; and as he wears his beard and moustache, and
so needs no dressing-case,—nothing but a toothbrush,—I do
not know a more independent personage. He learned his
travelling habits by drifting about, all over the South Seas,
with no other clothes or equipage than a red flannel shirt and
a pair of duck trousers. Yet we seldom see men of less criti-
cisable manners than he.' "

There is no record of these two men ever meeting again.

From the beginning, there had been, between Melville and
Hawthorne, a profound incompatibility. When they met, Melville was within one last step of absolute disenchantment.
One illusion, only, was to him still unblasted: The belief
in the possibility of a Utopian friendship that might solace all
of his earlier defeats. Ravished in solitude by his alienation
from hs fellows, Melville discovered that the author of *The
Scarlet Letter* was his neighbour. He came to know Hawthorne: and his eager soul rushed to embrace Hawthorne's as
that of a brother in despair. Exultant was his worship of
Hawthorne, absolute his desire for surrender. He craved of
Hawthorne an understanding and sympathy that neither Hawthorne, nor any other human being, perhaps, could ever have
given. His admiration for Hawthorne was, of course, as he
inevitably discovered, built upon a mistaken identity. Yet, on
the evidence of his letters, he for a time drew from this admiration moments both of tensest excitement and of miraculous
and impregnating peace. It would be interesting, indeed, to
know what *Moby-Dick* owed to this inspiration. It is patent
fact, however, that with the publication of *Moby-Dick,* and
Hawthorne's departure from Lenox, Melville's creative period
was at its close. At the age of thirty-two, so brilliant, so intense, so crowded had been the range of experience that burned
through him, that at the period of his life when most men are
just beginning to strike their gait, Melville found himself looking forward into utter night. Nearly forty years before his

death, he had come to be the most completely disenchanted of all considerable American writers.

From his youth, Melville had felt the flagrant and stubborn discord between aspiration and fact. He was born with an imagination of very extraordinary vigour, and with a constitution of corresponding vitality. In sheer capacity to feel, most American writers look pale beside him. Fired by his rebellious imagination, and abetted by his animal courage, he sallied forth in quest of happiness. Few men have ever compassed such a span of experience as he crowded within the thirty-two years of his quest; few men have lived with such daring, with such intensity. And one by one, as he put his illusions to the test, the bolts of his imagination, discharged against reality, but blazed out charred avenues to despair. It was Dante, he says in *Pierre,* who first "opened to his shuddering eyes the infinite cliffs and gulfs of human mystery and misery;—though still more in the way of experimental vision, than of sensational presentiment or experience." By the age of thirty-two, he had, by first-hand knowledge of life, learned to feel the justice of Schopenhauer's statement: "Where did Dante find the material for his *Inferno* if not from the world; and yet is not his picture exhaustively satisfactory? But look at his Paradise; when he attempted to describe it he had nothing to guide him, this pleasant world could not offer a single suggestion." This passage is marked in Melville's copy of Schopenhauer. And in *Pierre* he wrote: "By vast pains we mine into the pyramid; by horrible gropings we come to the central room; with joy we espy the sarcophagus; but we lift the lid—and nobody is there!—appallingly vacant, as vast as the soul of a man."

Melville's disillusionment began at home. The romantic idealisation of his mother gave place to a recoil into a realisation of the cold, "scaly, glittering folds of pride" that rebuffed his tormented love; and he studied the portrait of his father, and found it a defaming image. In *Pierre* this portrait thus addresses him: "To their young children, fathers are not wont to unfold themselves. . . . Consider this strange, ambiguous, smile; more narrowly regard this mouth. Behold,

what is this too ardent and, as it were, unchastened light in
these eyes. Consider. Is there no mystery here?" In *Pierre,*
he thought that there was.

In his boyhood, poverty added its goad to launch him forth
to find happiness in distance. He discovered hideousness; and
later, escaped into virgin savagery, he saw by contrast the
blatant defaults of civilisation; and he learned that it was the
dubious honour of the white civilised man of being "the most
ferocious animal on the face of the earth." In Tahiti he was
brought face to face with the bigotry and stupid self-righteousness of the proselyting Protestant mind; and there he learned
that Christianity—or what passes for it—may under some circumstances be not a blessing but a blight. In *Typee* and *Omoo*
he innocently turned his hand to right matters to a happier
adjustment, soon to reap the reward of such temerity. In the
navy he was made hideously aware of the versatility of the
human animal in evil. There he found not only a rich panorama of human unloveliness, but "evils which, like the suppressed domestic drama of Horace Walpole, will neither bear
representing, nor reading, and will hardly bear thinking of."
There, he was also struck by the criminal stupidity of war. In
White-Jacket he asked, "are there no Moravians in the Moon,
that not a missionary has yet visited this poor pagan planet
of ours, to civilise civilisation and Christianise Christendom?"
He was, as he calls himself, a "pondering man": and in his
evaluation of individual human life he soon came to share the
judgment of Josiah Royce, another "pondering man": "Call
it human life. You can not find a comparison more thoroughly condemning it." And he marked Schopenhauer's tribute to his fellows: "They are just what they seem to be, and
that is the worst that can be said of them."

As "the man who lived among the cannibals" he was famous
by the age of twenty-eight. But when he attempted to put his
earnest convictions on paper, he was to discover that the value
of the paper deteriorated thereby. When he made this discovery he was married, and a father: and debtors had to be
held at bay by the point of the pen. On April 30, 1851, Harper and Brothers denied him any further advance on his royal-

ties: they were making "extensive and expensive improvements"—and besides, he had already overdrawn nearly seven hundred dollars.

He had, too, sought personal happiness in the illusion of romantic love. The romantic lover is in especial peril of finding in marriage the sobered discovery that all his sublime and heroic effort has resulted simply in a vulgar satisfaction, and that, taking all things into consideration, he is no better off than he was before. In his poem *After the Pleasure Party* (in *Timoleon,* 1891) Melville tells such a "sad rosary of belittling pain." As a rule, Theseus once consoled, Ariadne is forsaken; and had Petrarch's passion been requited, his song would have ceased. Francesca and Paolo, romantic lovers who had experienced the limits of their desire, were by Dante put in Hell: and their sufficient punishment was their eternal companionship. By the very ardour of his idealisation, Melville was foredoomed to disappointment in marriage. Though both he and his wife were noble natures—indeed for that very reason—their marriage was for each a crucifixion. For between them there was deep personal loyalty without understanding. Bacon once said, "he that hath wife and children hath given hostages to fortune, for they are impediments to great enterprises, either of virtue or of mischief." Melville gave such hostages to fortune: but, such was his temperament, it is difficult to believe that unencumbered he would have magnified his achievement. Mrs. Melville is remembered as a gentle, gracious, loyal woman who bore with him for over forty years, in his disillusion, his loss of health, his poverty, his obscurity. And his father-in-law, Chief Justice Shaw, befriended him with forbearance and with more substantial gifts.

With the departure of Hawthorne from Lenox, Melville was left without companionship and without illusions. And he was aware of the approach of his Nemesis even before it overtook him. He confessed to Hawthorne while finishing *Moby-Dick* his feeling that he was approaching the limit of his power. And these intimations were prophetic. With *Moby-Dick* his creative period closed.

Of the end of this period his wife says: "Wrote *White*

Whale or *Moby-Dick* under unfavourable circumstances—
would sit at his desk all day not writing anything till four or
five o'clock—then ride to the village after dark—would be up
early and out walking before breakfast—sometimes splitting
wood for exercise. Published *White Whale* in 1851.—Wrote
Pierre: published 1852. We all felt anxious about the strain
on his health in Spring of 1853."

In *Pierre,* Melville coiled down into the night of his soul,
to write an anatomy of despair. The purpose of the book was
to show the impracticability of virtue: to give specific evidence,
freely plagiarised from his own psychology, that "the heavenly
wisdom of God is an earthly folly to man," "that although our
blessed Saviour was full of the wisdom of Heaven, yet his
gospel seems lacking in the practical wisdom of the earth;
that his nature was not merely human—was not that of a
mere man of the world"; that to try to live in this world
according to the strict letter of Christianity would result in
"the story of the Ephesian matron, allegorised." The
subtlety of the analysis is extraordinary; and in its probings
into unsuspected determinants from unconsciousness it is
prophetic of some of the most recent findings in psychology.
"Deep, deep, and still deep and deeper must we go," Melville
says, "if we would find out the heart of a man; descending
into which is as descending a spiral stair in a shaft, without
any end, and where that endlessness is only concealed by the
spiralness of the stair, and the blackness of the shaft." In
the winding ambiguities of *Pierre* Melville attempts to reveal
man's fatal facility at self-deception; to show that the human
mind is like a floating iceberg, hiding below the surface of
the sea most of its bulk; that from a great depth of thought
and feeling below the level of awareness, long silent hands are
ever reaching out, urging us to whims of the blood and ten-
sions of the nerves, whose origins we never suspect. "In
reserves men build imposing characters," Melville says; "not
in revelations." *Pierre* is not conspicuous for its reserves.

Pierre aroused the reviewers to such a storm of abuse that
legend has assigned Melville's swift obscuration to this dispraise. The explanation is too simple, as Mr. Mather con-

tends. But there is, doubtless, more than a half truth in this explanation. The abuse that *Pierre* reaped, coming when it did in Melville's career, and inspired by a book in which Melville with tragic earnestness attempted an apologia of worldly defeat, must have seemed to him in its heartlessness and total blindness to his purpose, a definitive substantiation of the thesis of his book.

Pierre has been very unsympathetically handled, even by Melville's most penetrating and sympathetic critics. Mr. Frank Jewett Mather, Jr., for example, in the second of his two essays on *Herman Melville* (*The Review,* August 9 and 16, 1919), says of *Pierre* that "it is perhaps the only positively ill-done book" of Melville's. Mr. Mather grants power to the book, but he finds it "repellent and overwrought." He recommends it only as a literary curiosity. And as a literary curiosity Mr. Arthur Johnson studied its stylistic convolutions in *The New Republic* of August 27, 1919. It is certainly true, as Mr. Johnson has said, that "the plot or theme, were it not so 'done' as to be hardly decipherable, would be to-day considered rather 'advanced.' " Mr. Johnson contends that for morbid unhealthy pathology, it has not been exceeded even by D. H. Lawrence. All this may be very excellent ethics, but it is not very enlightening criticism.

Melville wrote *Pierre* with no intent to reform the ways of the world. But he did write *Pierre* to put on record the reminder that the world's way is a hypocritic way in so far as it pretends to be any other than the Devil's way also. In *Pierre,* Melville undertook to dramatise this conviction. When he sat down to write, what seemed to him the holiest part of himself—his ardent aspirations—had wrecked itself against reality. So he undertook to present, in the character of Pierre, his own character purged of dross; and in the character of Pierre's parents, the essential outlines of his own parents. Then he started his hero forth upon a career of lofty and unselfish impulse, intent to show that the more transcendent a man's ideal, the more certain and devastating his worldly defeat; that the most innocent in heart are those most in peril of being eventually involved in "strange, *unique* follies and sins, unimagined before." Incidentally, Melville undertakes to show, in the tortuous ambiguities of *Pierre,* that even the purest impulses of Pierre were, in reality, tainted of clay. *Pierre* is an apologia of Melville's own defeat, in the sense that in *Pierre* Melville attempts to show that in so far as his own defeat—essentially paralleling Pierre's—was unblackened by incest, murder, and suicide, he had escaped these disasters through accident and inherent defect, rather than because of superior virtue. Pierre had followed the heavenly way that leads to damnation.

Such a thesis can be met by the worldly wisdom that Melville slanders in *Pierre,* only with uncompromising repugnance. There can be no forgiveness in this world for a man who calls the wisdom of this world a cowardly lie, and probes clinically into the damning imperfections of the best. His Kingdom is surely not of this world. And if this world evinces for his gospel neither understanding nor sympathy, he cannot reasonably complain if he reaps the natural fruits of his profession. Melville agreed with the Psalmist: "Verily there is a reward for the righteous." But he blasphemed when he dared teach that the reward of virtue and truth in this world must be wailing and gnashing of teeth. Like Dante, Melville set himself up against the world as a party of one. A majority judgment, though it has the power, has not necessarily the truth. It is theoretically possible that Melville, not the world, is right. But one can assent to Melville's creed only on penalty of destruction; and the race does not welcome annihilation. Hence this world must rejoice in its vengeance upon his blasphemy: and the self-righteous have washed their feet in the blood of the wicked.

After *Pierre,* any further writing from Melville was both an impertinence and an irrelevancy. No man who really believes that all is vanity can consistently go on taking elaborate pains to popularise his indifference. Schopenhauer did that thing, it is true; but Schopenhauer was an artist, not a moralist; and he was enchanted with disenchantment. Carlyle, too, through interminable volumes shrieked out the necessity of silence. But after *Pierre,* Melville was without internal urgings to write. "All profound things, and emotions of things," he wrote in *Pierre*, "are preceded and attended by silence." "When a man is really in a profound mood, then all merely verbal or written profundities are unspeakably repulsive, and seem downright childish to him." Infinitely greater souls than Melville's seem to have shared this conviction. Neither Buddha nor Socrates left a single written word; Christ wrote once only, and then in the sand.

As if the gods themselves were abetting Melville in his recoil from letters and his contempt for his hard-earned fame, the Harper's fire of 1853 destroyed the plates of all his novels, and practically all of the copies of his books then in stock. One hundred and eighty-five copies of *Typee* were burned; 276 copies of *Omoo;* 491 copies of *Mardi;* 296 copies of *Redburn;* 292 copies of *White-Jacket;* 297 copies of *Moby-Dick;* 494 copies of *Pierre.* There survived only 10 copies of *Mardi,* 60 copies of *Moby-Dick* and 110 copies of *Pierre.* All of these books except *Pierre* were reissued, but with no rich profit either to Harper's or to Melville. A typical royalty account is that covering the period between October 6, 1863, and August 1, 1864. During this period, 54 copies of *Typee* were sold; 56 of *Omoo;* 42 of *Redburn;* 49 of *Mardi;* 29 of *White-Jacket;* 48 of *Moby-Dick;* and 27 of *Pierre.* It was a fortunate year, indeed, for Melville that brought him in $100 royalties. During most of his life, Melville's account with Harper's was overdrawn: a fact that speaks more for the generosity of his publisher than for the appreciation of his public. Melville surely never achieved opulence by his pen. Convinced of the futility of writing and effort, Melville wanted only tranquillity for thought. But his health was breaking, and his family had to be fed. So he looked about him for some unliterary employment.

The following letter from Richard Henry Dana explains itself:

"BOSTON, May 10, 1853.

"DEAR SIR:

"I am informed by the Chief Justice that my friend, Mr. Herman Melville, has been named to the Government as a suitable person for the American Consulship at the Sandwich Islands.

"I acknowledge no little personal interest in Mr. Melville, but apart from that, I know, from my early experience, and from a practice of many years in Admiralty & Maritime causes, the great importance of having a consul at the Sandwich Islands who knows the wants of our vast Pacific Marine, and shall stand clear of those inducements of trade consignments which lead so many consuls to neglect seamen and lend their influence indiscriminately in favour of owners and masters.

"Mr. Melville has been all over the Pacific Ocean, in all sorts of maritime service & has the requisite acquaintance & interest to an unusual degree. Beyond this, his reputation, general intelligence & agreeable manners will be sure to make him a popular and useful officer among all our citizens who visit the Islands. I cannot conceive of a more appropriate appointment, & I sincerely hope it will be given him.

"If I knew the President or the Secretary of State, personally, I would take the liberty to write them. As I do not, I beg you will use whatever influence I may have in any quarter in his favour.

"Very truly yours,

"RICHARD H. DANA, JR.

"ALLAN MELVILLE, ESQ."

Melville was not appointed to a consular post in the Pacific: so his brother Allan busied himself in looking for an appointment elsewhere, as the following letter, addressed to Hon. Lemuel Shaw, shows:

"NEW YORK, June 11, 1853.

"MY DEAR SIR:

"Yours of the 8th reached me yesterday advising me of the recent information you have received through a confidential source from Washington respecting a consulate for Herman.

"There can be no consulship in Italy, not even Rome, where the fees would amount to sufficient to make it an object for Herman to accept a position there.

"I have positive information of the value of the Antwerp consulate and understand it to be worth from $2,500 to $3,000. Should this be tendered, Herman ought to accept it.

"I don't know that I can say anything more on this subject.

"Herman is in town and will see you on your arrival.

"Very truly yours,

"ALLAN MELVILLE.

"I may add that Herman has been specially urged for the Antwerp position & that Mr. Hawthorne spoke to Mr. Cushing of that place.

"A. M."

Of the domestic happenings at Arrowhead at this time, very little is known. One letter of Mrs. Melville's survives:

"ARROWHEAD, Aug. 10th, 1853.

"MY DEAR FATHER:

"I did not mean that so long a time should elapse, of your absence from home, without my writing you, especially when I have two letters of yours to answer. It is not because I have not thought of you much and often, but really because I can not find the time to seat myself quietly down to write a letter—that is more than for a hasty scrawl to mother occasionally—and inasmuch as my occupations are of the useful and not the frivolous kind I know you will appreciate the apology and accept it. Three little ones to look after and 'do for' takes up no little portion of the day, and my baby is as restless a little mortal as ever crowed. She is very well and healthy in every respect, but not very fat, as she sleeps very little comparatively and is very active. A few weeks since Malcolm made his début as a scholar at the white school house of Dr. Holmes'. I was afraid he would lose the little he already knew 'of letters' and as I could not find the time to give him regular instruction, I sent him to school rather earlier than I should have done otherwise. The neighbours' children call for him every morning, and he goes off with his pail of dinner in one hand and his primer in the other, to our no small amusement. The grand feature of the day to him seems to be the 'eating his dinner under the trees'—as he always gives that as his occupation when asked what he does at school—and as his pail is invariably empty when he returns, he does full justice to the noon-tide meal. Stannie begins to talk a great deal, and seems to be uncommonly forward for his age. He has a severe cough, which I think will prove the whooping-cough as there is a great deal of it about at present."

Failing of a consular appointment, Melville was forced to continue writing. He busied himself with the story of the "revolutionary beggar." Melville based his story upon "a little narrative, forlornly published on sleazy grey paper," that he had "rescued by the merest chance from the rag-pickers." Copies of this narrative are not excessively rare. The title page reads: *"Life and Remarkable Adventures of Israel R. Potter* (a native of Cranston, Rhode Island) who was a soldier in the American Revolution, and took a distinguished part in the Battle of Bunker Hill (in which he received three wounds) after which he was taken Prisoner by the British, conveyed to England, where for thirty years he obtained a livelihood for himself and family, by crying *'Old Chairs to Mend'* through the Streets of London.—In May last, by the assistance of the American Consul, he succeeded (in the 79th year of his age) in obtaining a passage to his native country, after an absence of 48 years. Providence: Printed by Henry Trumbull—1824 (Price 28 cents)." The result was *Israel Potter,* published in book form by G. P. Putnam in 1855, after having appeared serially in *Putnam's Monthly Magazine. Israel Potter* is, in most part, a spirited narrative containing, so Mr. Mather states, "the best account of a sea fight in American fiction." It was praised, too, by Hawthorne for its delineations of Franklin and John Paul Jones, and doubtless deserves a wider recognition than has ever been given it. Interestingly enough, the book is dedicated to Bunker Hill Monument.

Between 1853 and 1856, Melville published twelve articles, inclusive of *Israel Potter,* in *Putnam's Magazine* and in *Harper's Monthly.* Melville made from a selection from these his

Piazza Tales (1856), published in New York by Dix and Edwards, in London by Sampson Low. Of these, *The Bell Tower, Don Benito Cereno* and *The Encantadas* show the last glow of Melville's literary glamour, the final momentary brightening of the embers before they sank into blackness and ash. There exists a letter from *Putnam's Monthly,* dated May 12, 1854, and signed by Charles T. Briggs—refusing a still unpublished story of Melville's out of fear of "offending the religious sensibilities of the public and the Congregation of Grace Church." This letter is less important because of its exquisite sensitiveness, than because of its mention of a letter from Lowell; a letter in which Lowell is reported to have read *The Encantadas.* According to Briggs' communication, Lowell was so moved that "the figure of the cross on the .ass' neck brought tears into his eyes, and he thought it the finest touch of genius he had seen in prose." Swinburne speaks of "the generous pleasure of praising": this pleasure Lowell indulged frequently, and in his wholesome and wholehearted way. Of Hawthorne, Lowell said: "The rarest creative imagination of the century, the rarest in some ideal respects since Shakespeare." *The Confidence Man* was published in 1857: but it was a posthumous work. Thereafter, Melville was to try his hand at poetry, and with results little meriting the total oblivion into which his poetry has fallen; and in his old age he was again to turn to prose: but before Melville was half through his mortal life his signal literary achievement was done. The rest, if not silence, was whisper.

CHAPTER XVII

THE LONG QUIETUS

"The round face of the grub-man peered upon me now. 'His dinner is
ready. Won't he dine to-day, either? Or does he live without dining?'
" 'Lives without dining,' said I, and closed the eyes.
" 'Eh!—He's asleep, ain't he?'
" 'With kings and counsellors,' murmured I."
—HERMAN MELVILLE: *Bartleby the Scrivener.*

"THE death of Herman Melville," wrote Arthur Stedman,
"came as a surprise to the public at large, chiefly because it
revealed the fact that such a man had lived so long." The
New York *Times* missed the news of Melville's death (on
September 28, 1891) and published a few days later an editorial beginning:

"There has died and been buried in this city, during the
current week, at an advanced age, a man who is so little known,
even by name, to the generation now in the vigour of life,
that only one newspaper contained an obituary account of him,
and this was of but three or four lines."

In 1885, Robert Buchanan published in the London *Academy*
a pasquinade containing the following lines:

> ". . . Melville, sea-compelling man,
> Before whose wand Leviathan
> Rose hoary white upon the Deep,
> With awful sounds that stirred its sleep;
> Melville, whose magic drew Typee,
> Radiant as Venus, from the sea,
> Sits all forgotten or ignored,
> While haberdashers are adored!
> He, ignorant of the draper's trade,
>   Indifferent to the art of dress,
> Pictured the glorious South Sea maid
>   Almost in mother nakedness—
> Without a hat, or boot, or stocking,
> A want of dress to most so shocking,
> With just one chemisette to dress her

She *lives*—and still shall live, God bless her,
Long as the sea rolls deep and blue,
  While Heaven repeats the thunder of it,
Long as the White Whale ploughs it through,
  The shape my sea-magician drew
    Shall still endure, or I'm no prophet!

In a footnote, Buchanan added:

"I sought everywhere for this Triton, who is still living somewhere in New York. No one seemed to know anything of the one great writer fit to stand shoulder to shoulder with Whitman on that continent."

If this man, who had in mid-career been hailed at home and abroad as one of the glories of our literature, died "forgotten and ignored," it was, after all, in accordance with his own desires. Adventurous life and action was the stuff out of which his reputation had been made. But in the middle of his life, he turned his back upon the world, and in his recoil from life absorbed himself in metaphysics. He avoided all unnecessary associations and absorbed in his own thoughts he lived in sedulous isolation. He resisted all efforts to draw him out of retirement—though such efforts were very few indeed. Arthur Stedman tells us: "It is generally admitted that had Melville been willing to join freely in the literary movements of New York, his name would have remained before the public and a larger sale of his works would have been insured. But more and more, as he grew older, he avoided every action on his part and on the part of his family that might look in this direction, even declining to assist in founding the Authors Club in 1882." With an aggressive indifference he looked back in *Clarel* to

"Adventures, such as duly shown
Printed in books, seem passing strange
To clerks which read them by the fire,
Yet be the wonted common-place
Of some who in the Orient range,
Free-lances, spendthrifts of their hire,
And who in end, when they retrace
Their lives, see little to admire
Or wonder at, so dull they be."

When Titus Munson Coan was a student at Williams College, prompted by a youthful curiosity to hunt out celebrities, he called upon Melville at Arrowhead. In an undated letter to his mother he thus recounted the experience: "I have made my first literary pilgrimage—a call upon Herman Melville, the renowned author of *Typee,* &c. He lives in a spacious farm-house about two miles from Pittsfield, a weary walk through the .dust. But it was well repaid. I introduced myself as a Hawaiian-American and soon found myself in full tide of talk—or rather of monologue. But he would not repeat the experiences of which I had been reading with rapture in his books. In vain I sought to hear of Typee and those Paradise islands, but he preferred to pour forth his philosophy and his theories of life. The shade of Aristotle arose like a cold mist between myself and Fayaway. We have quite enough of Greek philosophy at Williams College, and I confess I was disappointed in this trend of the talk. But what a talk it was! Melville is transformed from a Marquesan to a gypsy student, the gypsy element still remaining strong in him. And this contradiction gives him the air of one who has suffered from opposition, both literary and social. With his liberal views he is apparently considered by the good people of Pittsfield as little better than a cannibal or a 'beach-comber.' His attitude seemed to me something like that of an Ishmael; but perhaps I judged hastily. I managed to draw him out very freely on everything but the Marquesas Islands, and when I left him he was in full tide of discourse on all things sacred and profane. But he seems to put away the objective side of life and to shut himself up in this cold North as a cloistered thinker."

An article appearing the New York *Times,* under the initials O. G. H., a week after Melville's death, said of him:

"He had shot his arrow and made his mark, and was satisfied. With considerable knowledge of the world, he had preferred to see it from a distance. . . . I asked the loan of some of his books which in early life had given me pleasure and was surprised when he said that he didn't own a single copy of them. . . . I had before noticed that though eloquent in discussing general literature he was dumb when the subject of his own writings was broached."

In her sketch of her husband's life, Mrs. Melville says: "In February, 1855, he had his first attack of severe rheumatism— and in the following June an attack of sciatica. Our neighbour in Pittsfield, Dr. O. W. Holmes, attended and prescribed for him. A severe attack of what he called crick in the back laid him up at his mother's in Gansevoort in March, 1858— and he never regained his former vigour and strength." In 1863, so runs the account of J. E. A. Smith, while Melville was in process of moving from Arrowhead, "he had occasion for some household articles he left behind, and, with a friend, started in a rude wagon to procure them. He was driving at a moderate pace over a perfectly smooth and level road, when a sudden start of the horse threw both occupants from the wagon; probably on account of an imperfectly secured seat. Mr. Melville fell with his back in a hollow of the frozen road, and was very severely injured. Being conveyed to his home by Col. George S. Willis, near whose farm on Williams Street the accident happened, he suffered painfully for many weeks. This prolonged agony and the confinement and interruption of work which it entailed, affected him strangely. He had been before on mountain excursions a driver daring almost to the point of recklessness. . . . After this accident he not only abandoned the rides of which he had been so fond, but for a time shrank from entering a carriage. It was long before the shock which his system had received was overcome; and it is doubtful whether it ever was completely." Ill health certainly contributed more to Melville's retirement from letters than any of his critics—Mr. Mather excepted—have ever even remotely suggested.

During the last half of his life, Melville twice journeyed far from home. In her journal Mrs. Melville says: "In October, 1856, his health being impaired by too close application, he again sailed for London. He went up the Mediterranean to Constantinople and the Holy Land. For much of his observation and reflection in that interesting quarter see his poem of *Clarel.* Sailed for home on the steamer *City of Manches-*

HERMAN MELVILLE IN 1868

ter May 6, 1857. In May, 1860, he made a voyage to San Francisco, sailing from Boston on the 30th of May with his brother Thomas Melville who commanded the *Meteor,* a fast sailing clipper in the China trade—and returning in November, he being the only passenger. He reached San Francisco Oct. 12th—returned in the *Carter* Oct. 20 to Panama—crossed the Isthmus &. sailed for New York on the *North Star.* This voyage to San Francisco has been incorrectly given in many of the papers of the day."

Of this trip to the Holy Land there survive, beside *Clarel* and Hawthorne's accounts of the meeting *en route,* a long and closely written journal that Melville kept during the trip, and twenty-one shorter poems printed in *Timoleon* under the caption "Fruit of Travel Long Ago." Typical of these shorter poems is

THE APPARITION

(The Parthenon uplifted on its rock first challenging the view
on the approach to Athens)

Abrupt the supernatural Cross,
Vivid in startled air,
Smote the Emperor Constantine
And turned his soul's allegiance there

With other power appealing down,
Trophy of Adam's best!
If cynic minds you scarce convert
You try them, shake them, or molest.

Diogenes, that honest heart,
Lived ere your date. began:
Thee had he seen, he might have swerved
In mood nor barked so much at man.

The journal was surely never written with a view to publication. It is a staccato jotting down of impressions, chiefly interesting (as is Dr. Johnson's French journal) as another evidence of Melville's scope of curiosity and keenness of observation. A typical entry is that for Saturday, December 13,— Melville's first day in Constantinople:

"Up early; went out; saw cemeteries where they dumped garbage. Sawing wood over a tomb. Forest of cemeteries. Intricacies of the streets. Started alone for Constantinople and after a terrible long walk found myself back where I started. Just like getting lost in a wood. No plan to streets. Pocket compass. Perfect labyrinth. Narrow. Close, shut in. If one could but get *up* aloft, it would be easy to see one's way out. If you could get up into a tree. Soar out of the maze. But no. No names to the streets no more than to natural alleys among the groves. No numbers, no anything. Breakfasted at 10 A. M. Took guide ($1.25 per day) and started for tour. Took Cargua for Seraglio. Holy ground. Crossed some extensive grounds and gardens. Fine buildings of the Saracenic style. Saw the Mosque of St. Sophia. Went in. Rascally priests demanding 'baksheesh.' Fleeced me out of ½ dollar; following me round, selling the fallen mosaics. Ascended a kind of hose way leading up, round and round. Came into a gallery fifty feet above the floor. Superb interior. Precious marbles. Prophyry & Verd antique. Immense magnitude of the building. Names of the prophets in great letters. Roman Catholic air to the whole. To the hippodrome, near which stands the six towered mosque of Sultan Achmed; soaring up with its snowy white spires into the pure blue sky. Like light-houses. Nothing finer. In the hippodrome saw the obelisk with Roman inscription on the base. Also a broken monument of bronze, representing three twisted serpents erect upon their tails. Heads broken off. Also a square monument of masoned blocks. Leaning over and frittered away,—like an old chimney stack. A Greek inscription shows it to be of the time of Theodoric. Sculpture about the base of the obelisk, representing Constantine & wife and sons, &c. Then saw the 'Burnt Column.' Black and grimy enough & hooped about with iron. Stands soaring up from among a bundle of old wooden stakes. A more striking fire mount than that of London. Then to the cistern of 1001 columns. You see a rounded knoll covered with close herbage. Then a kind of broken cellar-way you go down, and find yourself on a wooden, rickety platform, looking down into a grove of marble pillars, fading away into the darkness. A palatial sort of Tartarus. Two tiers of pillars, one standing on the other; lower tier half buried. Here and there a little light percolates through from breaks in the keys of the arches; where bits of green struggle down. Used to be a reservoir. Now full of boys twisting silk. Great hubbub. Flit about like imps. Whirr of the spinning Jenns. In going down, (as into a ship's hold) and wandering about, have to beware the innumerable skeins of silk. Terrible place to be robbed or murdered in. At whatever place you look, you see lines of pillars, like trees in an orchard arranged in the quincunx style.—Came out. Overhead looks like a mere shabby common, or worn out sheep pasture.—To the bazaar. A wilderness of traffic. Furniture, arms, silks, confectionery, shoes, saddles,—everything. (Cario) Covered overhead with stone arches, with wide openings. Immense crowds. Georgians, Armenians, Greeks, Jews & Turks are the merchants. Magnificent embroidered silk & gilt sabres & caparisons for horses. You lose yourself & are bewildered and confounded with the labyrinth, the din, the barbaric confusion of the whole.—Went to Watch Tower within a kind of arsenal (Immense arsenal) the tower of vast girth & height in the Saracenic style—a column. From the top, my God, what a view! Surpassing everything. The Propontis, the Bosphorus, the Golden Horn, the domes, the minarets, the bridges, the men-of-war, the cypresses.—Indescribable. Went to the Pigeon Mosque. In its court, the pigeons covered the pavement as thick as in the West they fly in hosts. A man feeding them. Some perched upon the roof of the colonnades & upon the fountain in the middle & on the cypresses. Took off my shoes and went in. Pigeons inside, flying round in the dome, in & out the lofty windows. Went to Mosque of Sultan Suleiman. The third one in point of size and splendour. The Mosque is a sort of marble mosque of which the minarets (four or six) are the stakes. In fact when inside it struck me that the idea of this kind of edifice was borrowed from the tent. Though it would make a noble ball room. Off shoes and went in. This custom more sensible than taking off hat. Muddy shoes; but never muddy head.

Floor covered with mats & on them beautiful rugs of great size & square. Fine light coming through the side slits below the dome. Blind dome. Many Turks at prayer; lowering head to the floor towards a kind of altar. Charity going on. In a gallery saw lot of portmanteaux, chests & bags; as in a R. R. baggage car.. Put there for safe-keeping by men who leave home, or afraid of robbers and taxation. 'Lay not up your treasures where moth and rust do corrupt' &c. Fountains (a row of them) outside along the side of the mosque for bathing the feet and hands of worshippers before going in. Natural rock.—Instead of going in in stockings (as I did) the Turks wear overshoes and doff them outside the mosque. The tent-like form of the Mosque broken up & dumbfounded with infinite number of arches, trellises, small domes, colonnades, &c, &c, &c. Went down to the Golden Horn. Crossed bridge of pontoons. Stood in the middle and not a cloud in the sky. Deep blue and clear. Delightful elastic atmosphere, although December. A kind of English June cooled and tempered sherbet-like with an American October; the serenity & beauty of summer without the heat.—Came home through the vast suburbs of Galatea, &c. Great crowds of all nations— money changers coins of all nations circulate—placards in four or five languages: (Turkish, French, Greek, Armenian) Lottery advertisements of boats the same. Sultan's ship in colours —no atmosphere like this for flags. You feel you are among the nations. Great curse that of Babel; not being able to talk to a fellow being, &c.—Have to tend to your pockets. My guide went with his hands to his.—The horrible grimy tragic air of the Streets. (Ruffians of Galatea) The rotten & wicked looking houses. So gloomy & grimy seem as if a suicide hung from every rafter within.—No open spaces—no squares or parks. You suffocate for room.—You pass close together. The cafés of the Turks. Dingy holes, faded splendour, moth eaten. On both sides rude seats and divans where the old musty Turks sit smoking like conjurers. Saw in certain kiosks (pavilions) the crowns of the late Sultan. You look through gilt gratings & between heavy curtains of lace, at the sparkling things. Near the Mosque of Sultan Suleiman saw the cemetery of his family—big as that of a small village, all his wives and children and servants. All gilt and carved. The women's tombs carved with heads (women no souls). The Sultan Suleiman's tomb & that of his three brothers in a kiosk. Gilded like mantel ornaments."

Clarel was, in 1876, printed at Melville's expense. More accurately, its printing was made possible by his uncle, Hon. Peter Gansevoort, who, as Melville says in the dedication, "in a personal interview provided for the publication of this poem, known to him by report, as existing in manuscript."

Not the least impressive thing about *Clarel* is its length: it extends to 571 pages. Mr. Mather states: "Of those who have actually perused the four books (of verse) and *Clarel,* I am presumably the only survivor." Mr. Mather is mistaken: there are two. But since, because of the excessive length of *Clarel* and the excessive scarcity of *John Marr* and *Timoleon* (both privately printed in an edition of only twenty-five copies) it would be over-optimistic to presume that there will soon be a third, some account must be given of Melville's poetry.

Stevenson once said: "There are but two writers who have touched the South Seas with any genius, both Americans: Melville and Charles Warren Stoddard; and at the christening of the first and greatest, some influential fairy must have been neglected; 'He shall be able to see'; 'He shall be able to tell'; 'He shall be able to charm,' said the friendly godmothers; 'But he shall not be able to hear!' exclaimed the last." When Stevenson wrote his passage, the artist in him seems for the moment to have slept; taking no account of Melville's frequent mastery of the magic of words, he berates Melville's genius for misspelling Polynesian names as a defect of genius. That Melville had an ear sensitive to the cadences of prose is shown by the facility with which he on occasion caught the rhythm both of the Psalms and of Sir Thomas Browne. Yet the same man who at his best is equalled only by Poe in the subtle melody of his prose, at times fell into ranting passages of obvious and intolerable parody of blank verse. The following from *Mardi* is an example: "From dawn till eve, the bright, bright days sped on, chased by the gloomy nights; and, in glory dying, lent their lustre to the starry skies. So, long the radiant dolphins fly before the sable sharks; but seized, and torn in flames —die, burning:—their last splendour left, in sparkling scales that float along the sea." In his poetry, as in his prose, is the same incongruous mating of astonishing facility and flagrant defect. It is the same paradox that one finds in Browning and in Meredith,—whose poetry Melville's more than superficially resembles. Melville shared with these men a greater interest in ideas than in verbal prettiness, and like the best of them, when mastered by a refractory idea, he was not over-exquisite in his regard for prosody and syntax in getting it said. When he had a mind to, however, he could pound with a lustiness that should endear him to those who delight in declamation contests: a contemptible distinction, perhaps—but even that has been denied him. The poem to the Swamp Angel, for example, the great gun that reduced Charleston, is fine in its irony and vigour. The poem begins:

> There is a coal-black Angel
>   With a thick Afric lip
> And he dwells (like the hunted and harried)
>   In a swamp where the green frogs dip
> But his face is against a City
>   Which is over a bay by the sea,
> And he breathes with a breath that is blastment
>   And dooms by a far degree.

Though there are memorable lines and stanzas in *Battle-Pieces,* only one of the poems in the volume has ever been at all noticed: *Sheridan at Cedar Creek,* beginning:

> Shoe the steed with silver
>   That bore him to the fray,
> When he heard the guns at dawning
>   Miles away;
> When he heard them calling, calling—
>   Mount! nor stay.

The following letter to his brother Tom bears upon Melville's *Battle-Pieces.*

"PITTSFIELD, May 25th, 1862.

"My DEAR BOY: (or, if that appears disrespectful)

"My DEAR CAPTAIN:

"Yesterday I received from Gansevoort your long and very entertaining letter to Mamma from Pernambuco. Yes, it was very entertaining. Particularly the account of that interesting young gentleman whom you so uncivilly stigmatise for a jack-ass, simply because he improves his opportunities in the way of sleeping, eating & other commendable customs. That's the sort of fellow, seems to me, to get along with. For my part I love sleepy fellows, and the more ignorant the better. Damn your wide-awake and knowing chaps. As for sleepiness, it is one of the noblest qualities of humanity. There is something sociable about it, too. Think of those sensible & sociable millions of good fellows all taking a good long friendly snooze together, under the sod—no quarrels, no imaginary grievances, no envies, heartburnings, & thinking how much better that other chap is off—none of this: but all equally free-&-easy, they sleep away & reel off their nine knots an hour, in perfect amity. If you see your sleepy ignorant jackass-friend again, give him my compliments, and say that however others may think of him, I honour and esteem him.—As for your treatment of the young man, there I entirely commend you. You remember what the Bible says:—

"Oh ye who teach the children of the nations,
Holland, France, England, Germany or Spain,
I pray ye *strap* them upon all occasions,
It mends their morals—never mind the pain."

"In another place the Bible says, you know, something about sparing the strap & spoiling the child.—Since I have quoted poetry above, it puts me in mind of my own doggerel. You will be pleased to learn that I have disposed of a lot of it at a great bargain. In fact, a trunk-maker took the whole lot off my hands at ten cents the pound. So, when you buy a new trunk again, just peep at the lining & perhaps you may be

rewarded by some glorious stanza staring you in the face &
claiming admiration. If you were not such a devil of a ways
off, I would send you a trunk, by way of presentation-copy.
I can't help thinking what a luckless chap you were that voyage you had a poetaster with you. You remember the romantic moonlight night, when the conceited donkey repeated to you
about three cables' length of his verses. But you bore it like
a hero. I can't in fact recall so much as a single *wince*. To
be sure, you went to bed immediately upon the conclusion of
the entertainment; but this much I am sure of, whatever were
your sufferings, you never gave them utterance. Tom, my
boy, I admire you. I say again, you are a hero.—By the way,
I hope in God's name, that rumour which reached your owners
(C. & P.) a few weeks since—that dreadful rumour is not true.
They heard that you had begun to take to—drink?—Oh no,
but worse—to sonnet-writing. That off Cape Horn instead
of being on deck about your business, you devoted your time
to writing a sonnet on your mistress' eyebrow, & another upon
her thumbnail.—'I'll be damned,' says Curtis (he was very
profane) 'if I'll have a sonneteer among my Captains.'—'Well,
if he has taken to poetising,' says Peabody—'God help the ship!'

.   .   .   .

And now, my boy, if you knew how much laziness I overcame
in writing you this letter, you would think me, what I am
              "Always your affectionate brother,
                                        "HERMAN."

Melville's family seem all to have been more sceptical of
his verse than they were of his prose. In 1859 Mrs. Melville
wrote to her mother "Herman has taken to writing poetry.
You need not tell any one, for you know how such things get
around." Mrs. Melville was too optimistic: her husband's
indiscreet practice is still pretty much a secret to the world at
large. And *Clarel*, his longest and most important poem, is
practically impossible to come by.

In 1884, Melville said of *Clarel* in a letter to Mr. James
Billson: "a metrical affair, a pilgrimage or what not, of several thousand lines, eminently adapted for unpopularity."

Though this is completely true, Melville used in *Clarel* more irony, vividness, and intellect than the whole congregation of practising poets of the present day (a few notable names excepted) could muster in aggregate. Yet with all this wealth of the stuff of poetry, the poem never quite fulfils itself. In *Clarel* Melville brings together in the Holy Land a group of pilgrims; pilgrims nearly all drawn from the life, as a study of his Journal of 1856-7 shows. In this group there are men devout and men sceptical, some suave in orthodoxy, and some militant in doubt. There are dreamers and men of action; unprincipled saints, and rakes without vice. In the bleak and legend-haunted Holy Land Melville places these men, and dramatises his own reactions to life in this setting. The problem of faith is the pivot of endless discussion: and upon this pivot is made to turn all of the problems of destiny that engage a "pondering man." These discussions take place against a panorama of desert and monastery and shrine. In some of the interpolated songs of *Clarel,* Melville almost achieved the lyric mood.

> My shroud is saintly linen,
>   In lavender 'tis laid;
> I have chosen a bed by the marigold
>   And supplied me a silver spade.

And there are, too, incidental legends and saints' tales:

> Those legends which, be it confessed
> Did nearer bring to them the sky—
> Did nearer woo it in their hope
> Of all that seers and saints avow—
> Than Galileo's telescope
> Can bid it unto prosing science now.

Clarel is by all odds the most important record we have of what was the temper of Melville's deeper thoughts during his long metaphysical period. Typical quotations have already been made.

The most recurrent note of the poem is a parched desire for companionship; a craving for

A brother that he well might own
In tie of friendship.

Could *I* but meet
Some stranger of a lore replete,
Who, marking how my looks betray
The dumb thoughts clogging here my feet
Would question me, expound and prove,
And make my heart to burn with love.

· · · · · · ·

Doubt's heavy hand
Is set against us; and his brand
Still warreth for his natural lord
King Common-place."

· · · · · · ·

Art thou the first soul tried by doubt?
Shall prove the last? Go, live it out.
But for thy fonder dream of love
In man towards man—the soul's caress—
The negatives of flesh should prove
Analogies of non-cordialness
In spirit.

· · · · · · ·

Why then
Remaineth to me what? the pen?
Dead feather of ethereal life!
Nor efficacious much, save when
It makes some fallacy more rife.
My kin—I blame them not at heart—
Would have me act some routine part.
Subserving family, and dreams
Alien to me—illusive schemes.
This world clean fails me: still I yearn.
Me then it surely does concern
Some other world to find. But where?
In creed? I do not find it there.

· · · · · · ·

This side the dark and hollow bound
Lies there no unexplored rich ground?
Some other world: well, there's the New—
Ah, joyless and ironic too!

Ay, Democracy
Lops, lops; but where's her planted bed?
The future, what is that to her
Who vaunts she's no inheritor?
'Tis in her mouth, not in her heart.
The past she spurns, though 'tis the past
From which she gets her saving part—
That Good which lets her evil last.

Behold her whom the panders crown,
Harlot on horseback, riding down
The very Ephesians who acclaim
This great Diana of ill fame!
Arch strumpet of an impious age,
Upstart from ranker villainage:
Asia shall stop her at the least
That old inertness of the East.

  .   .   .   .

But in the New World things make haste:
Not only men, the *state* lives fast—
Fast breed the pregnant eggs and shells,
The slumberous combustibles
Sure to explode. 'Twill come, 'twill come!
One demagogue can trouble much:
How of a hundred thousand such?

  .   .   .   .

Indeed, those germs one now may view:
Myriads playing pygmy parts—
Debased into equality:
Dead level of rank commonplace:
An Anglo-Saxon China, see,
May on your vast plains shame the race
In the Dark Ages of Democracy.

  .   .   .   .

Your arts advance in faith's decay:
You are but drilling the new Hun
Whose growl even now can some dismay;
Vindictive is his heart of hearts.
He schools him in your mines and marts
A skilled destroyer.

  .   .   .   .   .   .

Old ballads sing
Fair Christian children crucified
By impious Jews: you've heard the thing:
Yes, fable; but there's truth hard by:
How many Hughs of Lincoln, say,
Does Mammon, in his mills, to-day,
Crook, if he does not crucify?

The impieties of "Progress" speak;
What say *these,* in effect to God?
"How profits it? And who art Thou
That we should serve Thee? Of Thy ways
No knowledge we desire; *new* ways
We have found out, and better. Go—
Depart from us!"—And if He do?
Is aught betwixt us and the hells?

        .   .   .   .

Against all this stands Rome's array:
Rome is the Protestant to-day.
The Red Republic slinging flame
In Europe—she's your Scarlet Dame.
Rome stands: but who may tell the end?
Relapse barbaric may impend,
Dismission into ages blind—
Moral dispersion of mankind.
If Luther's day expand to Darwin's year,
Shall that exclude the hope—foreclose the fear?

        .   .   .   .

Yea, ape and angel, strife and old debate,
The harps of heaven and dreary gongs of hell;
Science the feud can only aggravate—
No umpire she betwixt the chimes and knell,
The running battle of the star and clod
Shall run forever—if there is no God.

        .   .   .   .

Then keep thy heart, though yet but ill resigned—
Clarel, thy heart, the issues there but mind;
That like the crocus budding through the snow—
That like a swimmer rising from the deep
That like a burning secret which doth go
Even from the bosom that would hoard and keep;
Emerge thou mayst from the last wheeling sea
And prove that death but routs life into victory.

Though *Clarel* is unconscionably long, and though there are arid wastes strewn throughout its length, a patient reading is rewarded by passages of beauty, and more frequently by passages of astonishing vigour and daring. And it speaks more for the orthodoxy of America than for her intellect, that *Clarel* —which reposes in the outer limbo of oblivion—is about all she has to show, as Mr. Mather has observed, for the poetical stirrings of the deeper theological waters which marked the age of Matthew Arnold, Clough, Tennyson, and Browning. We should blush for our neglect of a not unworthy representative.

Besides *Battle-Pieces* and *Clarel*, Melville printed for private circulation two slender volumes: *John Marr and Other Sailors* (1888) and *Timoleon* (1891): selections from a larger body of poetry, the remainder of which is still preserved in manuscript. In these, the inspiration flags throughout. Two of the better poems have already been quoted. *John Marr* was dedicated to W. Clark Russell, *Timoleon* to Elihu Vedder.

In 1886, according to Arthur Stedman, Melville "felt impelled to write Mr. Russell in regard to one of his newly published novels." This was the beginning of a correspondence between Russell and Melville. Melville's letters are not available. Russell's reply to Melville's first letter follows:

"July 21, 1886.

"My Dear Mr. Herman Melville:

"Your letter has given me a very great and singular pleasure. Your delightful books carry the imagination into a maritime period so remote that, often as you have been in my mind, I could never satisfy myself that you were still amongst the living. I am glad, indeed, to learn from Mr. Toft that you are still hale and hearty, and I do most heartily wish you many years yet of health and vigour.

"Your books I have in the American edition. I have *Typee, Omoo, Redburn,* and that noble piece, *Moby-Dick.* These are all I have been able to obtain. There have been many editions of your works in this country, particularly the lovely South Sea sketches; but the editions are not equal to those of the American publishers. Your reputation here is very great. It is hard to meet a man whose opinion as a reader is worth having who does not speak of your works in such terms as he might hesitate to employ, with all his patriotism, towards many renowned English writers.

"Dana is, indeed, great. There is nothing in literature more remarkable than the impression produced by Dana's portraiture of the homely inner life of a little brig's forecastle.

"I beg that you will accept my thanks for the kindly spirit in which you have read my books. I wish it were in my power to cross the Atlantic, for you assuredly would be the first whom it would be my happiness to visit. . . . The condition of my right hand obliges me to dictate this to my son; but painful as it is to me to hold a pen I cannot suffer this letter to reach the hands of a man of so admirable genius as Herman Melville without begging him to believe me to be, with my own hand, his most respectful and hearty admirer,

"W. CLARK RUSSELL."

Elihu Vedder and Melville never met or corresponded. The acknowledgment of the dedication came only after Melville's death. "I may not have been very successful in a worldly way," he said, "but the knowledge that my art has gained me so many friends—even if unknown to me—makes ample amends."

Schopenhauer was enabled to preserve his disillusions because he also preserved his income. If a man is blessed with a comfortable fortune, then it is easy for him to lead a tranquil and unpretentious existence, sheltered from all intruders. But for an unsuccessful writer with a wife, four children, and no income, to throw down the pen and retire from the world (except for a season in California and another in the Holy Land); the secret of such a feat should be popularised. The secret transpires in the following letter to Melville from his father-in-law, Justice Shaw.

"BOSTON, 15 May, 1860.

"MY DEAR HERMAN,

"I am very glad to learn from your letter that you intend to accept Thomas' invitation to go on his next voyage. I think

it affords a fair prospect of being a permanent benefit to your
health, and it will afford me the greatest pleasure to do anything in my power to aid your preparation, and make the voyage most agreeable and beneficial to you.

"The prospect of your early departure renders it proper and
necessary to bring to a definite conclusion the subject we have
had a considerable time under consideration, a settlement of
the matter of the Pittsfield estate, with a view to which you
handed me your deeds, when I was in Pittsfield last autumn.

"You will recollect that when you proposed to purchase a
house in N. York I advanced to you $2000. and afterwards,
when you purchased the Brewster place, I again advanced you
$3000. For these sums, as well as for another loan of $500.
afterwards, I took your notes. This I did, not because I had
then any fixed determination to treat the advances as debts, to
be certainly repaid, but I was in doubt at the time in reference
to other claims upon me, and how my affairs would be ultimately arranged, what I should be able to do by way of provision for my daughter, and I put these advances upon the
footing of loans until some future adjustment.

"I always supposed that you considered the two first of the
above-named advances as having substantially gone into the
purchase of the Brewster farm, and that I had some equitable
claim upon it as security. I presume it was upon that ground
that you once sent me a mortgage of the estate prepared by
your brother Allan. I never put that mortgage on record nor
made any use of it; and if the conveyances are made, which
I now propose, that mortgage will become superseded and utterly nugatory.

"What I now propose is to give up to you the above mentioned notes in full consideration of your conveyance to me of
your present homestead, being all the Brewster purchase except what you sold to Mr. Willis. This being done and the
estate vested in me, I propose to execute a deed conveying the
same in fee to Elizabeth. This will vest the fee as an estate
of inheritance in her, subject of course to your rights as her
husband during your life. If you wish to know more particularly what will be the legal effect and operation of these con-

veyances Mr. Colt will explain it to you fully. I have written to him and enclosed him a draft of a deed for you to execute to me and my deed executed to be delivered to you and your notes to be surrendered. I have explained the whole matter to Mr. Colt and I have full confidence in his prudence and fidelity. I do not see any advantage in giving the business any more notoriety than will arise from putting the deeds on record.

"Elizabeth now writes me that you wish the note for $600., given by the town and coming from the sale of the Brewster place, that part of it not sold to Mr. Willis, so placed that it may be applied as you have heretofore, in your own mind, appropriated it, for building a new barn.

"I propose to treat this as I did the estate itself: first purchase it of you for a full consideration and then apply it to Elizabeth's use. In looking for a consideration for this purchase there is the interest of the above notes not computed in the consideration for the deed and now amounting to several thousand dollars.

"But there is another consideration, respecting which I have never had any direct communication, I believe, but I can see no reason why it should not be now clearly understood. When you went to Europe in the fall of 1856 I advanced the money necessary for your outfit and the expenses of your tour. This was done through your brother Allan and amounted to about fourteen or fifteen hundred dollars. In my own mind, though I took no note or obligation for it, I treated it like the other advances, to be regarded as advance by way of loan or a gift according to some future arrangement. I propose now to consider that sum as a set off against the note of $600. and, as to all beyond that, to consider it cancelled and discharged. This will make the note mine. At the same time I propose to appropriate it to its original use, to build a barn, in which case it will go to increase the value of the estate already Elizabeth's, or should anything occur to prevent such use of the money I shall appropriate it in some other way to her use. The effect of this arrangement will be to cancel and discharge all debt and pecuniary obligation of every description from you to my-

ARROWHEAD
In the Olden Time
a. d. 1860

MELVILLE AS ARTIST

self. You will then leave home with the conscious satisfaction of knowing that you are free from debt: that if by a Providential dispensation you should be prevented from ever returning to your beloved family, provision will have been made at least for a home, for your wife and children.

"Affectionately and ever faithfully
"Your sincere friend
"LEMUEL SHAW."

After his return from the Holy Land, Melville tried to eke out the small income from his books and his farm by lecturing. J. E. A. Smith says: "Between 1857 and 1861, a rage for lyceum lectures prevailed all over the northern and western states. In Pittsfield the Burbank hall, now Mead's carriage repository, was filled at least once every week to its full capacity of over a thousand seats, with eager and intelligent listeners to the most brilliant orators in the country. Some of the most noted authors, as well as orators, were induced to mount the platform partly by the liberal pay which they received directly—and also for the increased sale which it gave their books. Among these was Herman Melville, who lectured in Burbank hall, and in Boston, New York, Philadelphia, Montreal, St. Louis, San Francisco as well as intermediate cities and towns. He did not take very kindly to the lecture platform, but had large and well pleased audiences."

If his audiences were composed of people of the jaunty and shallow provincialism of J. E. A. Smith—and J. E. A. Smith is a very fair product of his country and his time—Melville's distaste for their prim, bland receptivity does not pass understanding. The place and date of Melville's lectures, together with the "liberal pay directly received" follows.

1857-1858

November	24	Concord, Mass.	$30.00
December	2	Boston, Mass.	40.00
"	10	Montreal	50.00
"	30	New Haven, Conn.	50.00

January	5	Auburn, N. Y.	$40.00
"	7	Ithaca, N. Y.	50.00
"	10	Cleveland, Ohio	50.00
"	22	Clarksville	75.00
		Chillicothe, Ohio	40.00
n. d.		Cincinnati, Ohio	50.00
Feb.	10	Charleston, Mass.	20.00
"	23	Rochester, N. Y.	50.00
n. d.		New Bedford, Mass.	50.00

645.00

Travelling expenses 221.30

423.70

1858-9

Dec. 6,	1858	Yonkers, N. Y.	$30.00
" 14,	"	Pittsfield, Mass.	50.00
Jan. 31,	1859	Boston, Mass.	50.00
Feb. 7,	"	New York, N. Y.	55.00
" 8,	"	Baltimore, Md.	100.00
" 24,	"	Chicago, Ill.	50.00
" 25,	"	Milwaukee, Wisc.	50.00
" 28,	"	Rockford, Ill.	50.00
Mar. 2,	"	Quincy, Ill.	23.50
" 16,	"	Lynn, Mass. (2 lec)	60.00

518.50

1859-60

November 7,	Flushing, L. I.	$30.
February 14,	Danvers, Mass.	25.
" 21,	Cambridgeport, Mass.	55.

110.

For these lyceum gatherings, Melville prepared two lectures: one on the *South Seas,* one on *Statuary in Rome.*

On December 2, 1857, in competition with another Melville, a bareback rider, who at the circus at Bingo "nightly performed before the élite and respectability of the city," Melville lectured on *Statuary in Rome.* On December 3, 1857, the Boston *Journal* thus reported Melville's lecture:

"A large audience assembled last evening to listen to the author of *Omoo* and *Typee.* He began by asserting that in the realm of art there was no exclusiveness. Dilettanti might accumulate their technical terms, but that did not interfere with the substantial enjoyment of those who did not understand them. As the beauties of nature could be appreciated without a knowledge of botany, so art could be enjoyed without the artist's skill. With this principle in view, he, claiming to be neither critic nor artist, would make some plain remarks on the statuary of Rome.

"As you approach the city from Naples, you are first struck by the statues of the Church St. John Lateran. Here you have the sculptured biographies of ancient celebrities. The speaker then vividly described the statues of Demosthenes, Titus Vespasian, Socrates, looking like an Irish comedian. Julius Cæsar, so sensible and business-like of aspect that it might be taken for the bust of a railroad president; Seneca, with the visage of a pawn broker; Nero, the fast young man; Plato, with the locks and air of an exquisite, as if meditating on the destinies of the world under the hand of a hair-dresser. Thus these statues confessed, and, as it were, prattled to us of much that does not appear in history and the written works of those they represent. They seem familiar and natural to us—and yet there is about them all a heroic tone peculiar to ancient life. It is to be hoped that this is not wholly lost from the world, although the sense of earthly vanity inculcated by Christianity may have swallowed it up in humility.

"The lecturer next turned to the celebrated Apollo Belvedere. This stands alone by itself, and the impression made upon all beholders is such as to subdue the feelings with wonder and awe. The speaker gave a very eloquent description of the attitude and the spirit of Apollo. The elevating effect of such statues was exhibited in the influence they exerted upon the mind of Milton during his visit to Italy.

"Among the most wonderful works of statuary is that of Lucifer and his associates cast down from heaven. This is in Padua, and contains three-score figures cut out of solid rock. The variety and power of the group cannot be surpassed. The Venus de Medici, as compared with the Apollo, was lovely and not divine. Mr. Melville said he once surprised a native maiden in the precise attitude of the Venus. He then passed to a rapid review of the Laocoon and other celebrated sculptures, to show the human feeling and genius of the ancient artists. None but a gentle heart could have conceived the idea of the Dying Gladiator. The sculptured monuments of the early Christians, in the vaults of the Vatican, show the joyous triumph of the new religion—quite unlike the sombre momentoes of modern times.

"The lecturer then eloquently sketched the exterior of the Vatican. But nearly the whole of Rome was a Vatican—everywhere were fallen columns and sculptured fragments. Most of these, it is true, were works of Greek artists. And yet the grand spirit of Roman life inspired them. Passing from these ancient sculptures, tribute was paid to the colossal works of Benvenuto Cellini and Michael Angelo. He regretted that the time would not allow him to speak of the scenery and surroundings of the Roman sculptures—the old Coliseum, the, gardens, the Forum, and the villas in the environs. He sketched some of the most memorable of the latter, and the best works they contain.

"He concluded by summing up the obvious teachings of these deathless marbles. The lecture was quite interesting to those of artistic tastes, but we fancy the larger part of the audience would have preferred something more modern and personal."

The report of Melville's other lecture is quoted from the Boston *Journal*, January 31, 1859.

"At the Tremont Temple last evening, Herman Melville, Esq., the celebrated author and adventurer, delivered the ninth lecture of the course under the auspices of the Mechanic Apprentices' Association. Subject—'The South Seas.' The audience was not large, but about equal to the usual attendance at this and the Mercantile course.

"On being introduced to the audience, Mr. Melville said that the field of his subject was large, and he should not be expected to go over it all: nor should he be expected to read again what had long been in print, touching his own incidental adventures in Polynesia. But he proposed to view the subject in a general manner, in a random way, with here and there an incident by way of illustration.

"He first referred to the title of the lecture, and the origin and date of the name 'South Seas' which was older than the name 'Pacific,' to which preference is usually given now. The voyages of early navigators into the South Seas, and especially the Balboa, commander of the petty port of Darien, from whence he had taken formal possession of all the South Seas, and all lands and kingdoms therein, in behalf of his masters, the King of Castile and Leon, were noticed by the lecturer.

"Magellan was the man who, after the first hazardous and tortuous passage through the straits which now bear his name, gave the peaceful ocean to which he came out the name of 'Pacific.' It was California, said the lecturer, which first made the Pacific shores the home of the Anglo-Saxons. Even now, there were many places in this wide waste of waters which were not found upon the charts. But what was known, and well known, afforded an abundant theme for a lecture. The fish found in that water would furnish an abundant subject, of which he named the sword fish, a different fish from that of the same name found in our northern latitudes—and the devil fish, over which a mystery hangs, like that over the sea-serpent in northern waters. The birds, also, in those latitudes, might occupy a full hour. The lecturer said he wondered that the renowned Agassiz did not pack his carpet bag and betake himself to Nantucket, and from thence to the South Seas, than which he could find no richer field.

"Full of interest also were the fisheries of the South Seas and the life of the whaling crews on the broad waters, or visiting lands.. Seldom, if ever, touched by any but themselves, was covered over with a charm of novelty. Again the islands were an interesting study. Why, asked the lecturer, do northern Englishmen, who own large yachts, with which they sail up the Mediterranean, why don't they go yachting in the South Seas? The white race have a very bad reputation among the Polynesians. With few exceptions they were considered the most bloodthirsty, atrocious and diabolical race in the world. But there were no dangers to voyagers if they treated the natives with common kindness.

"In the Pacific there were yet unknown and unvisited isles. There were many places where a man might make himself a sylvan retreat and for years, at least, live as much removed from Christendom as if in another world.

"The lecturer described an interview he had with a poetical young man who called upon him to get his opinion upon what would be the prospects of a number, say four score, of disciples of Fourier to settle in the valley of Typee. He had not encouraged the scheme, having too much regard for his old friends, the Polynesians. The Mormons had also such a scheme in view—to discover a large island in the Pacific, upon which they could increase and multiply. The Polynesians themselves have ideas of the same nature. Every one has heard of the voyage of Ponce de Leon to find the fountain of perpetual youth. Equally poetical, and more unfamiliar, was the adventure of Cama Pecar, who set sail alone from Hawaii to find the fount of eternal joy, which was supposed to spring up in some distant island where the people lived in perpetual joy and youth. Like all who go to Paradise, he was never heard from again. A tranquil scene from the South Seas was remembered by the lecturer. In a ship from a port of the Pacific coast he had sailed five months, and came upon an island where the natives lived in a state of total laziness. Here they found a white man who was a permanent inhabitant, and comfortably settled with three wives, who, however, failed to keep his wardrobe in good order.

"Wonderful tales were told of the adventures in the South Seas, and the lecturer said that he believed that the books *Typee* and *Omoo* gave scarcely a full idea of them, except that part which tells of the long captivity in the valley of Typee. He had seen many of these story tellers of adventures in the South Seas with good vouchers of their tales in the shape of tattooing. A full and interesting description of the process of tattooing with its various styles was given. Tattooing was sometimes, like dress, an index of character, and worn as an ornament which would never wear off and could not be pawned, lost or stolen. The lecturer had successfully combated all attempts to naturalise him by marks as from a gridiron, on his face, for which he thanked God.

"A brief notice was made of the islands of the Pacific, where the Anglo-Saxons had settled, and civilised the people, and the lecturer had been disgusted, and threw down a paper published in the Sandwich Islands, which suggested the propriety of not having the native language taught in the common schools.

"In conclusion, the lecturer spoke of the desire of the natives of Georges Island to be annexed to the United States. He was sorry to see it, and, as a friend of humanity, and especially as a friend of the South Sea Islanders, he should pray, and call upon all Christians to pray with him, that the Polynesians might be delivered from all foreign and contaminating influences.

"The lecture gave the most ample satisfaction, and was frequently applauded."

Melville cut short his third year of lecturing to make the trip to California with his brother. Upon his return, he again made an unsuccessful attempt to be appointed to a consularship. Such a mission took him to Washington in 1861. This trip was chiefly notable because of the meeting of Melville and Lincoln. Melville recounted the experience in a letter to his wife: "The night previous to this I was at the second levee at the White House. There was a great crowd and a brilliant scene—ladies in full dress by the hundreds—a steady stream of two-and-two's wound through the apartments shaking hands with Old Abe and immediately passing on. This continued without cessation for an hour and a half. Of course I was one of the shakers. Old Abe is much better looking than I expected and younger looking. He shook hands like a good fellow—working hard at it like a man sawing wood at so much per cord."

Melville struggled on for two more years at Pittsfield, and in October, 1863, moved with his family to 104 East 26th Street, New York, where he spent the remaining years of his life. His house in New York he bought from his brother Allan, giving $7,750 (covered by mortgages and in time paid for by legacies of his wife) and the Arrowhead place, valued at $3,000.

The last years in Pittsfield and the early years in New York were, in financial hardship, perhaps the darkest in Melville's life. He was in ill health, and except for the pittance from his books he was without income. His lectures were a desperate if not lucrative measure. But for the generosity of his wife's father, he would have been in destitution.

On December 5, 1866, he was appointed Inspector of Customs in New York—a post he held until January 1, 1886. He was sixty-seven years old when he resigned. His wife had come into an inheritance that allowed him an ultimate serenity in his closing years.

R. H. Stoddard, in his *Recollections,* thus speaks of Melville:

"My good friend Benedict sent me, one gloomy November forenoon, this curt announcement of a new appointment in Herman Melville: 'He seems a good fellow, Dick, and says he knows you, though perhaps he doesn't, but anyhow be kind to him if this infernal weather will let you be so to anybody.' I bowed to the gentleman who handed the note to me, in whom I recognised a famous writer whom I had met some twenty-five years before; no American writer was more widely known in the late forties and early fifties in his own country and in England than Melville, who in his earlier books, *Typee, Omoo,*

MELVILLE'S CHILDREN
Malcolm, Frances, Elizabeth, Stanwix
(From left to right)

Mardi, and *White Jacket,* had made himself the prose poet of the strange islands and peoples of the South Seas.

"Whether any of Melville's readers understood the real drift of his mind, or whether he understood it himself, has often puzzled me. Next to Emerson he was the American mystic. He was more than that, however, he was one of our great unrecognised poets, as he manifested in his version of 'Sheridan's Ride,' which begins as all students of our serious war poetry ought to know: 'Shoe the steed with silver that bore him to the fray.' Melville's official duty during the last years of my Custom-House life confined him to the foot of Gansevoort Street, North River, and on a report that he might be changed to some district on the East River, he asked me to prevent the change, and Benedict said to me, 'He shan't be moved,' and he was not; and years later, on a second report of the same nature reaching him, I saw Benedict again, who declared with a profane expletive, 'He shall stay there.' And if he had not died about a dozen years ago he would probably be there to-day, at the foot of Gansevoort Street."

It is interesting that a man of the intellect of R. H. Stoddard should have found Melville's mind such a shadowed hieroglyph. With Stoddard so perplexed, it is less difficult to understand Melville's preference for solitude.

In his copy of Schopenhauer, Melville underlined the phrase —"this hellish society of men;" and he vigorously underscored the aphorism: "When two or three are gathered together, the devil is among them." Melville occupied himself with his books, with collecting etchings, with solitary walks; and for companionship he was satisfied with the society of his grandchildren. His grand-daughter, Mrs. Eleanor Melville Metcalf, thus records her recollections of such association:

"I was not yet ten years old when my grandfather died. To put aside all later impressions gathered from those who knew him longer and coloured by their personal reactions, all impressions made by subsequent reading of his books, results in a series of childish recollections, vivid homely scenes wherein he formed a palpable background for my own interested activities.

"Setting forth on a bright spring afternoon for a trip to Central Park, the Mecca of most of our pilgrimages, he made a brave and striking figure as he walked erect, head thrown back, cane in hand, inconspicuously dressed in a dark blue suit and a soft black felt hat. For myself, I skipped gaily beside him, anticipating the long jogging ride in the horse cars, the goats and shanty-topped granite of the upper reaches of our journey, the broad walks of the park, where the joy of all existence was best expressed by running down the hills, head back, skirts flying in the wind. He would follow more slowly and call 'Look out, or the "cop" may catch you!' I always thought he used funny words: 'cop' was surely a jollier word than 'policeman.'

"We never came in from a trip of this kind, nor indeed from any walk, but we stopped in the front hall under a coloured engraving of the Bay of Naples, its still blue dotted with tiny white sails. He would point to them with his cane and say, 'See the little boats sailing hither and thither.' 'Hither and thither'—more funny words, thought I, at the same time a little awed by something far away in the tone of voice.

"I remember mornings when even sugar on the oatmeal was not enough to tempt me to finish the last mouthful. It would be spring in the back yard too, and a tin cup full of little stones picked out of the garden meant a penny from my grandmother. He would say in a warning whisper, 'Jack Smoke will come down the chimney and take what you leave!' That was another matter. The oatmeal was laughingly finished and the yard gained. Across the back parlour and main hall upstairs ran a narrow iron-trimmed porch, furnished with Windsor and folding canvas chairs. There he would sit with a pipe and his most constant companion—his cane, and watch my busy activity below. Against the wall of the porch hung a match holder, more for ornament than utility, it seems. It was a gay red and blue china butterfly. Invariably he looked to see if it had flown away since we were there last.

"Once in a long while his interest in his grandchildren led him to cross the river and take the suburban train to East Orange, where we lived. He must have been an impressive figure, sitting silently on the piazza of our little house, while my sister and I pranced by with a neighbour's boy and his express wagon, filled with a satisfied sense of the strength and accomplishment of our years. When he had had enough of such exhibitions, he would suddenly rise and take the next train back to Hoboken.

"Chiefly do I think of him connected with different parts of the 26th Street house.

"His own room was a place of mystery and awe to me; there I never ventured unless invited by him. It looked bleakly north. The great mahogany desk, heavily bearing up four shelves of dull gilt and leather books; the high dim book-case, topped by strange plaster heads that peered along the ceiling level, or bent down, searching blindly with sightless balls; the small black iron bed, covered with dark cretonne; the narrow iron grate; the wide table in the alcove, piled with papers I would not dream of touching—these made a room even more to be fled than the back parlour, by whose door I always ran to escape the following eyes of his portrait, which hung there in a half light. Yet lo, the paper-piled table also held a little bag of figs, and one of the pieces of sweet stickiness was for me. 'Tittery-Eye' he called me, and awe melted into glee, as I skipped away to my grandmother's room, which adjoined.

"That was a very different place—sunny, comfortable and familiar, with a sewing machine and a *white* bed like other peoples' In the corner stood a big arm chair, where he always sat when he left the recesses of his own dark privacy. I used to climb on his knee, while he told me wild tales of cannibals and tropic isles. Little did I then know that he was reliving his own past. We came nearest intimacy at these times, and part of the fun was to put my hands in his thick beard and squeeze it hard. It was no soft silken beard, but tight curled like the horse hair breaking out of old upholstered chairs, firm and wiry to the grasp, and squarely chopped.

"Sad it is that he felt his grandchildren would turn against him as they grew older. He used to forebode as much. As it is, I have nothing but a remembrance of glorious fun, mixed with a childish awe, as of some one who knew far and strange things."

As the last meed of glory, Melville received this flattering letter:

"12 Lucknow Terrace,
"HALIFAX, N. S.
Nov. 21, 1889.

"DEAR SIR:

"Although a stranger, I take the liberty of addressing you on the ground of my ardent admiration for your works. For a number of years I have read and reread *Moby-Dick* with increasing pleasure in every perusal: and with this study, the conviction has grown up that the unique merits of that book have never received due recognition. I have been a student for ten years and have dabbled in literature more or less myself. And now I find myself in a position which enables me to give myself to literature as a life-work. I am anxious to set the merits of your books before the public and to that end, I beg the honour of corresponding with you. It would be of great assistance to me, if I could gather some particulars of your life and *literary methods* from you, other than given in such books as Duyckinck's dictionary. In the matter of style, apart from the matter altogether I consider your books, especially the earlier ones, the most thoroughly New World product in all American literature.

"Hoping that I am not asking too much, I remain,

"Yours most respectfully,

"ARCHD. MACMEEHAN, PH.D.

"Munro Professor of English at Dalhousie University."

Melville replied:

"104 E. 26th St.

"DEAR SIR:

"I beg you to overlook my delay in acknowledging yours of the 12th ult. It was unavoidable.

"Your note gave me pleasure, as how should it not, written in such a spirit.

"But you do not know, perhaps, that I have entered my 8th decade. After 20 years nearly, as an outdoor custom house officer, I have lately come into possession of unobstructed leisure, but only just as, in the course of nature, my vigour sensibly declines. What little of it is left I husband for certain matters as yet incomplete, and which indeed may never be completed.

"I appreciate, quite as much as you would have me, your friendly good will and shrink from any appearance to the contrary.

"Trusting that you will take all this, & what it implies, in the same spirit that prompts it, I am,

"Very truly yours,
"HERMAN MELVILLE.

"To

"Professor MacMeehan,
"Dec. 5, '89."

Melville was using his "unobstructed leisure" in a return to the writing of prose. Ten prose sketches and a novel were the result. But the result is not distinguished. The novel, *Billy Budd,* is built around the character of Jack Chase, the "Handsome Sailor." In the character of Billy Budd, Melville attempts to portray the native purity and nobility of the uncorrupted man. Melville spends elaborate pains in analysing "the mystery of iniquity," and in celebrating by contrast the god-like beauty of body and spirit of his hero. Billy Budd, by his heroic guilelessness is, like an angel of vengeance, precipitated into manslaughter; and for his very righteousness he is hanged. *Billy Budd,* finished within a few months before the end of Melville's life, would seem to teach that though the wages of sin is death, that sinners and saints alike toil for a common hire. In *Billy Budd* the orphic sententiousness is gone, it is true. But gone also is the brisk lucidity, the sparkle, the verve. Only the disillusion abided with him to the last.

Melville died at 104 East 26th Street, New York, on Monday, September 28, 1891. His funeral was attended by his wife and his two daughters—all of his immediate family that survived him—and a meagre scattering of relatives and family friends. The man who had created Moby-Dick died an obscure and elderly private citizen. He had in early manhood prayed that if indeed his soul missed its haven, that his might, at least, be an utter wreck. "All Fame is patronage," he had once written; "let me be infamous." But as if in contempt even for this preference, he had, during the last half of his life, cruised off and away upon boundless and uncharted waters; and in the end he sank down into death, without a ripple of renown.

"Oh, what quenchless feud is this, that Time hath with the sons of Men!"

BIBLIOGRAPHY

BIBLIOGRAPHY

Herman Melville's Sea Tales. 4 Volumes. Edited by Arthur Stedman. *New York*, 1892, 1896; *Boston*, 1900, 1910, 1919.
    Typee (with a biographical and critical introduction by
        the editor).
    Omoo.
    Moby-Dick.
    White-Jacket.

Typee: a Peep at Polynesian Life. During a Four Months' Residence
in a Valley of the Marquesas. . . . *New York*, 1846.

A Four Months' Residence among the Natives of a Valley of the
Marquesas Islands; or, a Peep at Polynesian Life. . . . *London*, 1846, 1847, 1855, 1861.

Typee: a Peep at Polynesian Life. . . . Revised edition, with a
Sequel, The Story of Toby. . . . *New York*, 1846, 1847, 1849,
1855, 1857, 1865, 1871. *London*, 1892, 1893 (ed. H. S. Salt),
1898, 1899. *Boston*, 1902 (ed. William P. Trent). *London*,
1903 (ed. William P. Trent). *London and New York*, 1904
(ed. W. Clark Russell); 1907 (ed. Ernest Rhys). *London*
1910; another edition 1910 (ed. W. Clark Russell). *New York*,
1911 (ed. W. Clark Russell); 1920 (ed. A. L. Sterling). *New
York and London*, 1921 (ed. Ernest Rhys).

    Translated into German by R. Garrique, *Leipzig*, 1846; into
    Dutch, *Haarlem*, 1847.

Omoo: a Narrative of Adventures in the South Seas. . . . *New York*,
1847 (five editions the same year). *London*, 1847, 1849. *New
York and London*, 1855. *London*, 1861. *New York*, 1863, 1868.
London, 1892, 1893 (ed. H. S. Salt). *London and New York*,
1904 (ed. W. Clark Russell); 1908 (ed. Ernest Rhys); 1911
(ed. W. Clark Russell); 1921 (ed. Ernest Rhys).

    Translated into German by F. Gerstäcker, *Leipzig*, 1847.

Mardi: and a Voyage Thither. . . . *New York*, 1849 (2 volumes).
London, 1849 (3 volumes). *New York*, 1855, 1864.

Redburn: His First Voyage. Being the Sailor-Boy Confessions and Reminiscences of the Son-of-a-Gentleman, in the Merchant Service. . . . *New York,* 1849. *London,* 1849 (2 volumes). *New York,* 1855, 1863.

Translated into German by L. Marezoll, *Grimma,* 1850.

White-Jacket: **or,** The World in a Man-of-War. . . . *New York,* 1850. *London,* 1850 (2 volumes). *New York and London,* 1855. *London,* 1892, 1893, 1901.

Moby-Dick; or, the Whale. . . . *New York,* 1851.

The Whale. . . . *London,* 1851, 1853 (3 volumes).

Moby-Dick; or, the Whale. . . . *New York,* 1863. *London,* 1901 (ed. L. Becke). *London and New York,* 1907 (ed. Ernest Rhys). *London,* 1912; 1920 (ed. Violet Maynell). *London and New York,* 1921 (ed. Ernest Rhys). The editions since 1892 have borne the title Moby-Dick; (or) the (Great) White Whale.

Pierre: or The Ambiguities. . . . *New York,* 1852, 1855.

Israel Potter: His Fifty Years of Exile. . . . *New York,* 1855 (three editions in the same year). *London,* 1855, 1861. (The book appeared serially in *Putnam's Monthly Magazine,* July, 1854– March, 1855. It was pirated at *Philadelphia,* n. d. (entered 1865), as The Refugee, with the original dedication and table of contents omitted).

The Piazza Tales. . . . *New York,* 1856. *London,* 1856. (Contains: The Piazza; Bartleby; Benito Cereno; The Lightning-Rod Man; The Encantadas; The Bell-Tower).

The Confidence-Man: His Masquerade. . . . *New York,* 1857. *London,* 1857.

Battle-Pieces and Aspects of the War. . . . *New York,* 1866.

Clarel: a Poem and Pilgrimage in the Holy Land. . . . *New York,* 1878.

John Marr and Other Sailors. . . . *New York,* 1888. (Privately printed).

Timoleon, etc. *New York,* 1891. (Privately printed).

CONTRIBUTIONS TO MAGAZINES, ETC.

Fragments from a Writing Desk. *The Democratic Press and Lansingburgh Advertiser,* 4 May; 18 May; 1849.

Hawthorne and His Mosses, By a Virginian Spending a July in Vermont. *Literary World.* 17 Aug.; 24 Aug.; 1850.

The Town-Ho's Story. (Ch. 54 of Moby-Dick.) *Harper's New Monthly Magazine.* Oct., 1851.

A Memorial to James Fenimore Cooper. Discourses and tributes by Bryant, Bancroft, Irving, Melville, etc., etc. *New York,* 1852.

Bartleby, the Scrivener. A story of Wall-Street. *Putnam's Monthly Magazine.* Nov.-Dec., 1853.

Cock-a-Doodle-Doo! or, The Crowing of the Cock of Benentano. *Harper's New Monthly Magazine.* Dec., 1853.

The Encantadas, or Enchanted Isles, by Salvator R. Tarnmoor. *Putnam's Monthly Magazine.* March-May, 1854.

The Lightning-Rod Man. *Putnam's Monthly Magazine.* Aug., 1854.

Poor Man's Pudding and Rich Man's Crumbs. *Harper's New Monthly Magazine.* June, 1854.

Happy Failure. A Story of the River Hudson. *Harper's New Monthly Magazine.* July, 1854.

The Fiddler. *Harper's New Monthly Magazine.* Sept., 1854.

Paradise of Bachelors and Tartarus of Maids. *Harper's New Monthly Magazine.* April, 1855.

The Bell-Tower. *Putnam's Monthly Magazine.* Aug., 1855.

Benito Cereno. *Putnam's Monthly Magazine.* Oct.-Dec., 1855.

Jimmy Rose. *Harper's New Monthly Magazine.* Nov., 1855.

The 'Gees. *Harper's New Monthly Magazine.* March, 1856.

I and My Chimney. *Putnam's Monthly Magazine.* March, 1856.

The Apple-Tree Table: or, Original Spiritual Manifestations. *Putnam's Monthly Magazine.* May, 1856.

The March to the Sea (poem). *Putnam's Monthly Magazine.* Feb., 1856.

The Cumberland (poem). *Putnam's Monthly Magazine.* March, 1866.

Philip (poem). *Putnam's Monthly Magazine.* April, 1866.

Chattanooga (poem). *Harper's New Monthly Magazine.* June, 1866.

Gettysburg: July, 1863 (poem). *Harper's New Monthly's Magazine.* July, 1866.

The History of Pittsfield, Mass., Compiled and written, under the general direction of a committee, by J. E. A. Smith, Pittsfield, 1876. (The account of Major Thomas Melville, pp. 399-400, was written by Melville.)

INDEX OF NAMES

INDEX OF NAMES